Editor
DIANA SCHUTZ

Digital Production
RYAN HILL

Designer
CARY GRAZZINI

Publisher
MIKE RICHARDSON

This volume collects issues 83-89
of the Dark Horse comic book series *Usagi Yojimbo Volume Three.*

Visit the Usagi Yojimbo Dojo website
usagiyojimbo.com

Published by Dark Horse Books
A division of Dark Horse Comics, Inc.
10956 SE Main Street
Milwaukie, Oregon 97222

DarkHorse.com

First edition: July 2007
ISBN 978-1-59307-783-9

3 5 7 9 10 8 6 4
Printed by 1010 Printing International, Ltd., Guangdong Province, China.

USAGI YOJIMBO™

— THE MOTHER OF MOUNTAINS —

Created, Written, and Illustrated by
STAN SAKAI

Introduction by
JOHN LANDIS

DARK HORSE BOOKS®

Usagi Yojimbo

Introduction

I grew up in West Los Angeles, California. As a kid, I could take a bus all the way from Sepulveda down Wilshire Boulevard to La Brea Avenue, where for many years there was a movie theater called the Toho La Brea. The Toho La Brea screened only Japanese films in their original versions, with English subtitles. There were Japanese-owned nurseries all over West L.A. then, and many of my schoolmates were Japanese-American. And it was those kids who introduced me to the Toho La Brea Theater and the Samurai movie!

While most of the population of the United States was first introduced to Japanese cinema by the bastardized *Godzilla, King of the Monsters*, I had already seen the glories of Kurosawa and the magnificent Toshiro Mifune!

So, many, many years later, when I was with my (then little) son Max at the legendary Golden Apple comic-book store on Melrose, my eye was naturally drawn to the colorful cover of a comic featuring what appeared to be a samurai rabbit! After leafing through just a few pages, I was hooked. *Yojimbo* is now not just the title of one of my favorite movies, but *Usagi Yojimbo* has become the title of one my favorite comics, too!

I hold Stan Sakai right up there with Winsor McCay, Chester Gould, Art Spiegelman, Jack Davis, Wally Wood, Al Capp, Charles Schulz, Robert Crumb, Jules Feiffer, Will Eisner, and all the others who can move me and tell such wonderful stories with just drawings on the page.

This collection of nine issues of *Usagi Yojimbo* in one volume tells the epic tale of two cousins and a lost mine. The evil Noriko can hold her place among the great villainesses—like Cruella de Ville, but with deadly martial arts skills! This whole saga reminds me again of how close the samurai stories are to our Westerns. If Italians can make Westerns in Spain, why can't Stan make realistic samurai tales about a brave and accomplished and honorable rabbit? Stan Sakai can, and he does!

The similarities between comics and film are well known. Movie storyboards—illustrated shot lists—are just comics, after all. When a movie— or play or book or graphic novel or painting— succeeds, it's called "suspension of disbelief." Simply, you believe it.

You're there. Stan's work does that. In some weird feudal Japan where these strange lizards run around and anthropomorphic warriors and peasants live, I lose myself entirely.

I love this stuff!

JOHN LANDIS
LOS ANGELES, CALIFORNIA
MARCH, 2007

Director John Landis and Stan Sakai. *Photo by Sharon Sakai*

CONTENTS

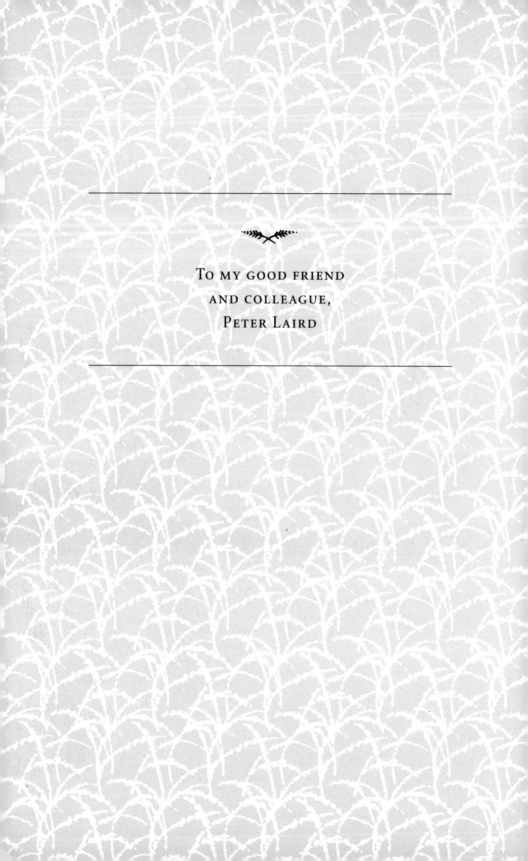

To my good friend
and colleague,
Peter Laird

KLAK!
KLAK!
KLAK!
KLAK!
KLAK!
KLAK!
KLAK!
KLAK!
KLAK!
HIIIYAHHHHHHH
KIAHHHHHHHHH

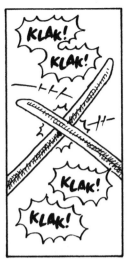

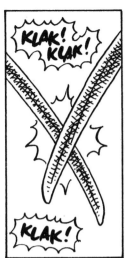

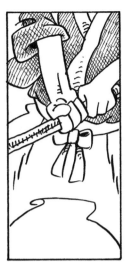

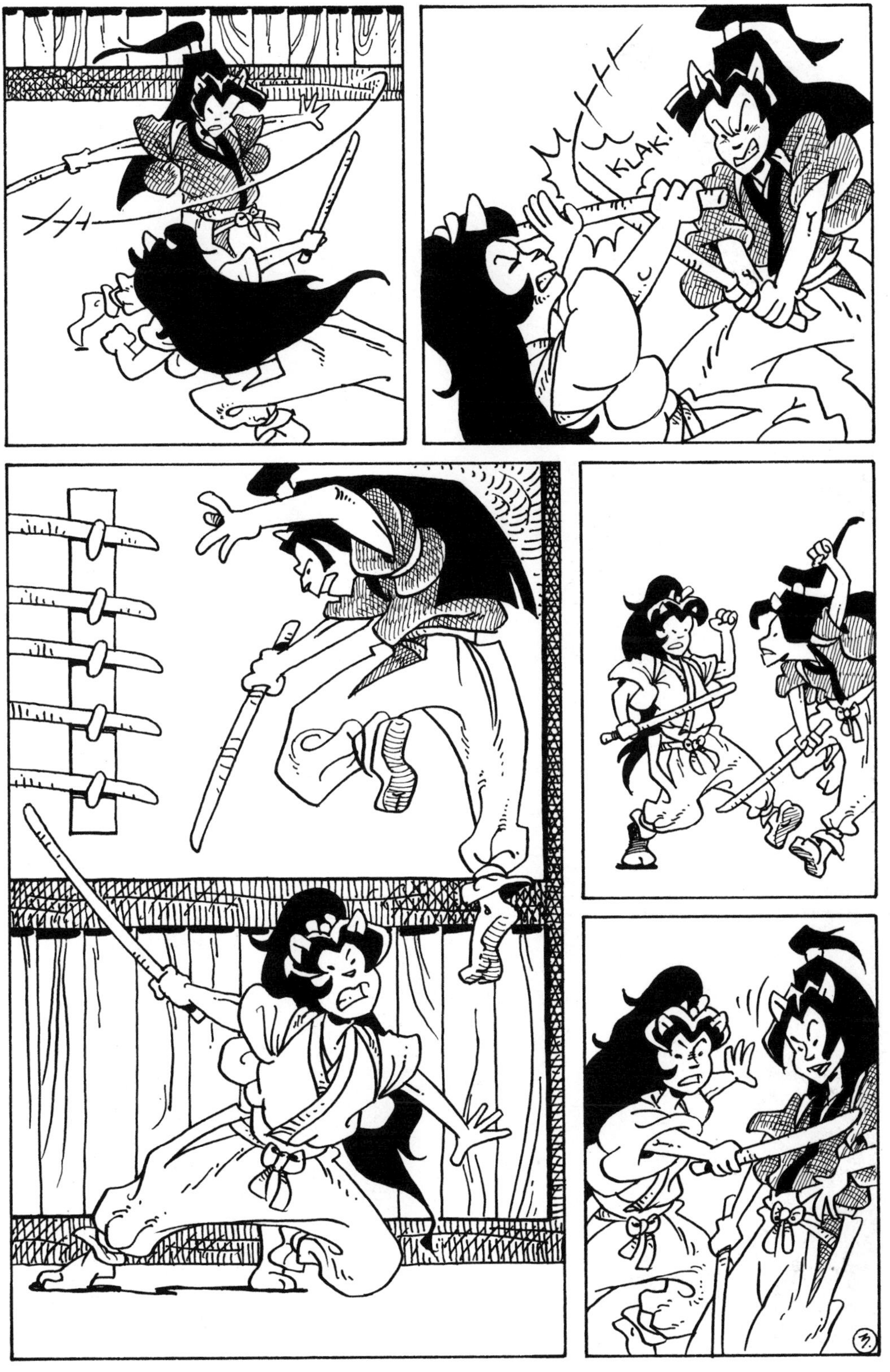
KLAK!

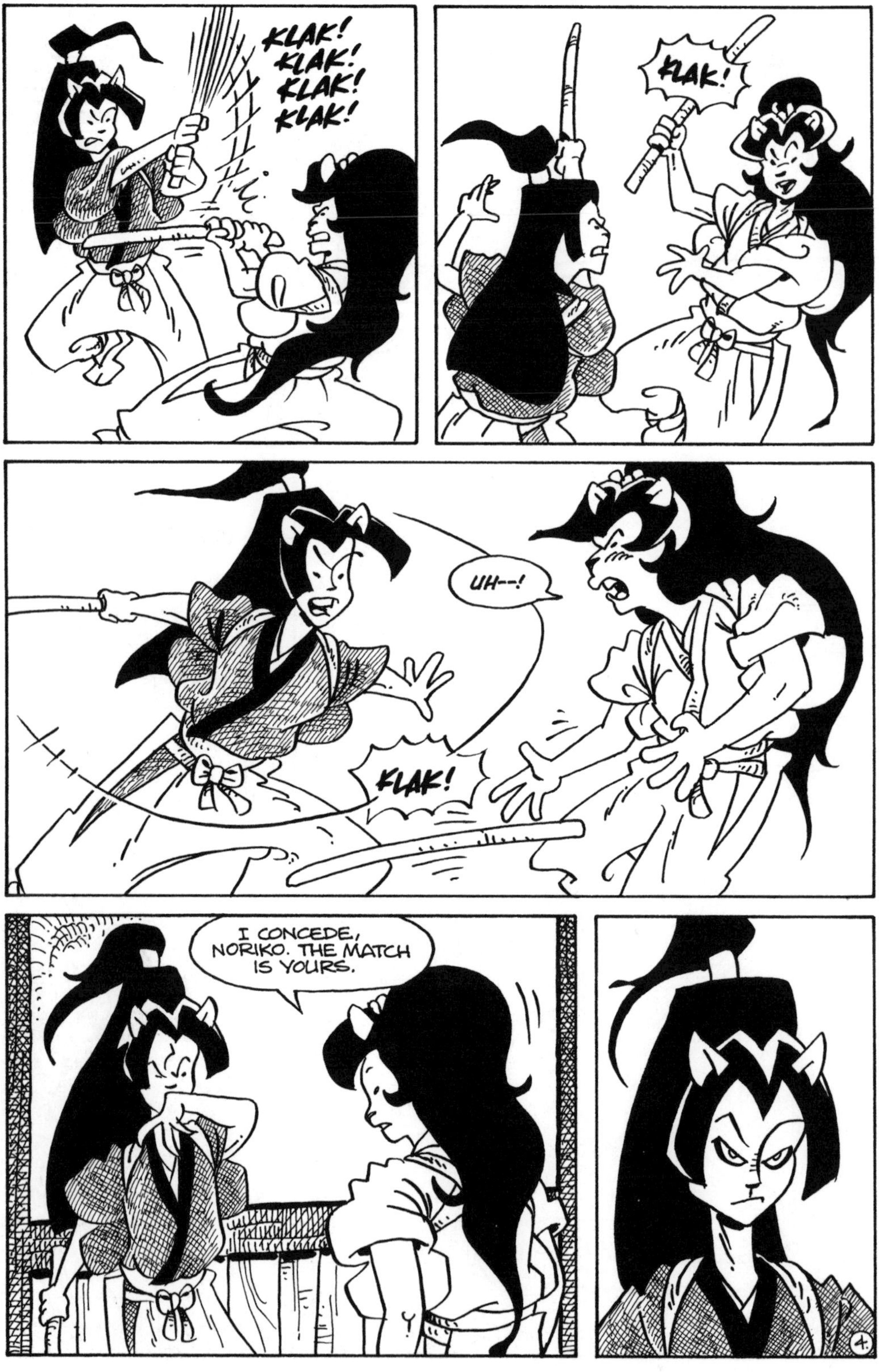
KLAK! KLAK! KLAK! KLAK!
KLAK!
UH--!
KLAK!
I CONCEDE, NORIKO. THE MATCH IS YOURS.
4.

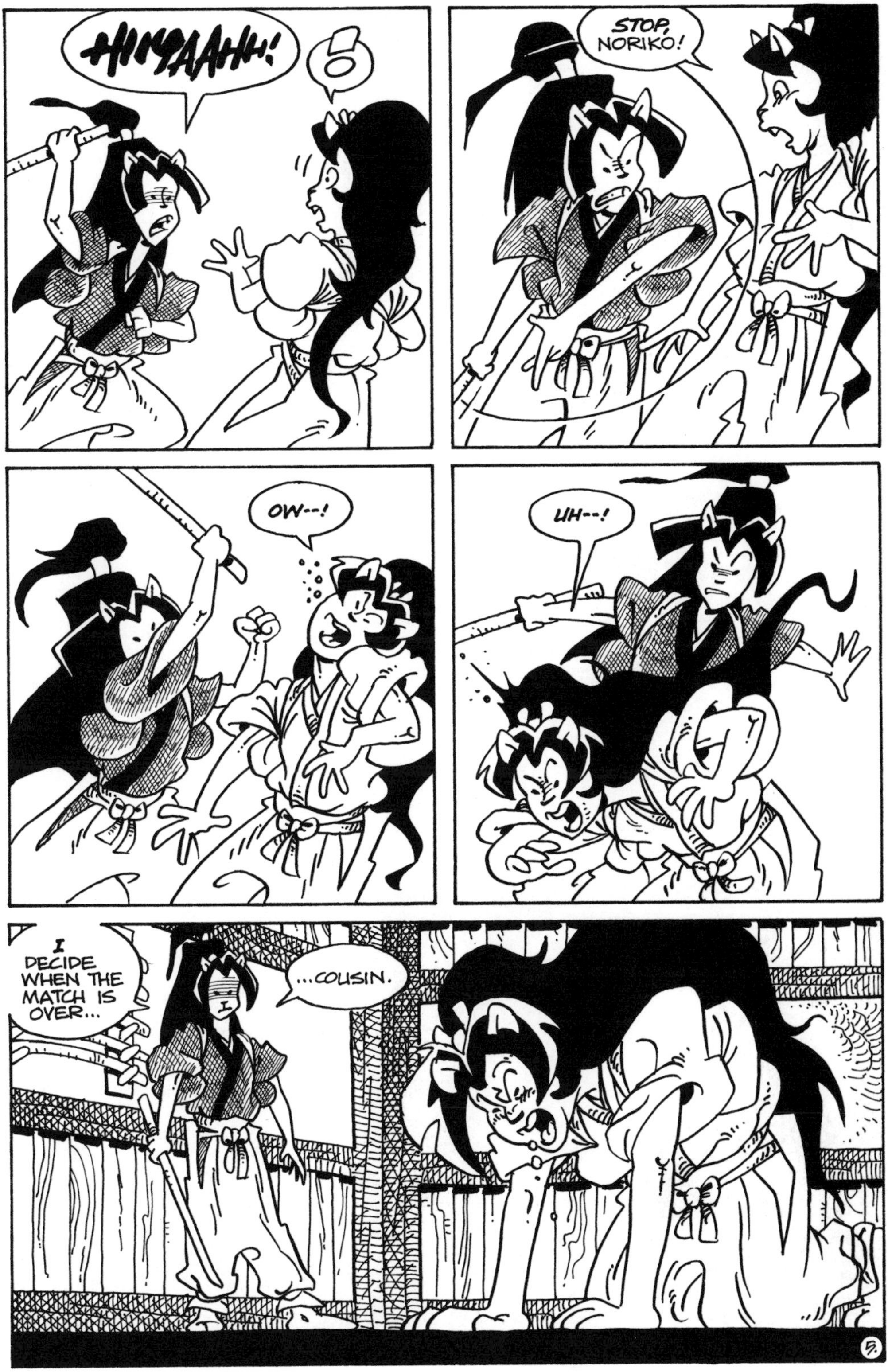
HIIYAAHH!
!
STOP, NORIKO!
OW--!
UH--!
I DECIDE WHEN THE MATCH IS OVER...
...COUSIN.

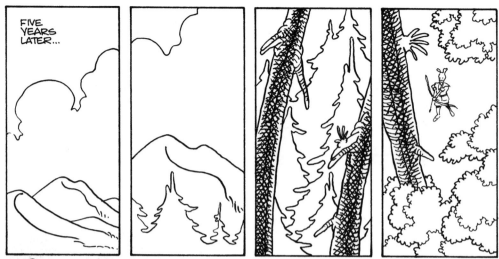

THE TREASURE OF THE MOTHER OF MOUNTAINS

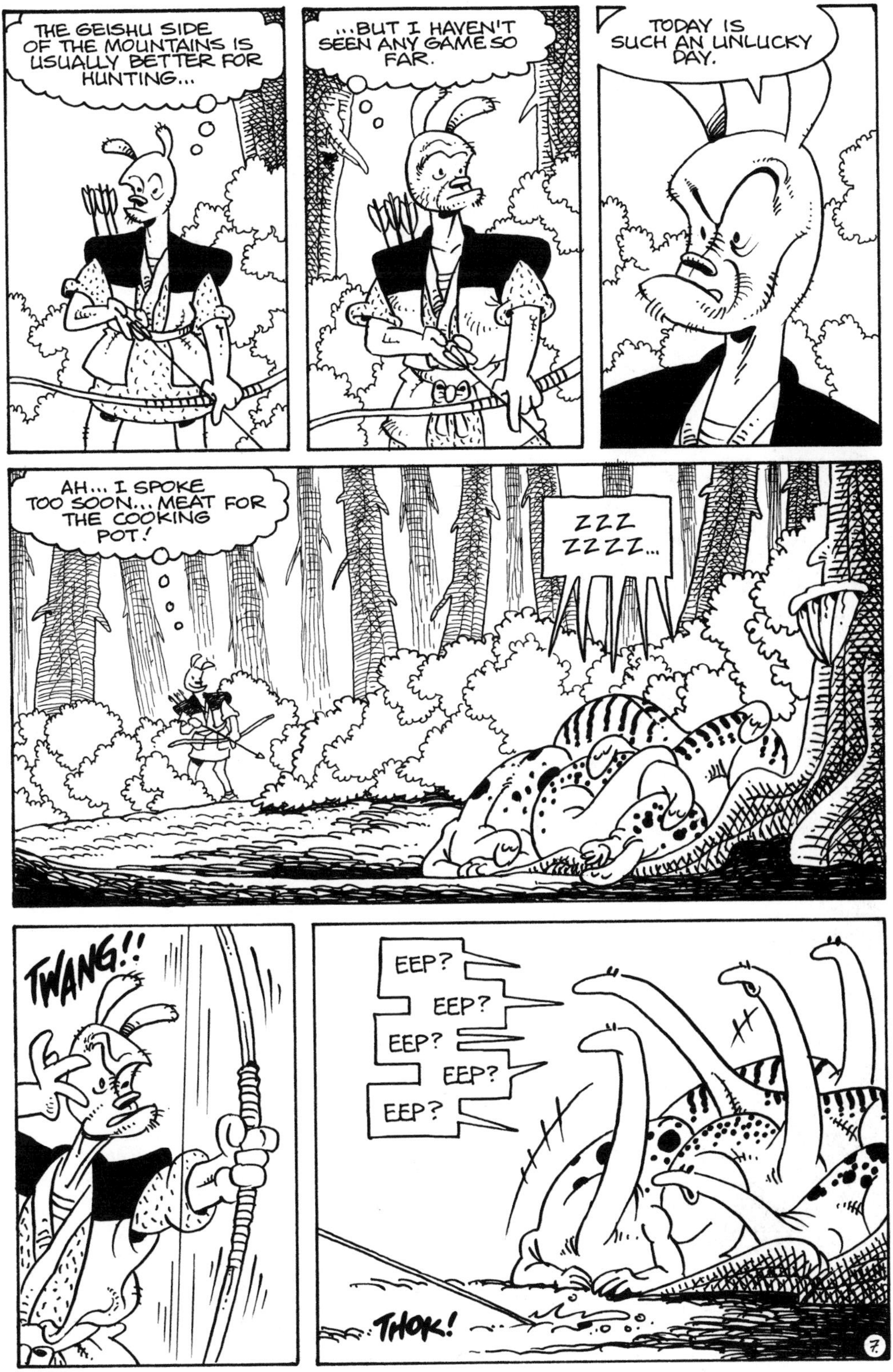
THE GEISHU SIDE OF THE MOUNTAINS IS USUALLY BETTER FOR HUNTING...
...BUT I HAVEN'T SEEN ANY GAME SO FAR.
TODAY IS SUCH AN UNLUCKY DAY.
AH... I SPOKE TOO SOON... MEAT FOR THE COOKING POT!
ZZZ ZZZZ...
TWANG!!
EEP?
EEP?
EEP?
EEP?
EEP?
THOK!
7.

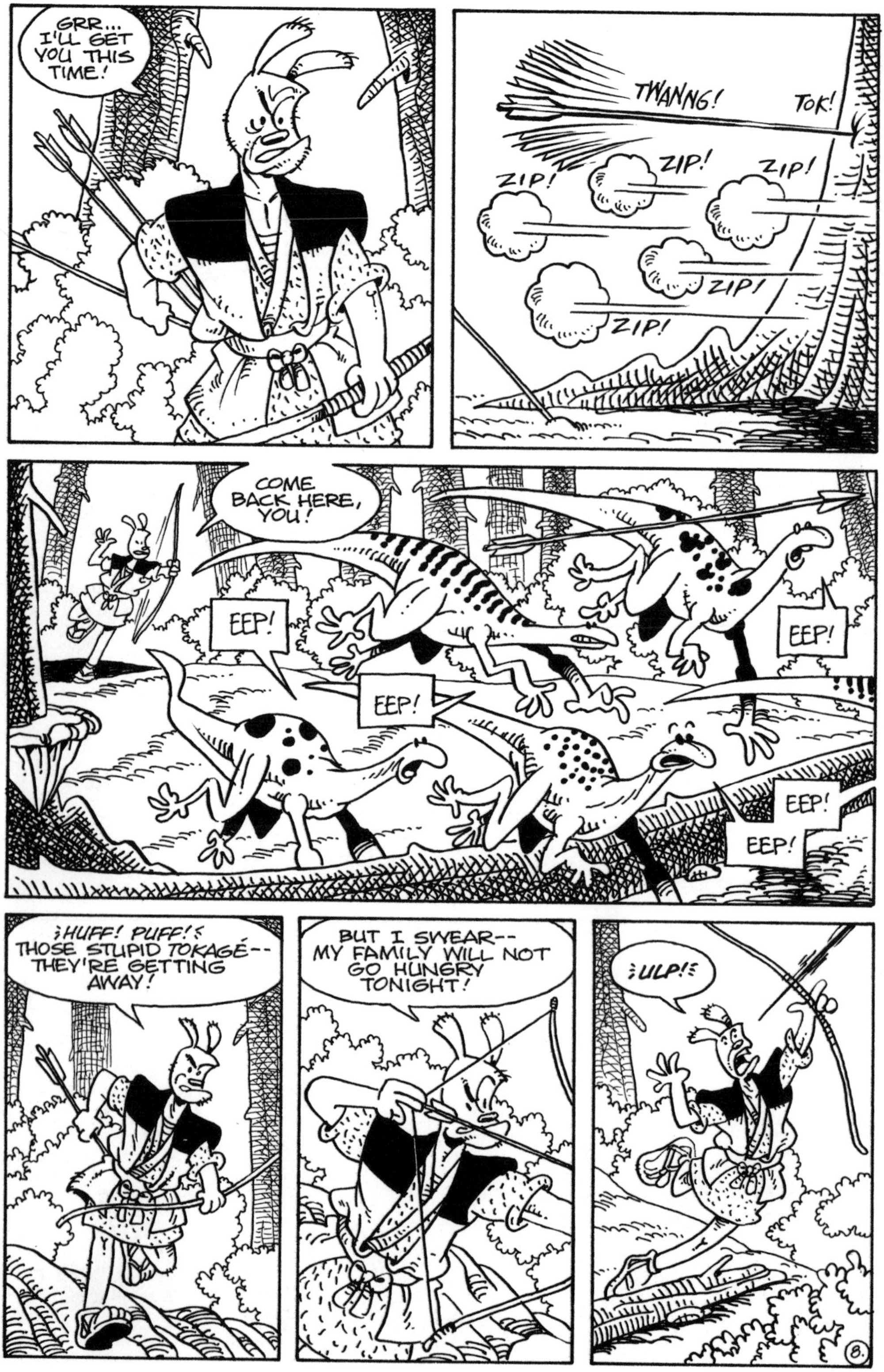
GRR... I'LL GET YOU THIS TIME!
TWANNG!
TOK!
ZIP!
ZIP!
ZIP!
ZIP!
ZIP!
COME BACK HERE, YOU!
EEP!
EEP!
EEP!
EEP!
EEP!
¡HUFF! PUFF!¡ THOSE STUPID TOKAGÉ-- THEY'RE GETTING AWAY!
BUT I SWEAR-- MY FAMILY WILL NOT GO HUNGRY TONIGHT!
¡ULP!¡
8.

CHHHHHHHHHHHH ook!

OOOOOHHH... THIS IS THE WORST DAY OF MY LIFE. MY BOW IS BROKEN..., I'VE LOST ALL MY ARROWS... I THINK I BROKE MY...MY...

WHAT'S THIS?!

I-I CAN'T BELIEVE IT! A GROMWELL BUSH!

HOORAY! THIS IS THE BEST DAY OF MY LIFE!

OOOOOOHHH...

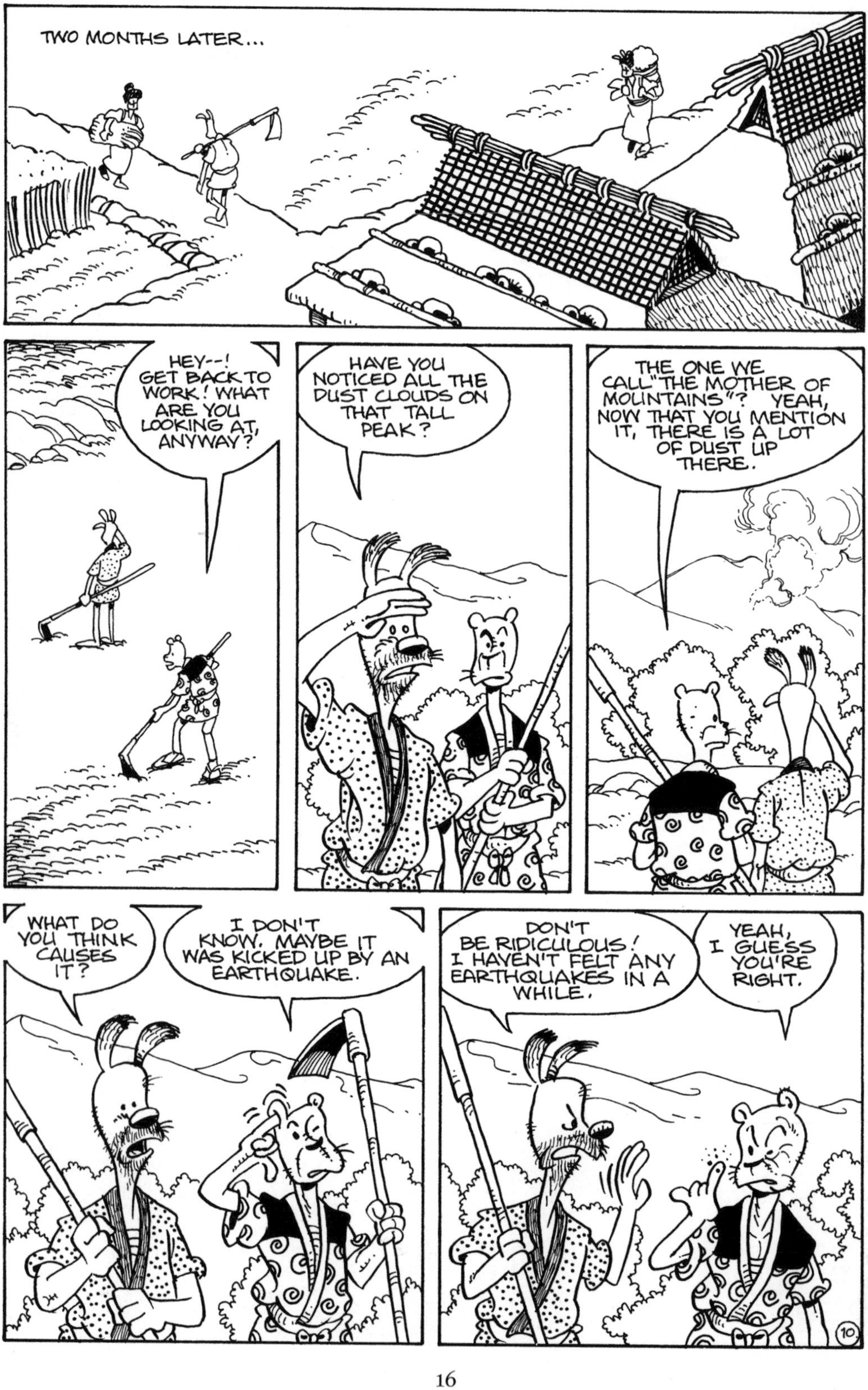
TWO MONTHS LATER...
HEY--! GET BACK TO WORK! WHAT ARE YOU LOOKING AT, ANYWAY?
HAVE YOU NOTICED ALL THE DUST CLOUDS ON THAT TALL PEAK?
THE ONE WE CALL "THE MOTHER OF MOUNTAINS"? YEAH, NOW THAT YOU MENTION IT, THERE IS A LOT OF DUST UP THERE.
WHAT DO YOU THINK CAUSES IT?
I DON'T KNOW. MAYBE IT WAS KICKED UP BY AN EARTHQUAKE.
DON'T BE RIDICULOUS! I HAVEN'T FELT ANY EARTHQUAKES IN A WHILE.
YEAH, I GUESS YOU'RE RIGHT.
10

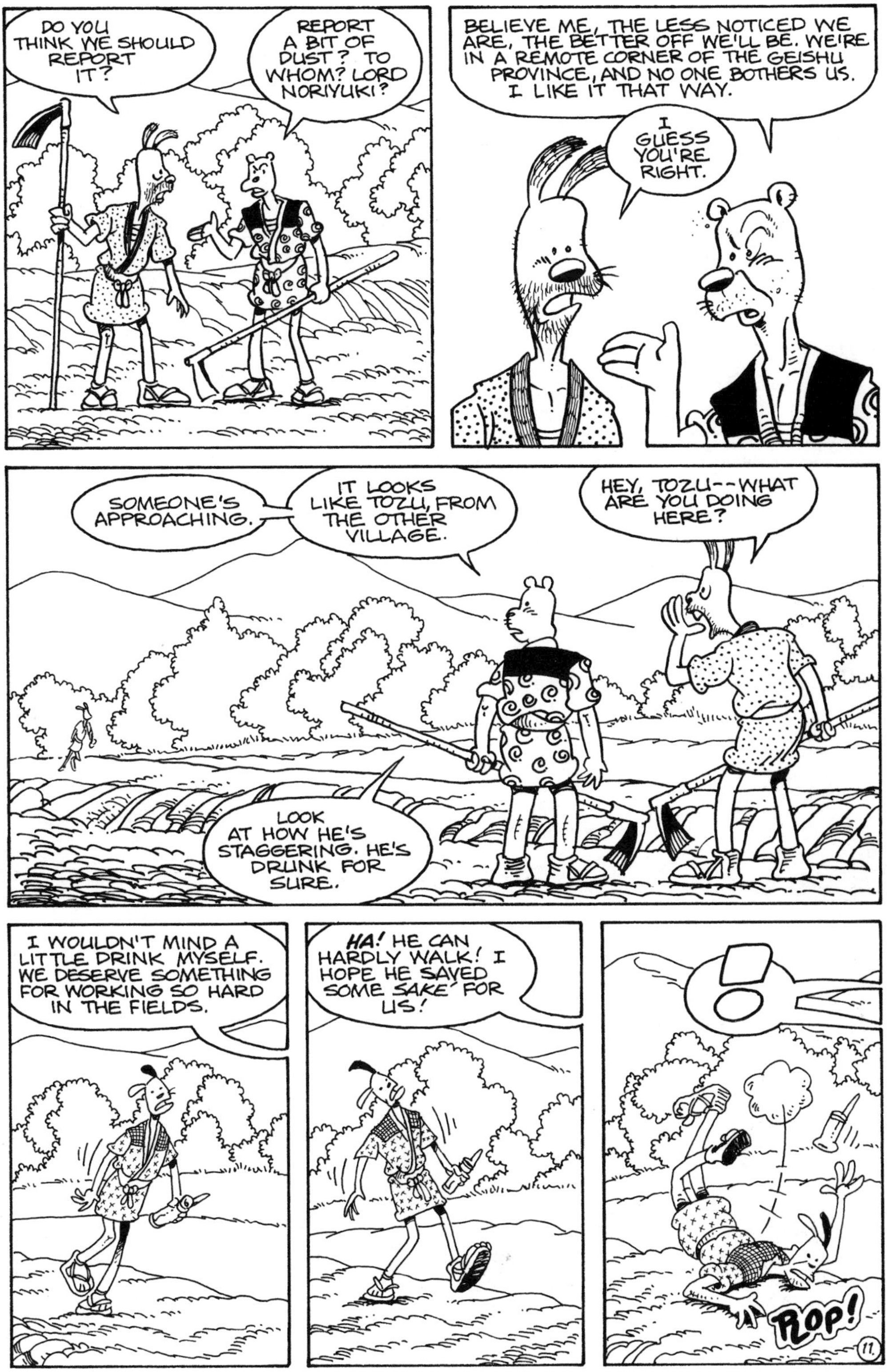
DO YOU THINK WE SHOULD REPORT IT?
REPORT A BIT OF DUST? TO WHOM? LORD NORIYUKI?
BELIEVE ME, THE LESS NOTICED WE ARE, THE BETTER OFF WE'LL BE. WE'RE IN A REMOTE CORNER OF THE GEISHU PROVINCE, AND NO ONE BOTHERS US. I LIKE IT THAT WAY.
I GUESS YOU'RE RIGHT.
SOMEONE'S APPROACHING.
IT LOOKS LIKE TOZU, FROM THE OTHER VILLAGE.
HEY, TOZU--WHAT ARE YOU DOING HERE?
LOOK AT HOW HE'S STAGGERING. HE'S DRUNK FOR SURE.
I WOULDN'T MIND A LITTLE DRINK MYSELF. WE DESERVE SOMETHING FOR WORKING SO HARD IN THE FIELDS.
HA! HE CAN HARDLY WALK! I HOPE HE SAVED SOME SAKE FOR US!
!
PLOP!
11.

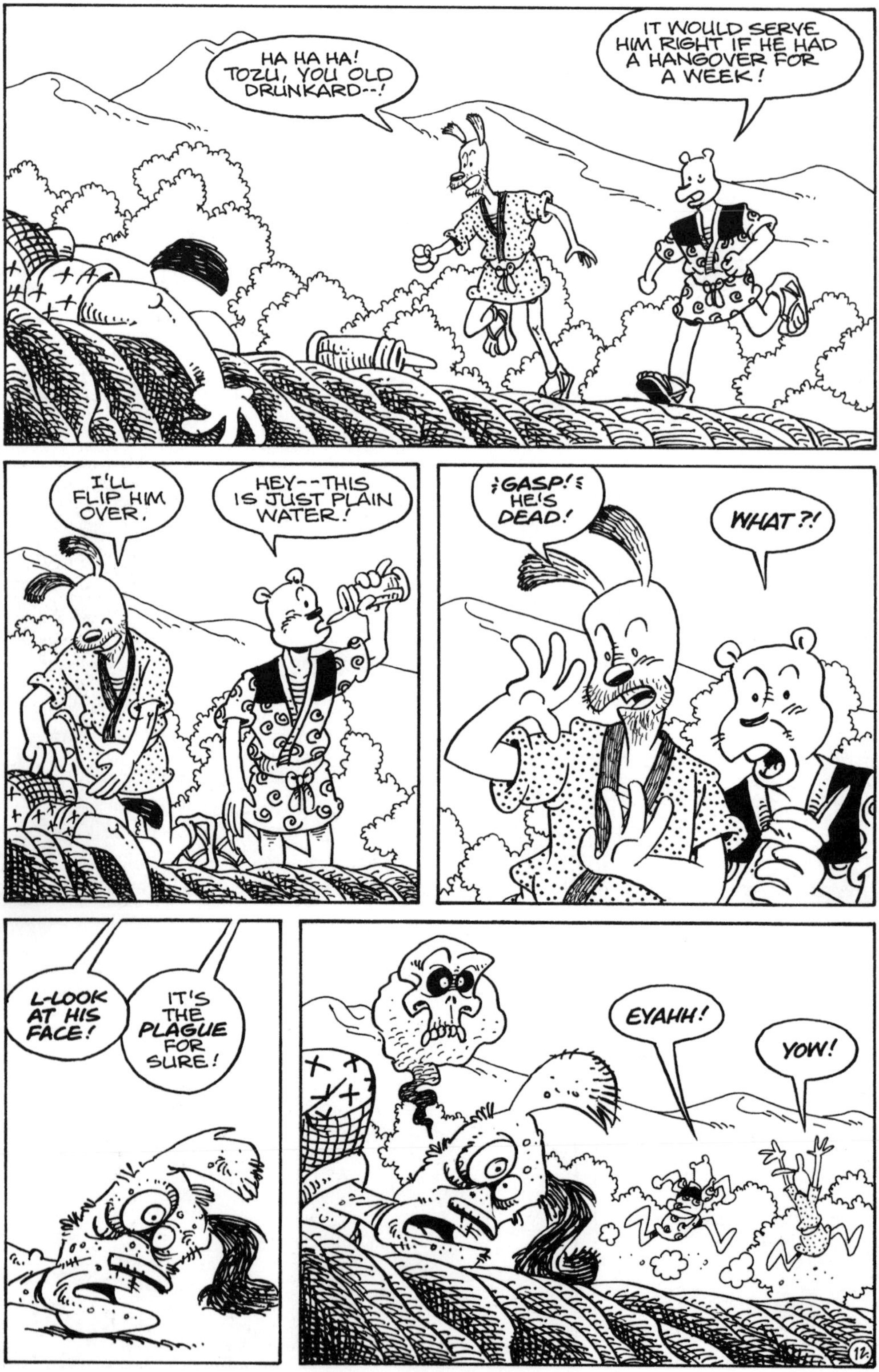
HA HA HA! TOZU, YOU OLD DRUNKARD--!
IT WOULD SERVE HIM RIGHT IF HE HAD A HANGOVER FOR A WEEK!
I'LL FLIP HIM OVER.
HEY--THIS IS JUST PLAIN WATER!
GASP! HE'S DEAD!
WHAT?!
L-LOOK AT HIS FACE!
IT'S THE PLAGUE FOR SURE!
EYAHH!
YOW!
12

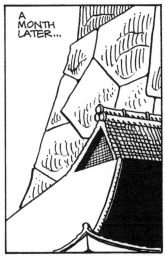

A MONTH LATER...

...AND I DEMAND THAT LADY TOMOE EITHER PRESENT PROOF OF HER ALLEGATIONS...

...OR APOLOGIZE.

LORD HORIKAWA, BE REASONABLE.

"REASONABLE"? SHE ALL BUT ACCUSED MY ANCESTOR OF INCOMPETENCE... OF BEING RESPONSIBLE FOR OUR CLAN'S DEFEAT IN A BATTLE TWO HUNDRED YEARS AGO.

I FEEL I AM BEING *VERY* REASONABLE.

NOW SHE MUST OFFER EITHER HER EVIDENCE....OR AN APOLOGY AND ADMIT HER ERROR.

VERY WELL, TO MAINTAIN PEACE WITHIN OUR CLAN...

TOMOE...?

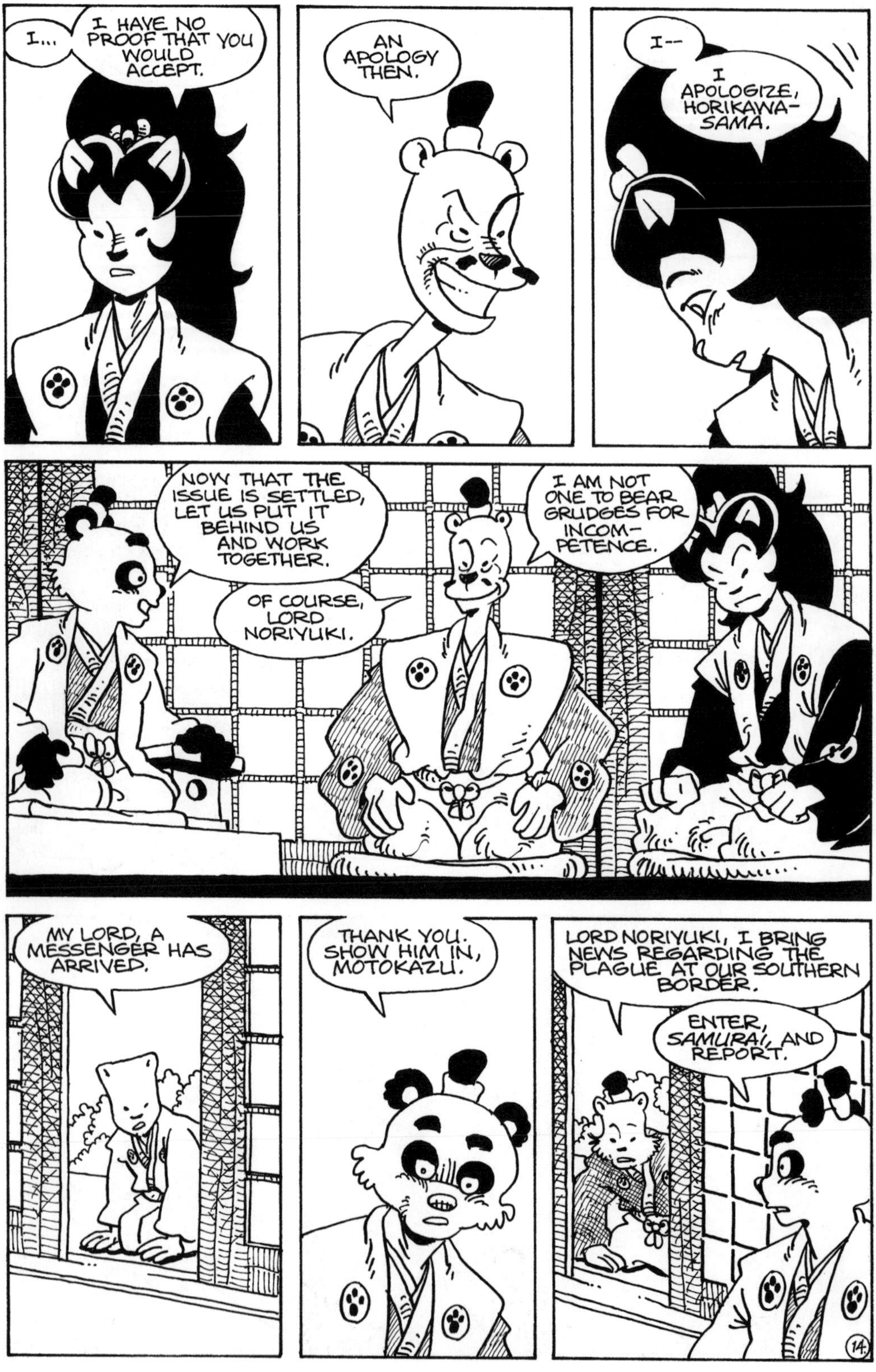
I...
I HAVE NO PROOF THAT YOU WOULD ACCEPT.
AN APOLOGY THEN.
I--
I APOLOGIZE, HORIKAWA-SAMA.
NOW THAT THE ISSUE IS SETTLED, LET US PUT IT BEHIND US AND WORK TOGETHER.
OF COURSE, LORD NORIYUKI.
I AM NOT ONE TO BEAR GRUDGES FOR INCOMPETENCE.
MY LORD, A MESSENGER HAS ARRIVED.
THANK YOU. SHOW HIM IN, MOTOKAZU.
LORD NORIYUKI, I BRING NEWS REGARDING THE PLAGUE AT OUR SOUTHERN BORDER.
ENTER, SAMURAI, AND REPORT.
14.

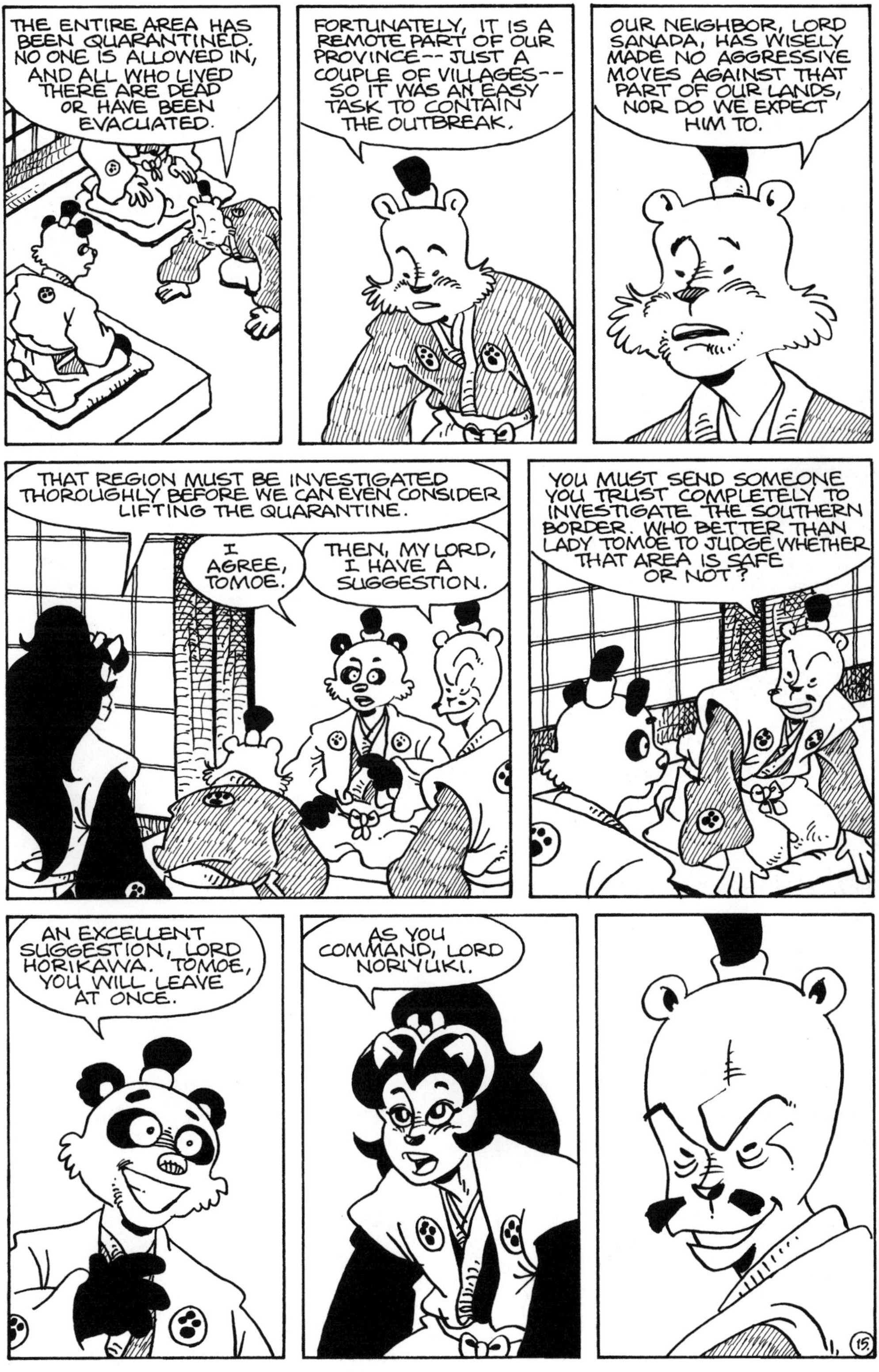
THE ENTIRE AREA HAS BEEN QUARANTINED. NO ONE IS ALLOWED IN, AND ALL WHO LIVED THERE ARE DEAD OR HAVE BEEN EVACUATED.
FORTUNATELY, IT IS A REMOTE PART OF OUR PROVINCE-- JUST A COUPLE OF VILLAGES-- SO IT WAS AN EASY TASK TO CONTAIN THE OUTBREAK.
OUR NEIGHBOR, LORD SANADA, HAS WISELY MADE NO AGGRESSIVE MOVES AGAINST THAT PART OF OUR LANDS, NOR DO WE EXPECT HIM TO.
THAT REGION MUST BE INVESTIGATED THOROUGHLY BEFORE WE CAN EVEN CONSIDER LIFTING THE QUARANTINE.
I AGREE, TOMOE.
THEN, MY LORD, I HAVE A SUGGESTION.
YOU MUST SEND SOMEONE YOU TRUST COMPLETELY TO INVESTIGATE THE SOUTHERN BORDER. WHO BETTER THAN LADY TOMOE TO JUDGE WHETHER THAT AREA IS SAFE OR NOT?
AN EXCELLENT SUGGESTION, LORD HORIKAWA. TOMOE, YOU WILL LEAVE AT ONCE.
AS YOU COMMAND, LORD NORIYUKI.
15

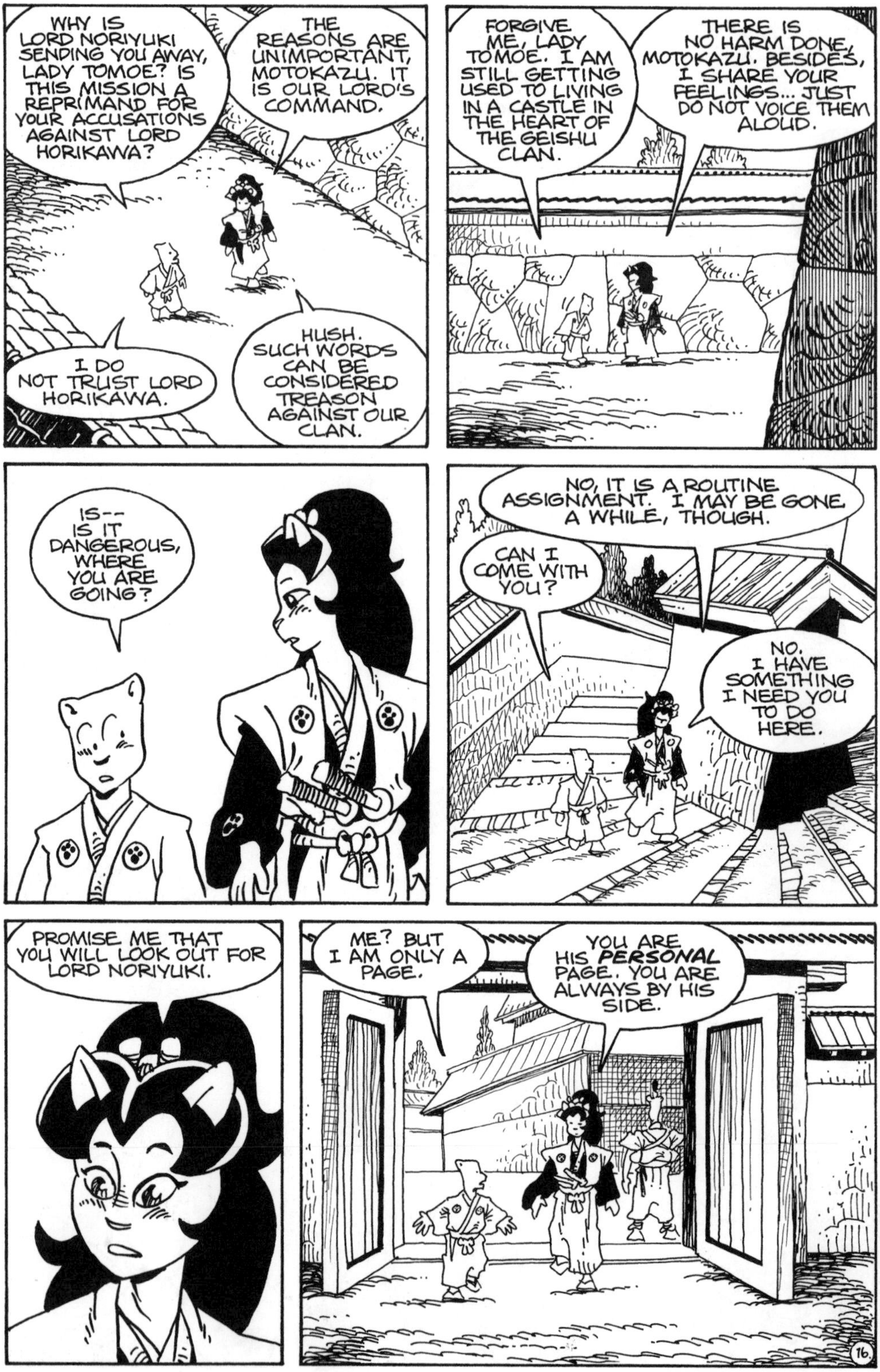

WHY IS LORD NORIYUKI SENDING YOU AWAY, LADY TOMOE? IS THIS MISSION A REPRIMAND FOR YOUR ACCUSATIONS AGAINST LORD HORIKAWA?
THE REASONS ARE UNIMPORTANT, MOTOKAZU. IT IS OUR LORD'S COMMAND.
I DO NOT TRUST LORD HORIKAWA.
HUSH. SUCH WORDS CAN BE CONSIDERED TREASON AGAINST OUR CLAN.
FORGIVE ME, LADY TOMOE. I AM STILL GETTING USED TO LIVING IN A CASTLE IN THE HEART OF THE GEISHU CLAN.
THERE IS NO HARM DONE, MOTOKAZU. BESIDES, I SHARE YOUR FEELINGS... JUST DO NOT VOICE THEM ALOUD.
IS-- IS IT DANGEROUS, WHERE YOU ARE GOING?
NO, IT IS A ROUTINE ASSIGNMENT. I MAY BE GONE A WHILE, THOUGH.
CAN I COME WITH YOU?
NO. I HAVE SOMETHING I NEED YOU TO DO HERE.
PROMISE ME THAT YOU WILL LOOK OUT FOR LORD NORIYUKI.
ME? BUT I AM ONLY A PAGE.
YOU ARE HIS PERSONAL PAGE. YOU ARE ALWAYS BY HIS SIDE.
16.

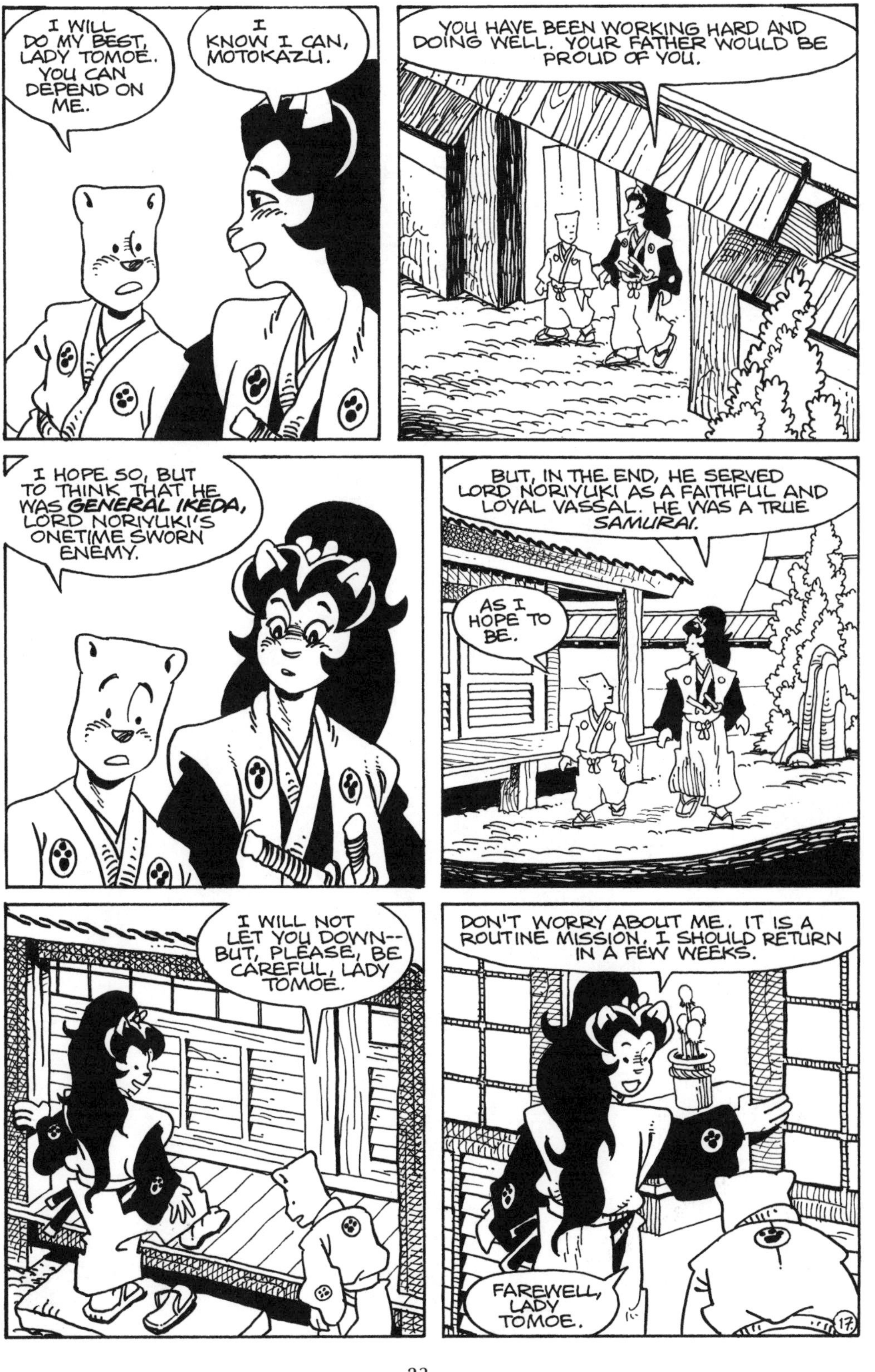
I WILL DO MY BEST, LADY TOMOE. YOU CAN DEPEND ON ME.
I KNOW I CAN, MOTOKAZU.
YOU HAVE BEEN WORKING HARD AND DOING WELL. YOUR FATHER WOULD BE PROUD OF YOU.
I HOPE SO, BUT TO THINK THAT HE WAS GENERAL IKEDA, LORD NORIYUKI'S ONETIME SWORN ENEMY.
BUT, IN THE END, HE SERVED LORD NORIYUKI AS A FAITHFUL AND LOYAL VASSAL. HE WAS A TRUE SAMURAI.
AS I HOPE TO BE.
I WILL NOT LET YOU DOWN-- BUT, PLEASE, BE CAREFUL, LADY TOMOE.
DON'T WORRY ABOUT ME. IT IS A ROUTINE MISSION. I SHOULD RETURN IN A FEW WEEKS.
FAREWELL, LADY TOMOE.
17.

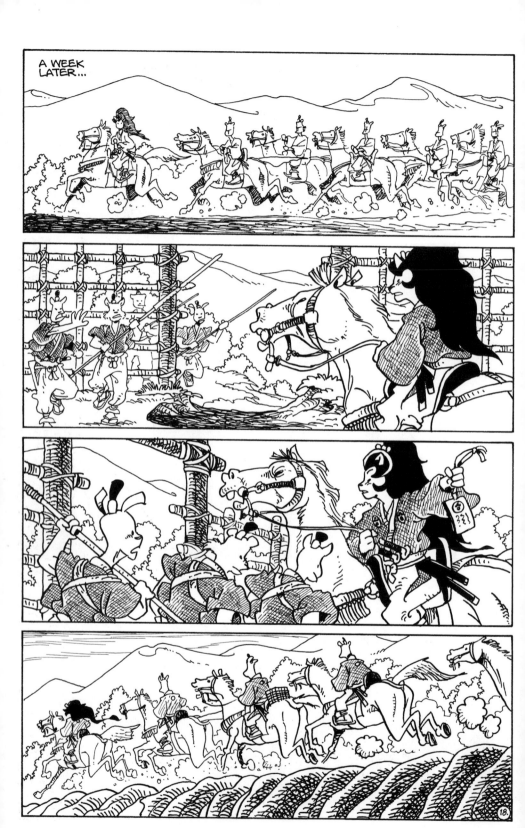

A WEEK
LATER...

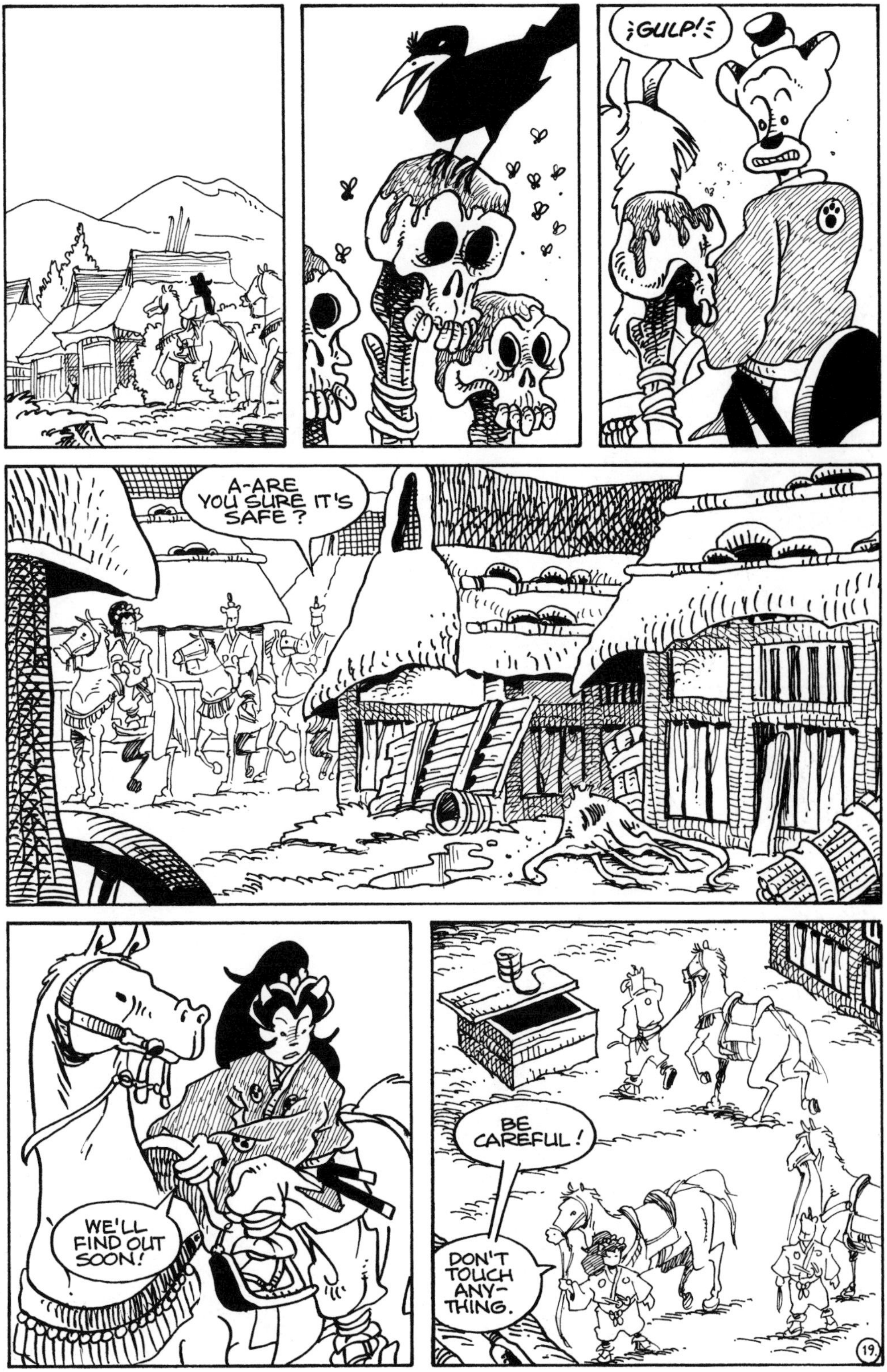
¡GULP!
A-ARE YOU SURE IT'S SAFE?
WE'LL FIND OUT SOON!
BE CAREFUL!
DON'T TOUCH ANY-THING.
19.

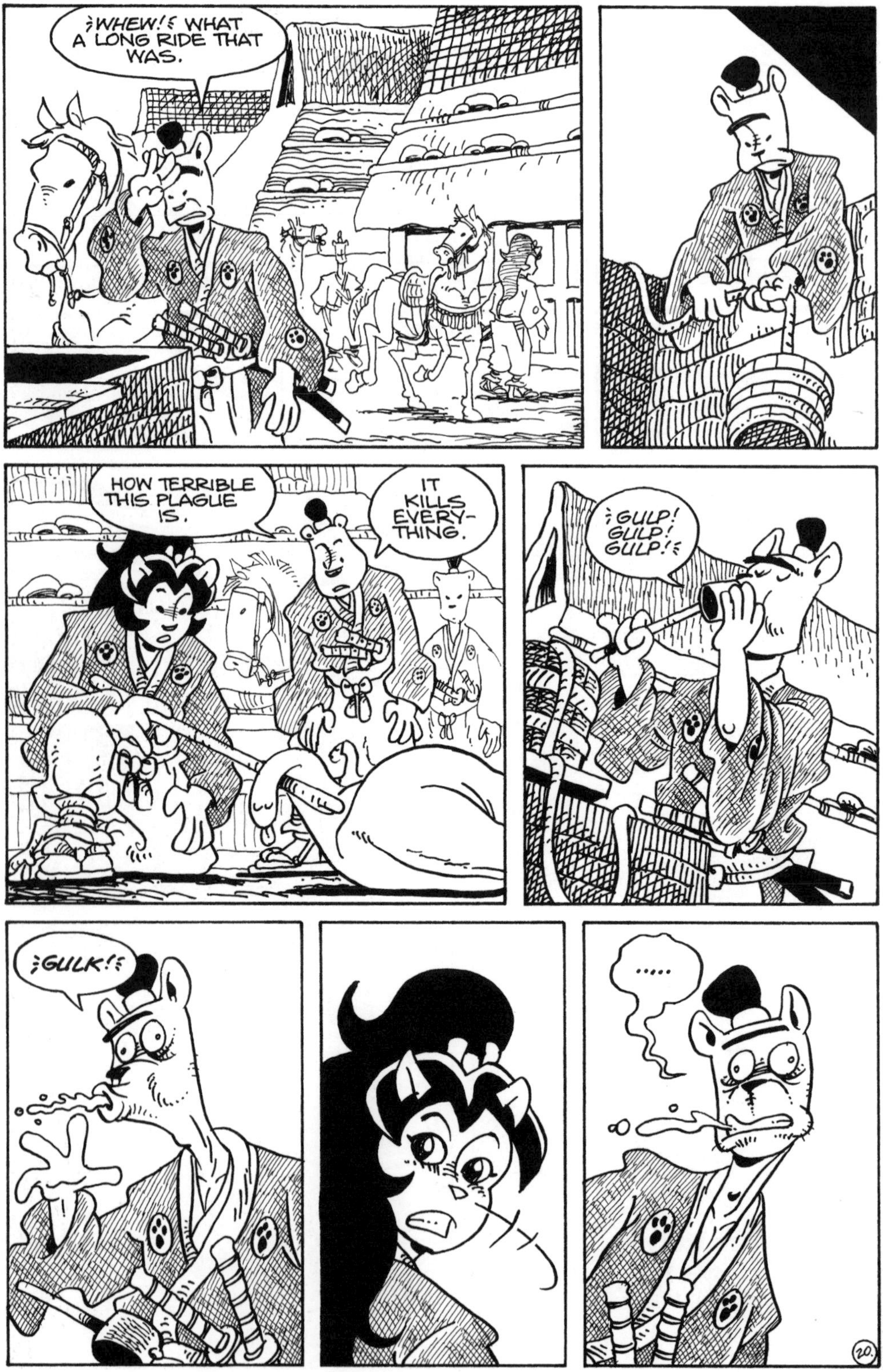
WHEW! WHAT A LONG RIDE THAT WAS.
HOW TERRIBLE THIS PLAGUE IS.
IT KILLS EVERYTHING.
GULP! GULP! GULP!
GULK!
.....
20.

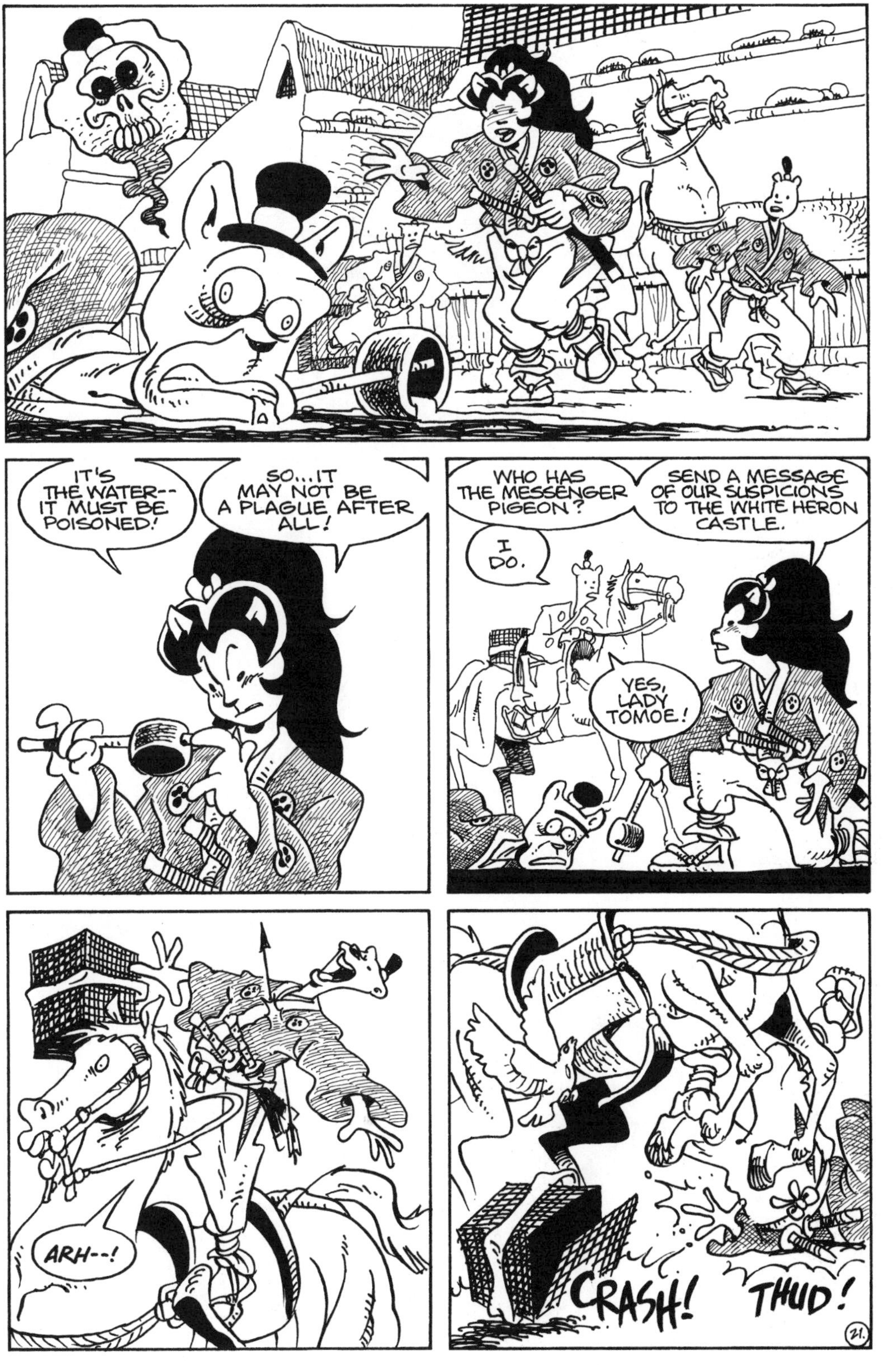
IT'S THE WATER-- IT MUST BE POISONED!
SO...IT MAY NOT BE A PLAGUE AFTER ALL!
WHO HAS THE MESSENGER PIGEON?
SEND A MESSAGE OF OUR SUSPICIONS TO THE WHITE HERON CASTLE.
I DO.
YES, LADY TOMOE!
ARH--!
CRASH!
THUD!
21.

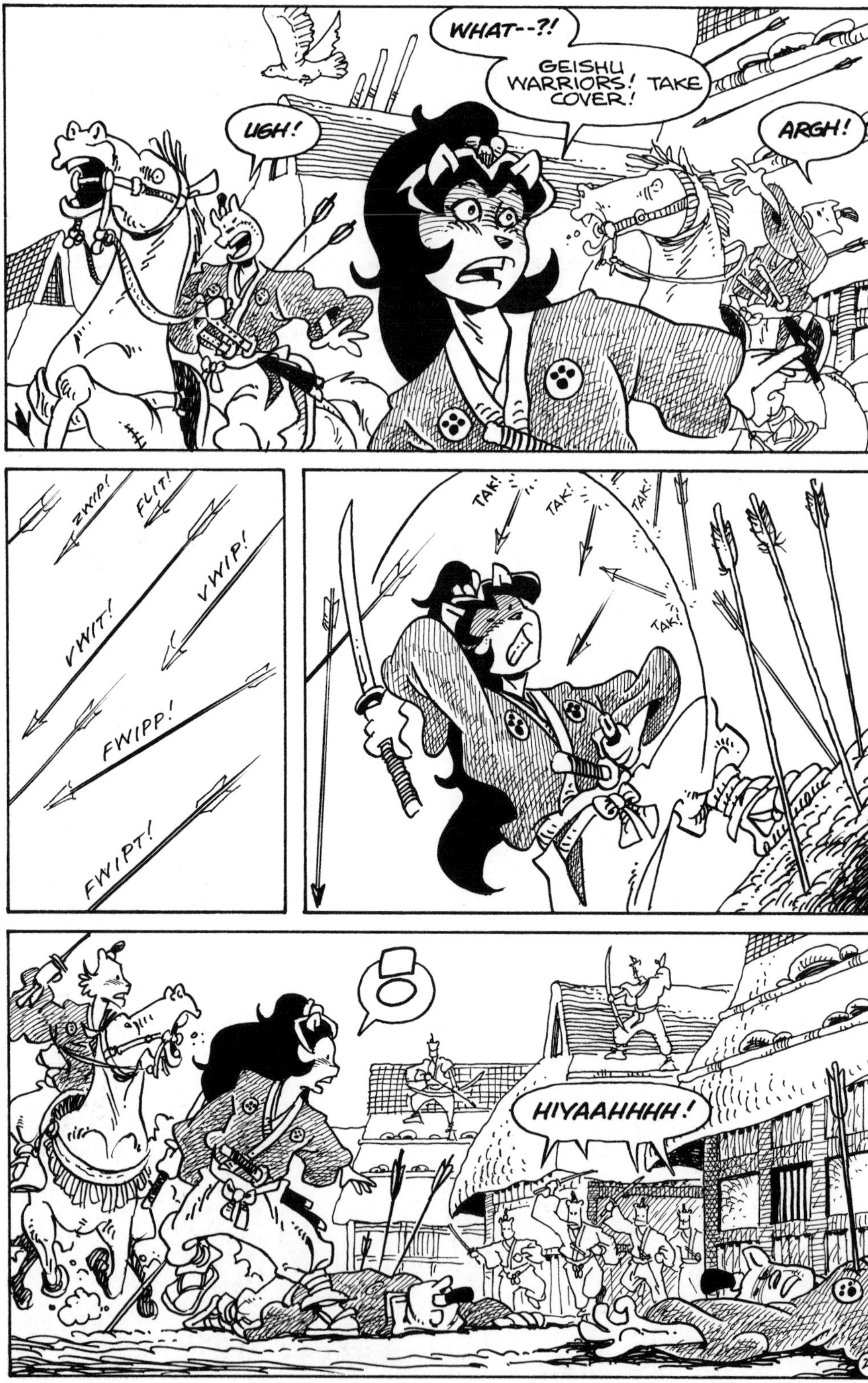
WHAT--?!
GEISHU WARRIORS! TAKE COVER!
UGH!
ARGH!
ZWIP!
FLIT!
VWIP!
VWIT!
FWIPP!
FWIPT!
TAK!
TAK!
TAK!
TAK!
HIYAAHHHH!
22

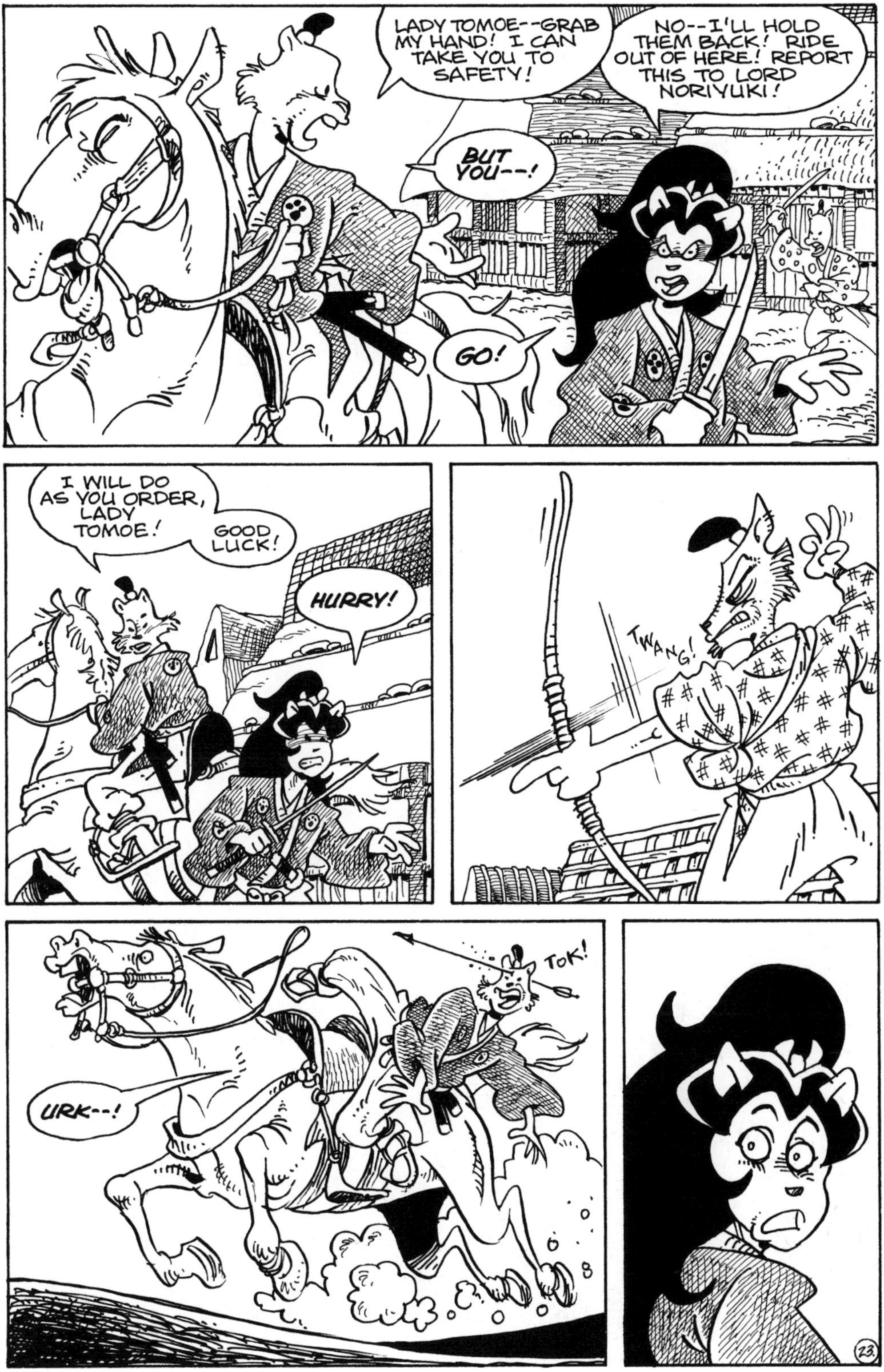
LADY TOMOE--GRAB MY HAND! I CAN TAKE YOU TO SAFETY!
NO--I'LL HOLD THEM BACK! RIDE OUT OF HERE! REPORT THIS TO LORD NORIYUKI!
BUT YOU--!
GO!
I WILL DO AS YOU ORDER, LADY TOMOE!
GOOD LUCK!
HURRY!
TWANG!
TOK!
URK--!
23.

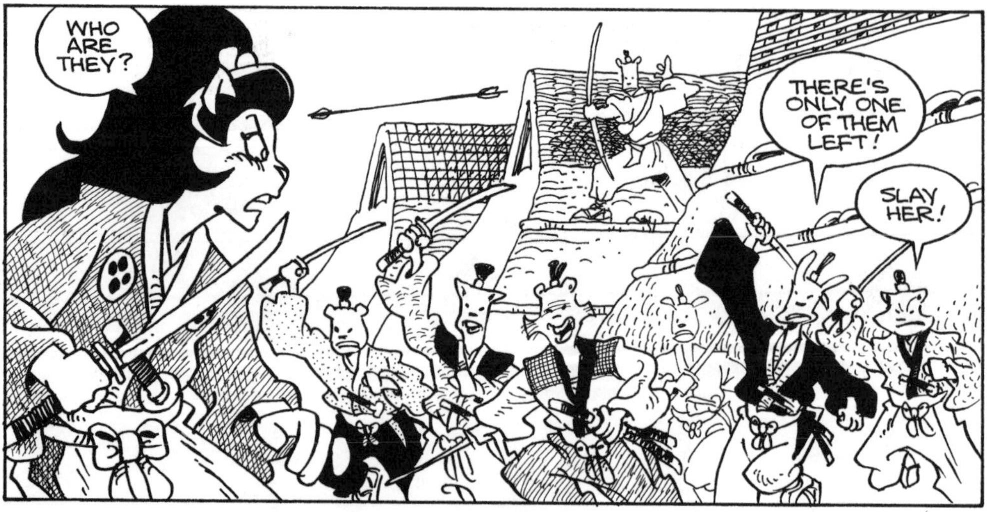
WHO ARE THEY?
THERE'S ONLY ONE OF THEM LEFT!
SLAY HER!

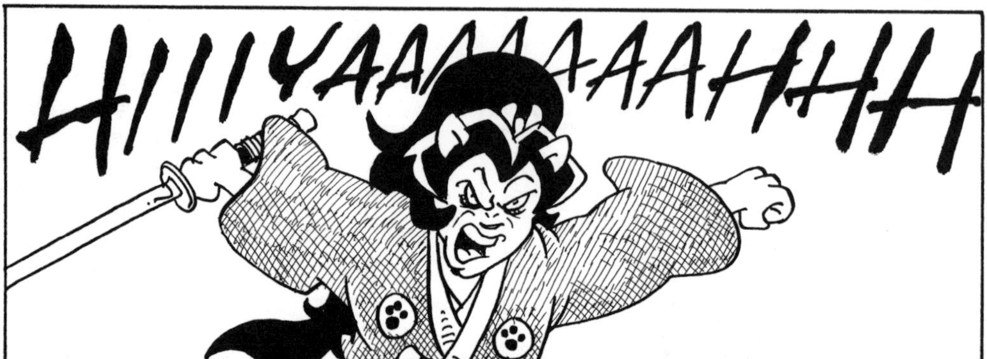
HIIIYAAAAAAAAHHHH

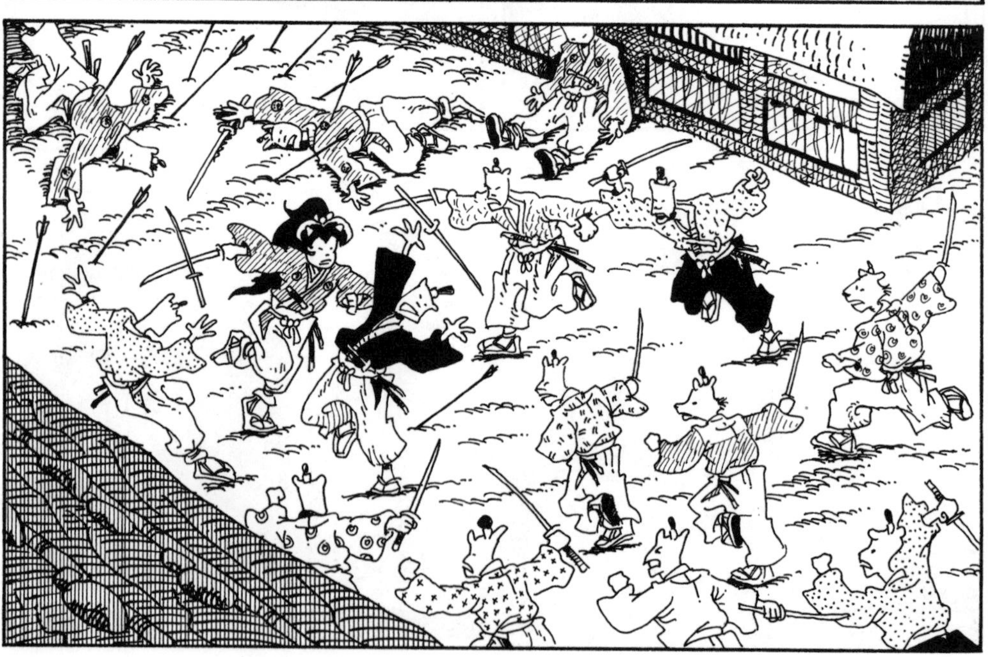

THE TREASURE of the MOTHER of MOUNTAINS

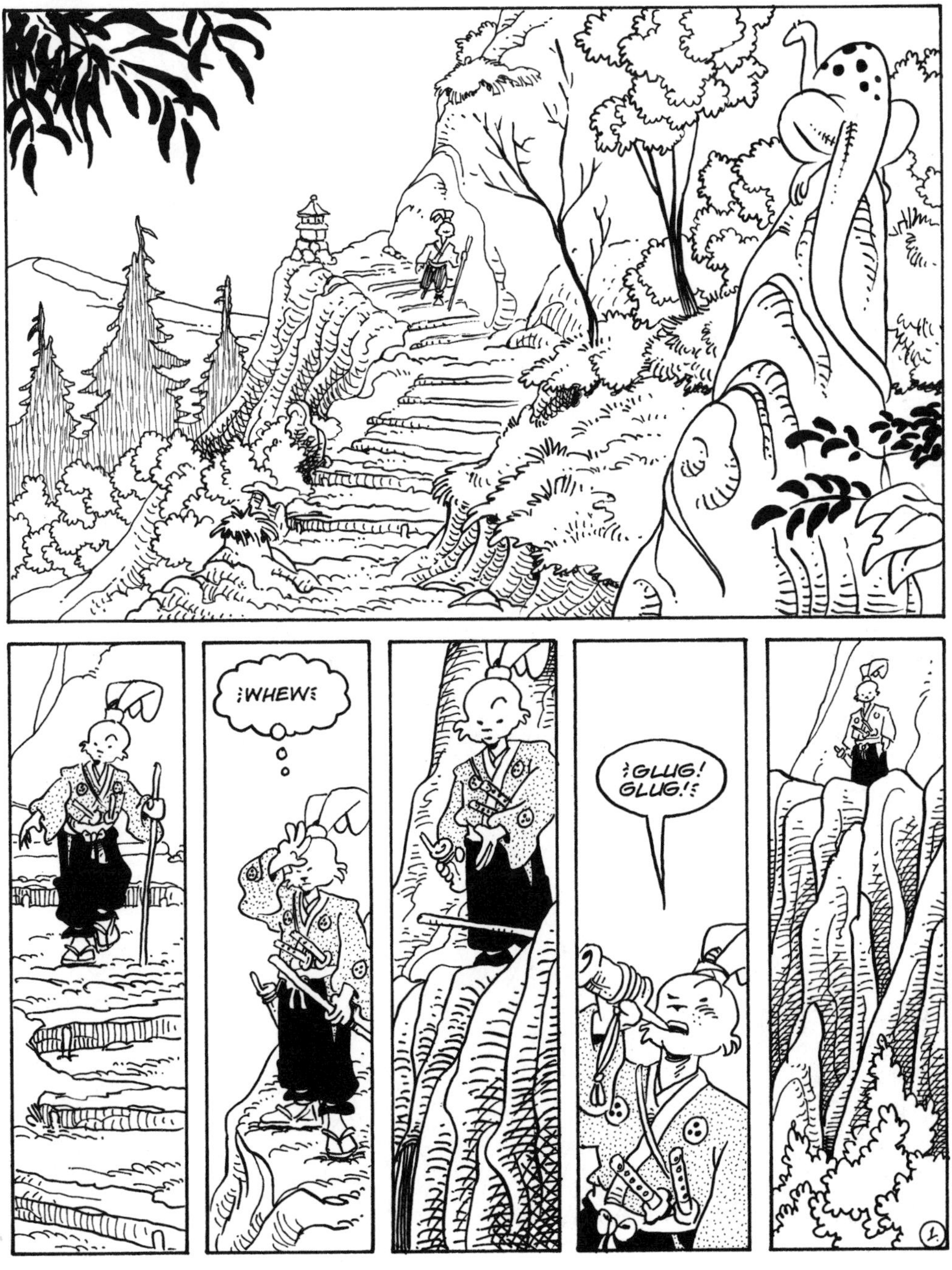
WHEW
GLUG! GLUG!

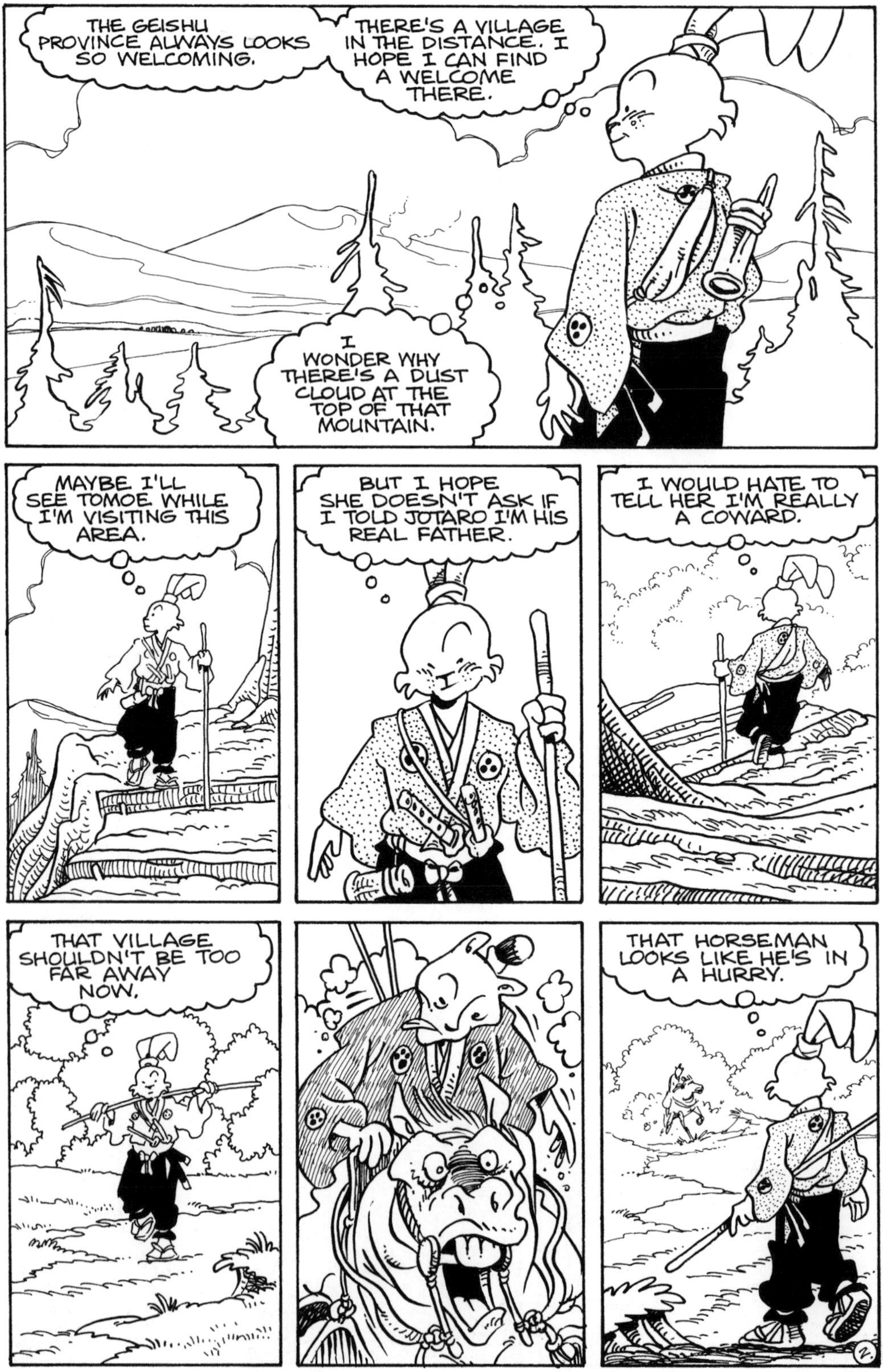
THE GEISHU PROVINCE ALWAYS LOOKS SO WELCOMING.
THERE'S A VILLAGE IN THE DISTANCE. I HOPE I CAN FIND A WELCOME THERE.
I WONDER WHY THERE'S A DUST CLOUD AT THE TOP OF THAT MOUNTAIN.
MAYBE I'LL SEE TOMOE WHILE I'M VISITING THIS AREA.
BUT I HOPE SHE DOESN'T ASK IF I TOLD JOTARO I'M HIS REAL FATHER.
I WOULD HATE TO TELL HER I'M REALLY A COWARD.
THAT VILLAGE SHOULDN'T BE TOO FAR AWAY NOW.
THAT HORSEMAN LOOKS LIKE HE'S IN A HURRY.

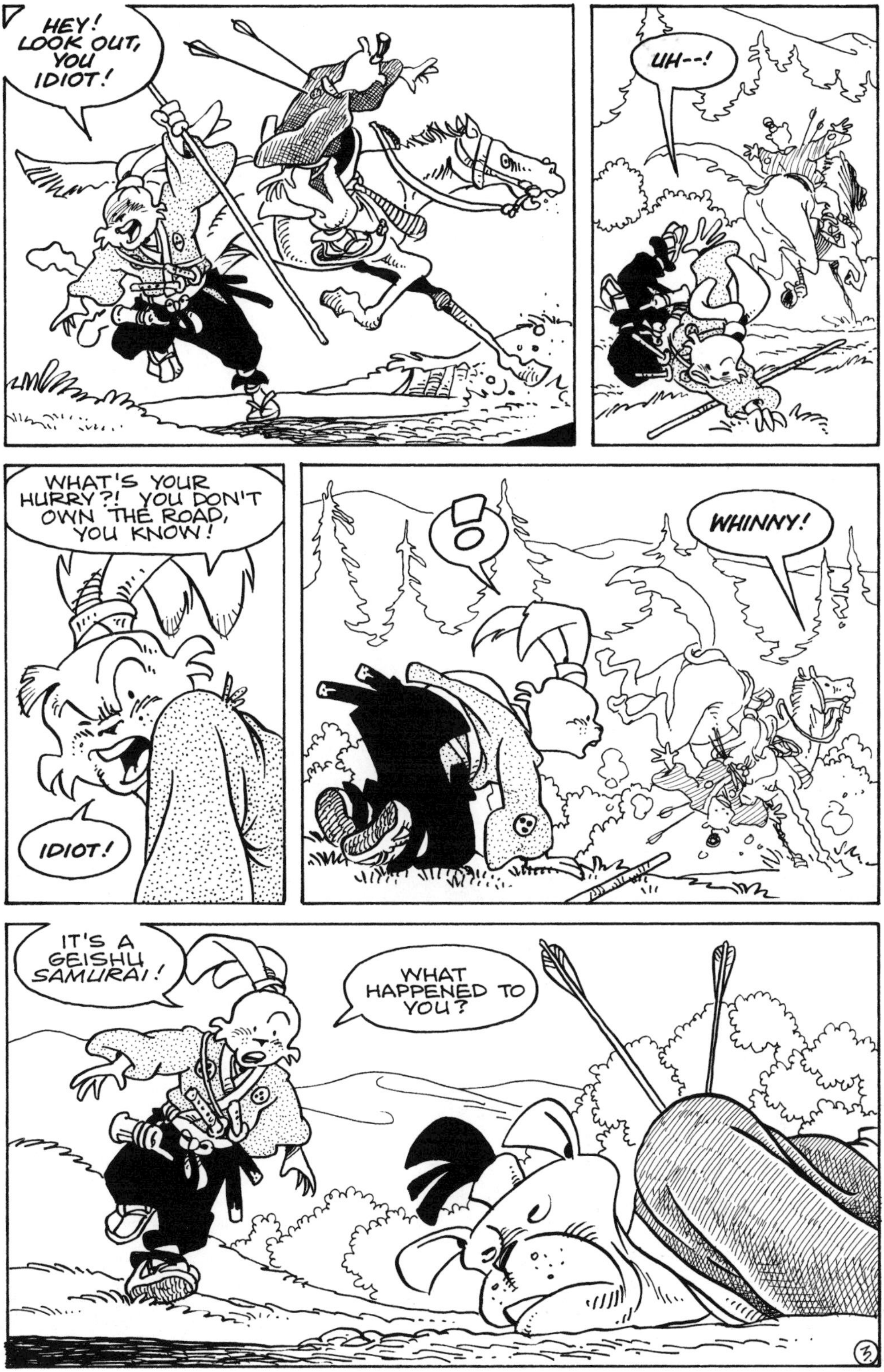
HEY! LOOK OUT, YOU IDIOT!
UH--!
WHAT'S YOUR HURRY?! YOU DON'T OWN THE ROAD, YOU KNOW!
IDIOT!
!
WHINNY!
IT'S A GEISHU SAMURAI!
WHAT HAPPENED TO YOU?
3.

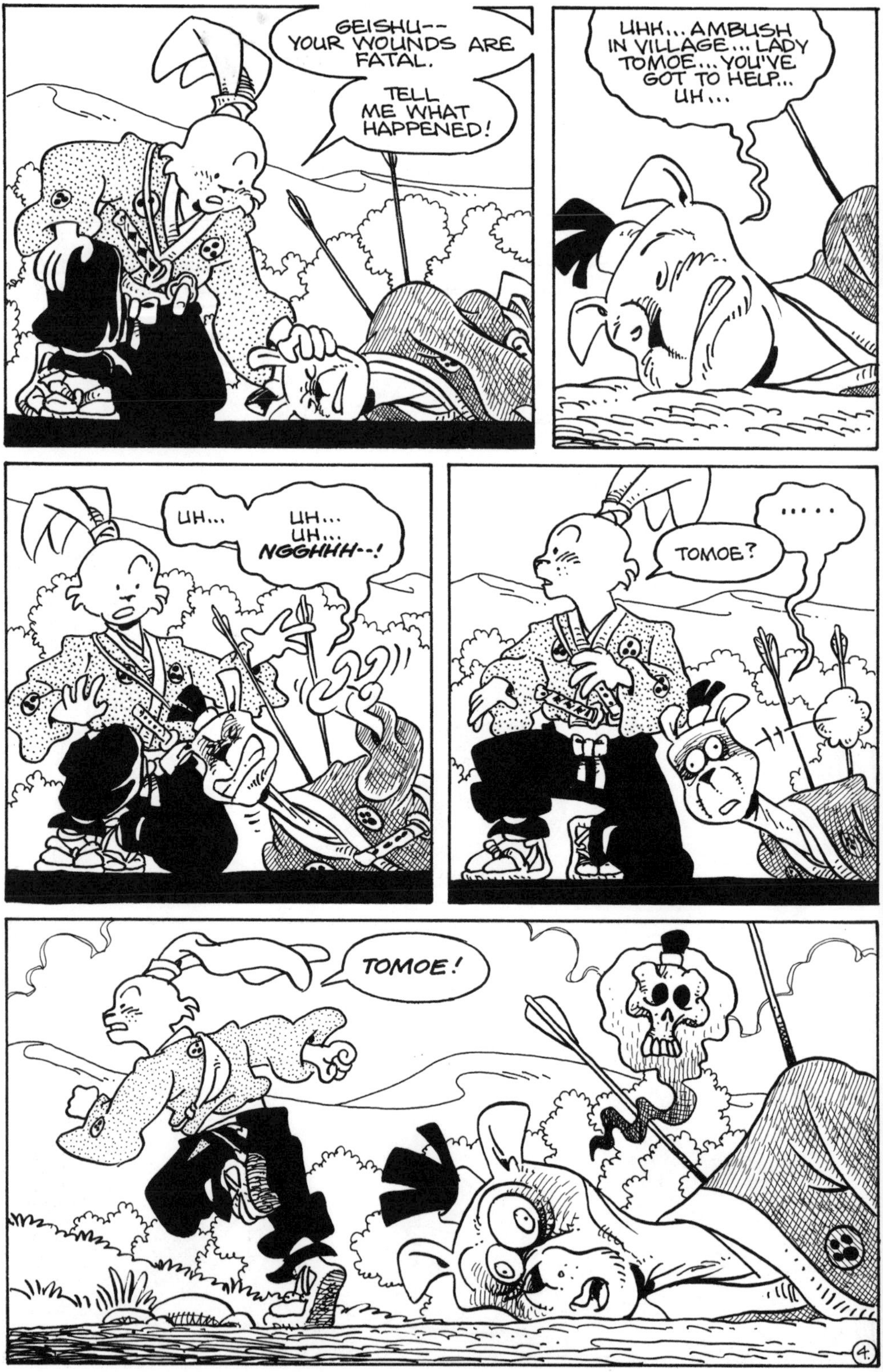
GEISHU-- YOUR WOUNDS ARE FATAL.
TELL ME WHAT HAPPENED!
UHH... AMBUSH IN VILLAGE... LADY TOMOE... YOU'VE GOT TO HELP... UH...
UH...
UH... UH... NGGHHH--!
TOMOE?
....
TOMOE!
4.

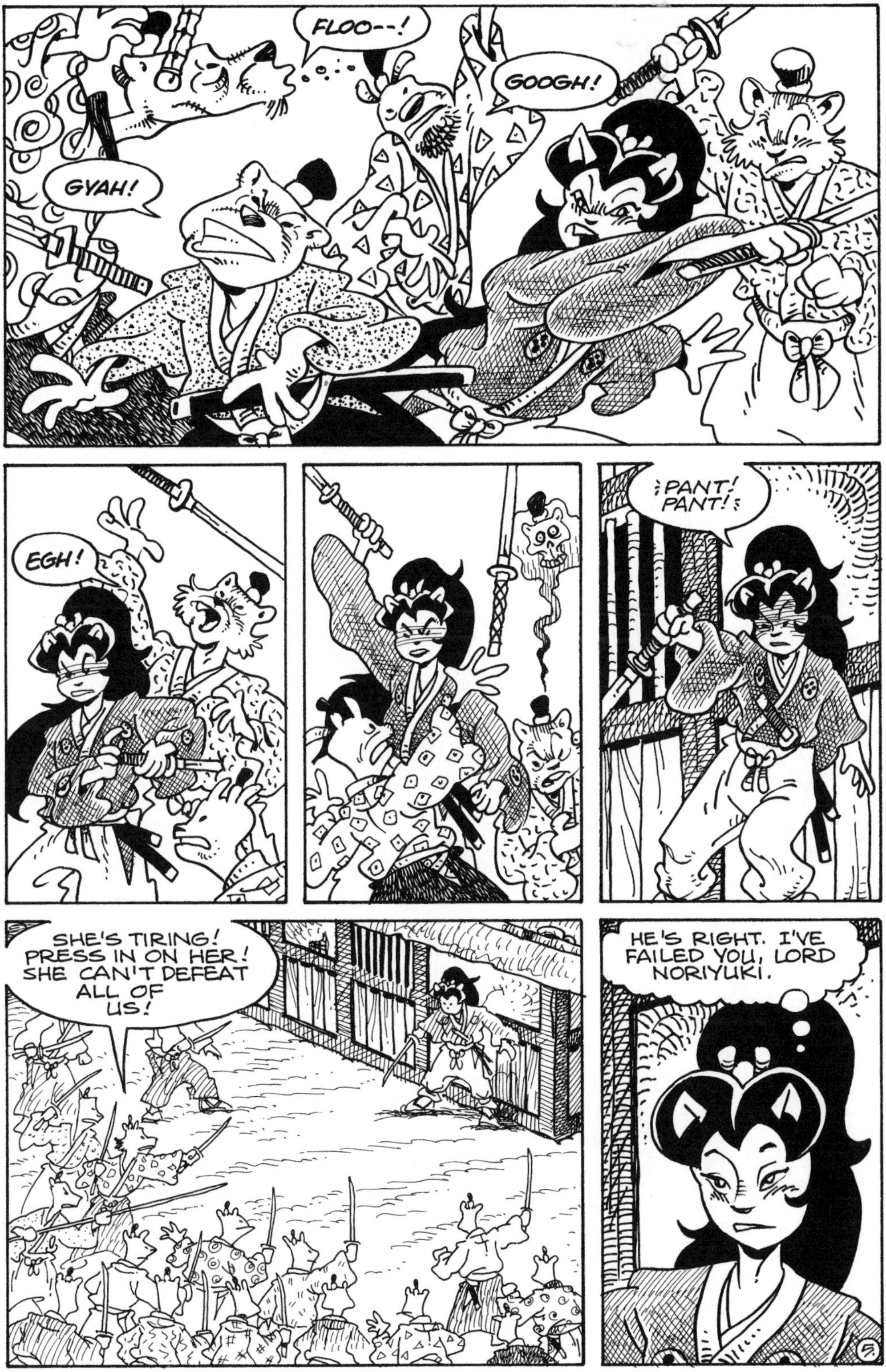
FLOO--!
GOOGH!
GYAH!
EGH!
PANT! PANT!
SHE'S TIRING! PRESS IN ON HER! SHE CAN'T DEFEAT ALL OF US!
HE'S RIGHT. I'VE FAILED YOU, LORD NORIYUKI.

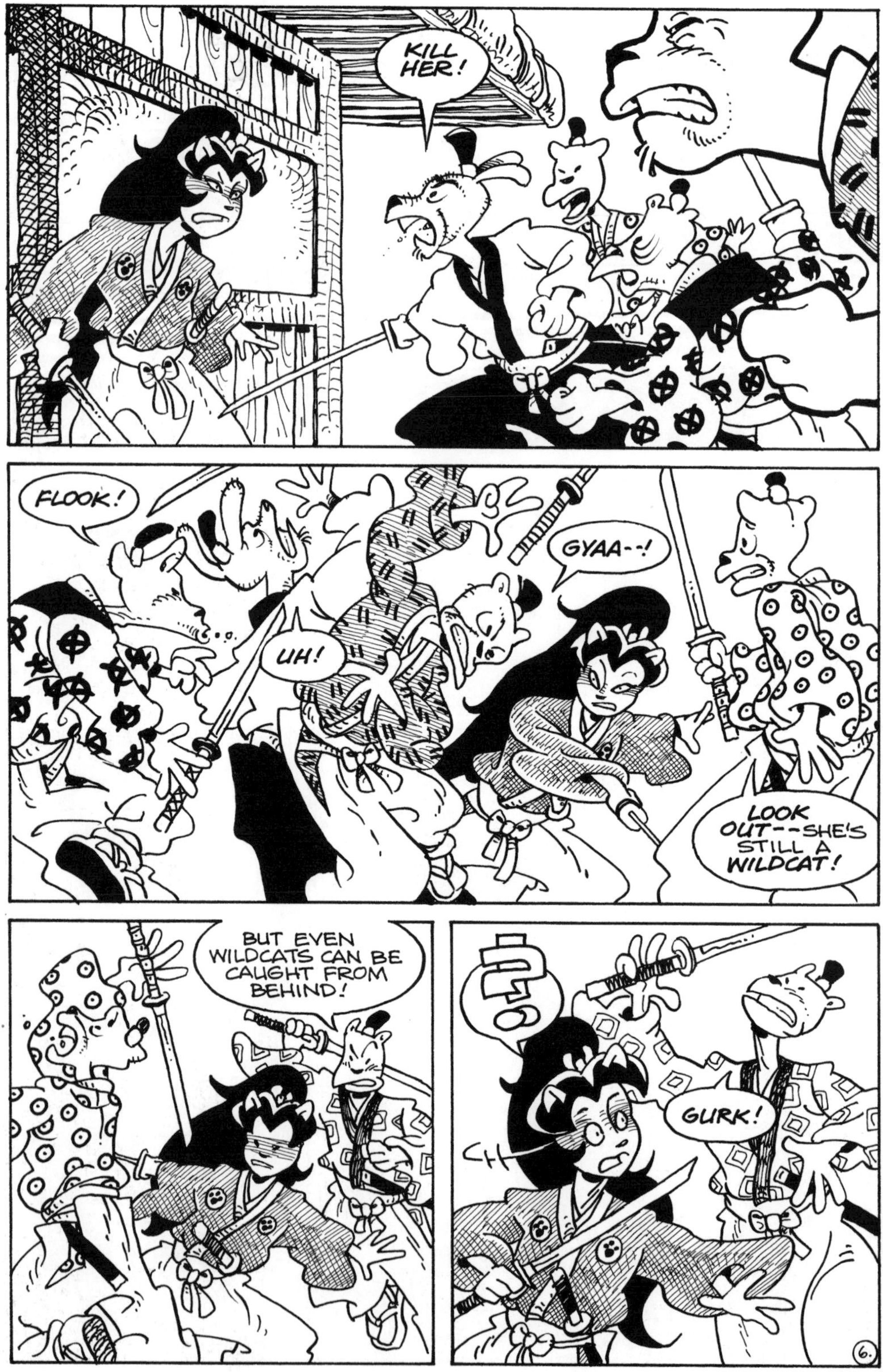
KILL HER!
FLOOK!
UH!
GYAA--!
LOOK OUT--SHE'S STILL A WILDCAT!
BUT EVEN WILDCATS CAN BE CAUGHT FROM BEHIND!
?
GURK!
6.

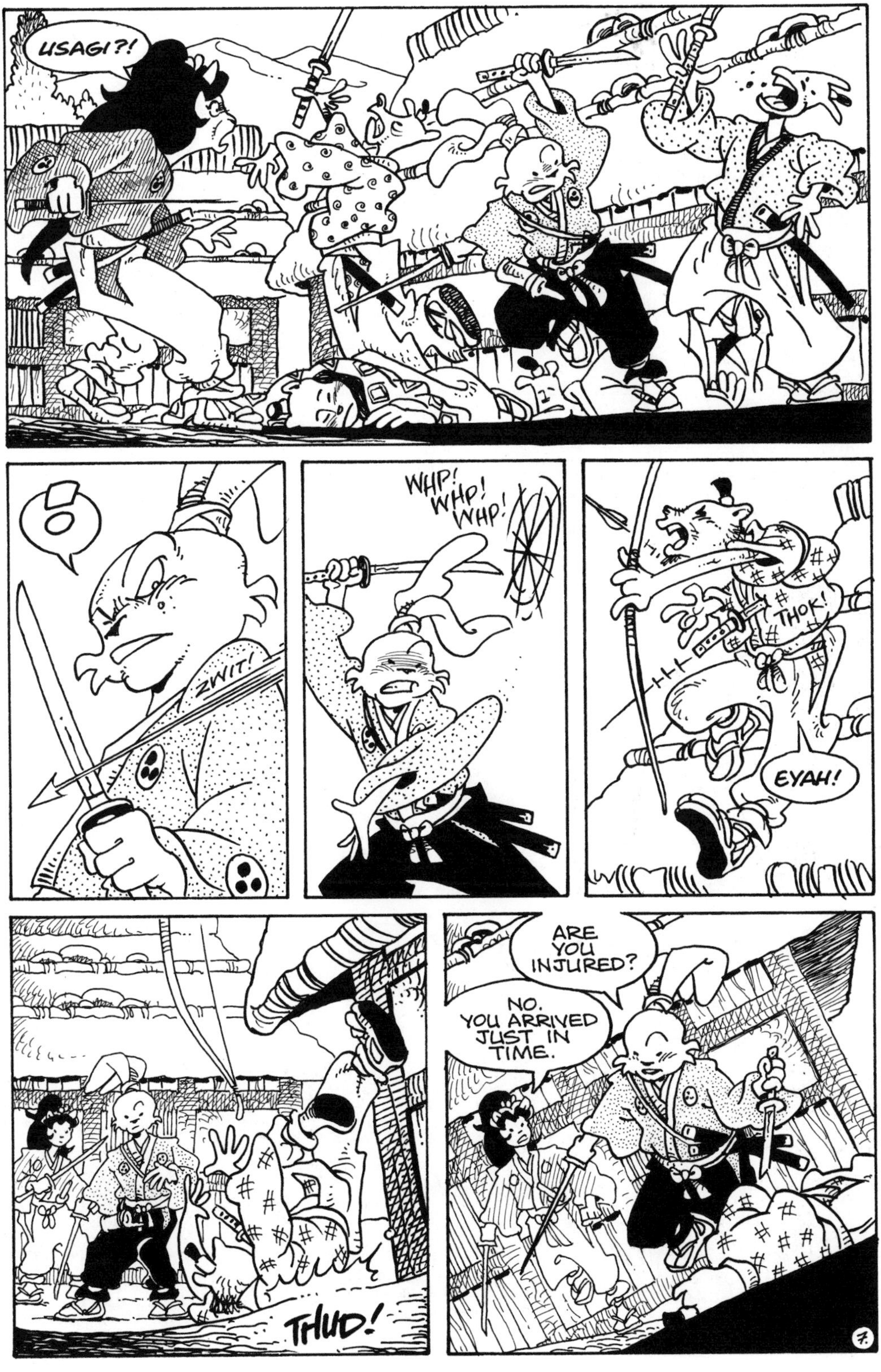
USAGI?!
!
ZWIT!
WHP! WHP! WHP!
THOK!
EYAH!
THUD!
ARE YOU INJURED?
NO. YOU ARRIVED JUST IN TIME.
7.

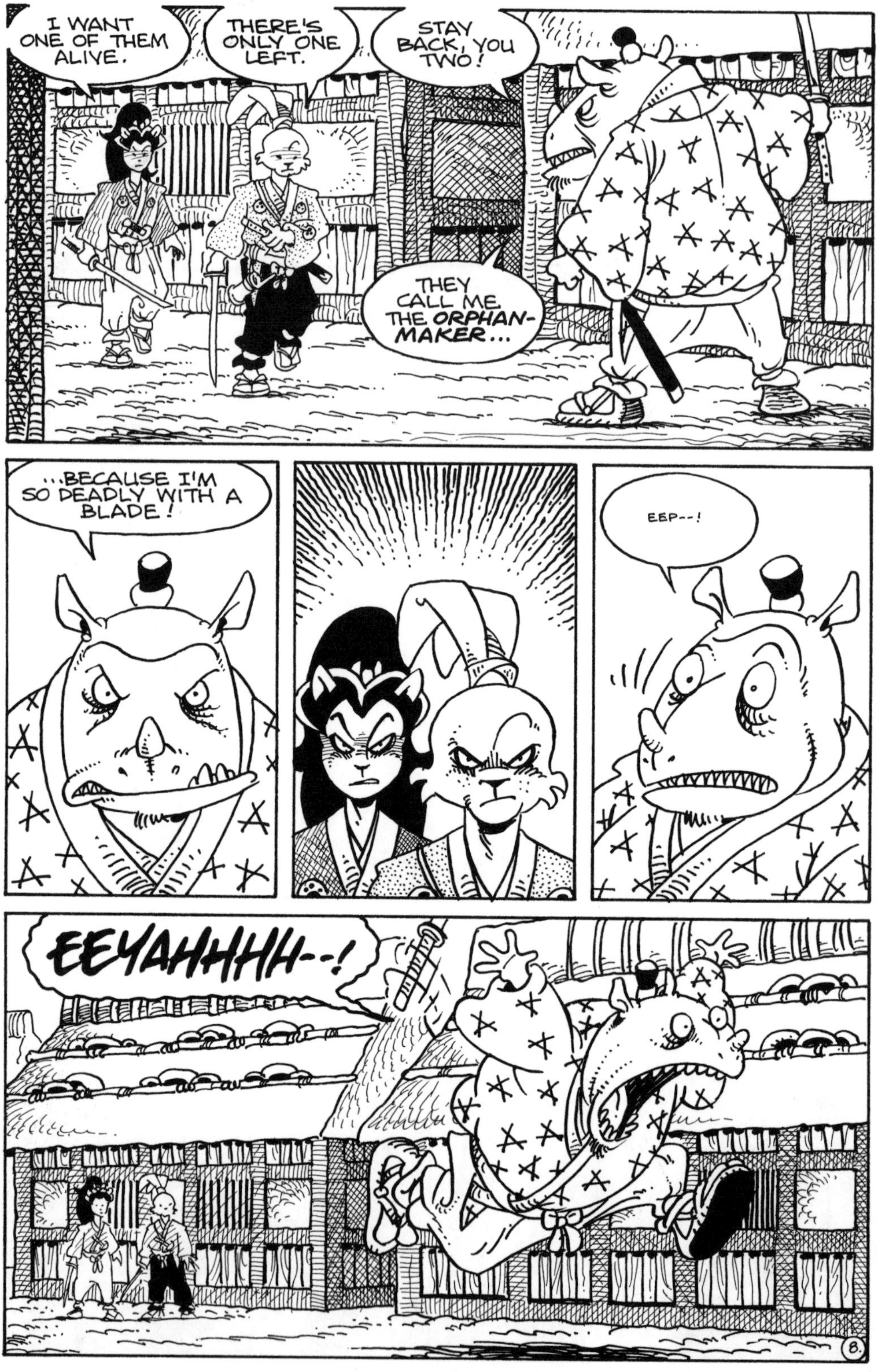

I WANT ONE OF THEM ALIVE.
THERE'S ONLY ONE LEFT.
STAY BACK, YOU TWO!
THEY CALL ME THE ORPHAN-MAKER...
...BECAUSE I'M SO DEADLY WITH A BLADE!
EEP--!
EEYAHHHH--!
8.

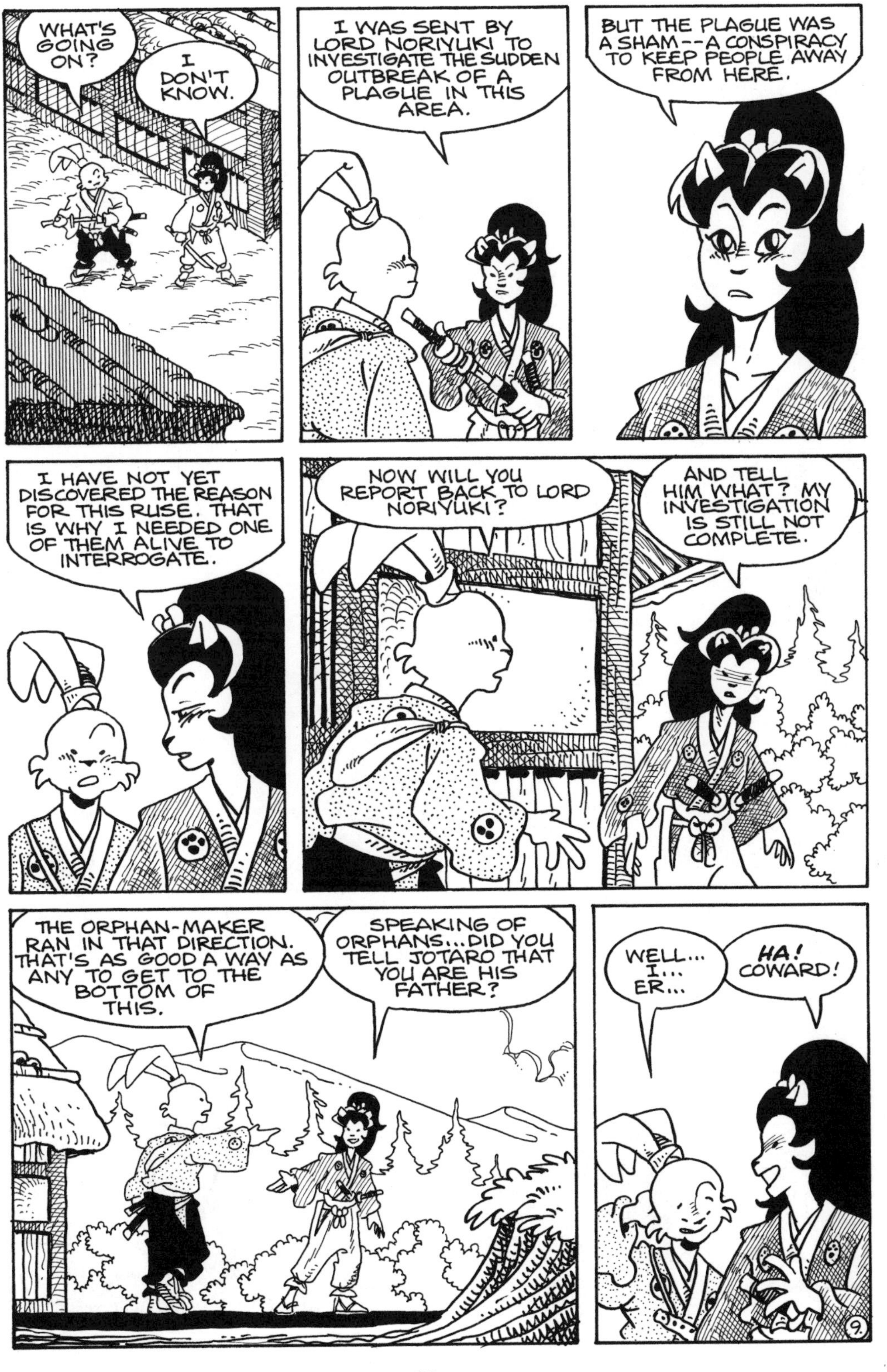
WHAT'S GOING ON?
I DON'T KNOW.
I WAS SENT BY LORD NORIYUKI TO INVESTIGATE THE SUDDEN OUTBREAK OF A PLAGUE IN THIS AREA.
BUT THE PLAGUE WAS A SHAM--A CONSPIRACY TO KEEP PEOPLE AWAY FROM HERE.
I HAVE NOT YET DISCOVERED THE REASON FOR THIS RUSE. THAT IS WHY I NEEDED ONE OF THEM ALIVE TO INTERROGATE.
NOW WILL YOU REPORT BACK TO LORD NORIYUKI?
AND TELL HIM WHAT? MY INVESTIGATION IS STILL NOT COMPLETE.
THE ORPHAN-MAKER RAN IN THAT DIRECTION. THAT'S AS GOOD A WAY AS ANY TO GET TO THE BOTTOM OF THIS.
SPEAKING OF ORPHANS...DID YOU TELL JOTARO THAT YOU ARE HIS FATHER?
WELL... I... ER...
HA! COWARD!
9.

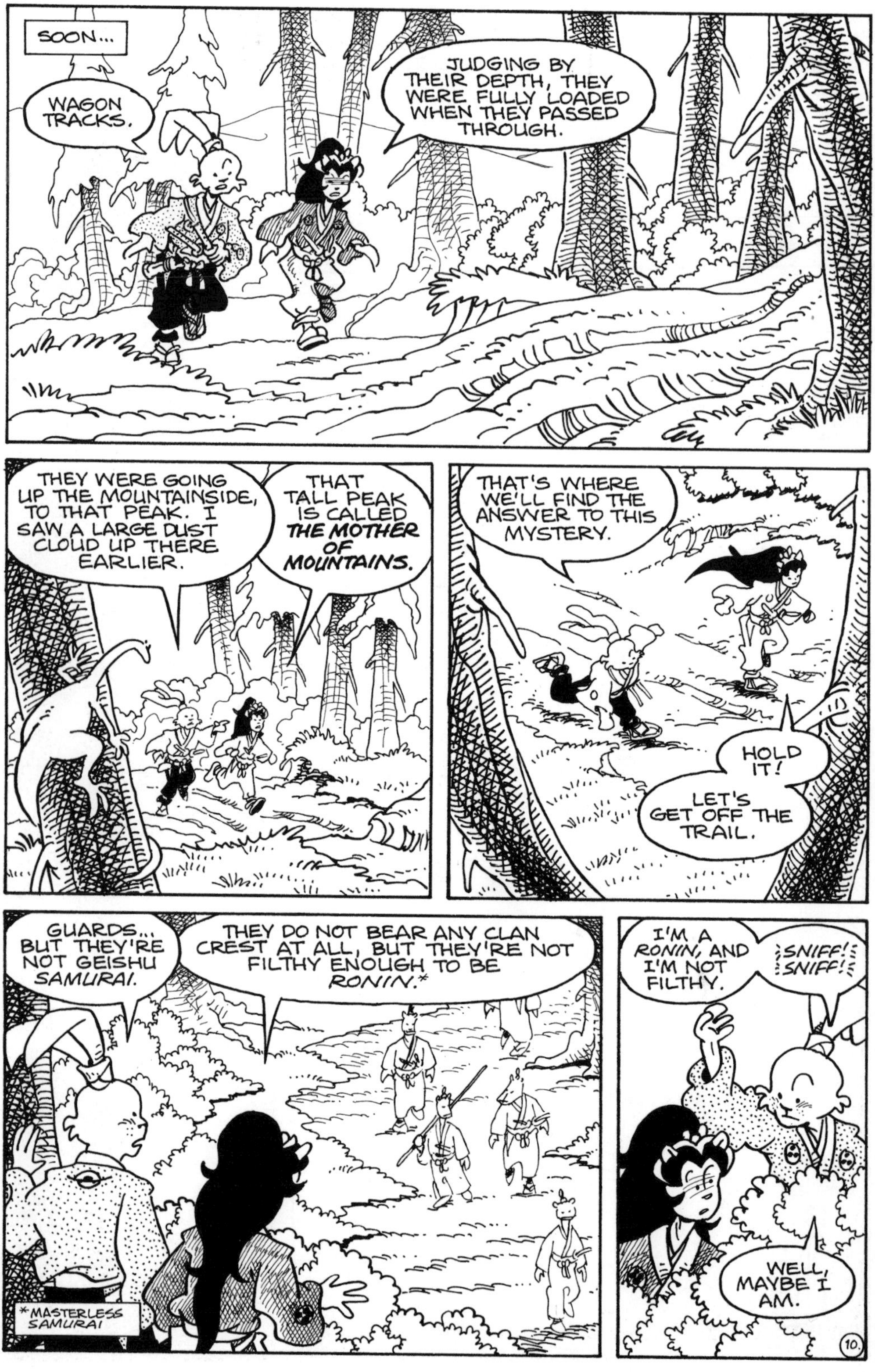
SOON...
WAGON TRACKS.
JUDGING BY THEIR DEPTH, THEY WERE FULLY LOADED WHEN THEY PASSED THROUGH.
THEY WERE GOING UP THE MOUNTAINSIDE, TO THAT PEAK. I SAW A LARGE DUST CLOUD UP THERE EARLIER.
THAT TALL PEAK IS CALLED **THE MOTHER OF MOUNTAINS.**
THAT'S WHERE WE'LL FIND THE ANSWER TO THIS MYSTERY.
HOLD IT!
LET'S GET OFF THE TRAIL.
GUARDS... BUT THEY'RE NOT GEISHU *SAMURAI.*
THEY DO NOT BEAR ANY CLAN CREST AT ALL, BUT THEY'RE NOT FILTHY ENOUGH TO BE *RONIN.**
*MASTERLESS SAMURAI
I'M A *RONIN,* AND I'M NOT FILTHY.
SNIFF! SNIFF!
WELL, MAYBE I AM.
10.

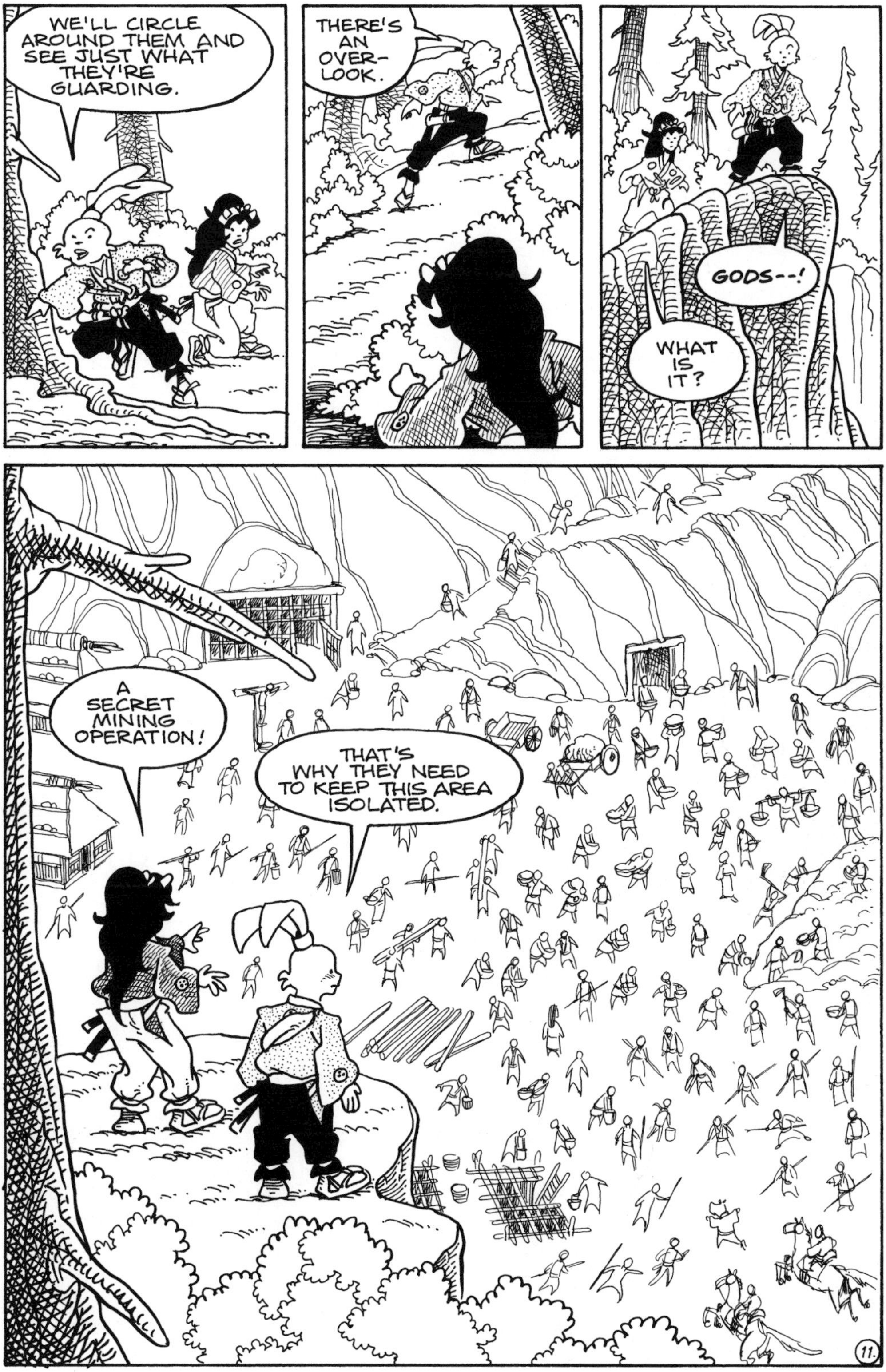
WE'LL CIRCLE AROUND THEM AND SEE JUST WHAT THEY'RE GUARDING.
THERE'S AN OVER-LOOK.
GODS--!
WHAT IS IT?
A SECRET MINING OPERATION!
THAT'S WHY THEY NEED TO KEEP THIS AREA ISOLATED.
11.

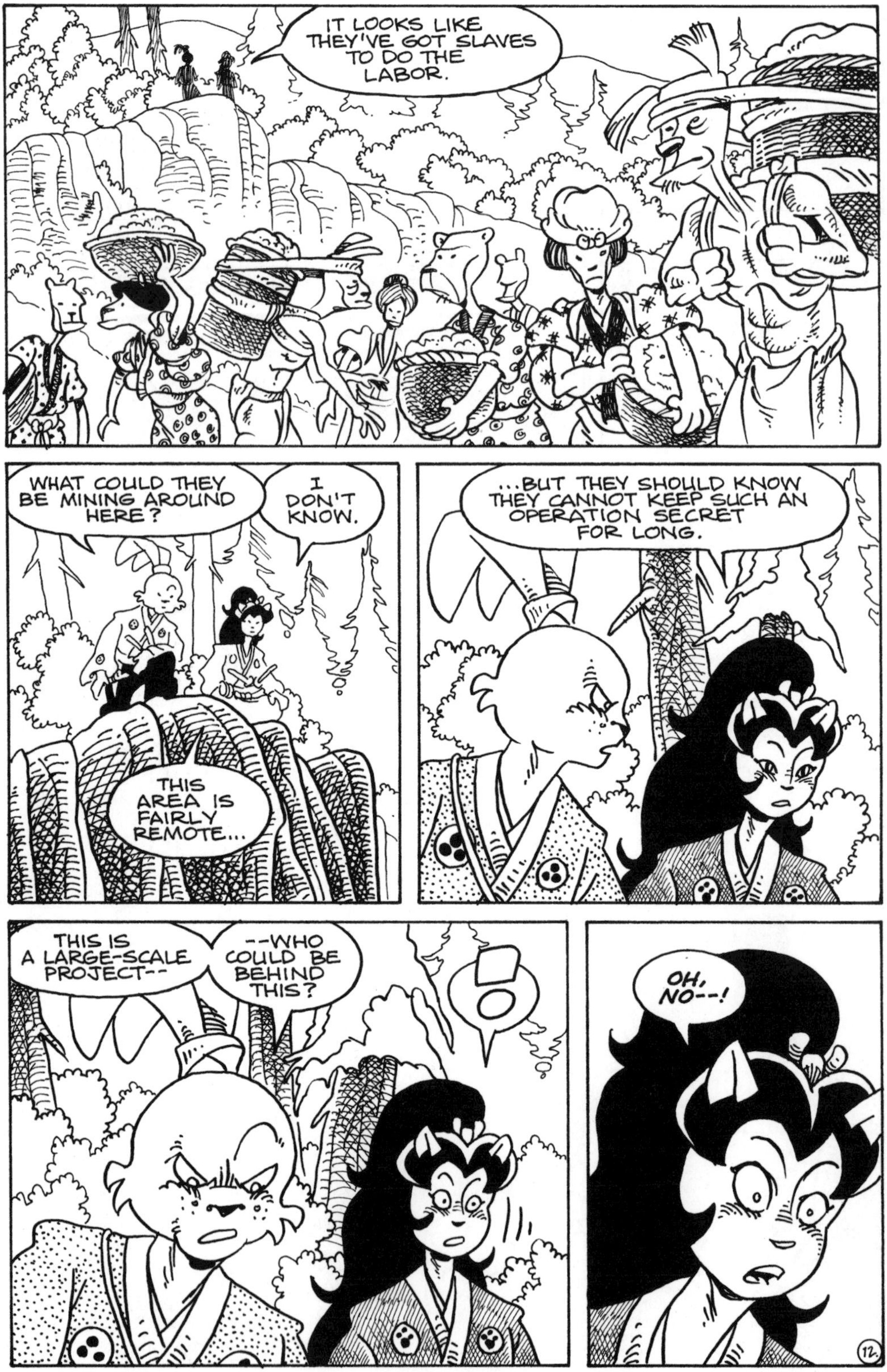
IT LOOKS LIKE THEY'VE GOT SLAVES TO DO THE LABOR.
WHAT COULD THEY BE MINING AROUND HERE?
I DON'T KNOW.
THIS AREA IS FAIRLY REMOTE...
...BUT THEY SHOULD KNOW THEY CANNOT KEEP SUCH AN OPERATION SECRET FOR LONG.
THIS IS A LARGE-SCALE PROJECT--
--WHO COULD BE BEHIND THIS?
!
OH, NO--!
12.

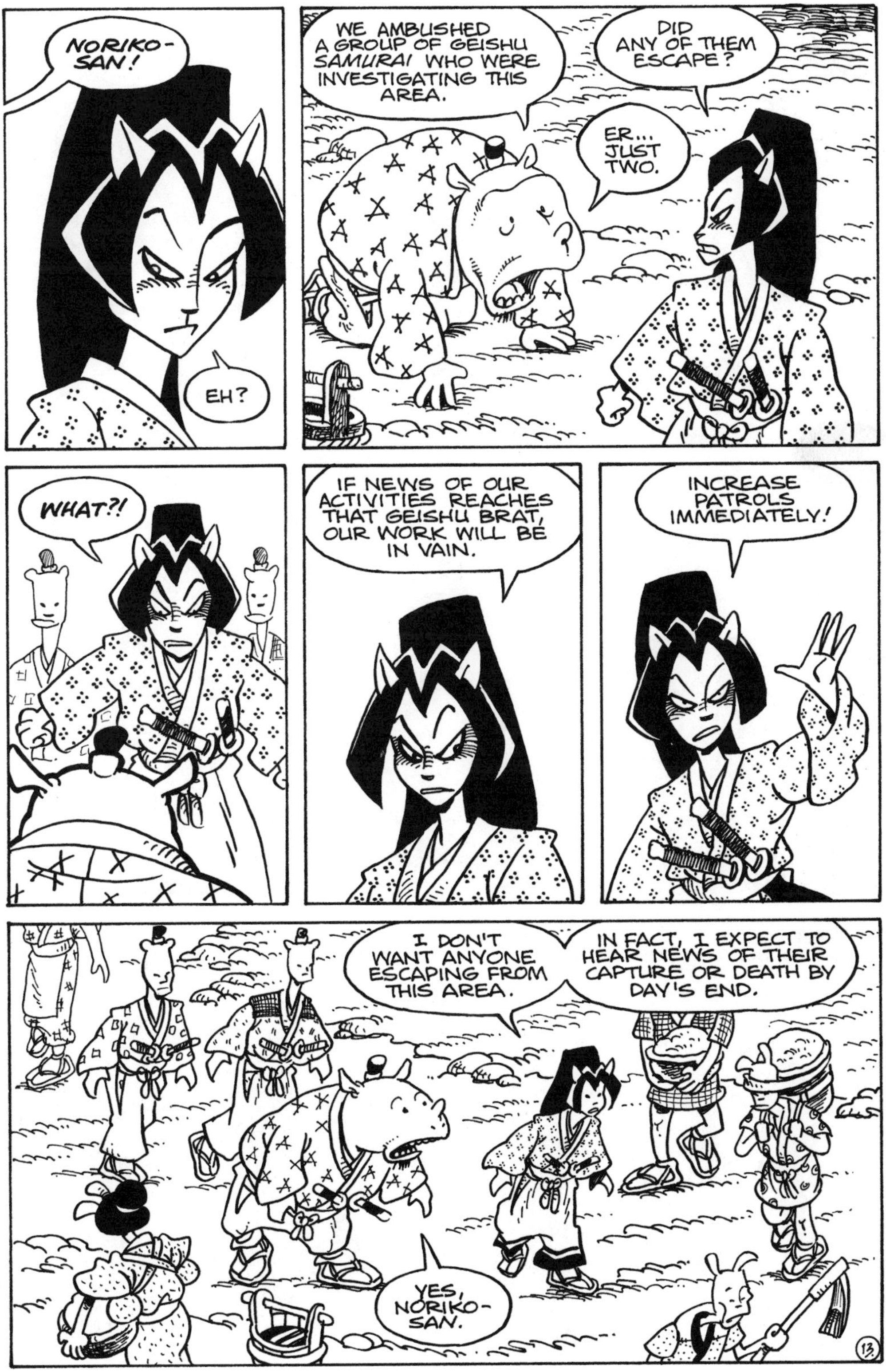
NORIKO-SAN!
EH?
WE AMBUSHED A GROUP OF GEISHU SAMURAI WHO WERE INVESTIGATING THIS AREA.
DID ANY OF THEM ESCAPE?
ER... JUST TWO.
WHAT?!
IF NEWS OF OUR ACTIVITIES REACHES THAT GEISHU BRAT, OUR WORK WILL BE IN VAIN.
INCREASE PATROLS IMMEDIATELY!
I DON'T WANT ANYONE ESCAPING FROM THIS AREA.
IN FACT, I EXPECT TO HEAR NEWS OF THEIR CAPTURE OR DEATH BY DAY'S END.
YES, NORIKO-SAN.
13

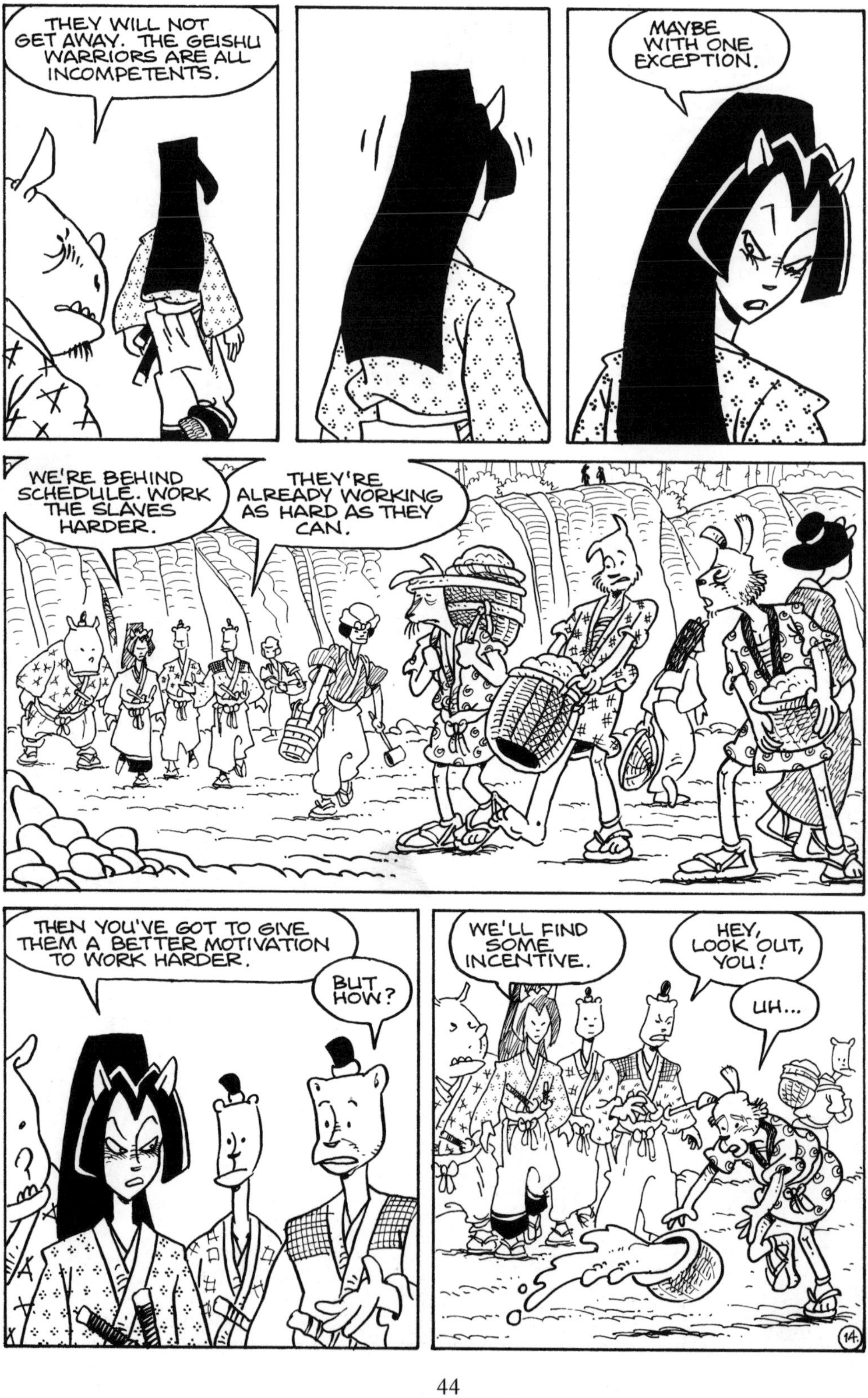
THEY WILL NOT GET AWAY. THE GEISHU WARRIORS ARE ALL INCOMPETENTS.
MAYBE WITH ONE EXCEPTION.
WE'RE BEHIND SCHEDULE. WORK THE SLAVES HARDER.
THEY'RE ALREADY WORKING AS HARD AS THEY CAN.
THEN YOU'VE GOT TO GIVE THEM A BETTER MOTIVATION TO WORK HARDER.
BUT HOW?
WE'LL FIND SOME INCENTIVE.
HEY, LOOK OUT, YOU!
UH...
14.

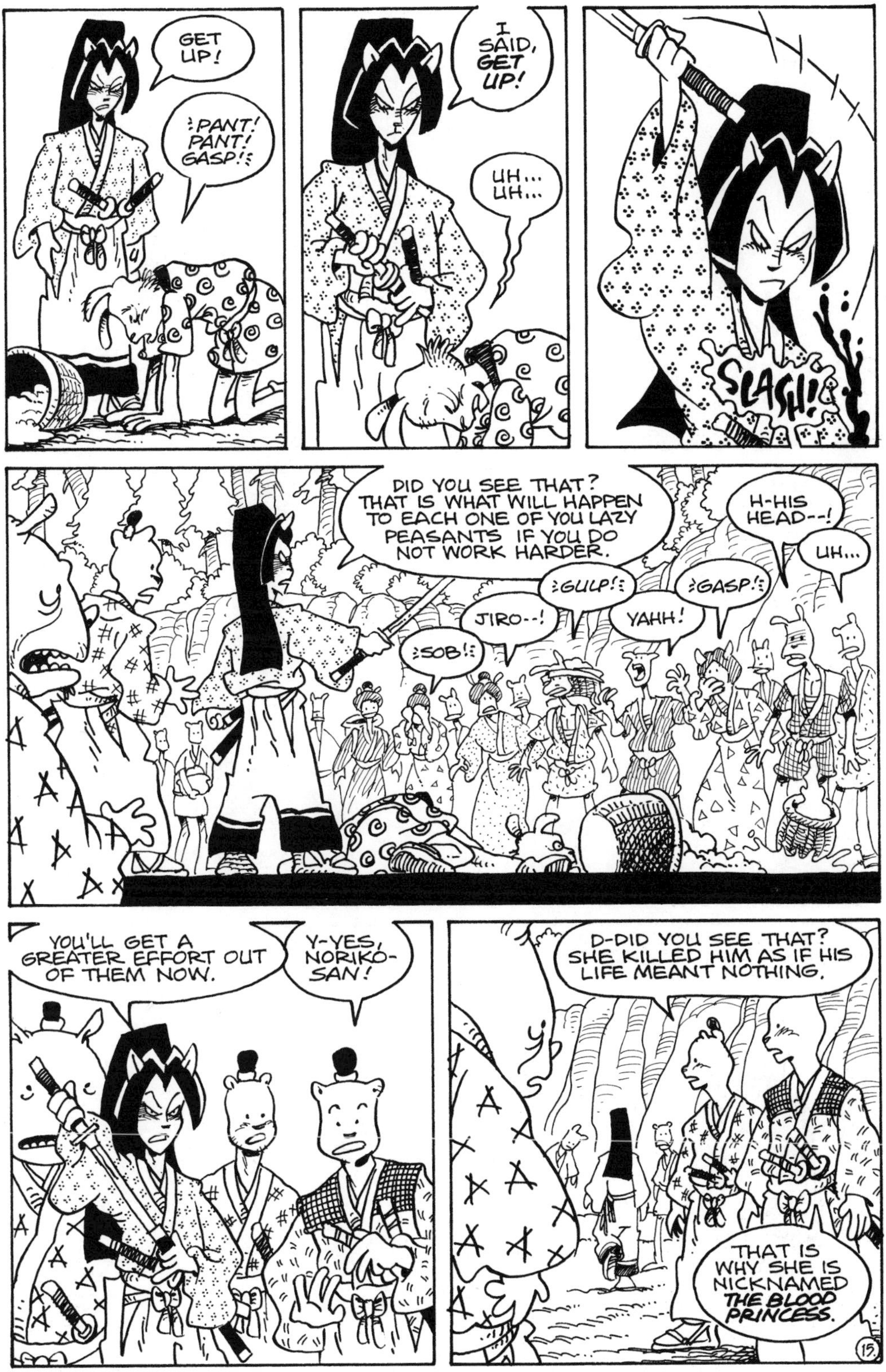
GET UP!
:PANT! PANT! GASP!:
I SAID, GET UP!
UH... UH...
SLASH!
DID YOU SEE THAT? THAT IS WHAT WILL HAPPEN TO EACH ONE OF YOU LAZY PEASANTS IF YOU DO NOT WORK HARDER.
H-HIS HEAD--!
UH...
:GULP!:
:GASP!:
JIRO--!
YAHH!
:SOB!:
YOU'LL GET A GREATER EFFORT OUT OF THEM NOW.
Y-YES, NORIKO-SAN!
D-DID YOU SEE THAT? SHE KILLED HIM AS IF HIS LIFE MEANT NOTHING.
THAT IS WHY SHE IS NICKNAMED THE BLOOD PRINCESS.
15

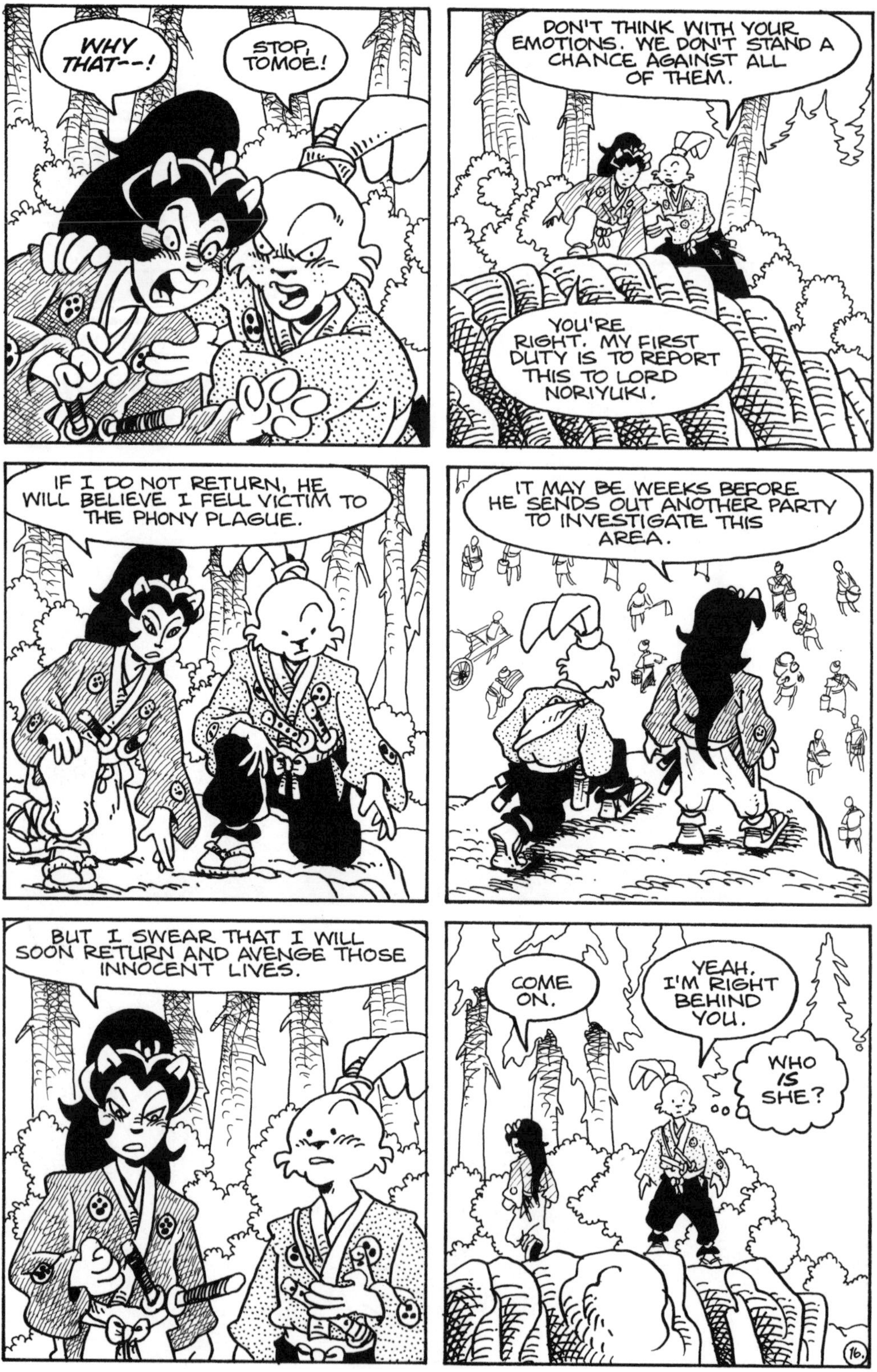
WHY THAT--!
STOP, TOMOE!
DON'T THINK WITH YOUR EMOTIONS. WE DON'T STAND A CHANCE AGAINST ALL OF THEM.
YOU'RE RIGHT. MY FIRST DUTY IS TO REPORT THIS TO LORD NORIYUKI.
IF I DO NOT RETURN, HE WILL BELIEVE I FELL VICTIM TO THE PHONY PLAGUE.
IT MAY BE WEEKS BEFORE HE SENDS OUT ANOTHER PARTY TO INVESTIGATE THIS AREA.
BUT I SWEAR THAT I WILL SOON RETURN AND AVENGE THOSE INNOCENT LIVES.
COME ON.
YEAH. I'M RIGHT BEHIND YOU.
WHO IS SHE?
16.

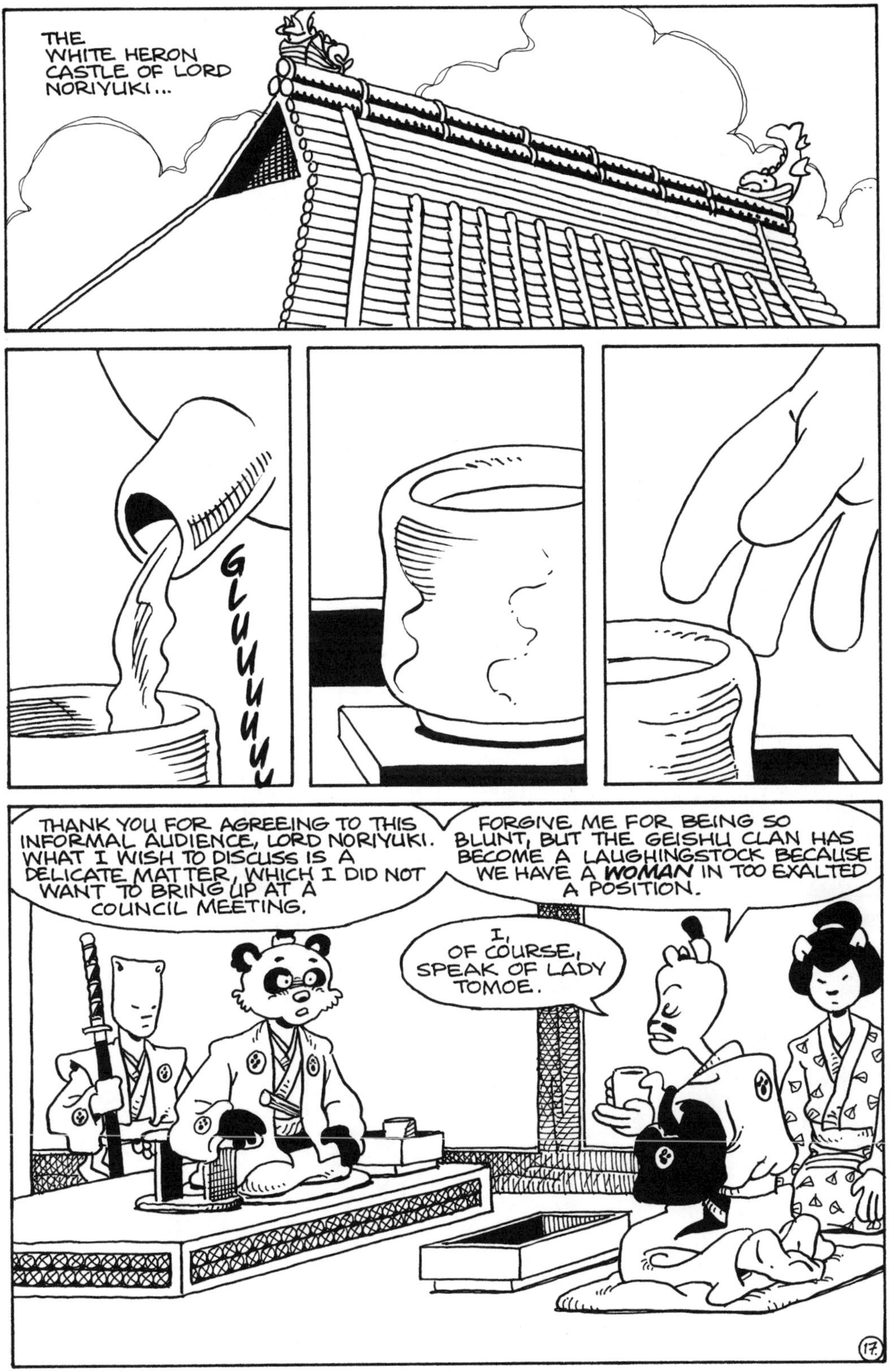
THE WHITE HERON CASTLE OF LORD NORIYUKI...
GLUUUUUUU
THANK YOU FOR AGREEING TO THIS INFORMAL AUDIENCE, LORD NORIYUKI. WHAT I WISH TO DISCUSS IS A DELICATE MATTER, WHICH I DID NOT WANT TO BRING UP AT A COUNCIL MEETING.
FORGIVE ME FOR BEING SO BLUNT, BUT THE GEISHU CLAN HAS BECOME A LAUGHINGSTOCK BECAUSE WE HAVE A *WOMAN* IN TOO EXALTED A POSITION.
I, OF COURSE, SPEAK OF LADY TOMOE.
17.

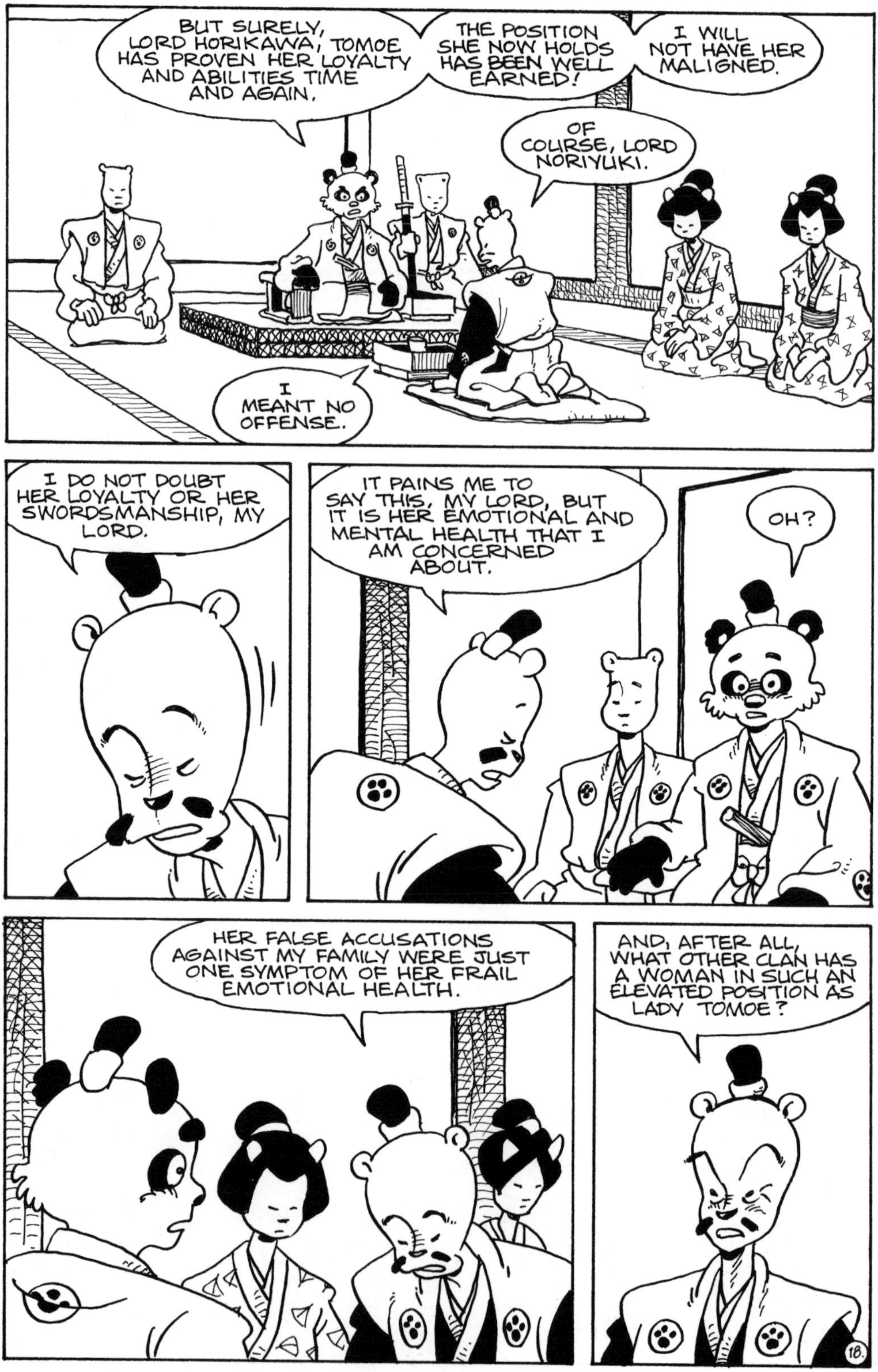
BUT SURELY, LORD HORIKAWA, TOMOE HAS PROVEN HER LOYALTY AND ABILITIES TIME AND AGAIN.
THE POSITION SHE NOW HOLDS HAS BEEN WELL EARNED!
I WILL NOT HAVE HER MALIGNED.
OF COURSE, LORD NORIYUKI.
I MEANT NO OFFENSE.
I DO NOT DOUBT HER LOYALTY OR HER SWORDSMANSHIP, MY LORD.
IT PAINS ME TO SAY THIS, MY LORD, BUT IT IS HER EMOTIONAL AND MENTAL HEALTH THAT I AM CONCERNED ABOUT.
OH?
HER FALSE ACCUSATIONS AGAINST MY FAMILY WERE JUST ONE SYMPTOM OF HER FRAIL EMOTIONAL HEALTH.
AND, AFTER ALL, WHAT OTHER CLAN HAS A WOMAN IN SUCH AN ELEVATED POSITION AS LADY TOMOE?
18.

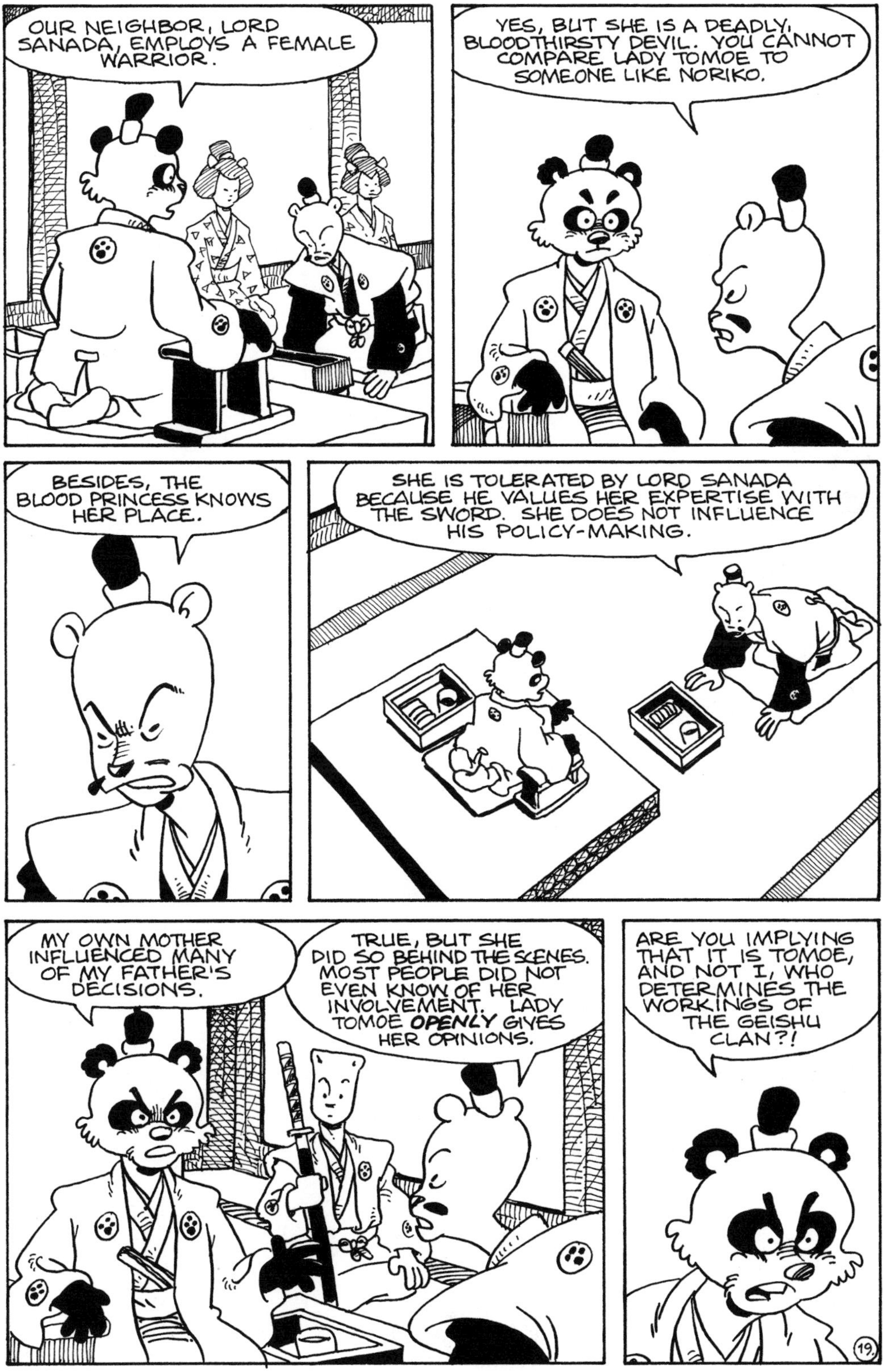
OUR NEIGHBOR, LORD SANADA, EMPLOYS A FEMALE WARRIOR.
YES, BUT SHE IS A DEADLY, BLOODTHIRSTY DEVIL. YOU CANNOT COMPARE LADY TOMOE TO SOMEONE LIKE NORIKO.
BESIDES, THE BLOOD PRINCESS KNOWS HER PLACE.
SHE IS TOLERATED BY LORD SANADA BECAUSE HE VALUES HER EXPERTISE WITH THE SWORD. SHE DOES NOT INFLUENCE HIS POLICY-MAKING.
MY OWN MOTHER INFLUENCED MANY OF MY FATHER'S DECISIONS.
TRUE, BUT SHE DID SO BEHIND THE SCENES. MOST PEOPLE DID NOT EVEN KNOW OF HER INVOLVEMENT. LADY TOMOE **OPENLY** GIVES HER OPINIONS.
ARE YOU IMPLYING THAT IT IS TOMOE, AND NOT I, WHO DETERMINES THE WORKINGS OF THE GEISHU CLAN?!
19.

OH, NO, THAT IS NOT WHAT I MEANT AT ALL. HOWEVER, IN THE RIGHT CIRCUMSTANCES, LADY TOMOE CAN BE AN EVEN MORE EFFECTIVE VASSAL FOR OUR CLAN.

OH? WHAT DO YOU SUGGEST?

?

ITO NOREN, A VASSAL OF LORD KOJIMA OF THE WEST, HAS SEEN LADY TOMOE AND HAS BECOME QUITE SMITTEN WITH HER.

A MARRIAGE WOULD UNITE BOTH OUR CLANS. I DON'T HAVE TO TELL YOU WHAT A POWERFUL ALLY LORD KOJIMA WOULD BE.

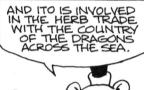

AND ITO IS INVOLVED IN THE HERB TRADE WITH THE COUNTRY OF THE DRAGONS ACROSS THE SEA.

A MARRIAGE TO SUCH A VASSAL IS MORE THAN LADY TOMOE COULD HOPE FOR. IT WOULD BE A HAPPY UNION. DON'T YOU THINK SHE DESERVES IT?

HMM... I NEVER THOUGHT OF IT LIKE THAT. TOMOE HAS GIVEN MUCH TO THE GEISHU CLAN. IT'S ABOUT TIME SHE RECEIVED SOME HAPPINESS FOR HERSELF...

YOU MAY BE RIGHT. PERHAPS TOMOE SHOULD GET MARRIED.

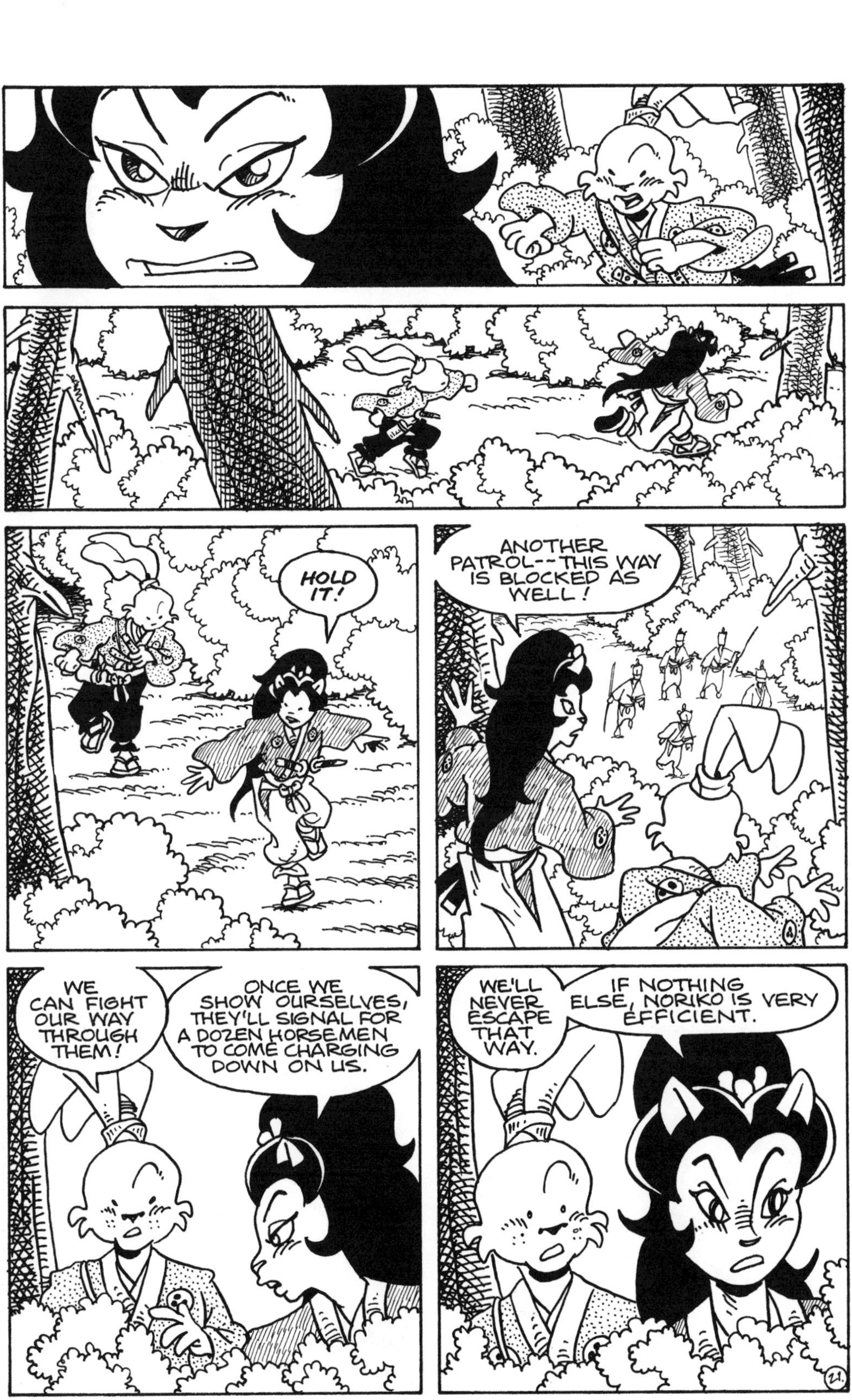
HOLD IT!
ANOTHER PATROL--THIS WAY IS BLOCKED AS WELL!
WE CAN FIGHT OUR WAY THROUGH THEM!
ONCE WE SHOW OURSELVES, THEY'LL SIGNAL FOR A DOZEN HORSEMEN TO COME CHARGING DOWN ON US.
WE'LL NEVER ESCAPE THAT WAY.
IF NOTHING ELSE, NORIKO IS VERY EFFICIENT.
21.

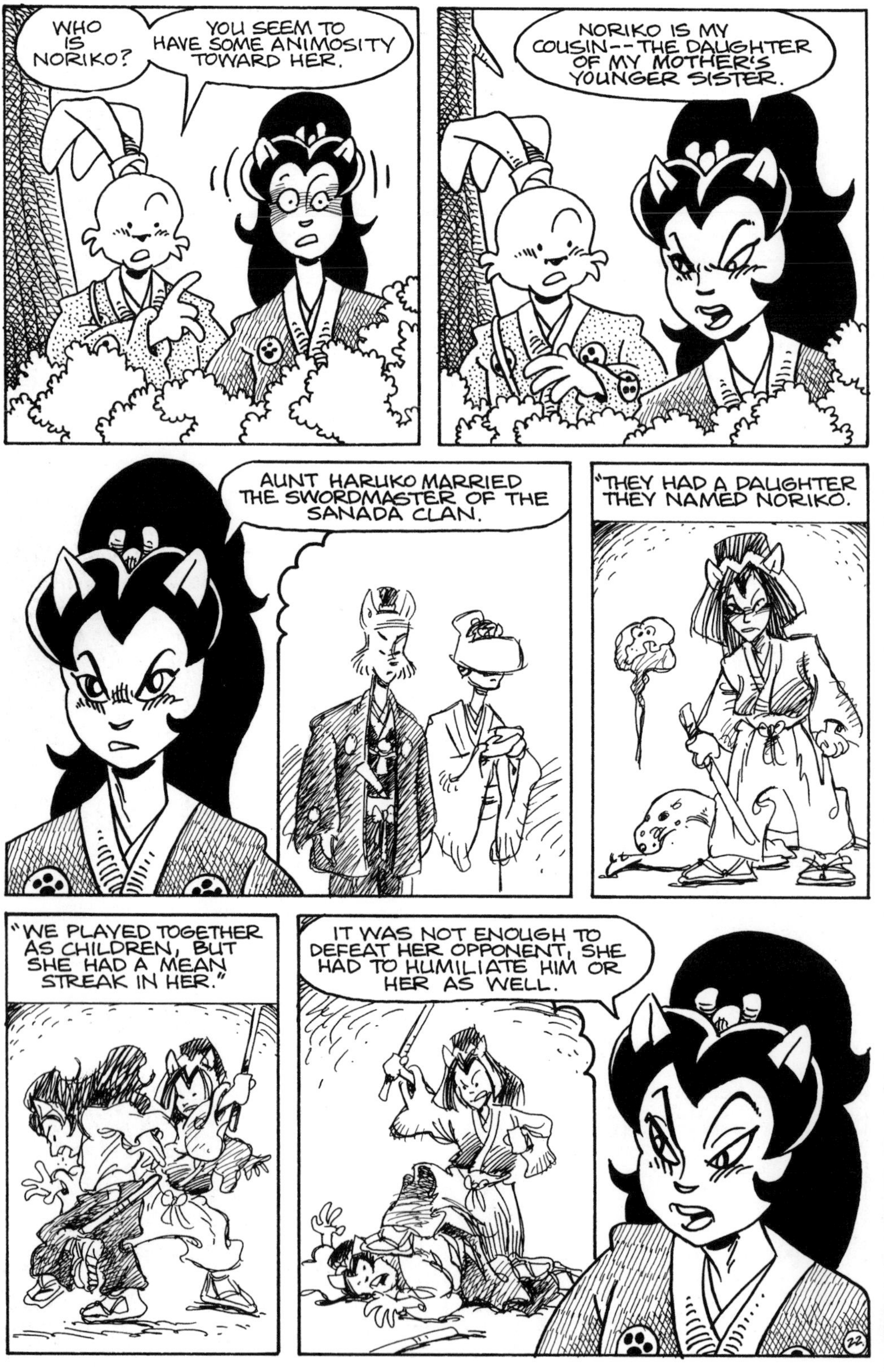
WHO IS NORIKO?
YOU SEEM TO HAVE SOME ANIMOSITY TOWARD HER.
NORIKO IS MY COUSIN--THE DAUGHTER OF MY MOTHER'S YOUNGER SISTER.
AUNT HARUKO MARRIED THE SWORDMASTER OF THE SANADA CLAN.
"THEY HAD A DAUGHTER THEY NAMED NORIKO.
"WE PLAYED TOGETHER AS CHILDREN, BUT SHE HAD A MEAN STREAK IN HER."
IT WAS NOT ENOUGH TO DEFEAT HER OPPONENT, SHE HAD TO HUMILIATE HIM OR HER AS WELL.
22.

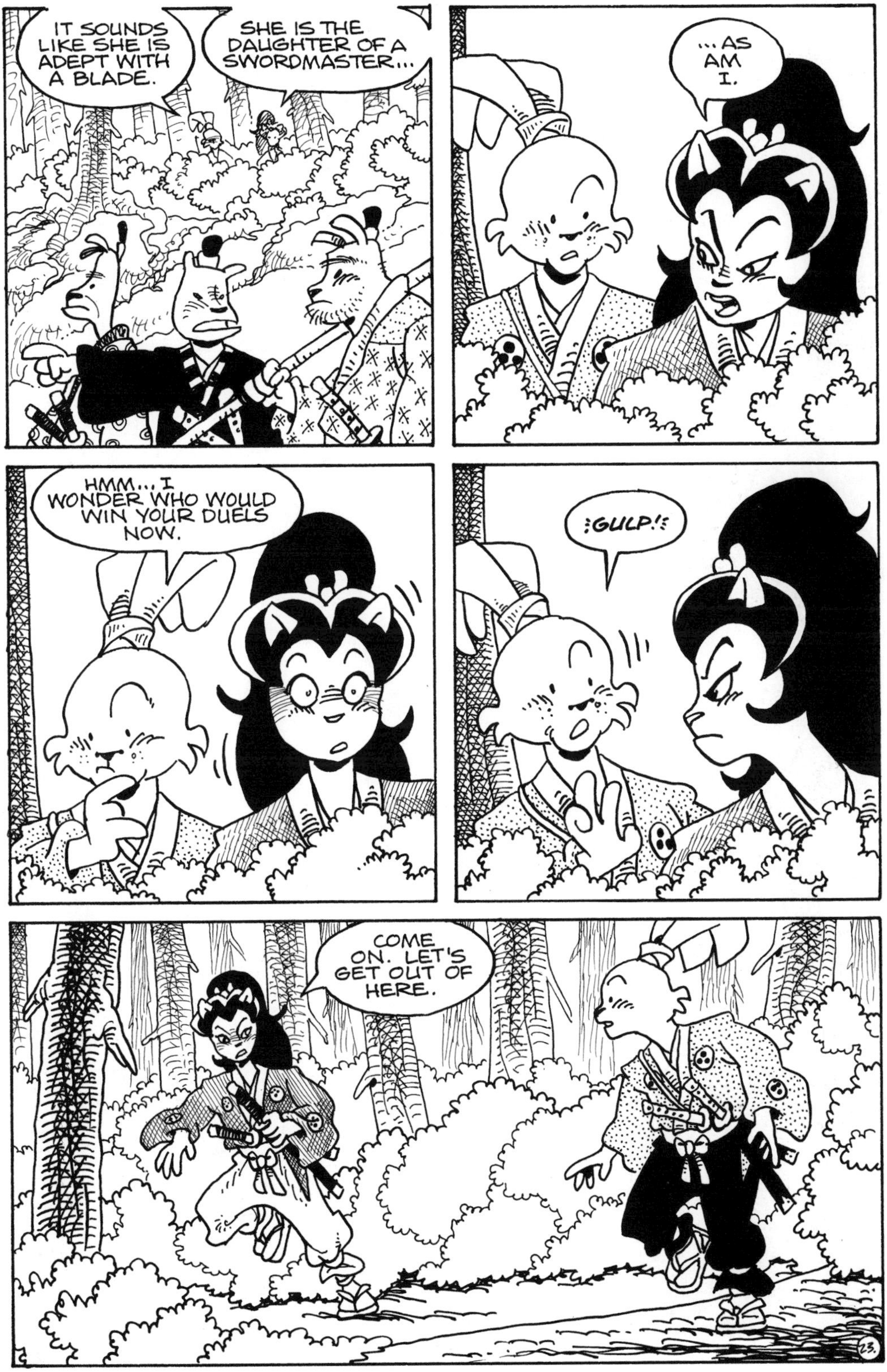
IT SOUNDS LIKE SHE IS ADEPT WITH A BLADE.
SHE IS THE DAUGHTER OF A SWORDMASTER...
...AS AM I.
HMM... I WONDER WHO WOULD WIN YOUR DUELS NOW.
GULP!
COME ON. LET'S GET OUT OF HERE.
23.

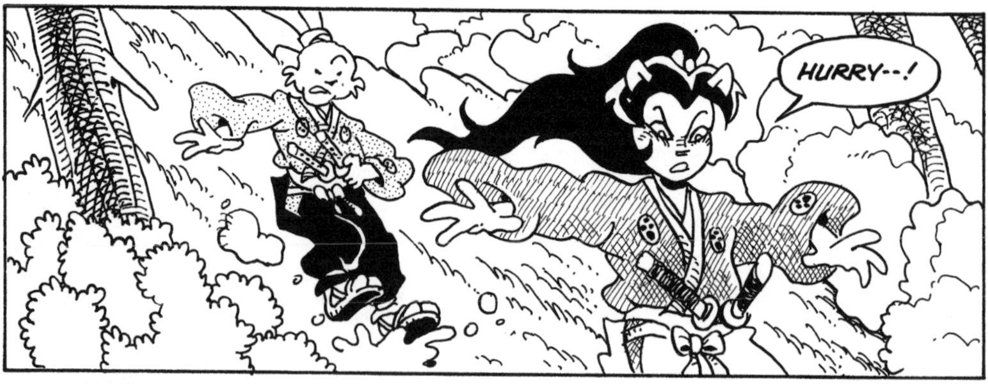
HURRY--!

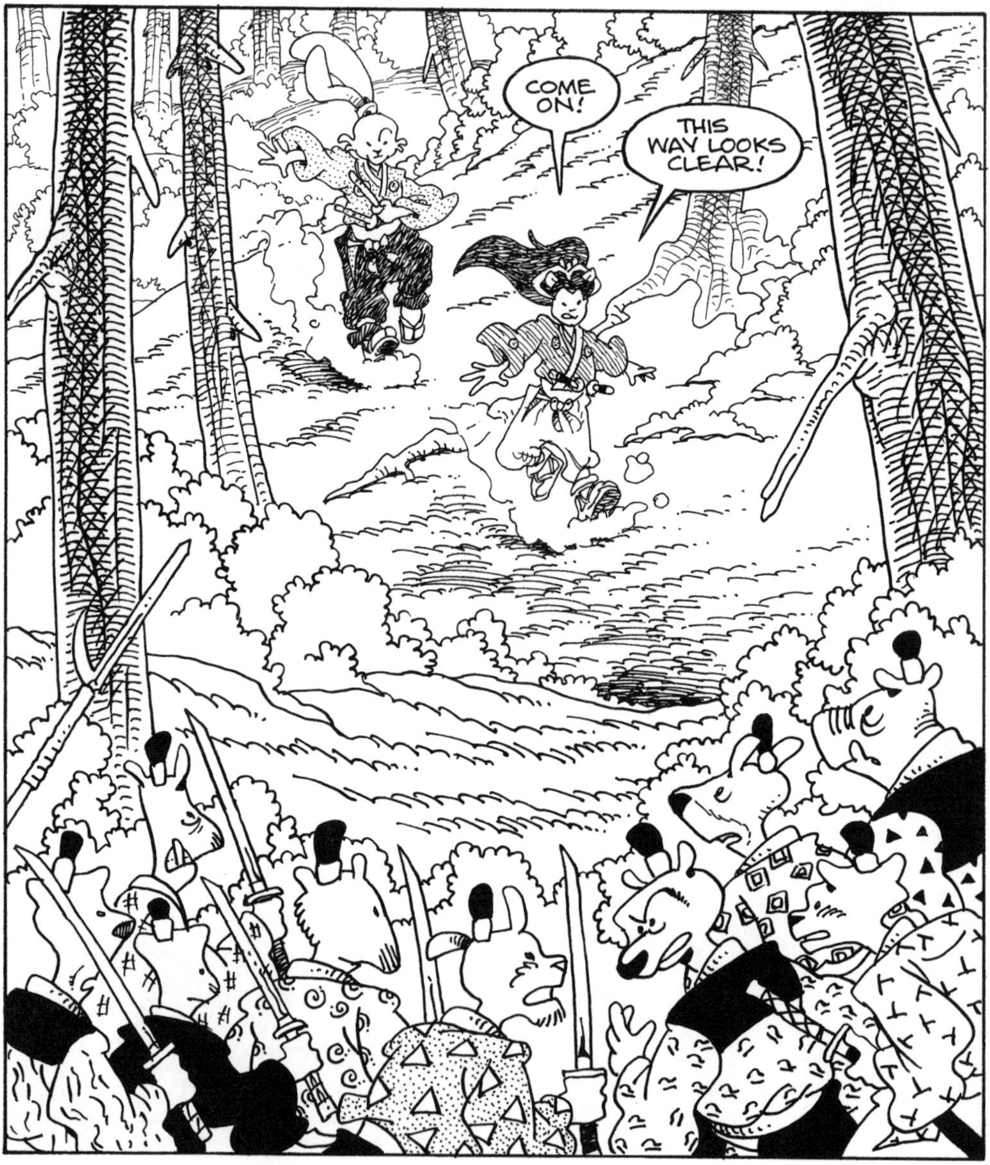
COME ON!
THIS WAY LOOKS CLEAR!

THE TREASURE of the MOTHER of MOUNTAINS

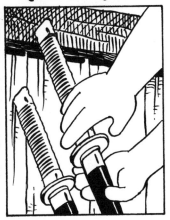

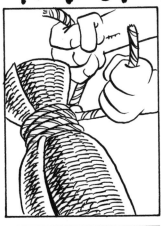

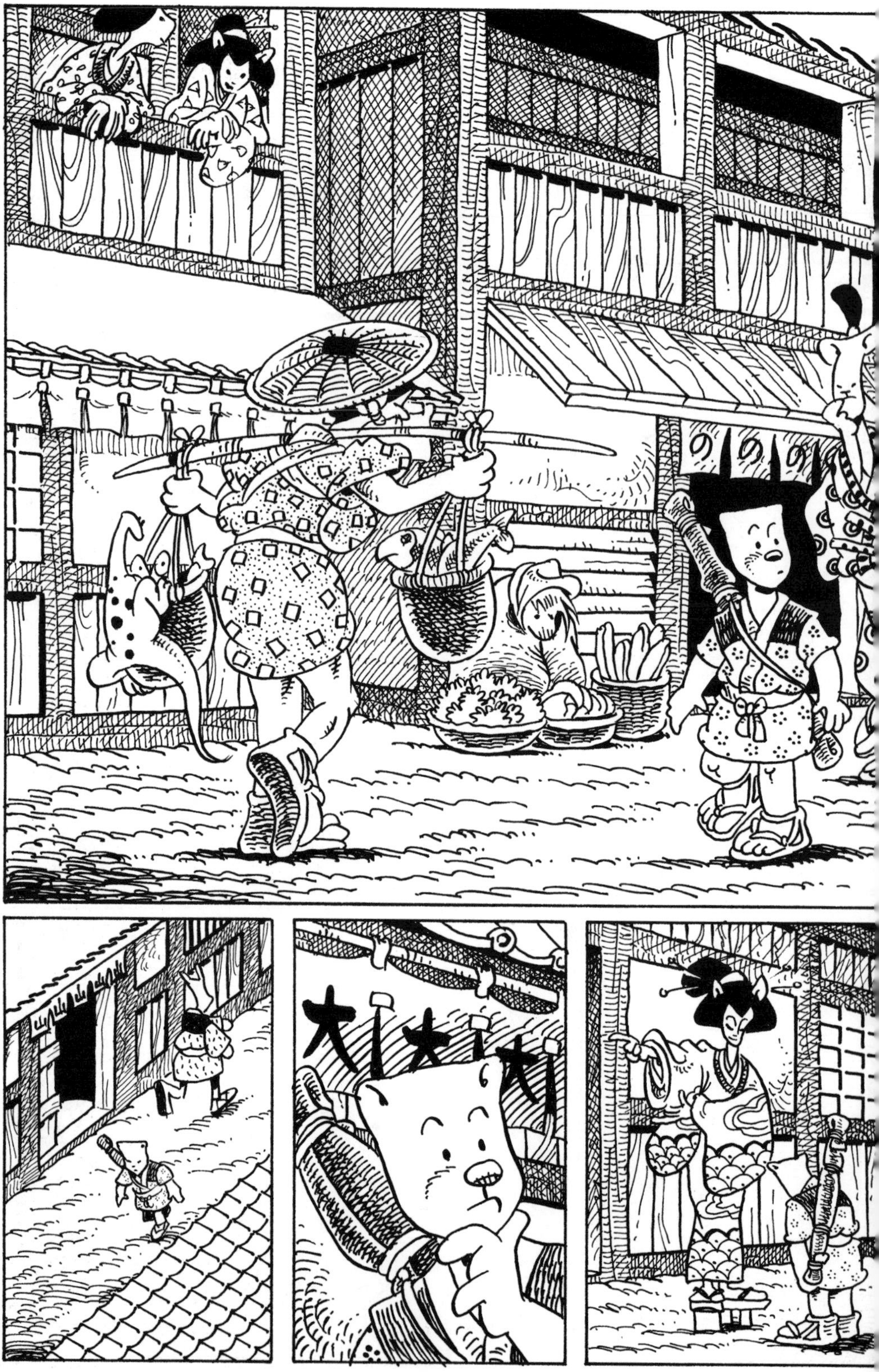

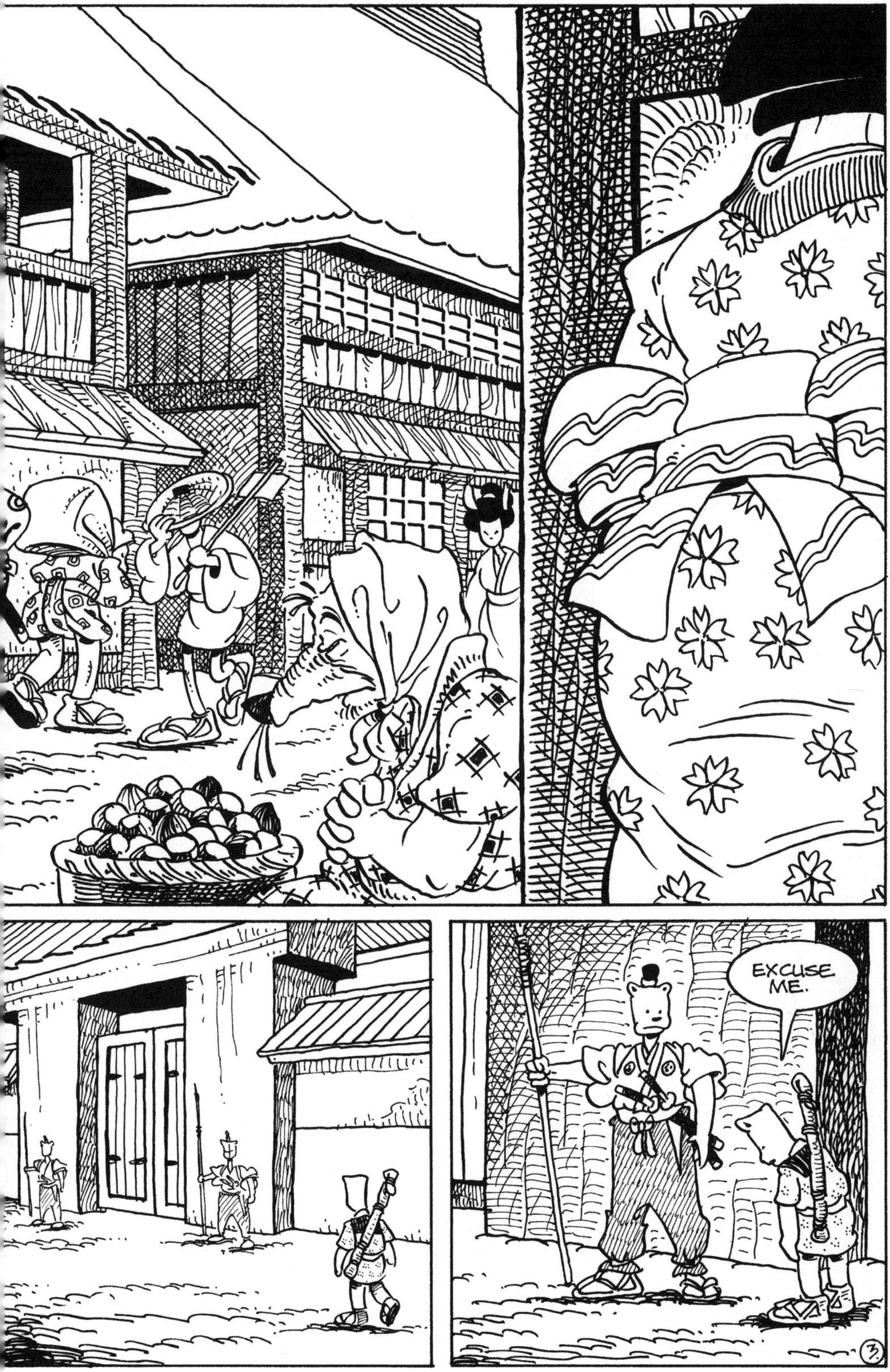
EXCUSE ME.
3

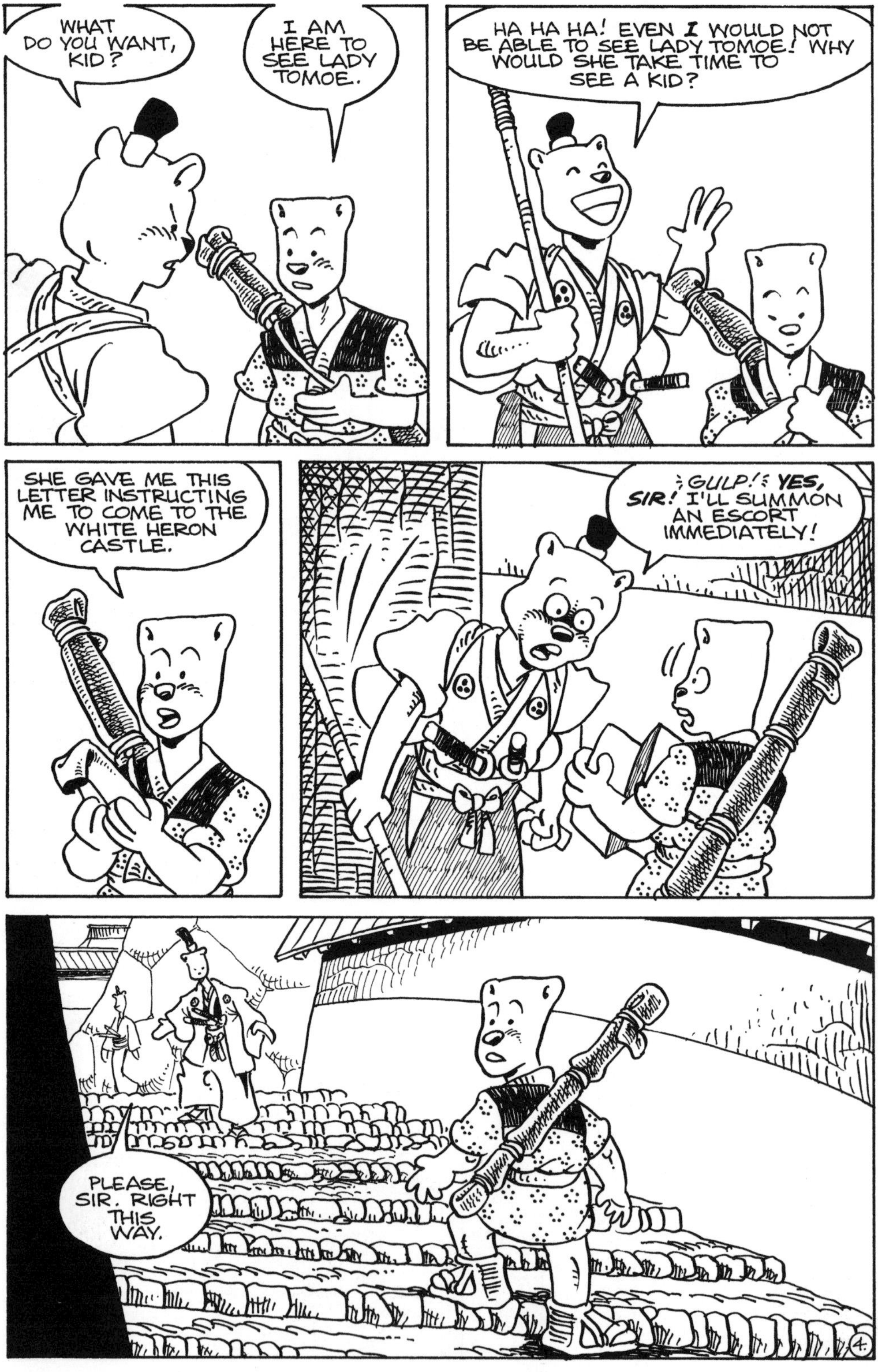
WHAT DO YOU WANT, KID?
I AM HERE TO SEE LADY TOMOE.
HA HA HA! EVEN I WOULD NOT BE ABLE TO SEE LADY TOMOE! WHY WOULD SHE TAKE TIME TO SEE A KID?
SHE GAVE ME THIS LETTER INSTRUCTING ME TO COME TO THE WHITE HERON CASTLE.
GULP! YES, SIR! I'LL SUMMON AN ESCORT IMMEDIATELY!
PLEASE, SIR. RIGHT THIS WAY.
4.

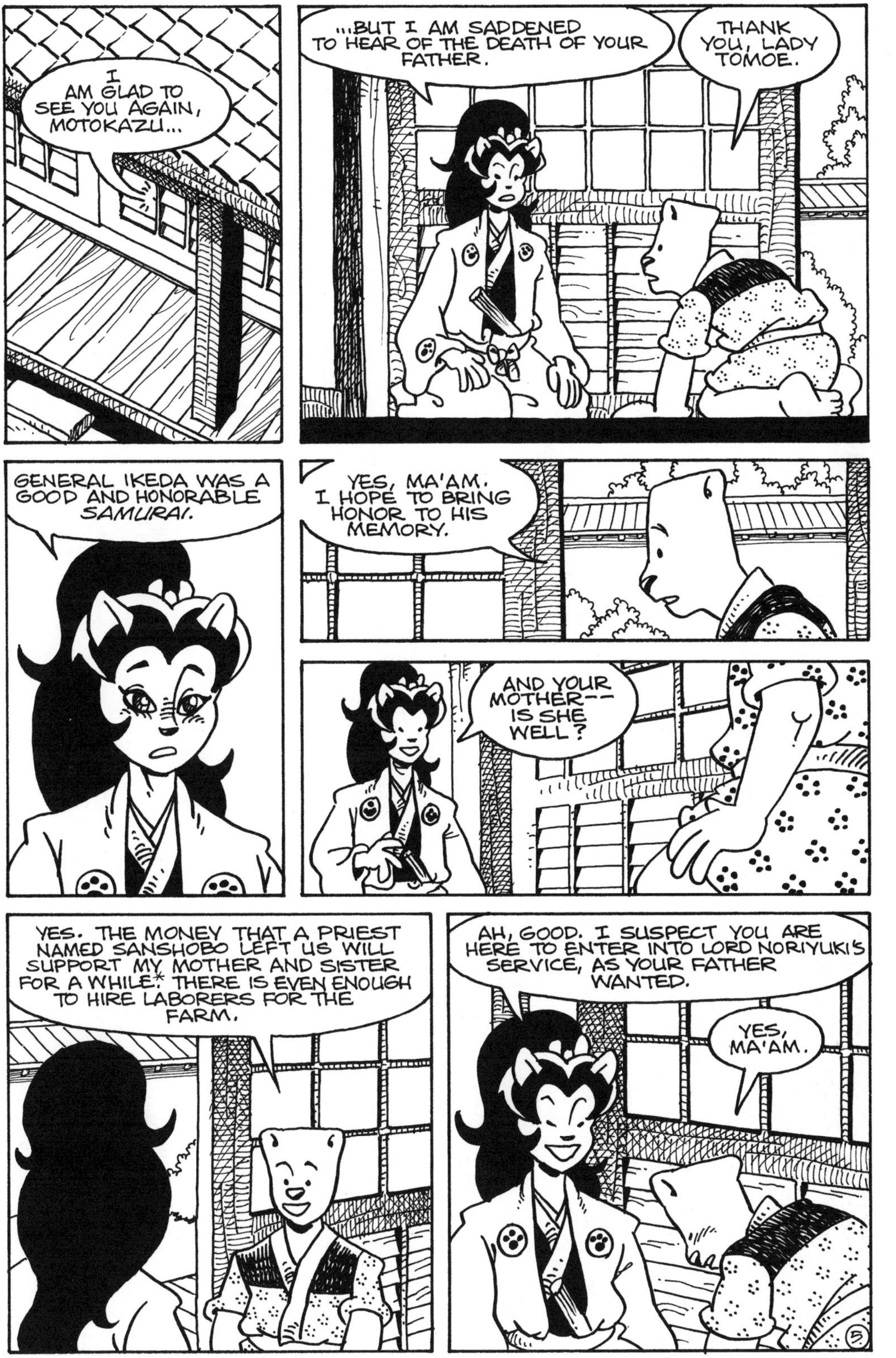
I AM GLAD TO SEE YOU AGAIN, MOTOKAZU...
...BUT I AM SADDENED TO HEAR OF THE DEATH OF YOUR FATHER.
THANK YOU, LADY TOMOE.
GENERAL IKEDA WAS A GOOD AND HONORABLE *SAMURAI*.
YES, MA'AM. I HOPE TO BRING HONOR TO HIS MEMORY.
AND YOUR MOTHER-- IS SHE WELL?
YES. THE MONEY THAT A PRIEST NAMED SANSHOBO LEFT US WILL SUPPORT MY MOTHER AND SISTER FOR A WHILE.* THERE IS EVEN ENOUGH TO HIRE LABORERS FOR THE FARM.
AH, GOOD. I SUSPECT YOU ARE HERE TO ENTER INTO LORD NORIYUKI'S SERVICE, AS YOUR FATHER WANTED.
YES, MA'AM.

*UY BOOK 16: THE SHROUDED MOON

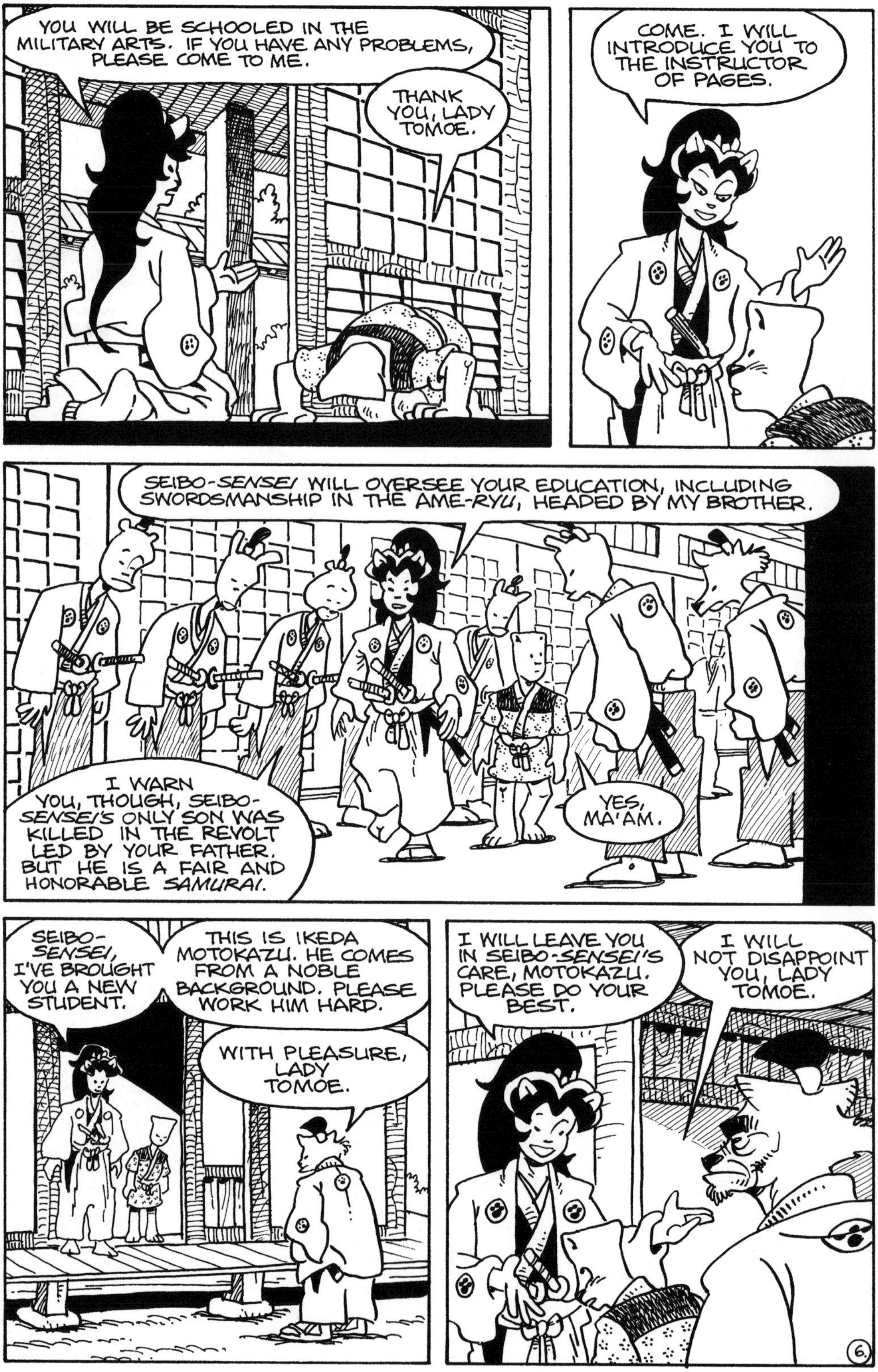
YOU WILL BE SCHOOLED IN THE MILITARY ARTS. IF YOU HAVE ANY PROBLEMS, PLEASE COME TO ME.
THANK YOU, LADY TOMOE.
COME. I WILL INTRODUCE YOU TO THE INSTRUCTOR OF PAGES.
SEIBO-SENSEI WILL OVERSEE YOUR EDUCATION, INCLUDING SWORDSMANSHIP IN THE AME-RYU, HEADED BY MY BROTHER.
I WARN YOU, THOUGH, SEIBO-SENSEI'S ONLY SON WAS KILLED IN THE REVOLT LED BY YOUR FATHER. BUT HE IS A FAIR AND HONORABLE SAMURAI.
YES, MA'AM.
SEIBO-SENSEI, I'VE BROUGHT YOU A NEW STUDENT.
THIS IS IKEDA MOTOKAZU. HE COMES FROM A NOBLE BACKGROUND. PLEASE WORK HIM HARD.
WITH PLEASURE, LADY TOMOE.
I WILL LEAVE YOU IN SEIBO-SENSEI'S CARE, MOTOKAZU. PLEASE DO YOUR BEST.
I WILL NOT DISAPPOINT YOU, LADY TOMOE.
6.

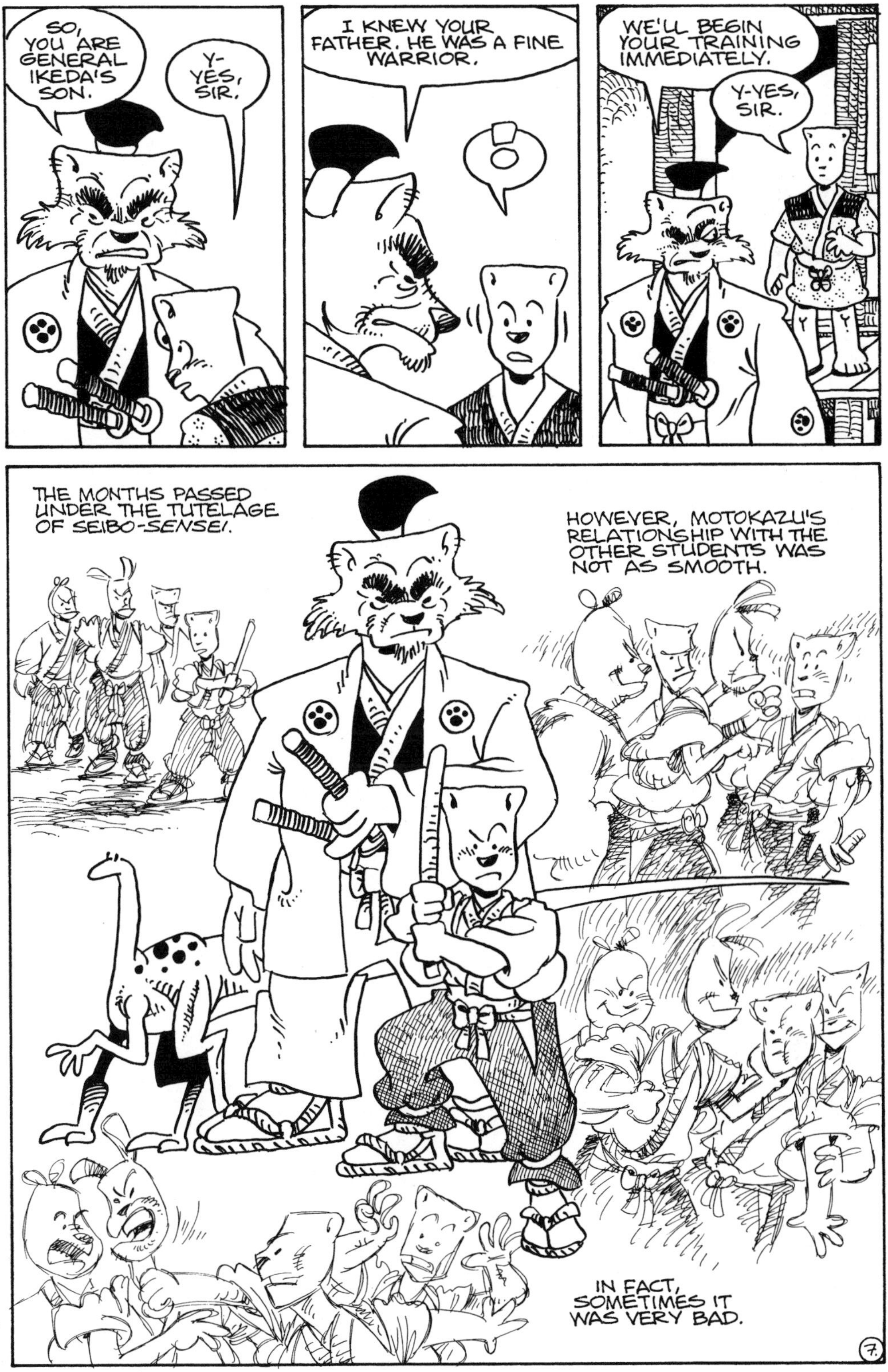
SO, YOU ARE GENERAL IKEDA'S SON.
Y-YES, SIR.
I KNEW YOUR FATHER. HE WAS A FINE WARRIOR.
!
WE'LL BEGIN YOUR TRAINING IMMEDIATELY.
Y-YES, SIR.
THE MONTHS PASSED UNDER THE TUTELAGE OF SEIBO-SENSEI.
HOWEVER, MOTOKAZU'S RELATIONSHIP WITH THE OTHER STUDENTS WAS NOT AS SMOOTH.
IN FACT, SOMETIMES IT WAS VERY BAD.
7.

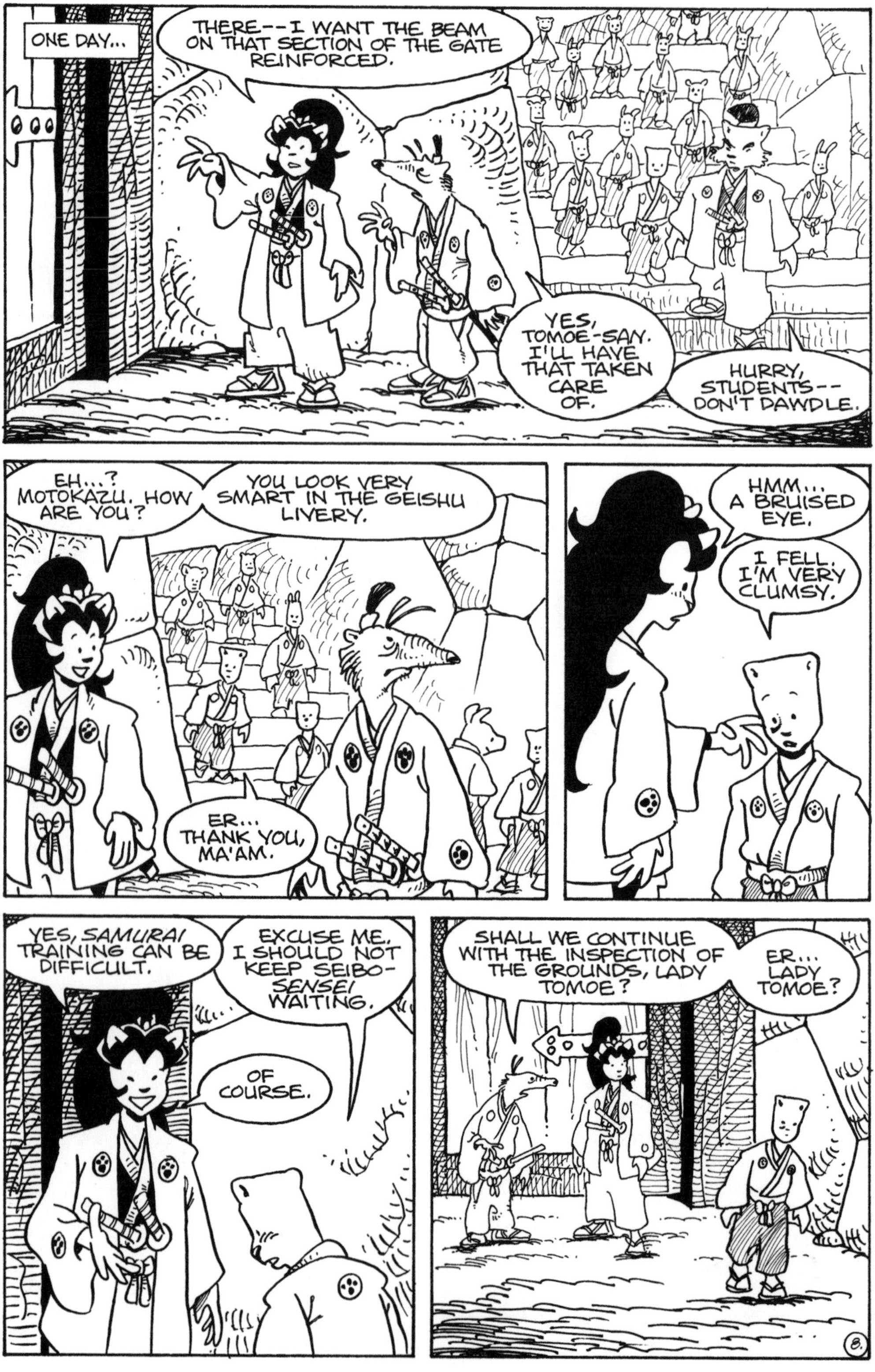
ONE DAY...
THERE--I WANT THE BEAM ON THAT SECTION OF THE GATE REINFORCED.
YES, TOMOE-SAN. I'LL HAVE THAT TAKEN CARE OF.
HURRY, STUDENTS-- DON'T DAWDLE.
EH...? MOTOKAZU. HOW ARE YOU?
YOU LOOK VERY SMART IN THE GEISHU LIVERY.
ER... THANK YOU, MA'AM.
HMM... A BRUISED EYE.
I FELL. I'M VERY CLUMSY.
YES, *SAMURAI* TRAINING CAN BE DIFFICULT.
EXCUSE ME. I SHOULD NOT KEEP SEIBO-*SENSEI* WAITING.
OF COURSE.
SHALL WE CONTINUE WITH THE INSPECTION OF THE GROUNDS, LADY TOMOE?
ER... LADY TOMOE?
8.

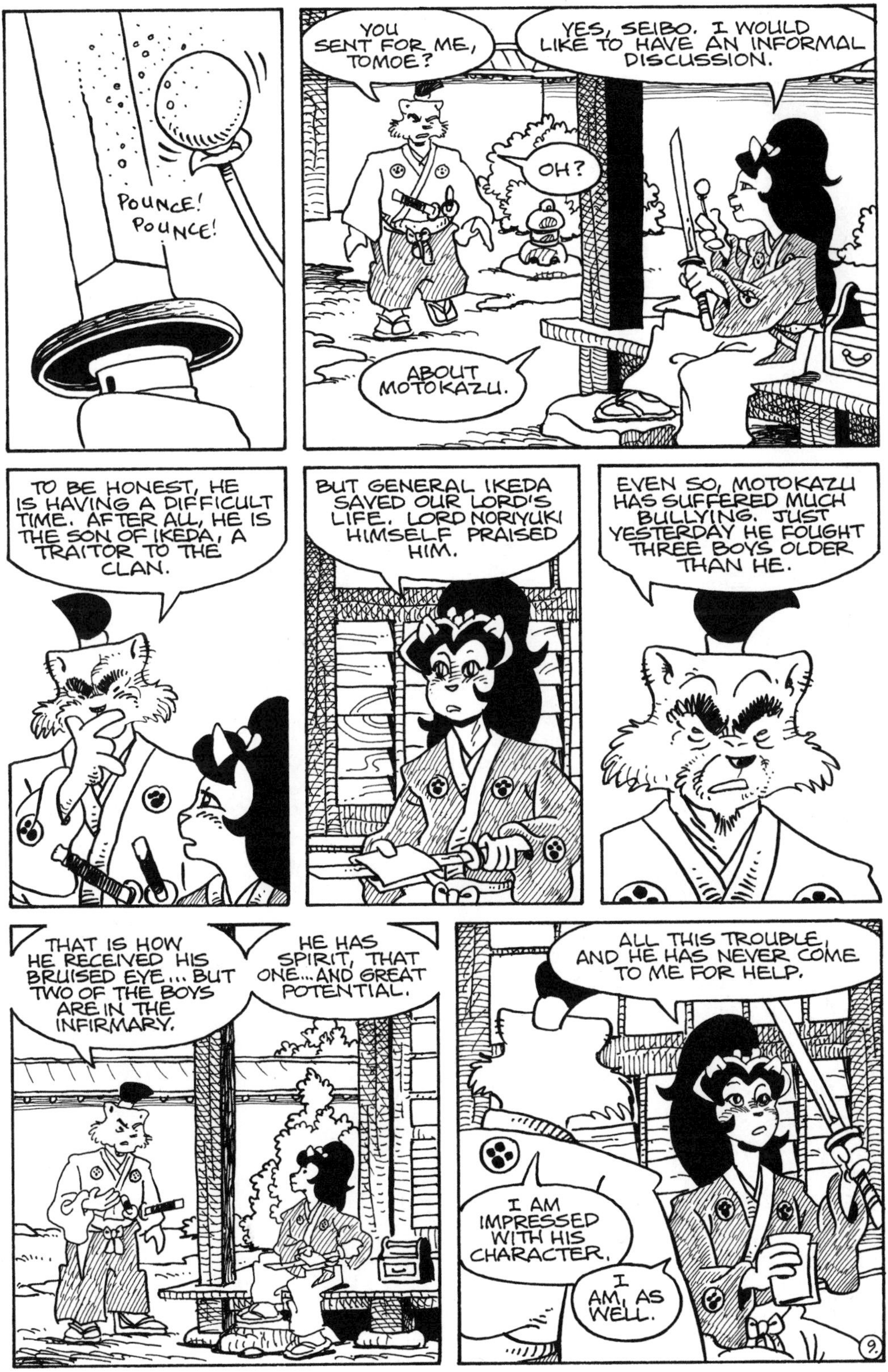

POUNCE! POUNCE!
YOU SENT FOR ME, TOMOE?
YES, SEIBO. I WOULD LIKE TO HAVE AN INFORMAL DISCUSSION.
OH?
ABOUT MOTOKAZU.
TO BE HONEST, HE IS HAVING A DIFFICULT TIME. AFTER ALL, HE IS THE SON OF IKEDA, A TRAITOR TO THE CLAN.
BUT GENERAL IKEDA SAVED OUR LORD'S LIFE. LORD NORIYUKI HIMSELF PRAISED HIM.
EVEN SO, MOTOKAZU HAS SUFFERED MUCH BULLYING. JUST YESTERDAY HE FOUGHT THREE BOYS OLDER THAN HE.
THAT IS HOW HE RECEIVED HIS BRUISED EYE... BUT TWO OF THE BOYS ARE IN THE INFIRMARY.
HE HAS SPIRIT, THAT ONE... AND GREAT POTENTIAL.
ALL THIS TROUBLE, AND HE HAS NEVER COME TO ME FOR HELP.
I AM IMPRESSED WITH HIS CHARACTER.
I AM, AS WELL.
9.

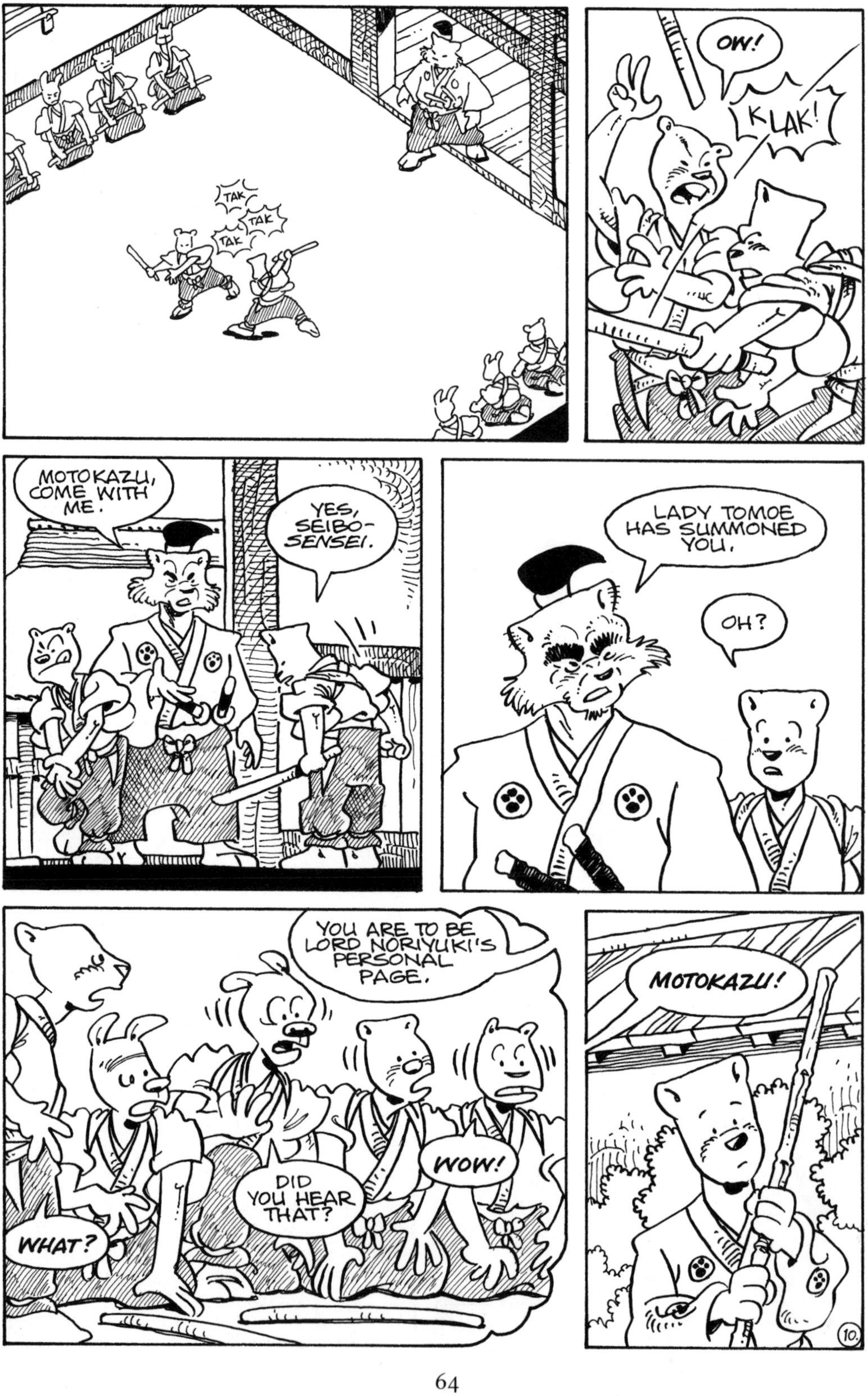
TAK
TAK
TAK
OW!
KLAK!
MOTOKAZU, COME WITH ME.
YES, SEIBO-SENSEI.
LADY TOMOE HAS SUMMONED YOU.
OH?
YOU ARE TO BE LORD NORIYUKI'S PERSONAL PAGE.
WHAT?
DID YOU HEAR THAT?
WOW!
MOTOKAZU!
10.

MOTOKAZU! DAYDREAMING AGAIN?

HUH?

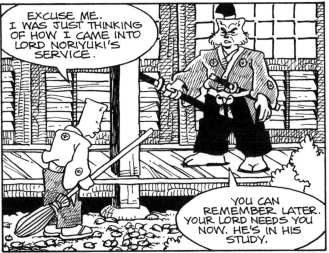

EXCUSE ME. I WAS JUST THINKING OF HOW I CAME INTO LORD NORIYUKI'S SERVICE.

YOU CAN REMEMBER LATER. YOUR LORD NEEDS YOU NOW. HE'S IN HIS STUDY.

THAT AFTERNOON...

WHAT? THE CARRIER PIGEON RETURNED WITHOUT A MESSAGE FROM TOMOE?

IT MUST HAVE FALLEN OFF DURING FLIGHT. SHE PROBABLY DID NOT SECURE IT PROPERLY.

I'M SURE IT'S NOTHING TO BE CONCERNED ABOUT.

BUT SHE DID GO TO INVESTIGATE A PLAGUE. WHAT IF SHE ENCOUNTERED SOME OTHER DANGER?

AFTER ALL, THAT PART OF OUR LAND BORDERS LORD SANADA'S PROVINCE.

NONSENSE. WE HAVE BEEN AT PEACE WITH LORD SANADA FOR YEARS. WHAT REASON HAS HE TO START TROUBLE NOW?

YOU'RE PROBABLY RIGHT.

11.

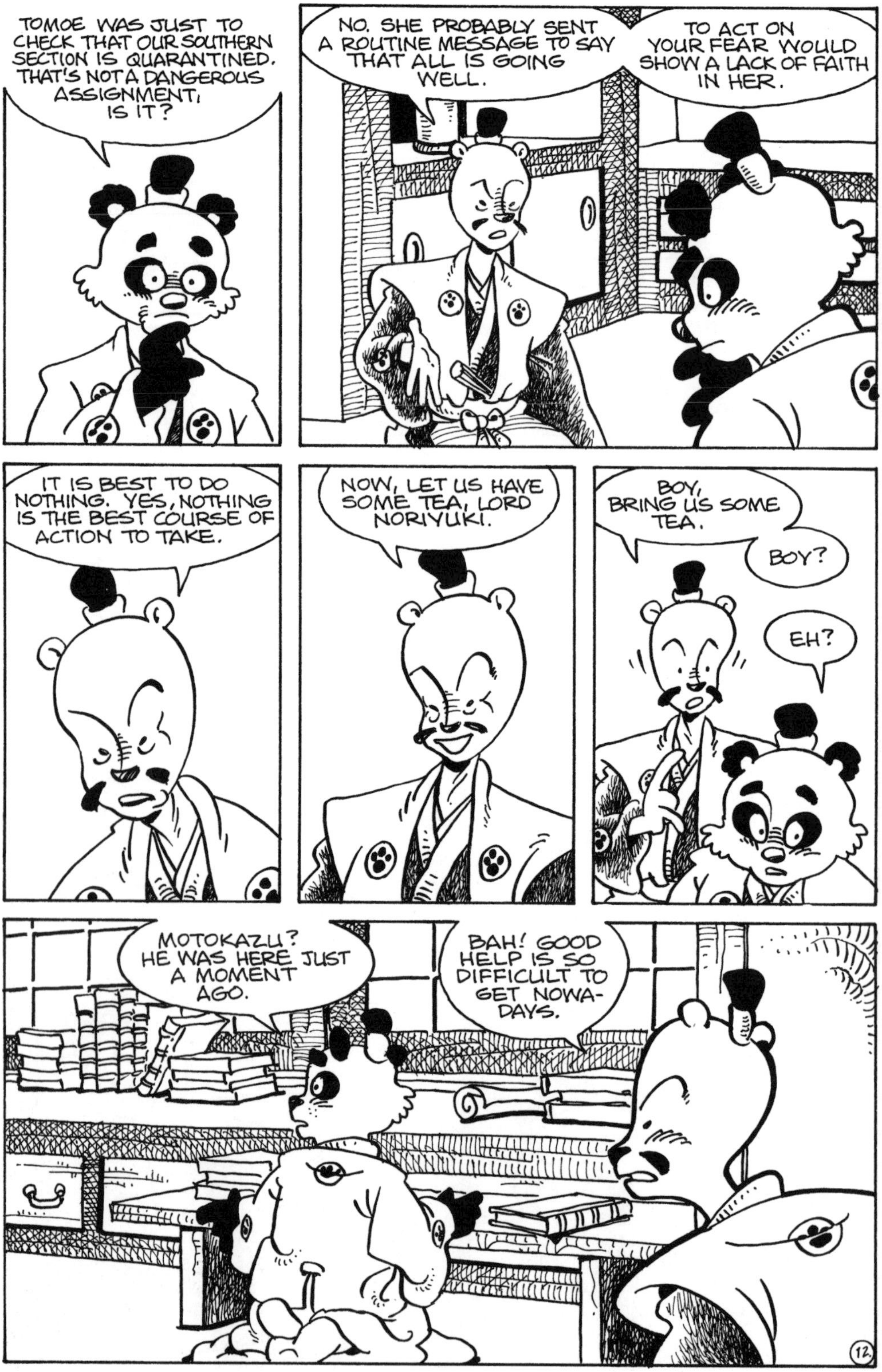
TOMOE WAS JUST TO CHECK THAT OUR SOUTHERN SECTION IS QUARANTINED. THAT'S NOT A DANGEROUS ASSIGNMENT, IS IT?
NO. SHE PROBABLY SENT A ROUTINE MESSAGE TO SAY THAT ALL IS GOING WELL.
TO ACT ON YOUR FEAR WOULD SHOW A LACK OF FAITH IN HER.
IT IS BEST TO DO NOTHING. YES, NOTHING IS THE BEST COURSE OF ACTION TO TAKE.
NOW, LET US HAVE SOME TEA, LORD NORIYUKI.
BOY, BRING US SOME TEA.
BOY?
EH?
MOTOKAZU? HE WAS HERE JUST A MOMENT AGO.
BAH! GOOD HELP IS SO DIFFICULT TO GET NOWA-DAYS.
12

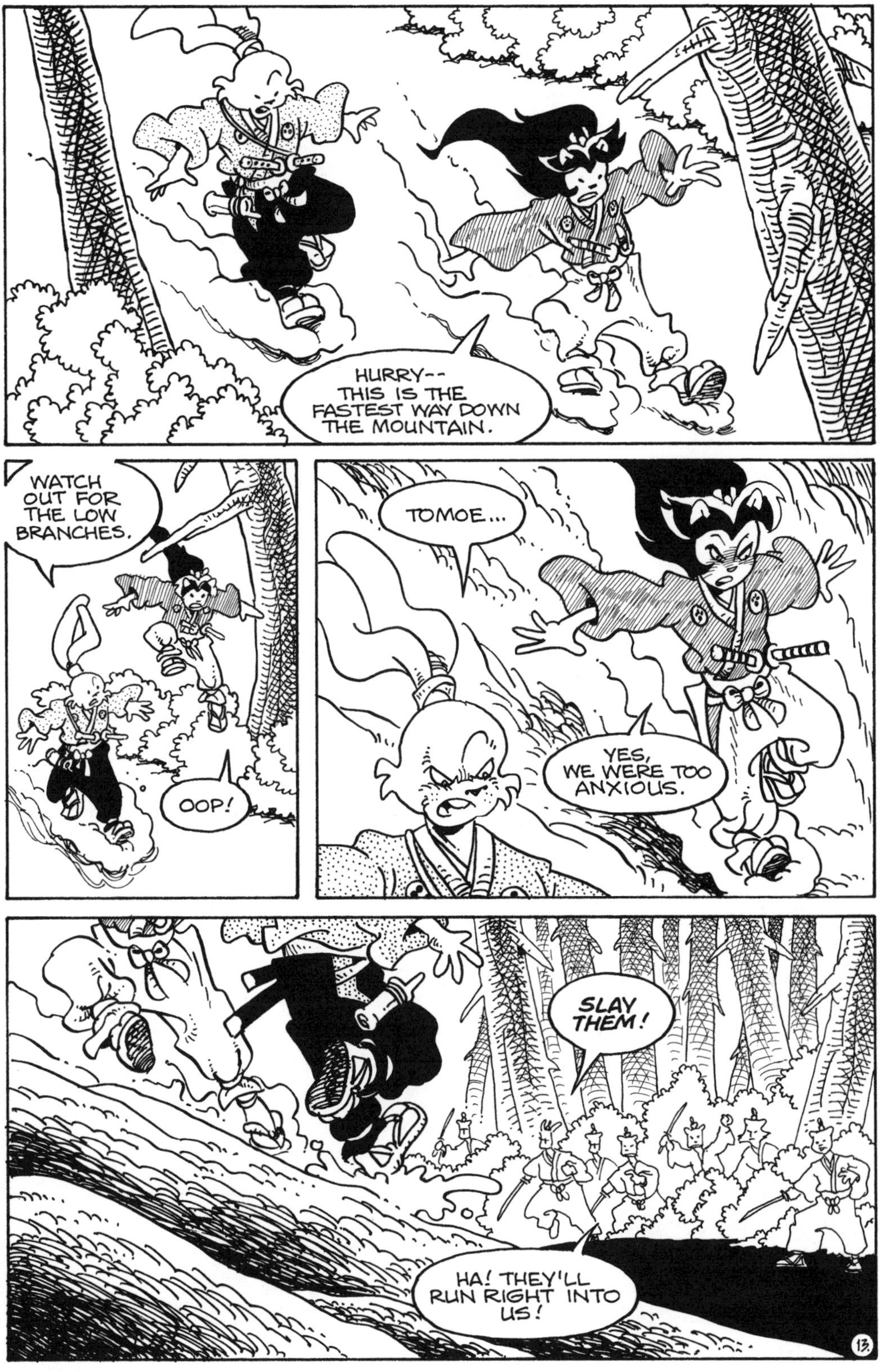
HURRY-- THIS IS THE FASTEST WAY DOWN THE MOUNTAIN.
WATCH OUT FOR THE LOW BRANCHES.
OOP!
TOMOE...
YES, WE WERE TOO ANXIOUS.
SLAY THEM!
HA! THEY'LL RUN RIGHT INTO US!
13

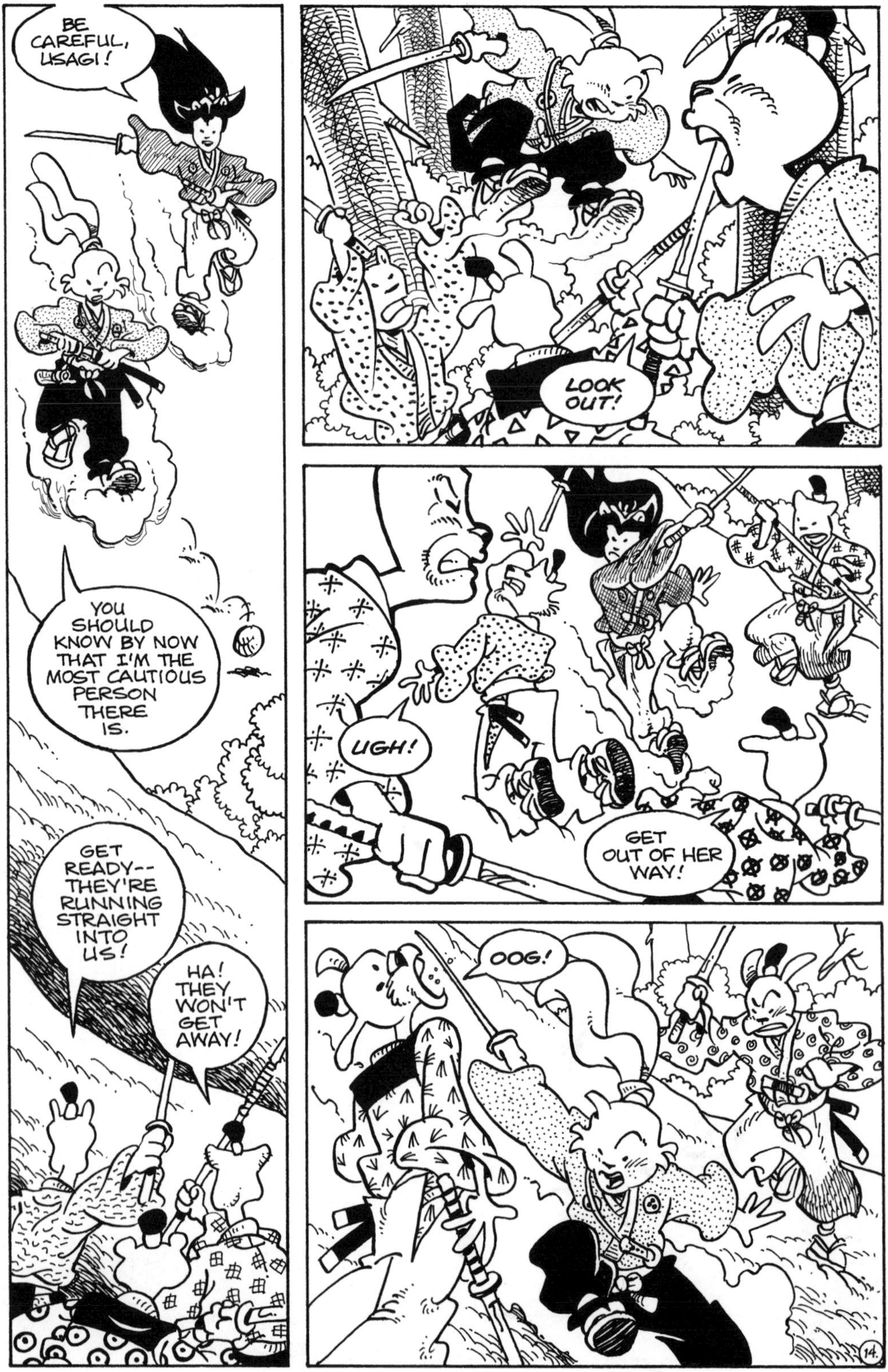
BE CAREFUL, USAGI!
YOU SHOULD KNOW BY NOW THAT I'M THE MOST CAUTIOUS PERSON THERE IS.
GET READY-- THEY'RE RUNNING STRAIGHT INTO US!
HA! THEY WON'T GET AWAY!
LOOK OUT!
UGH!
GET OUT OF HER WAY!
OOG!
14.

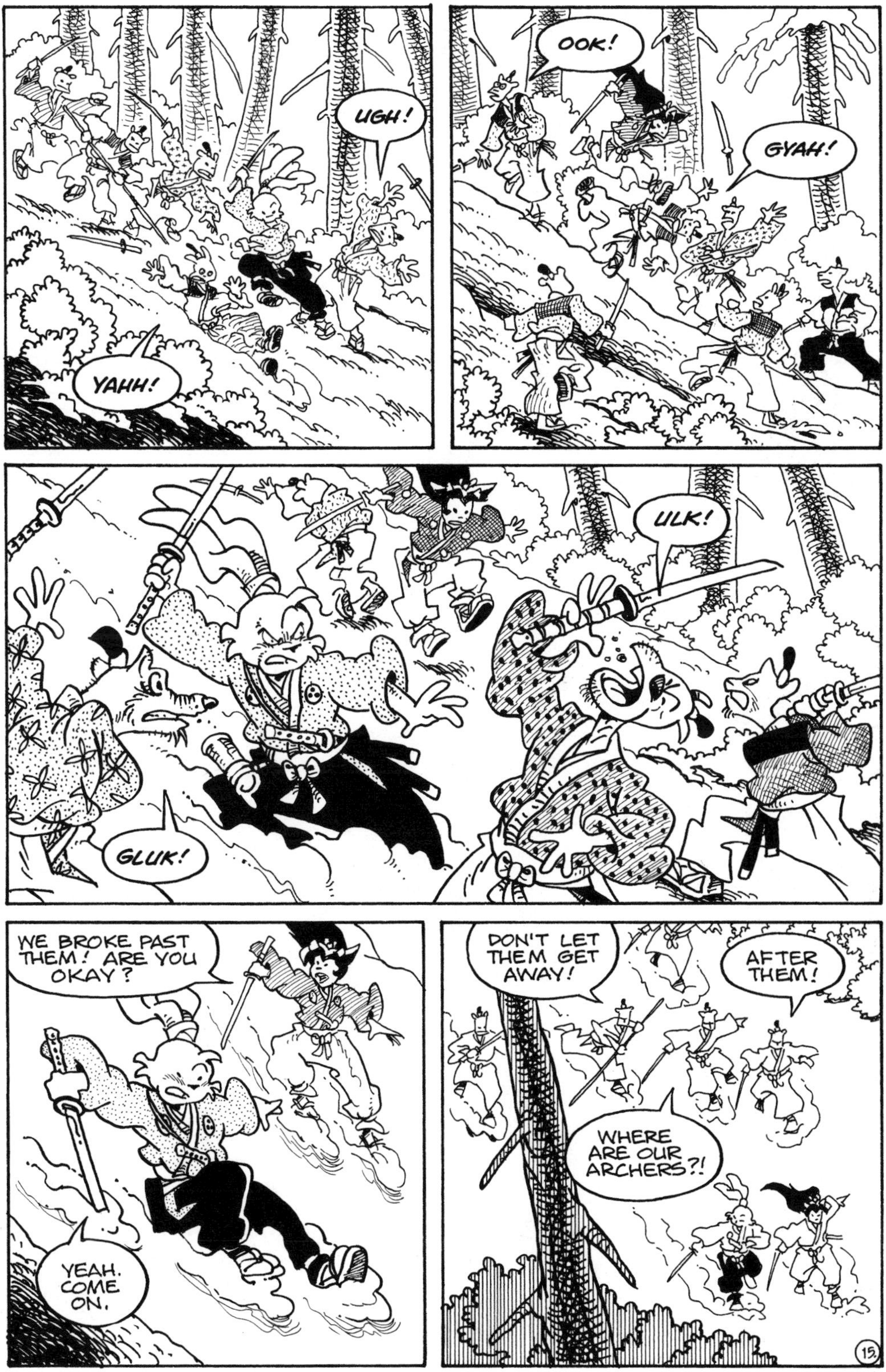
UGH!
YAHH!
OOK!
GYAH!
ULK!
GLUK!
WE BROKE PAST THEM! ARE YOU OKAY?
YEAH. COME ON.
DON'T LET THEM GET AWAY!
AFTER THEM!
WHERE ARE OUR ARCHERS?!
15

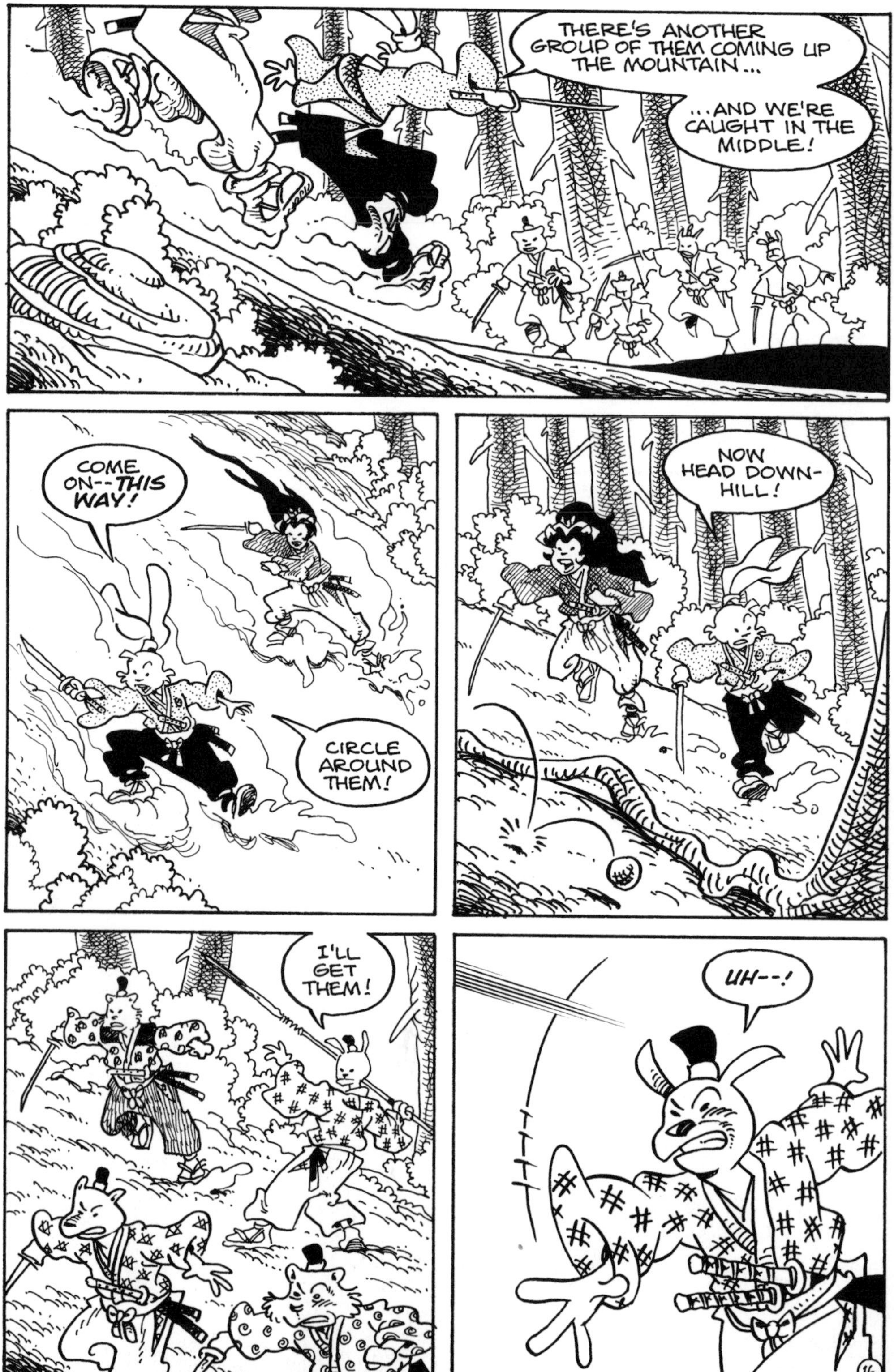
THERE'S ANOTHER GROUP OF THEM COMING UP THE MOUNTAIN...
...AND WE'RE CAUGHT IN THE MIDDLE!
COME ON--THIS WAY!
CIRCLE AROUND THEM!
NOW HEAD DOWN-HILL!
I'LL GET THEM!
UH--!
16.

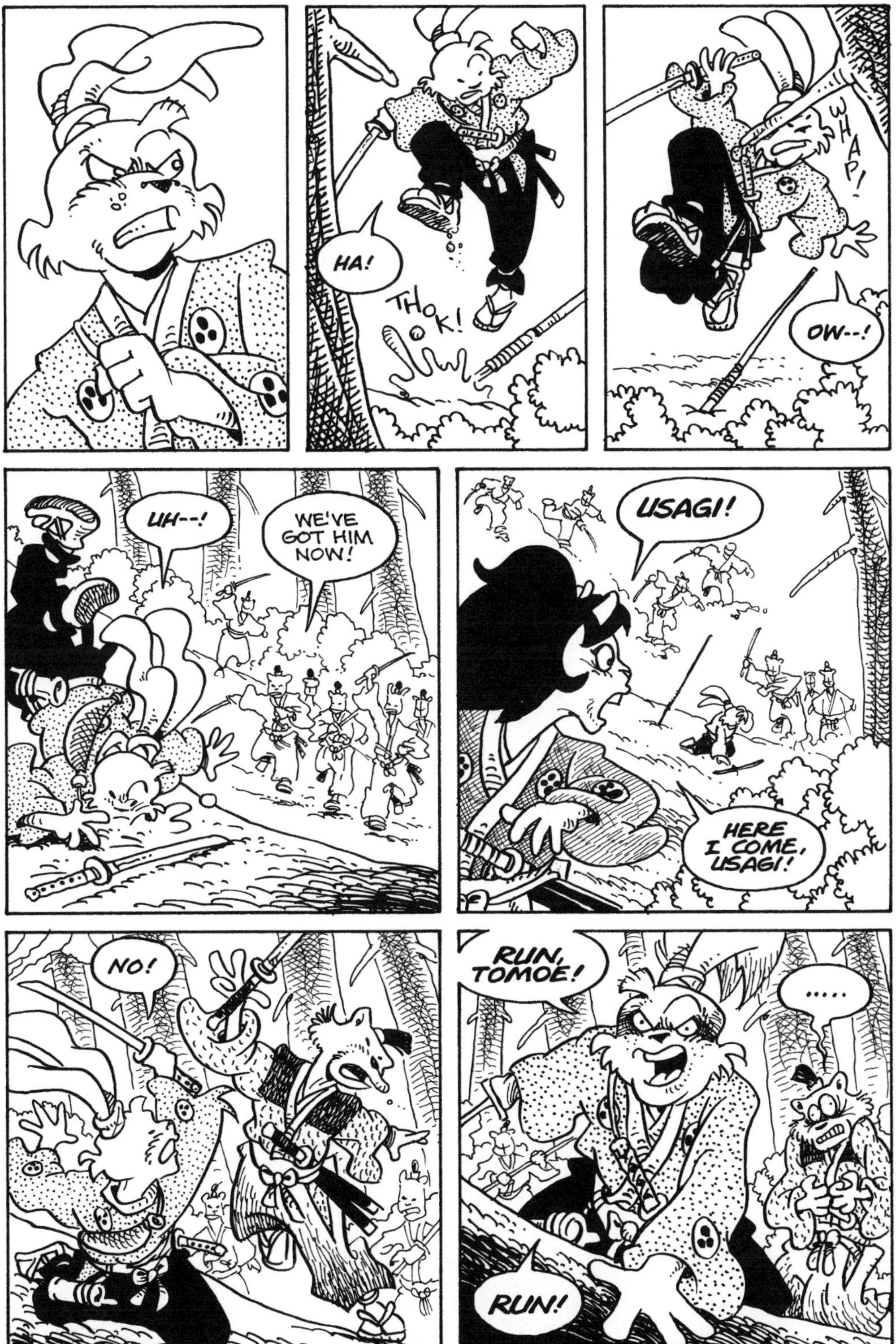
HA!
THOK!
WHAP!
OW--!
UH--!
WE'VE GOT HIM NOW!
USAGI!
HERE I COME, USAGI!
NO!
RUN, TOMOE!
.....
RUN!
17

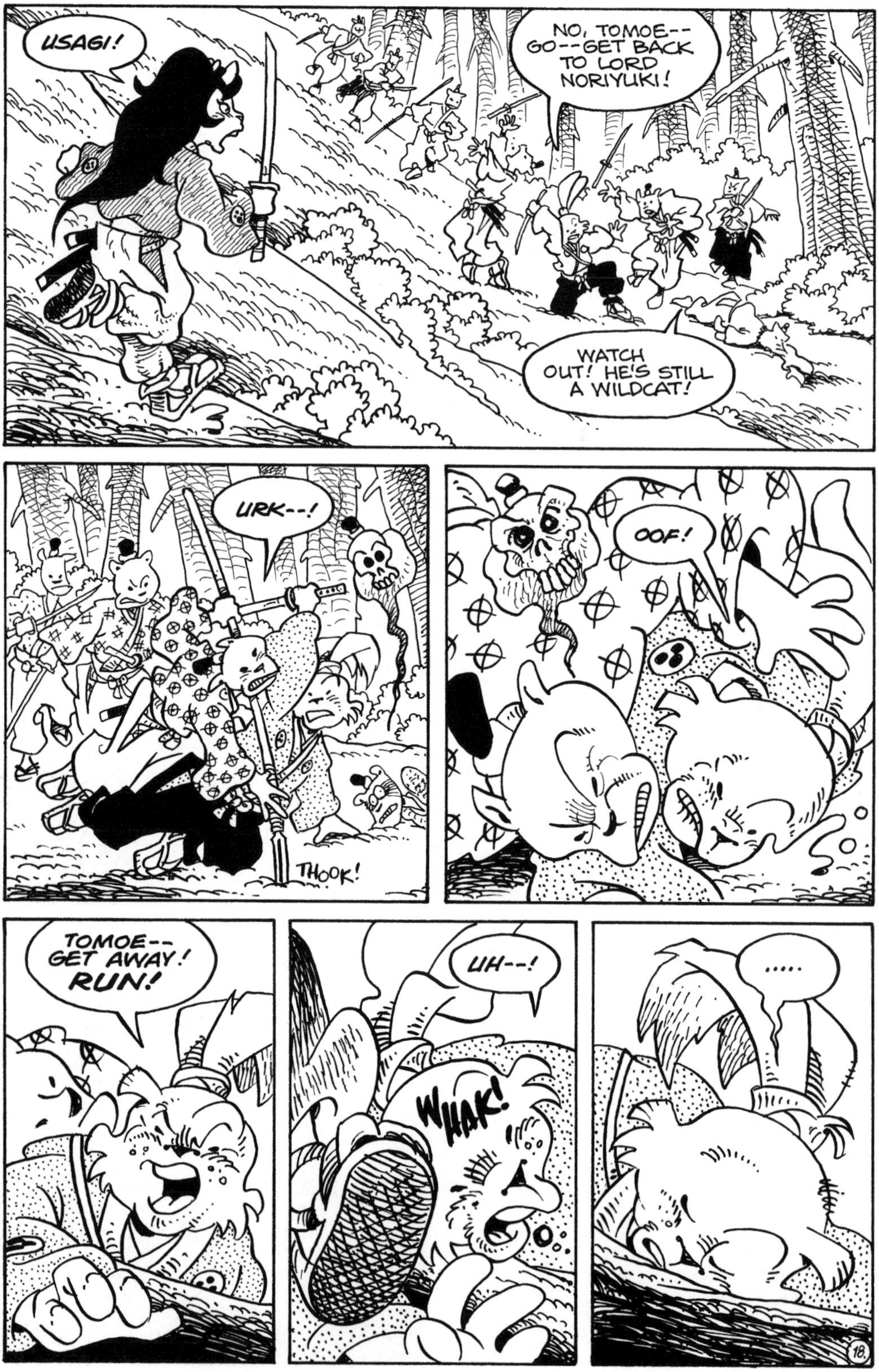
USAGI!
NO, TOMOE-- GO--GET BACK TO LORD NORIYUKI!
WATCH OUT! HE'S STILL A WILDCAT!
URK--!
THOOK!
OOF!
TOMOE-- GET AWAY! RUN!
UH--!
WHAK!
.....
18.

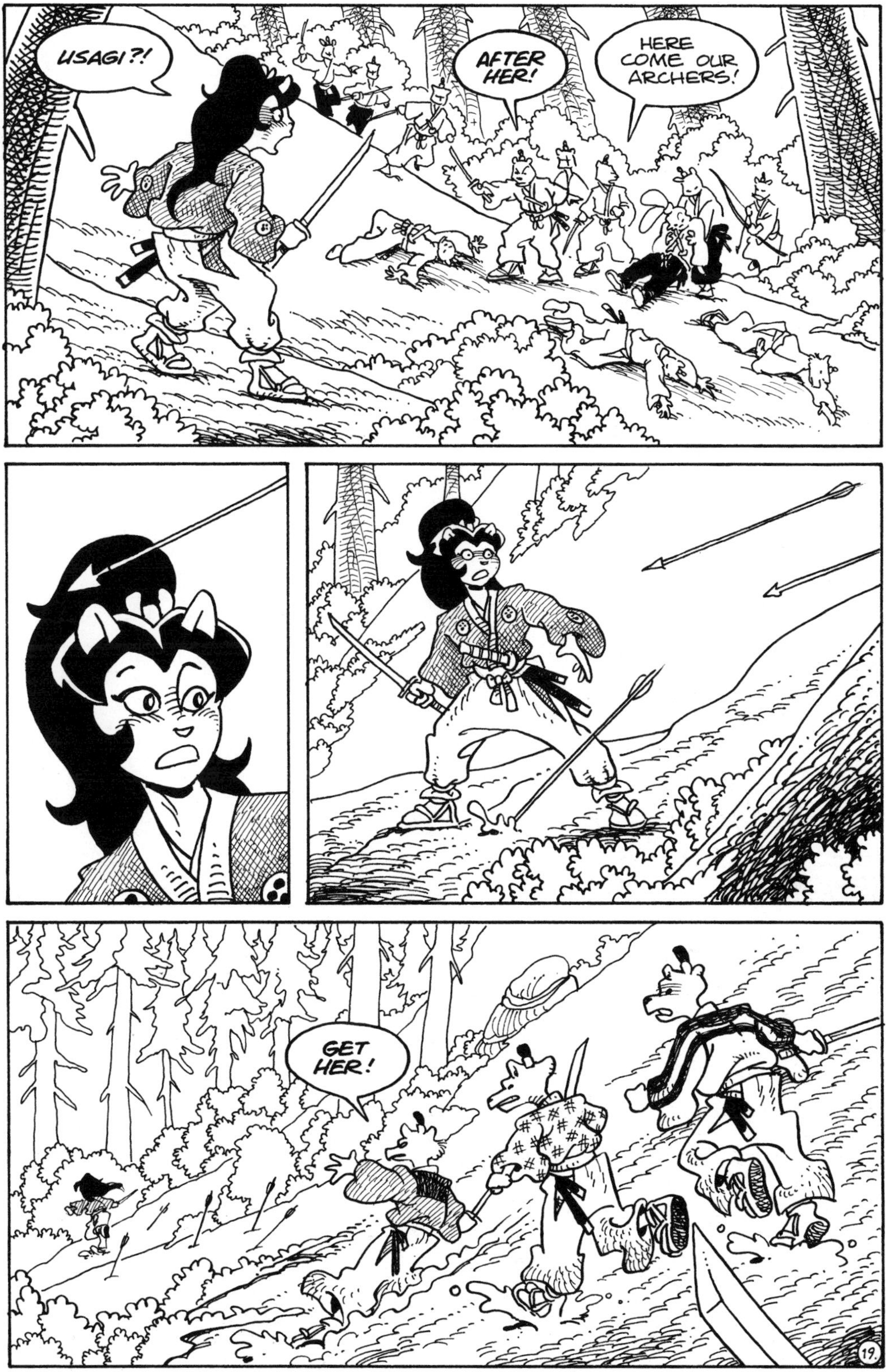
USAGI?!
AFTER HER!
HERE COME OUR ARCHERS!
GET HER!
19.

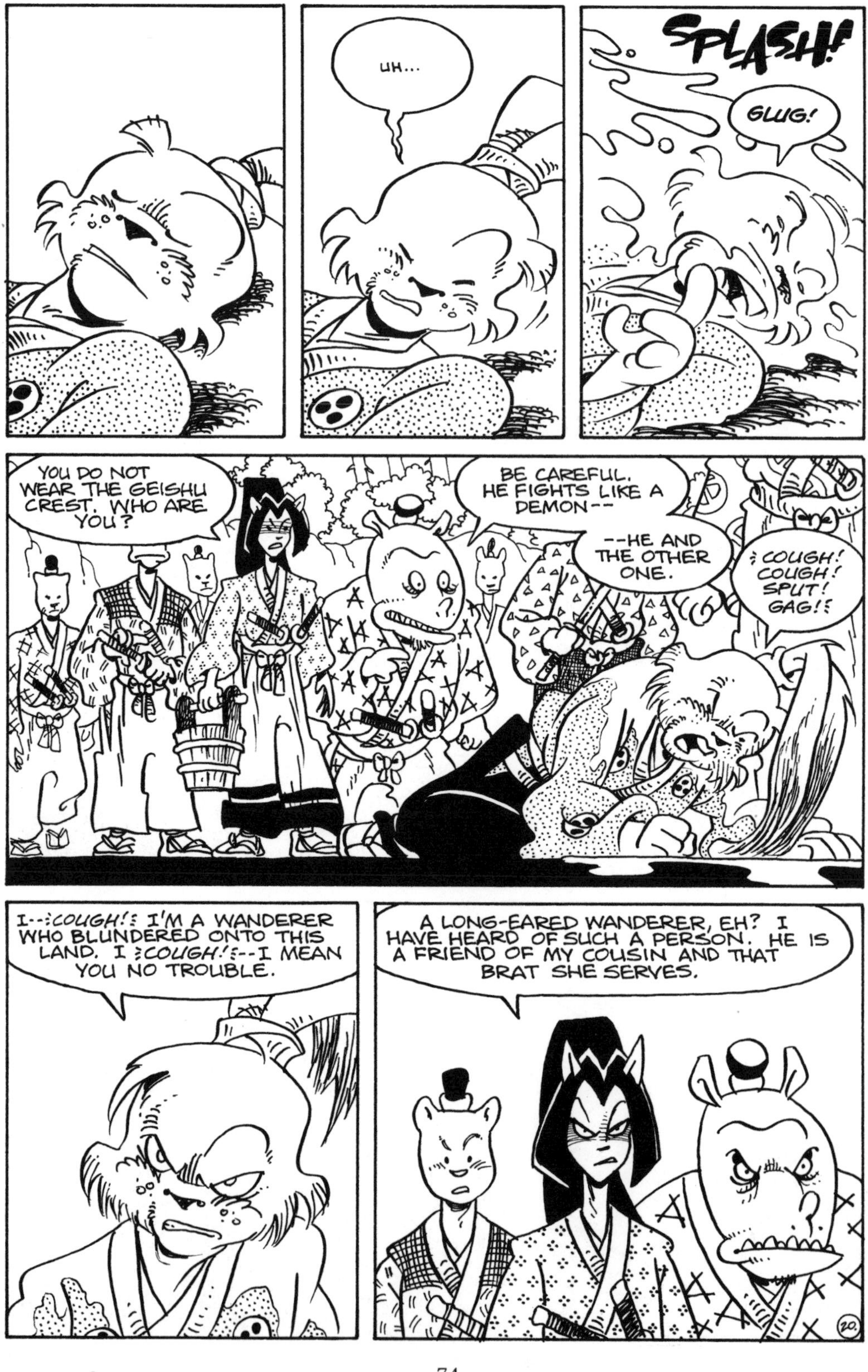
UH...
SPLASH!
GLUG!
YOU DO NOT WEAR THE GEISHU CREST. WHO ARE YOU?
BE CAREFUL. HE FIGHTS LIKE A DEMON--
--HE AND THE OTHER ONE.
COUGH! COUGH! SPUT! GAG!
I--COUGH! I'M A WANDERER WHO BLUNDERED ONTO THIS LAND. I COUGH!--I MEAN YOU NO TROUBLE.
A LONG-EARED WANDERER, EH? I HAVE HEARD OF SUCH A PERSON. HE IS A FRIEND OF MY COUSIN AND THAT BRAT SHE SERVES.
20.

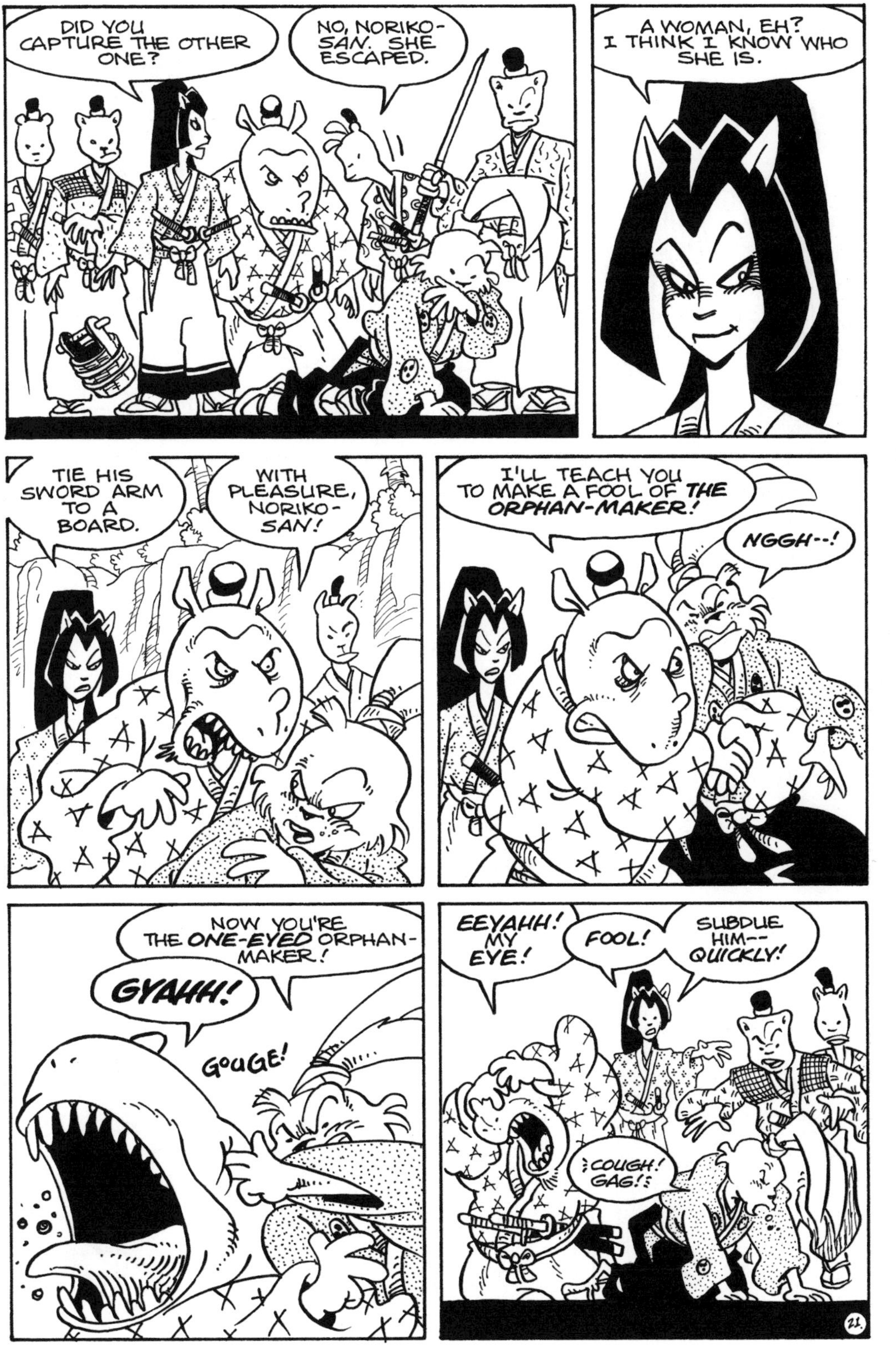
DID YOU CAPTURE THE OTHER ONE?
NO, NORIKO-SAN. SHE ESCAPED.
A WOMAN, EH? I THINK I KNOW WHO SHE IS.
TIE HIS SWORD ARM TO A BOARD.
WITH PLEASURE, NORIKO-SAN!
I'LL TEACH YOU TO MAKE A FOOL OF THE ORPHAN-MAKER!
NGGH--!
NOW YOU'RE THE ONE-EYED ORPHAN-MAKER!
GYAHH!
GOUGE!
EEYAHH! MY EYE!
FOOL!
SUBDUE HIM-- QUICKLY!
COUGH! GAG!
21.

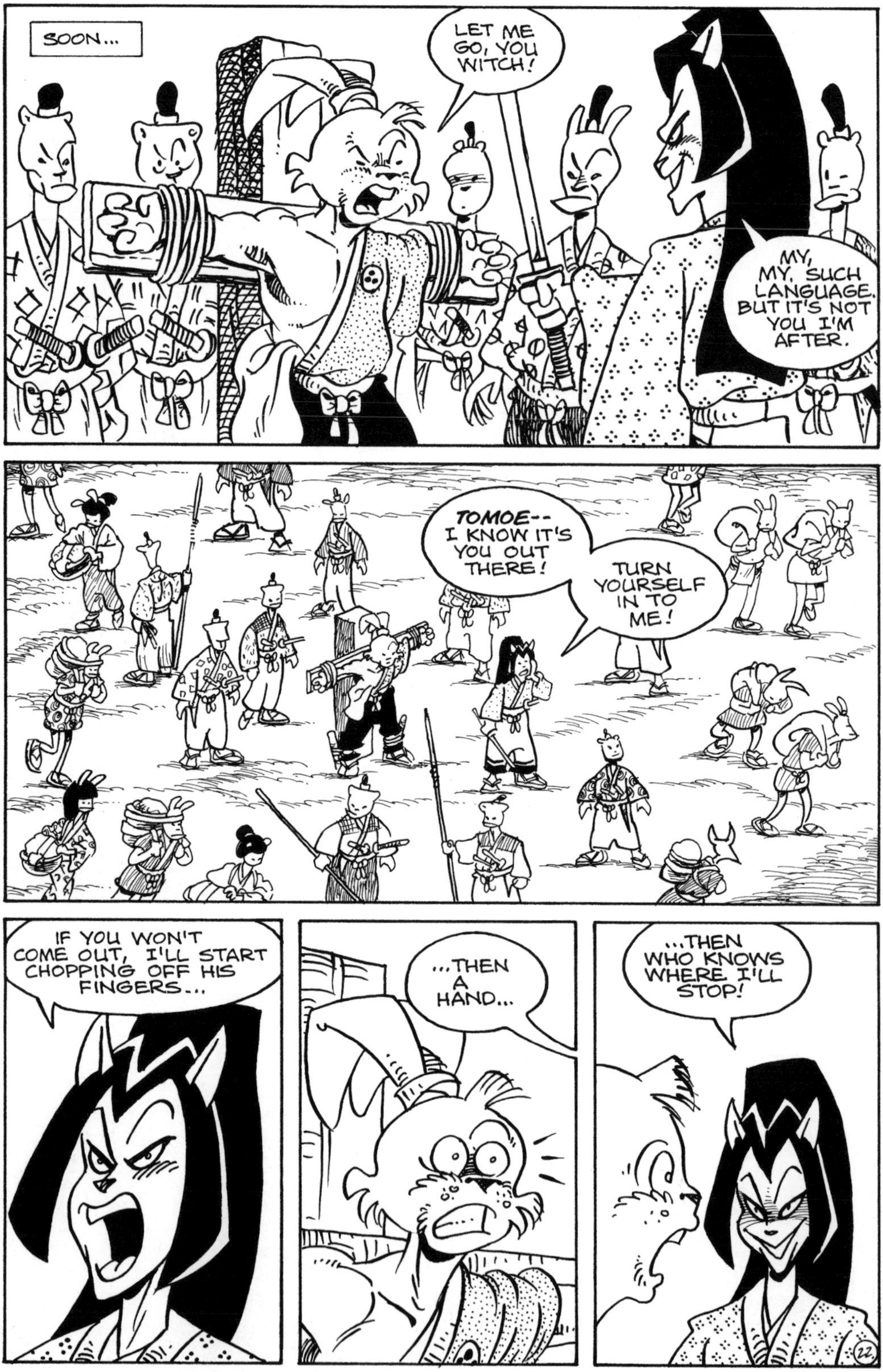
SOON...
LET ME GO, YOU WITCH!
MY, MY, SUCH LANGUAGE. BUT IT'S NOT YOU I'M AFTER.
TOMOE-- I KNOW IT'S YOU OUT THERE!
TURN YOURSELF IN TO ME!
IF YOU WON'T COME OUT, I'LL START CHOPPING OFF HIS FINGERS...
...THEN A HAND...
...THEN WHO KNOWS WHERE I'LL STOP!
22

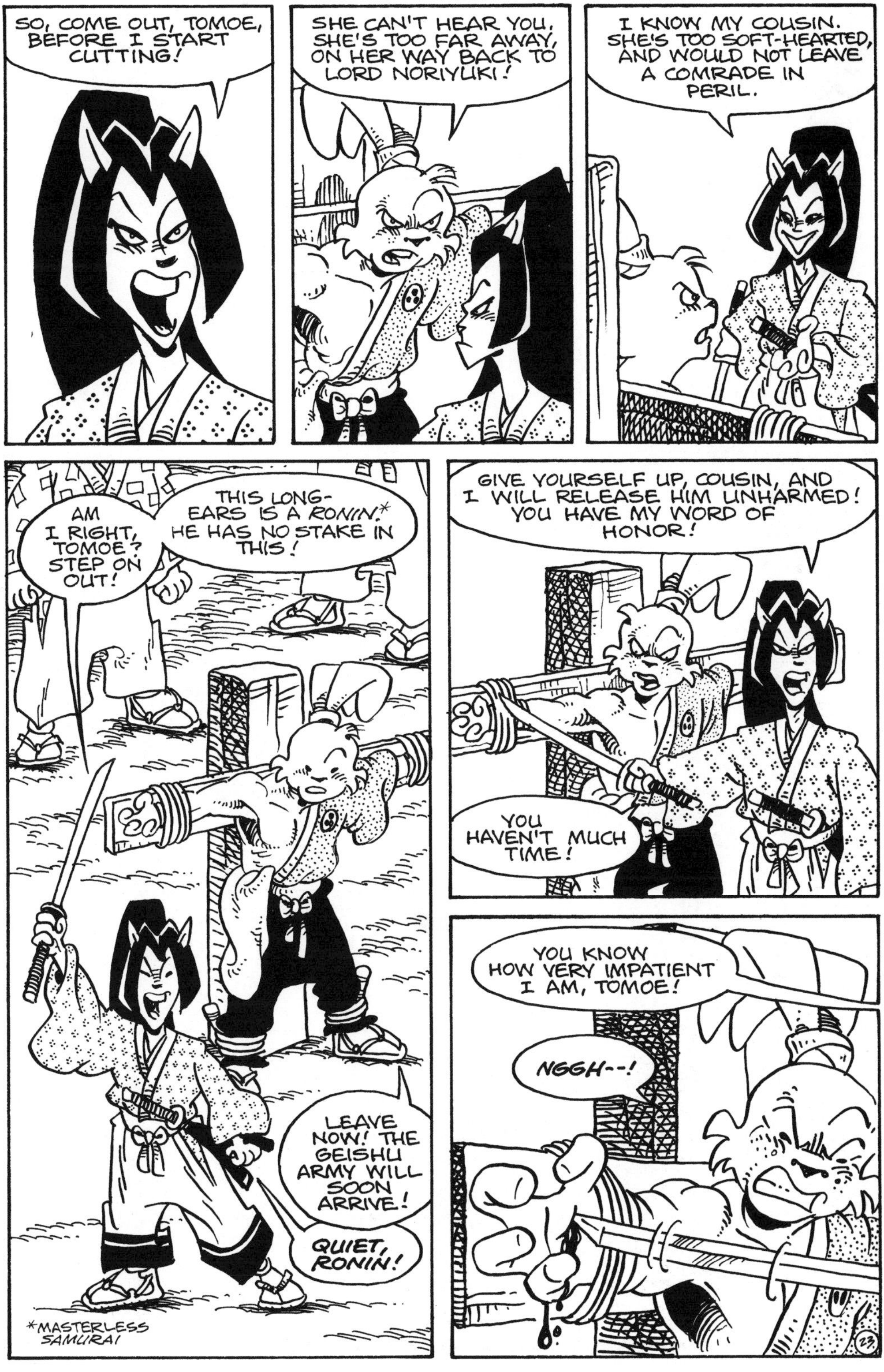
SO, COME OUT, TOMOE, BEFORE I START CUTTING!
SHE CAN'T HEAR YOU. SHE'S TOO FAR AWAY, ON HER WAY BACK TO LORD NORIYUKI!
I KNOW MY COUSIN. SHE'S TOO SOFT-HEARTED, AND WOULD NOT LEAVE A COMRADE IN PERIL.
THIS LONG-EARS IS A RONIN!* HE HAS NO STAKE IN THIS!
AM I RIGHT, TOMOE? STEP ON OUT!
LEAVE NOW! THE GEISHU ARMY WILL SOON ARRIVE!
QUIET, RONIN!
*MASTERLESS SAMURAI
GIVE YOURSELF UP, COUSIN, AND I WILL RELEASE HIM UNHARMED! YOU HAVE MY WORD OF HONOR!
YOU HAVEN'T MUCH TIME!
YOU KNOW HOW VERY IMPATIENT I AM, TOMOE!
NGGH--!
23

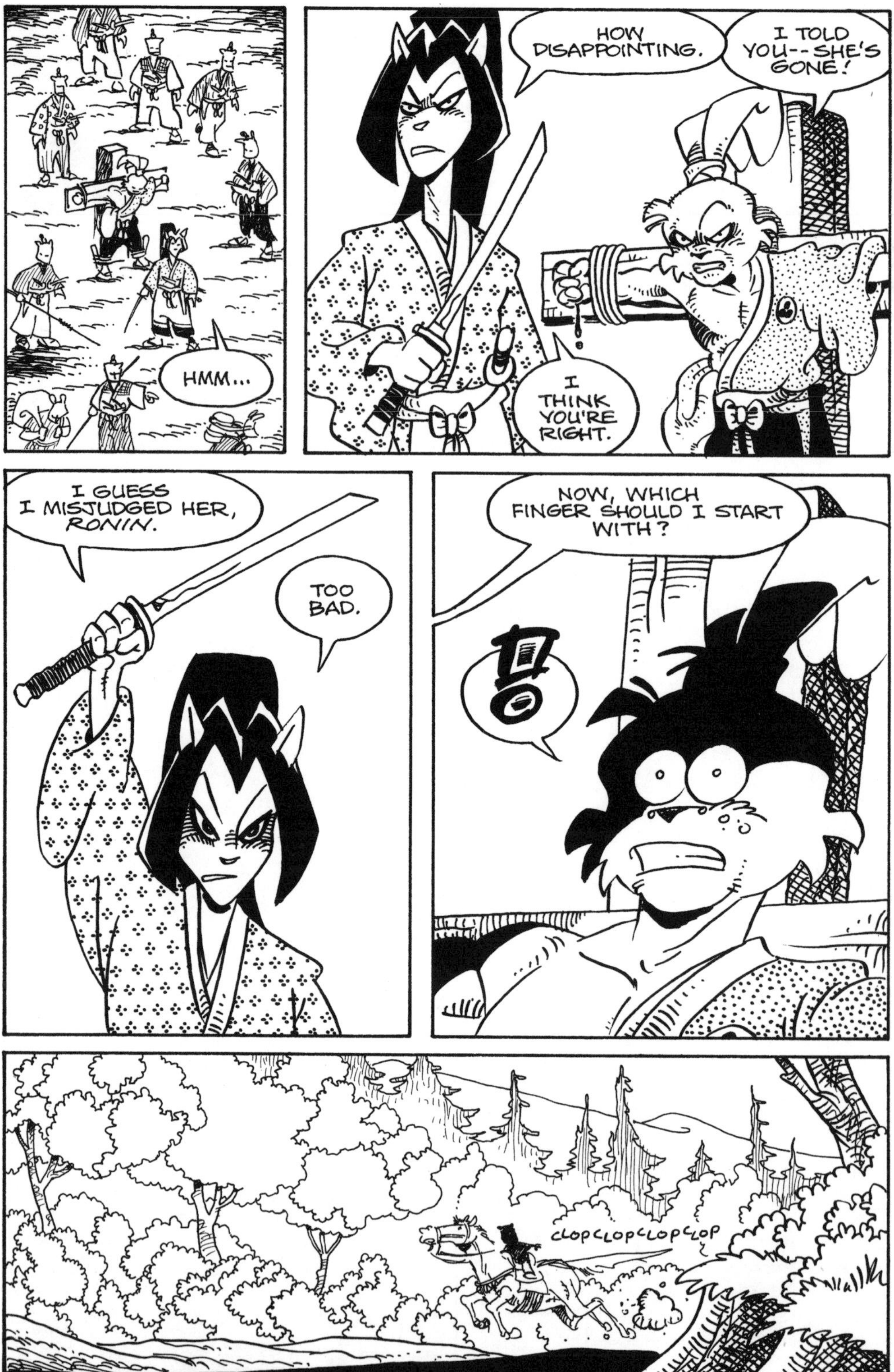
HMM...
HOW DISAPPOINTING.
I TOLD YOU--SHE'S GONE!
I THINK YOU'RE RIGHT.
I GUESS I MISJUDGED HER, *RONIN*.
TOO BAD.
NOW, WHICH FINGER SHOULD I START WITH?
CLOPCLOPCLOPCLOP

THE TREASURE of the MOTHER of MOUNTAINS

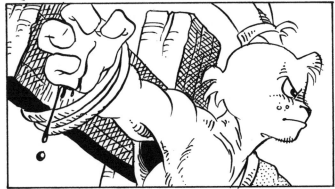

ANSWER ME, *RONIN*. WHICH FINGER SHOULD I CUT OFF FIRST?

YOU HAVE NO RESPONSE FOR ME, *RONIN*?

THEN *I* WILL CHOOSE.

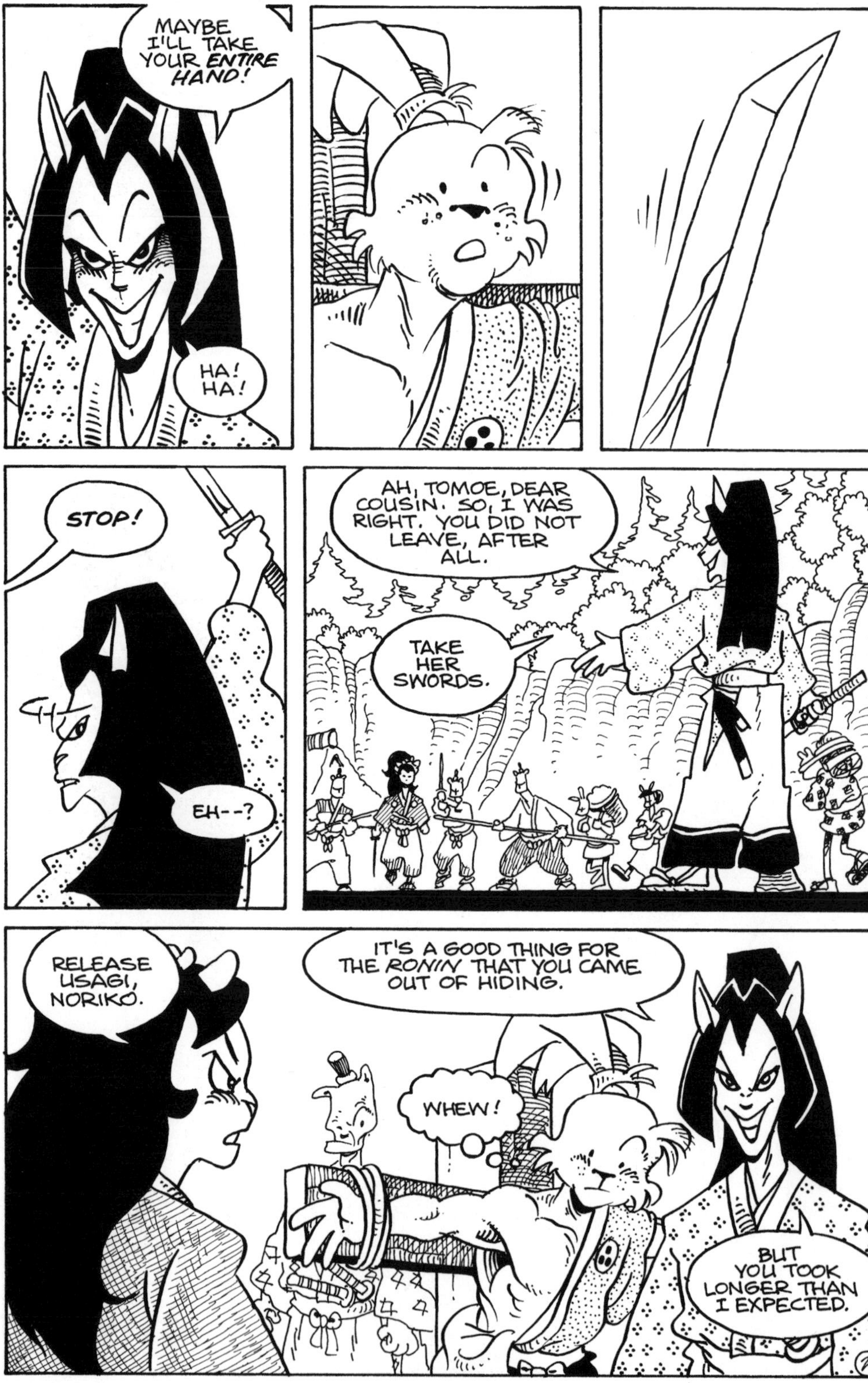
MAYBE I'LL TAKE YOUR *ENTIRE HAND!*
HA! HA!
STOP!
EH--?
AH, TOMOE, DEAR COUSIN. SO, I WAS RIGHT. YOU DID NOT LEAVE, AFTER ALL.
TAKE HER SWORDS.
RELEASE USAGI, NORIKO.
IT'S A GOOD THING FOR THE *RONIN* THAT YOU CAME OUT OF HIDING.
WHEW!
BUT YOU TOOK LONGER THAN I EXPECTED.

AND I DON'T LIKE TO BE KEPT WAITING!
HIYAHH!
NO!
CHOP!

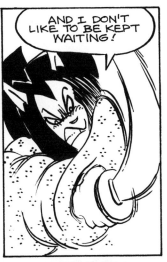

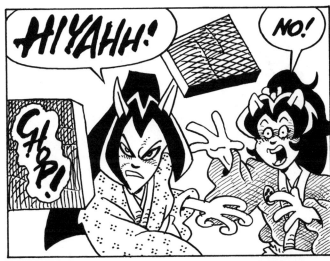

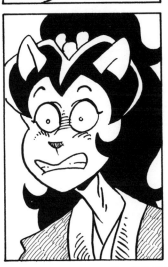

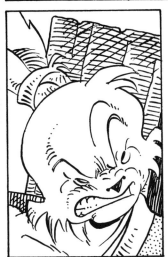

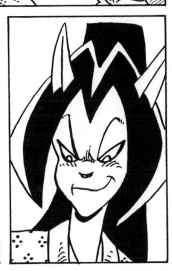

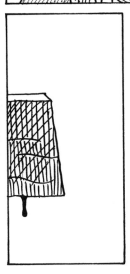

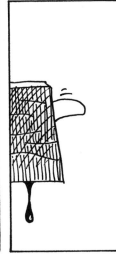

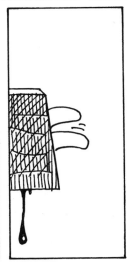

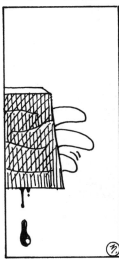

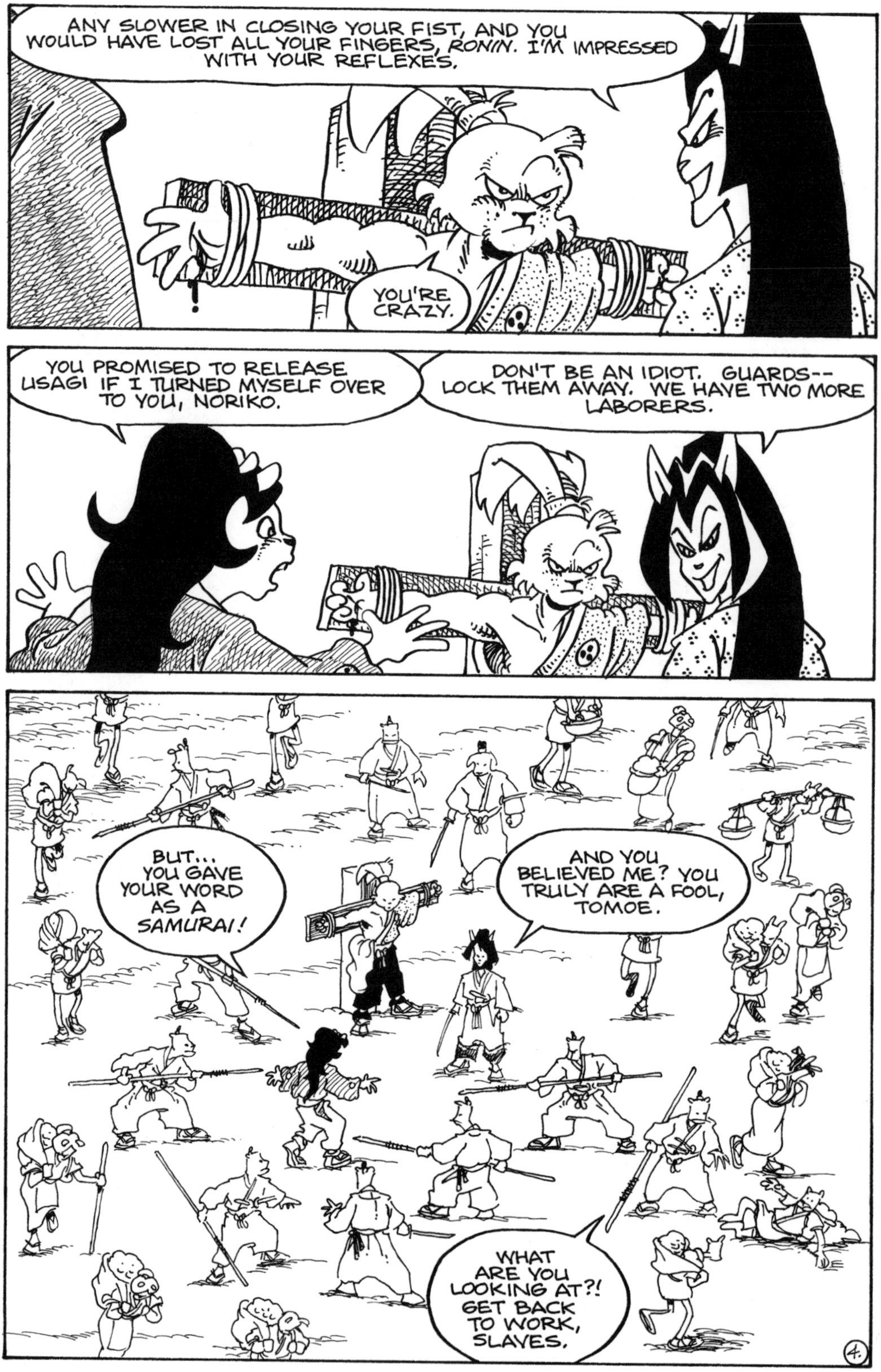
ANY SLOWER IN CLOSING YOUR FIST, AND YOU WOULD HAVE LOST ALL YOUR FINGERS, *RONIN*. I'M IMPRESSED WITH YOUR REFLEXES.
YOU'RE CRAZY.
YOU PROMISED TO RELEASE USAGI IF I TURNED MYSELF OVER TO YOU, NORIKO.
DON'T BE AN IDIOT. GUARDS-- LOCK THEM AWAY. WE HAVE TWO MORE LABORERS.
BUT... YOU GAVE YOUR WORD AS A SAMURAI!
AND YOU BELIEVED ME? YOU TRULY ARE A FOOL, TOMOE.
WHAT ARE YOU LOOKING AT?! GET BACK TO WORK, SLAVES.
4.

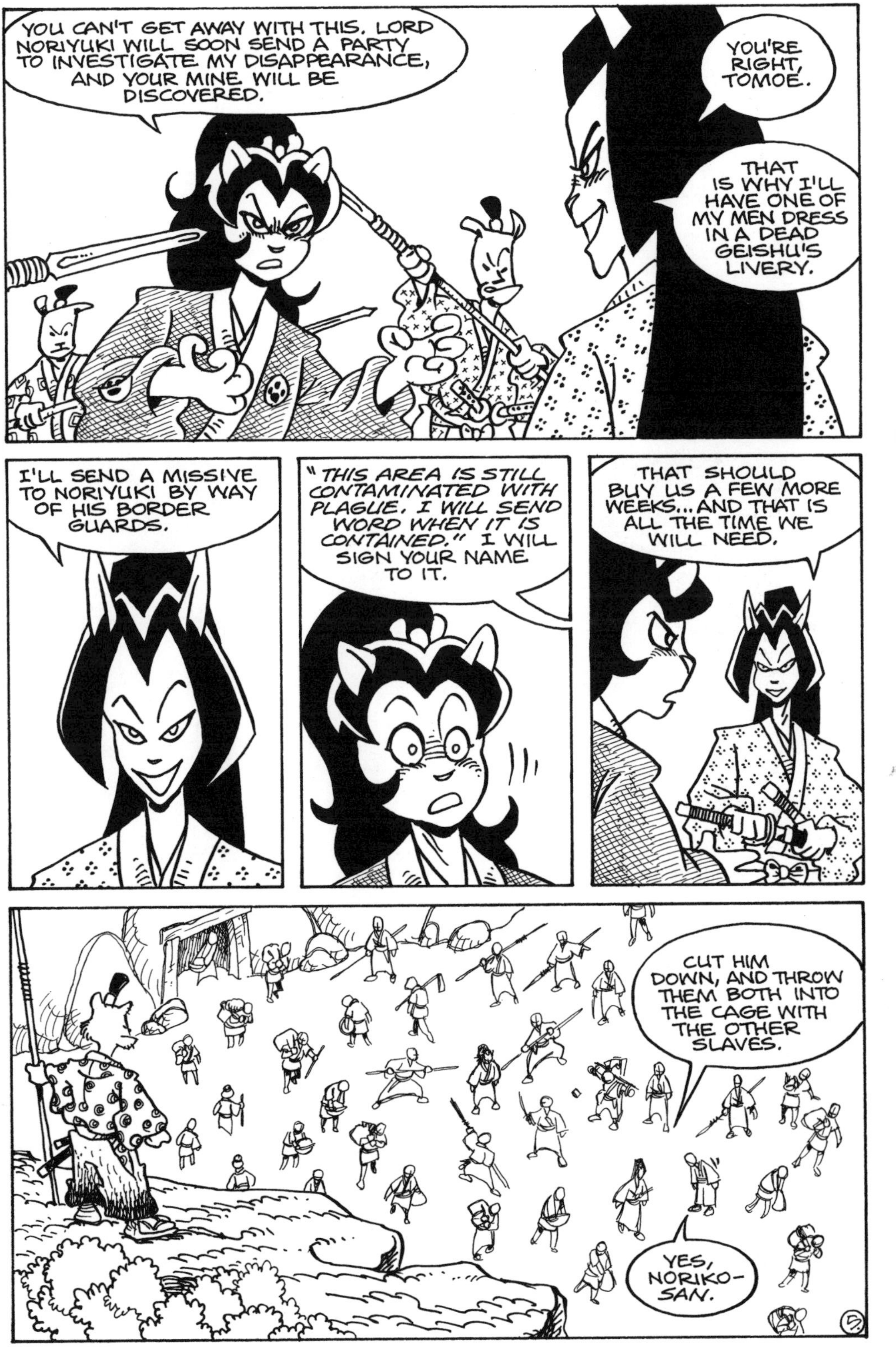
YOU CAN'T GET AWAY WITH THIS. LORD NORIYUKI WILL SOON SEND A PARTY TO INVESTIGATE MY DISAPPEARANCE, AND YOUR MINE WILL BE DISCOVERED.
YOU'RE RIGHT, TOMOE.
THAT IS WHY I'LL HAVE ONE OF MY MEN DRESS IN A DEAD GEISHU'S LIVERY.
I'LL SEND A MISSIVE TO NORIYUKI BY WAY OF HIS BORDER GUARDS.
"THIS AREA IS STILL CONTAMINATED WITH PLAGUE. I WILL SEND WORD WHEN IT IS CONTAINED." I WILL SIGN YOUR NAME TO IT.
THAT SHOULD BUY US A FEW MORE WEEKS...AND THAT IS ALL THE TIME WE WILL NEED.
CUT HIM DOWN, AND THROW THEM BOTH INTO THE CAGE WITH THE OTHER SLAVES.
YES, NORIKO-SAN.
5

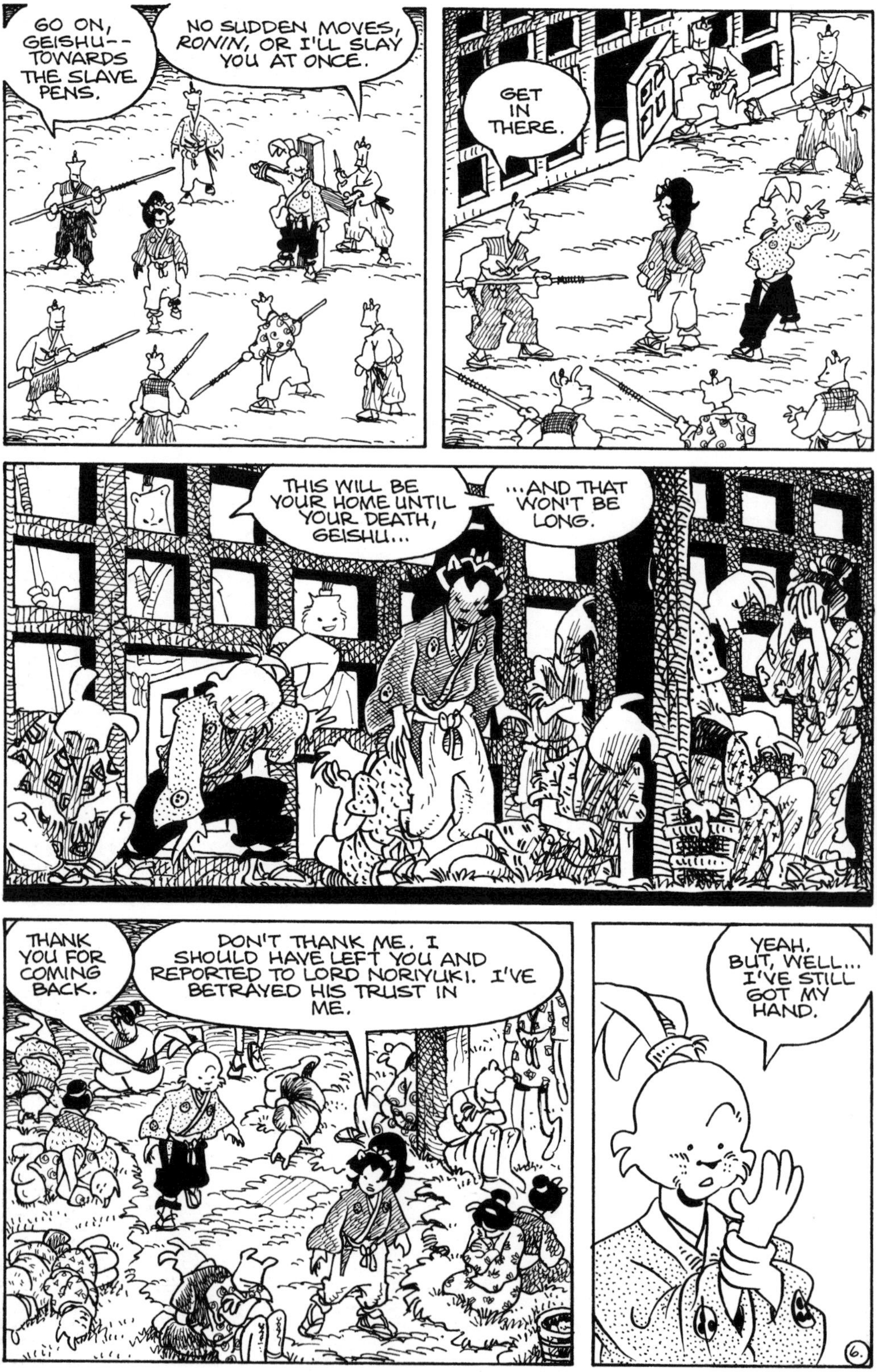
GO ON, GEISHU-- TOWARDS THE SLAVE PENS.
NO SUDDEN MOVES, RONIN, OR I'LL SLAY YOU AT ONCE.
GET IN THERE.
THIS WILL BE YOUR HOME UNTIL YOUR DEATH, GEISHU...
...AND THAT WON'T BE LONG.
THANK YOU FOR COMING BACK.
DON'T THANK ME. I SHOULD HAVE LEFT YOU AND REPORTED TO LORD NORIYUKI. I'VE BETRAYED HIS TRUST IN ME.
YEAH, BUT, WELL... I'VE STILL GOT MY HAND.
6.

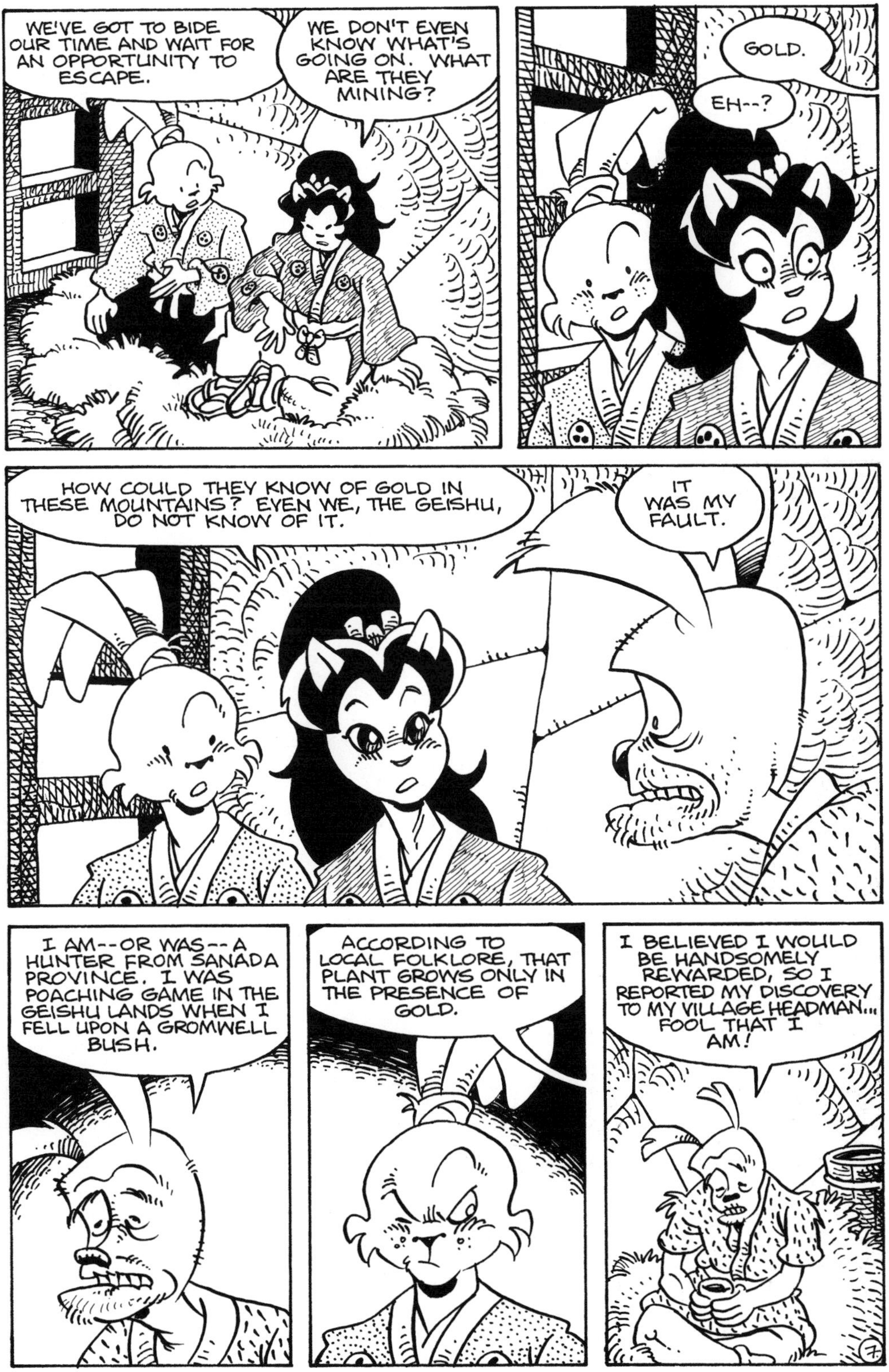
WE'VE GOT TO BIDE OUR TIME AND WAIT FOR AN OPPORTUNITY TO ESCAPE.
WE DON'T EVEN KNOW WHAT'S GOING ON. WHAT ARE THEY MINING?
GOLD.
EH--?
HOW COULD THEY KNOW OF GOLD IN THESE MOUNTAINS? EVEN WE, THE GEISHU, DO NOT KNOW OF IT.
IT WAS MY FAULT.
I AM--OR WAS--A HUNTER FROM SANADA PROVINCE. I WAS POACHING GAME IN THE GEISHU LANDS WHEN I FELL UPON A GROMWELL BUSH.
ACCORDING TO LOCAL FOLKLORE, THAT PLANT GROWS ONLY IN THE PRESENCE OF GOLD.
I BELIEVED I WOULD BE HANDSOMELY REWARDED, SO I REPORTED MY DISCOVERY TO MY VILLAGE HEADMAN... FOOL THAT I AM!
7.

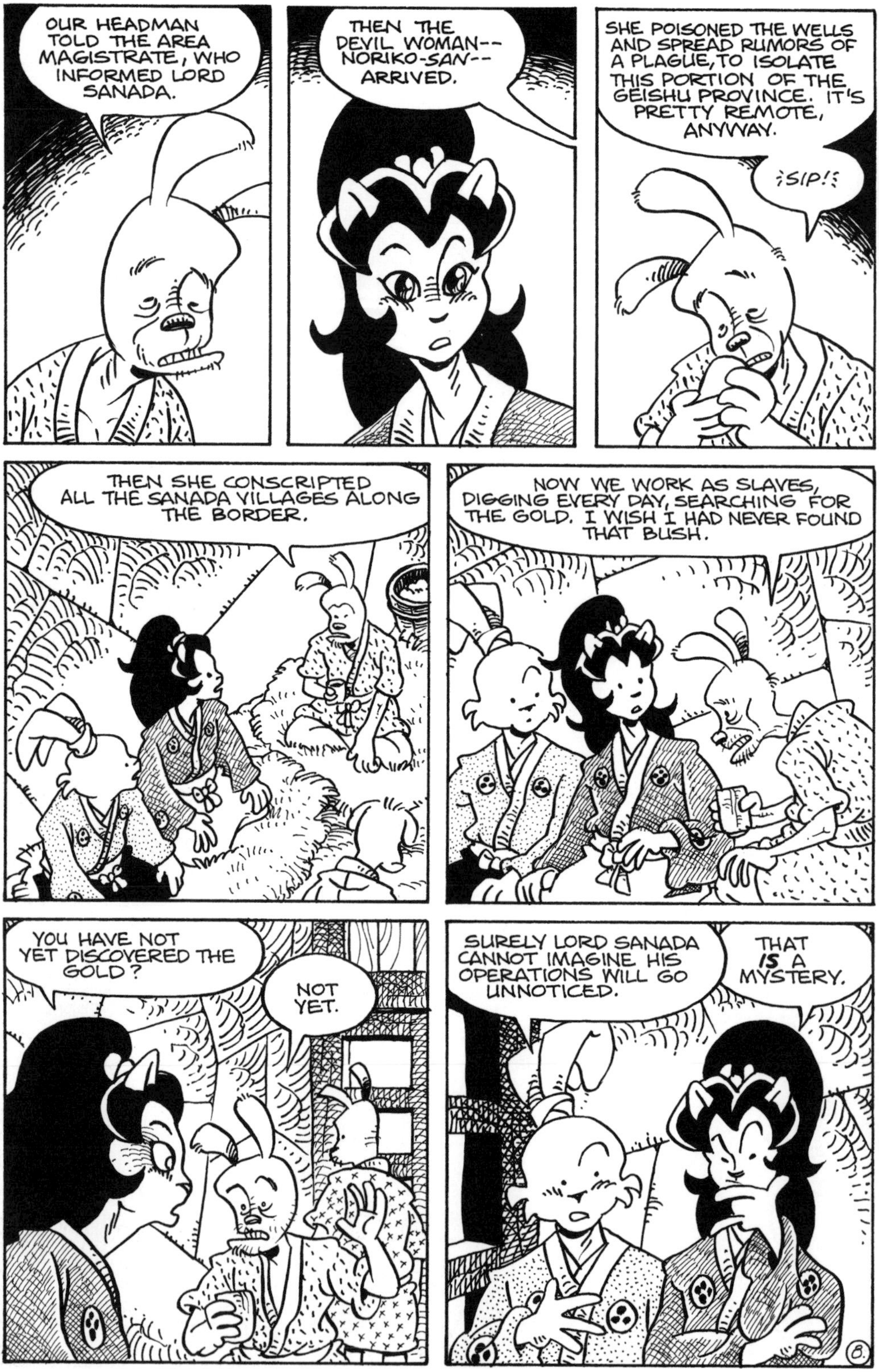
OUR HEADMAN TOLD THE AREA MAGISTRATE, WHO INFORMED LORD SANADA.
THEN THE DEVIL WOMAN-- NORIKO-SAN-- ARRIVED.
SHE POISONED THE WELLS AND SPREAD RUMORS OF A PLAGUE, TO ISOLATE THIS PORTION OF THE GEISHU PROVINCE. IT'S PRETTY REMOTE, ANYWAY.
SIP!
THEN SHE CONSCRIPTED ALL THE SANADA VILLAGES ALONG THE BORDER.
NOW WE WORK AS SLAVES, DIGGING EVERY DAY, SEARCHING FOR THE GOLD. I WISH I HAD NEVER FOUND THAT BUSH.
YOU HAVE NOT YET DISCOVERED THE GOLD?
NOT YET.
SURELY LORD SANADA CANNOT IMAGINE HIS OPERATIONS WILL GO UNNOTICED.
THAT IS A MYSTERY.
8.

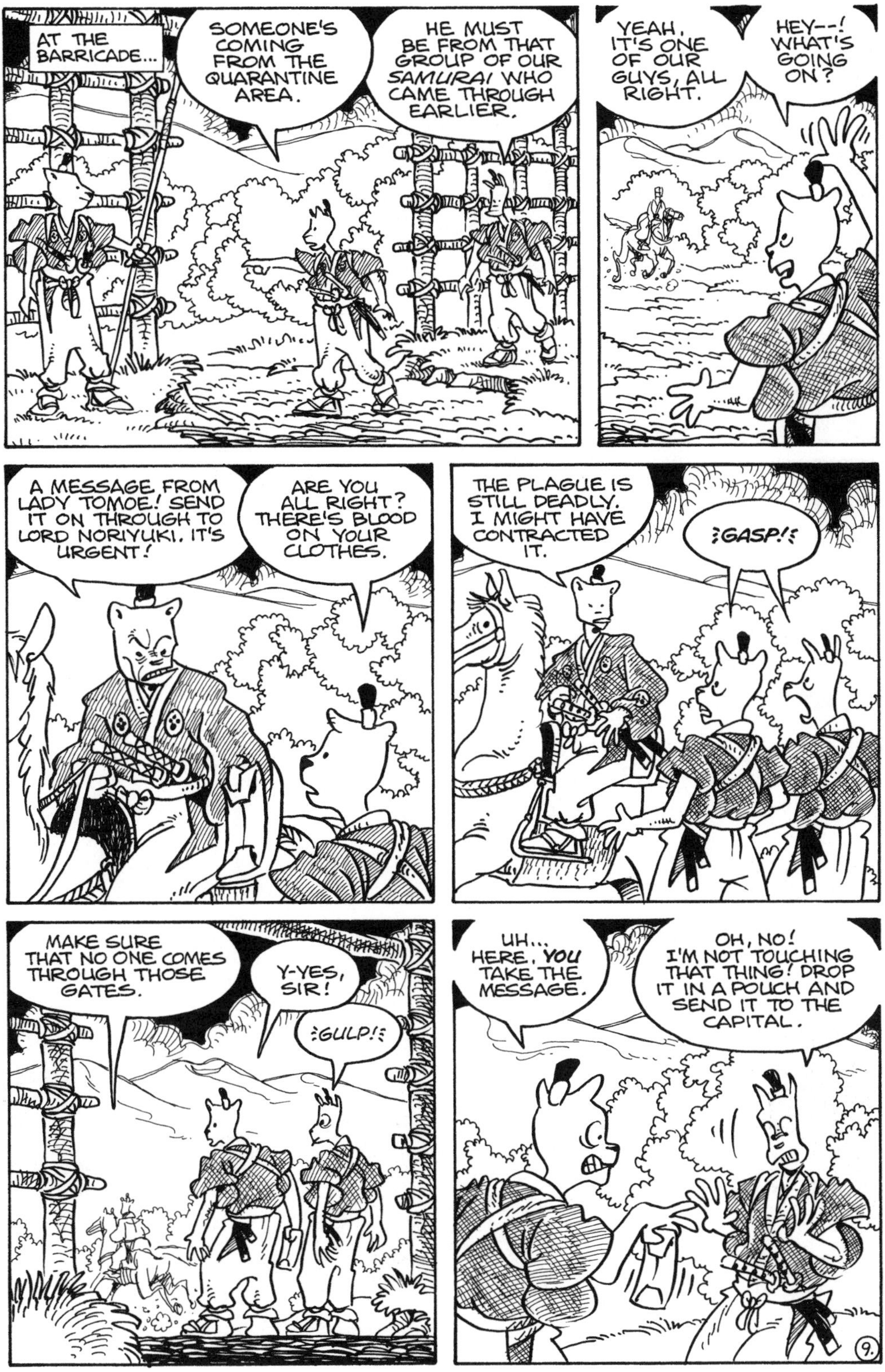
AT THE BARRICADE...
SOMEONE'S COMING FROM THE QUARANTINE AREA.
HE MUST BE FROM THAT GROUP OF OUR SAMURAI WHO CAME THROUGH EARLIER.
YEAH, IT'S ONE OF OUR GUYS, ALL RIGHT.
HEY--! WHAT'S GOING ON?
A MESSAGE FROM LADY TOMOE! SEND IT ON THROUGH TO LORD NORIYUKI. IT'S URGENT!
ARE YOU ALL RIGHT? THERE'S BLOOD ON YOUR CLOTHES.
THE PLAGUE IS STILL DEADLY. I MIGHT HAVE CONTRACTED IT.
GASP!
MAKE SURE THAT NO ONE COMES THROUGH THOSE GATES.
Y-YES, SIR!
GULP!
UH... HERE. YOU TAKE THE MESSAGE.
OH, NO! I'M NOT TOUCHING THAT THING! DROP IT IN A POUCH AND SEND IT TO THE CAPITAL.
9.

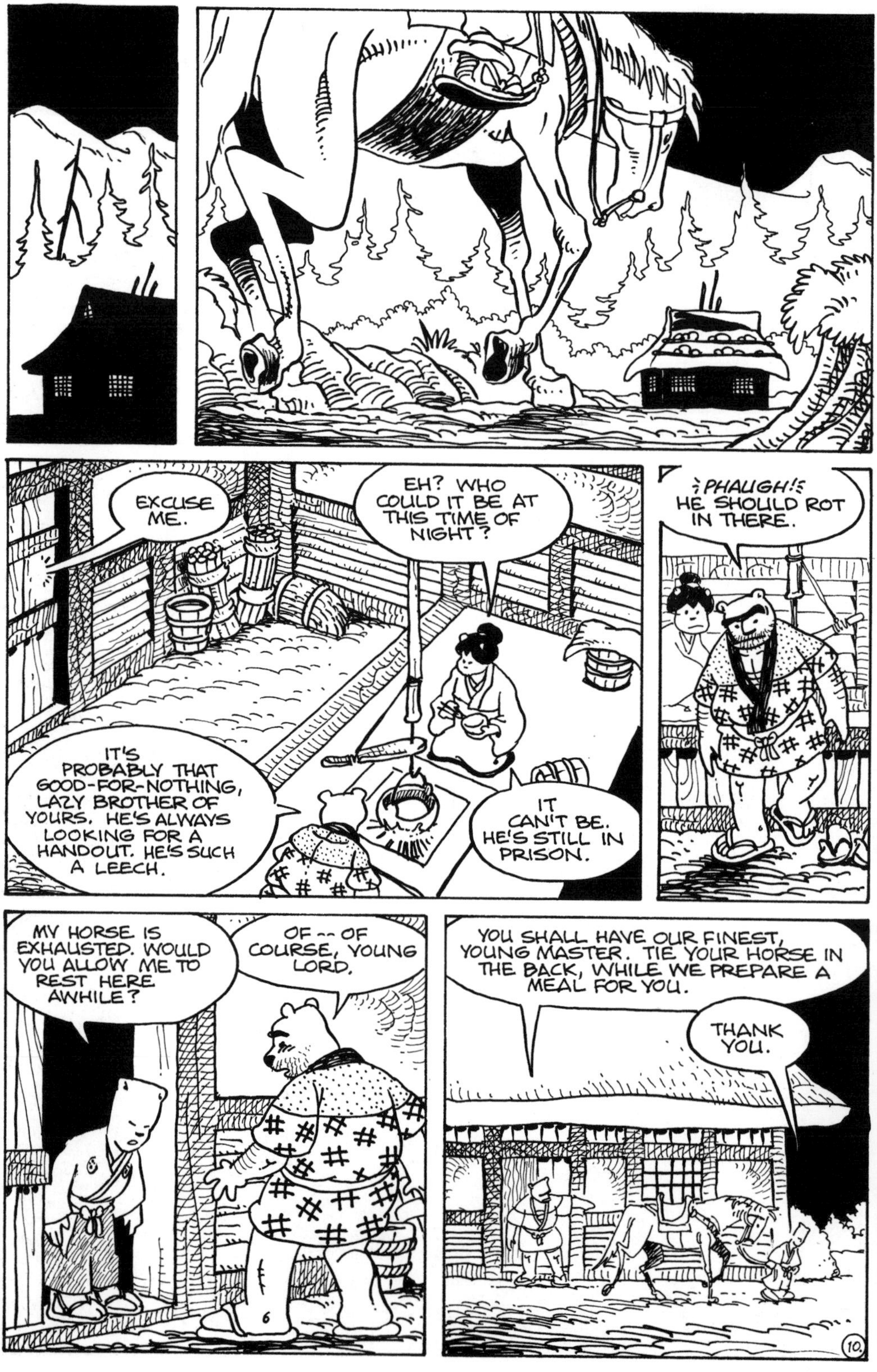
EXCUSE ME.
EH? WHO COULD IT BE AT THIS TIME OF NIGHT?
IT'S PROBABLY THAT GOOD-FOR-NOTHING, LAZY BROTHER OF YOURS. HE'S ALWAYS LOOKING FOR A HANDOUT. HE'S SUCH A LEECH.
IT CAN'T BE. HE'S STILL IN PRISON.
PHAUGH! HE SHOULD ROT IN THERE.
MY HORSE IS EXHAUSTED. WOULD YOU ALLOW ME TO REST HERE AWHILE?
OF -- OF COURSE, YOUNG LORD.
YOU SHALL HAVE OUR FINEST, YOUNG MASTER. TIE YOUR HORSE IN THE BACK, WHILE WE PREPARE A MEAL FOR YOU.
THANK YOU.
10.

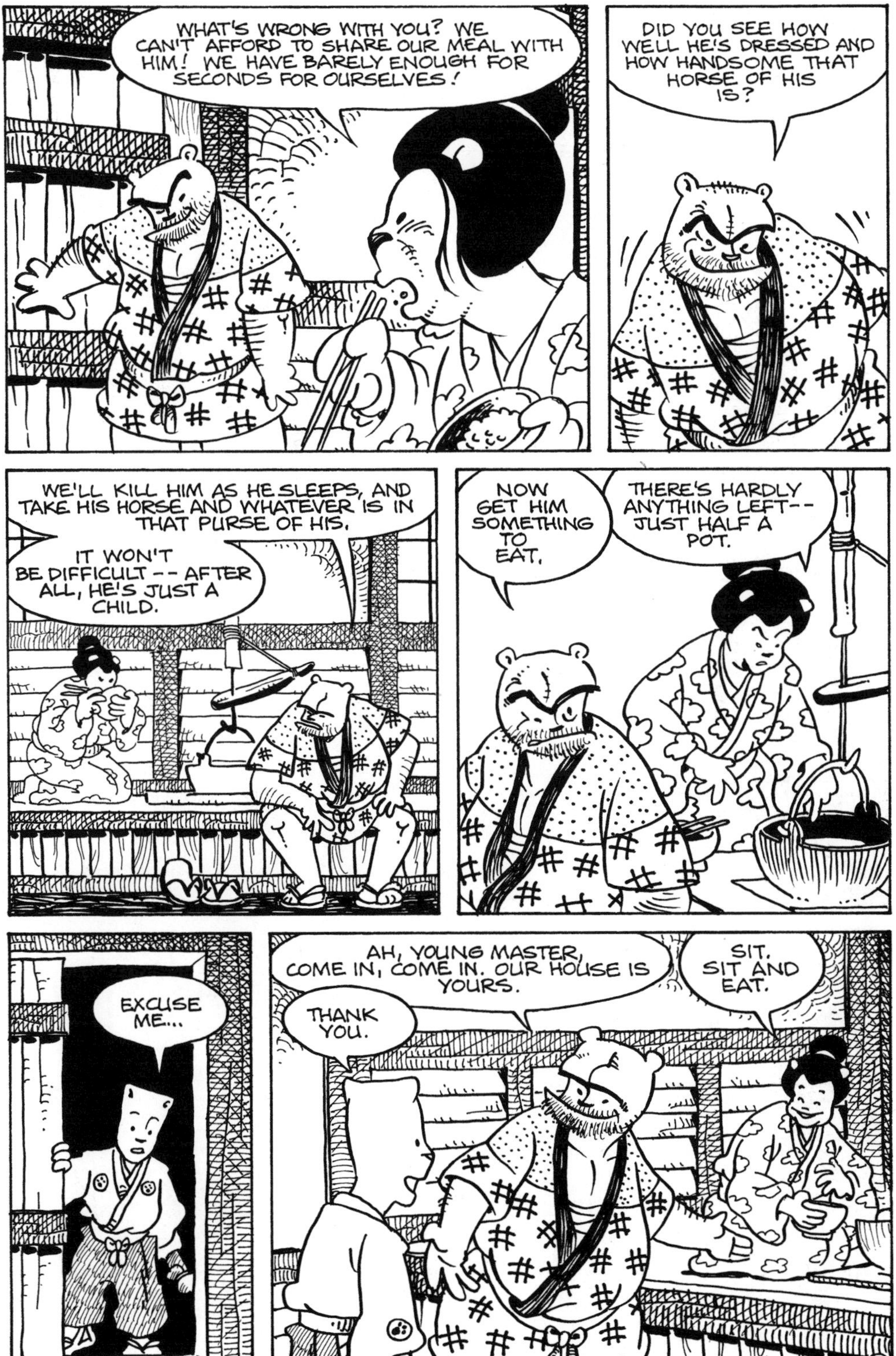
WHAT'S WRONG WITH YOU? WE CAN'T AFFORD TO SHARE OUR MEAL WITH HIM! WE HAVE BARELY ENOUGH FOR SECONDS FOR OURSELVES!
DID YOU SEE HOW WELL HE'S DRESSED AND HOW HANDSOME THAT HORSE OF HIS IS?
WE'LL KILL HIM AS HE SLEEPS, AND TAKE HIS HORSE AND WHATEVER IS IN THAT PURSE OF HIS.
IT WON'T BE DIFFICULT -- AFTER ALL, HE'S JUST A CHILD.
NOW GET HIM SOMETHING TO EAT.
THERE'S HARDLY ANYTHING LEFT-- JUST HALF A POT.
EXCUSE ME...
AH, YOUNG MASTER, COME IN, COME IN. OUR HOUSE IS YOURS.
THANK YOU.
SIT. SIT AND EAT.
11.

LATER...

HE'S ASLEEP. HE MUST HAVE BEEN RIDING ALL DAY. HE MUST BE DEAD TIRED.

BUT SOON, HE'LL JUST BE DEAD. NOW GO ON-- KILL HIM.

DON'T RUSH ME! DON'T RUSH ME!

ZZZZ....

IT WILL BE LIKE FILLETING A FISH.

JUST THINK OF HOW MUCH MONEY HE COULD BE CARRYING.

YEAH. YEAH.

GO ON, GO ON.

HEH. HEH. HEH.

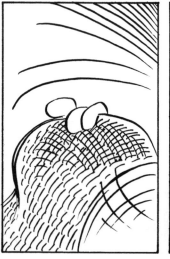

YAHHHHH!!

12

90

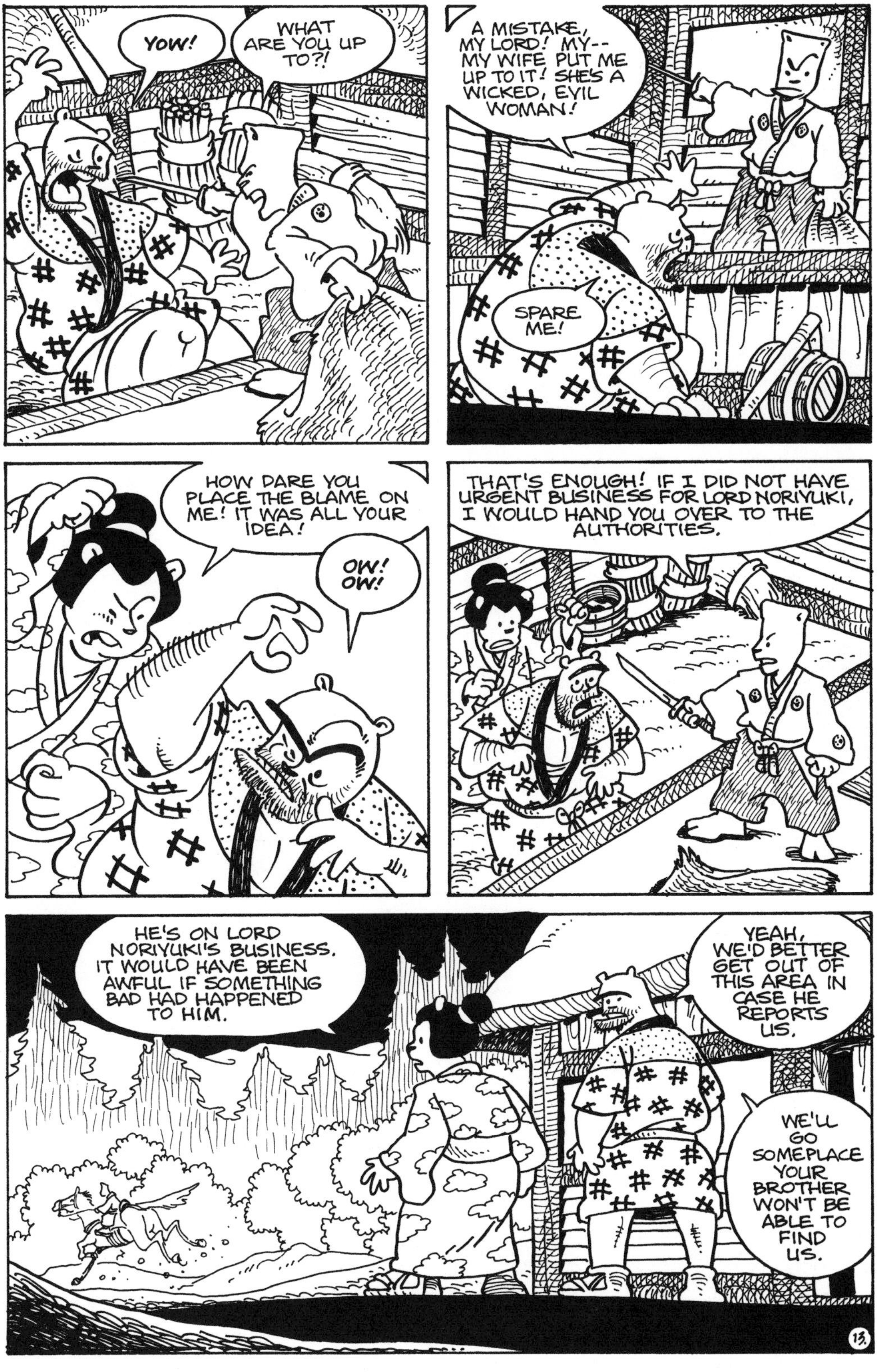
YOW!
WHAT ARE YOU UP TO?!
A MISTAKE, MY LORD! MY-- MY WIFE PUT ME UP TO IT! SHE'S A WICKED, EVIL WOMAN!
SPARE ME!
HOW DARE YOU PLACE THE BLAME ON ME! IT WAS ALL YOUR IDEA!
OW! OW!
THAT'S ENOUGH! IF I DID NOT HAVE URGENT BUSINESS FOR LORD NORIYUKI, I WOULD HAND YOU OVER TO THE AUTHORITIES.
HE'S ON LORD NORIYUKI'S BUSINESS. IT WOULD HAVE BEEN AWFUL IF SOMETHING BAD HAD HAPPENED TO HIM.
YEAH, WE'D BETTER GET OUT OF THIS AREA IN CASE HE REPORTS US.
WE'LL GO SOMEPLACE YOUR BROTHER WON'T BE ABLE TO FIND US.
13

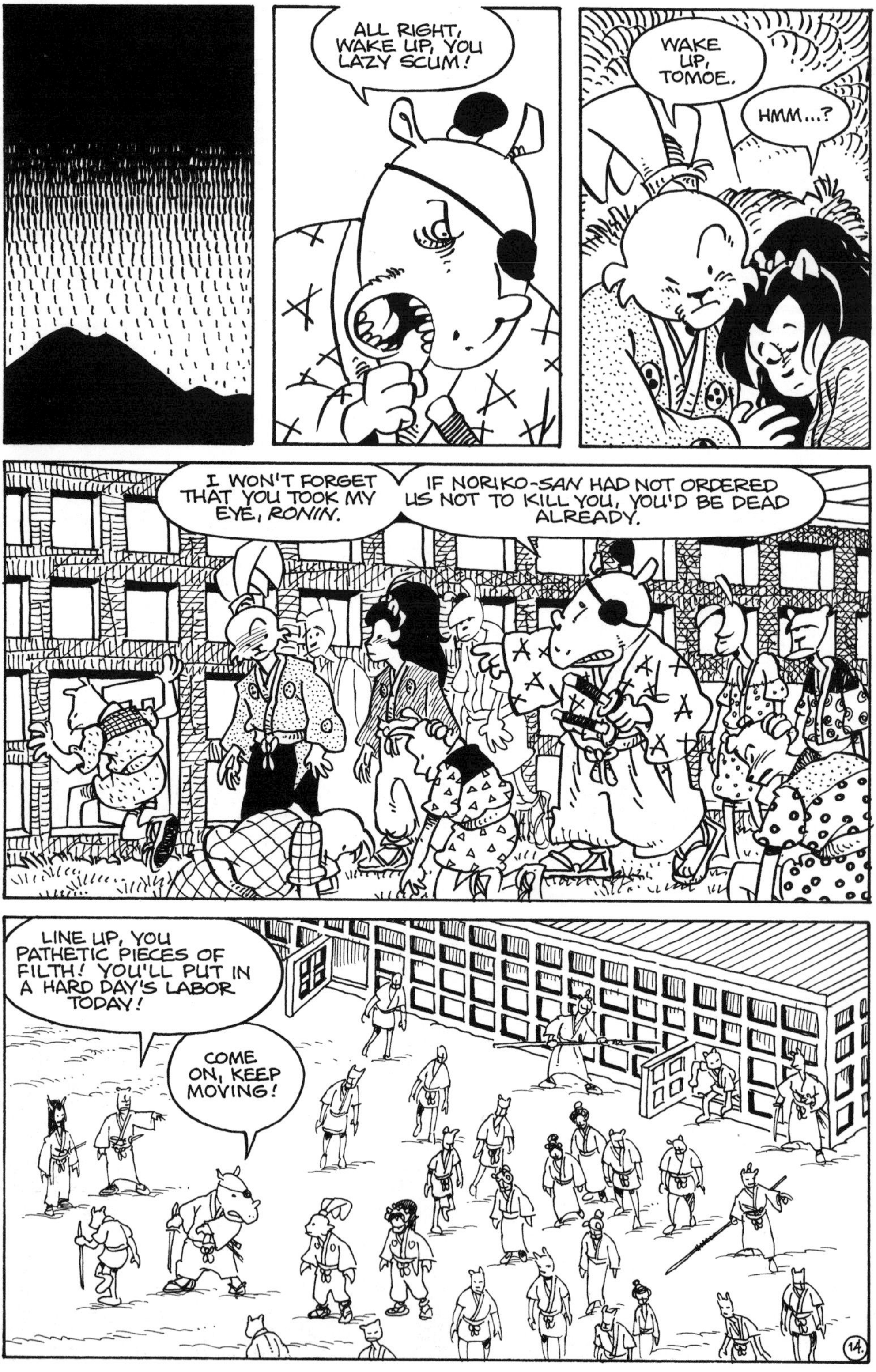
ALL RIGHT, WAKE UP, YOU LAZY SCUM!
WAKE UP, TOMOE.
HMM...?
I WON'T FORGET THAT YOU TOOK MY EYE, RONIN.
IF NORIKO-SAN HAD NOT ORDERED US NOT TO KILL YOU, YOU'D BE DEAD ALREADY.
LINE UP, YOU PATHETIC PIECES OF FILTH! YOU'LL PUT IN A HARD DAY'S LABOR TODAY!
COME ON, KEEP MOVING!
14.

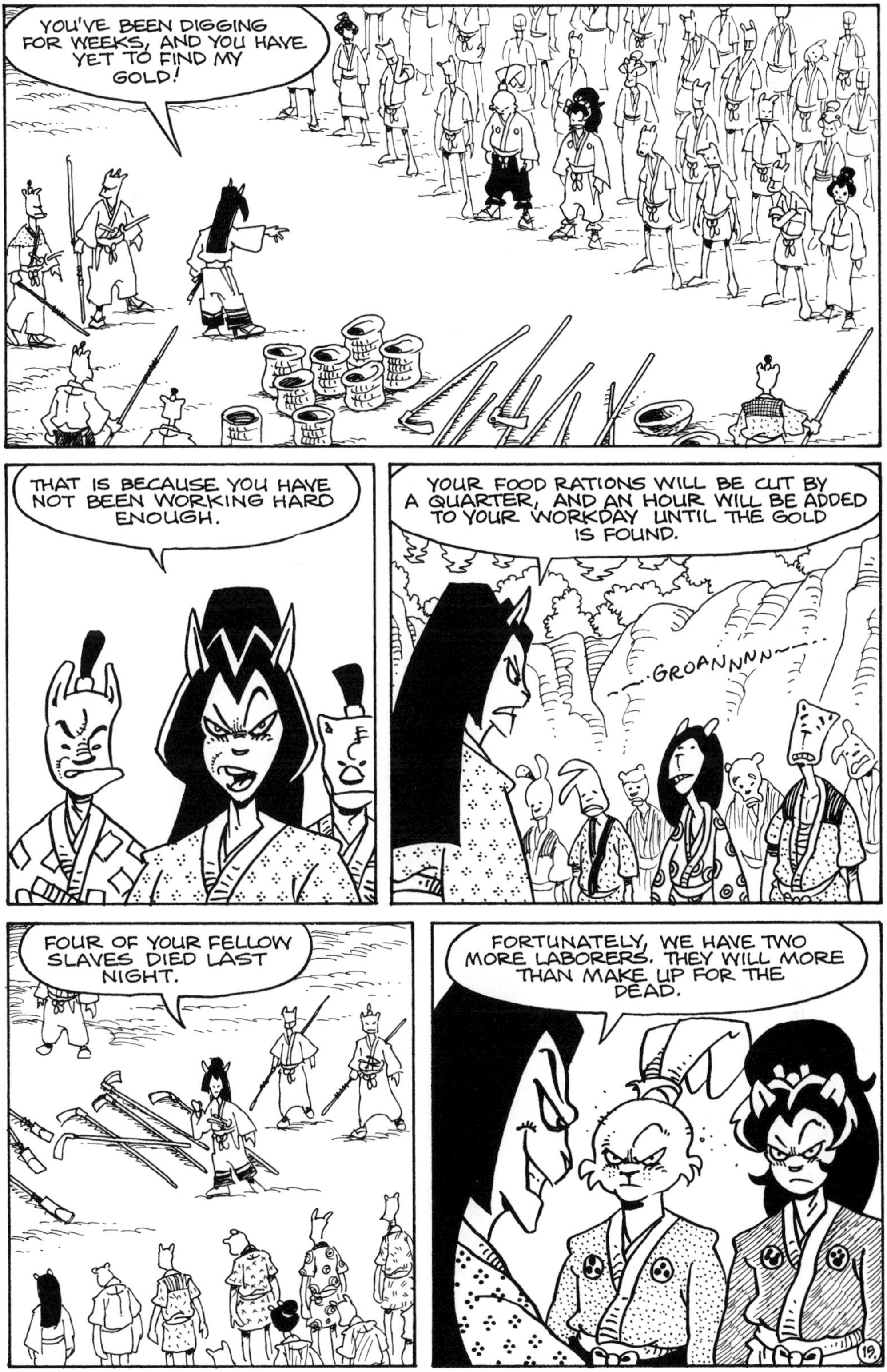

YOU'VE BEEN DIGGING FOR WEEKS, AND YOU HAVE YET TO FIND MY GOLD!
THAT IS BECAUSE YOU HAVE NOT BEEN WORKING HARD ENOUGH.
YOUR FOOD RATIONS WILL BE CUT BY A QUARTER, AND AN HOUR WILL BE ADDED TO YOUR WORKDAY UNTIL THE GOLD IS FOUND.
GROANNNN
FOUR OF YOUR FELLOW SLAVES DIED LAST NIGHT.
FORTUNATELY, WE HAVE TWO MORE LABORERS. THEY WILL MORE THAN MAKE UP FOR THE DEAD.
15.

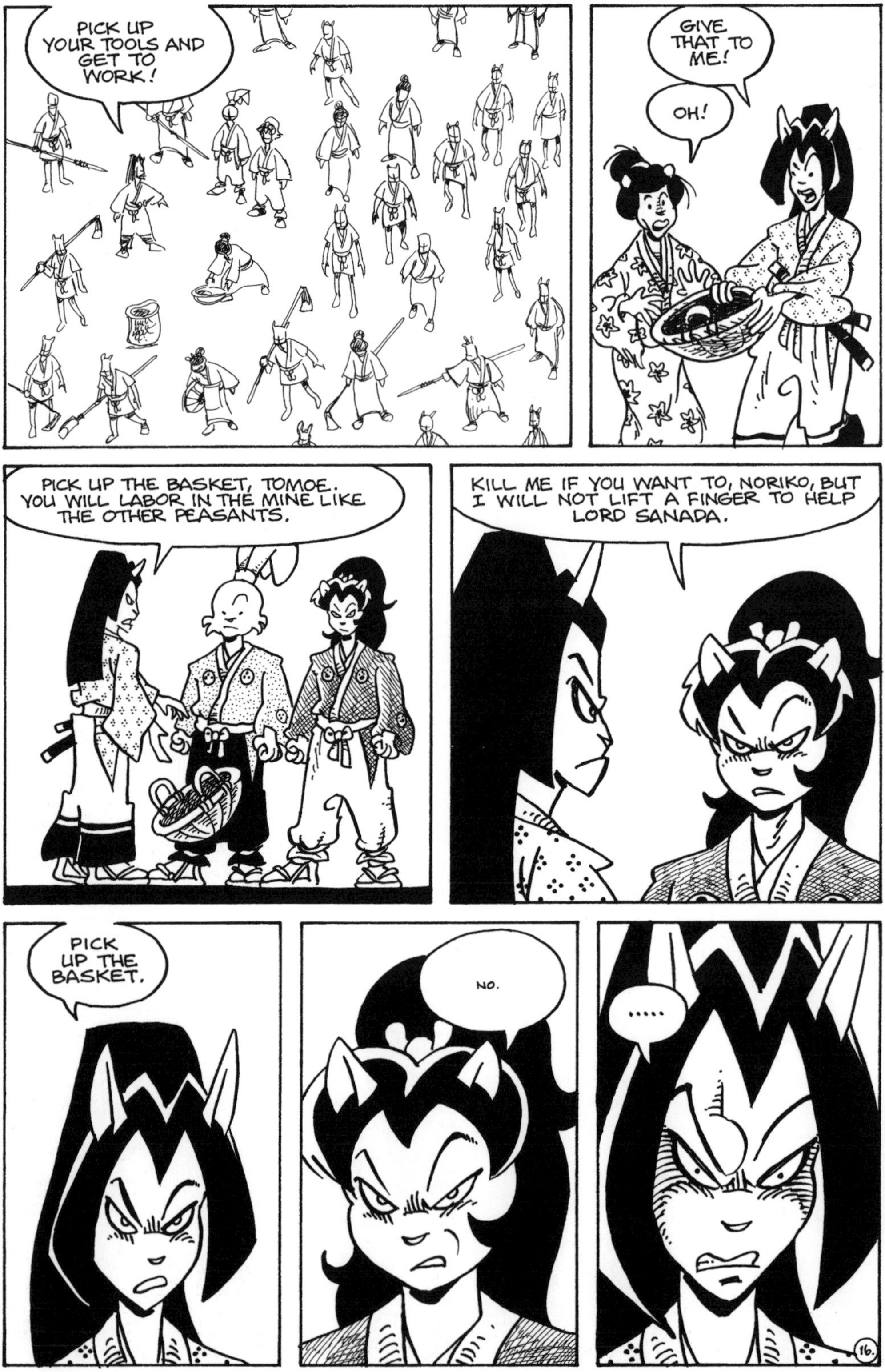
PICK UP YOUR TOOLS AND GET TO WORK!
GIVE THAT TO ME!
OH!
PICK UP THE BASKET, TOMOE. YOU WILL LABOR IN THE MINE LIKE THE OTHER PEASANTS.
KILL ME IF YOU WANT TO, NORIKO, BUT I WILL NOT LIFT A FINGER TO HELP LORD SANADA.
PICK UP THE BASKET.
NO.
.....
16.

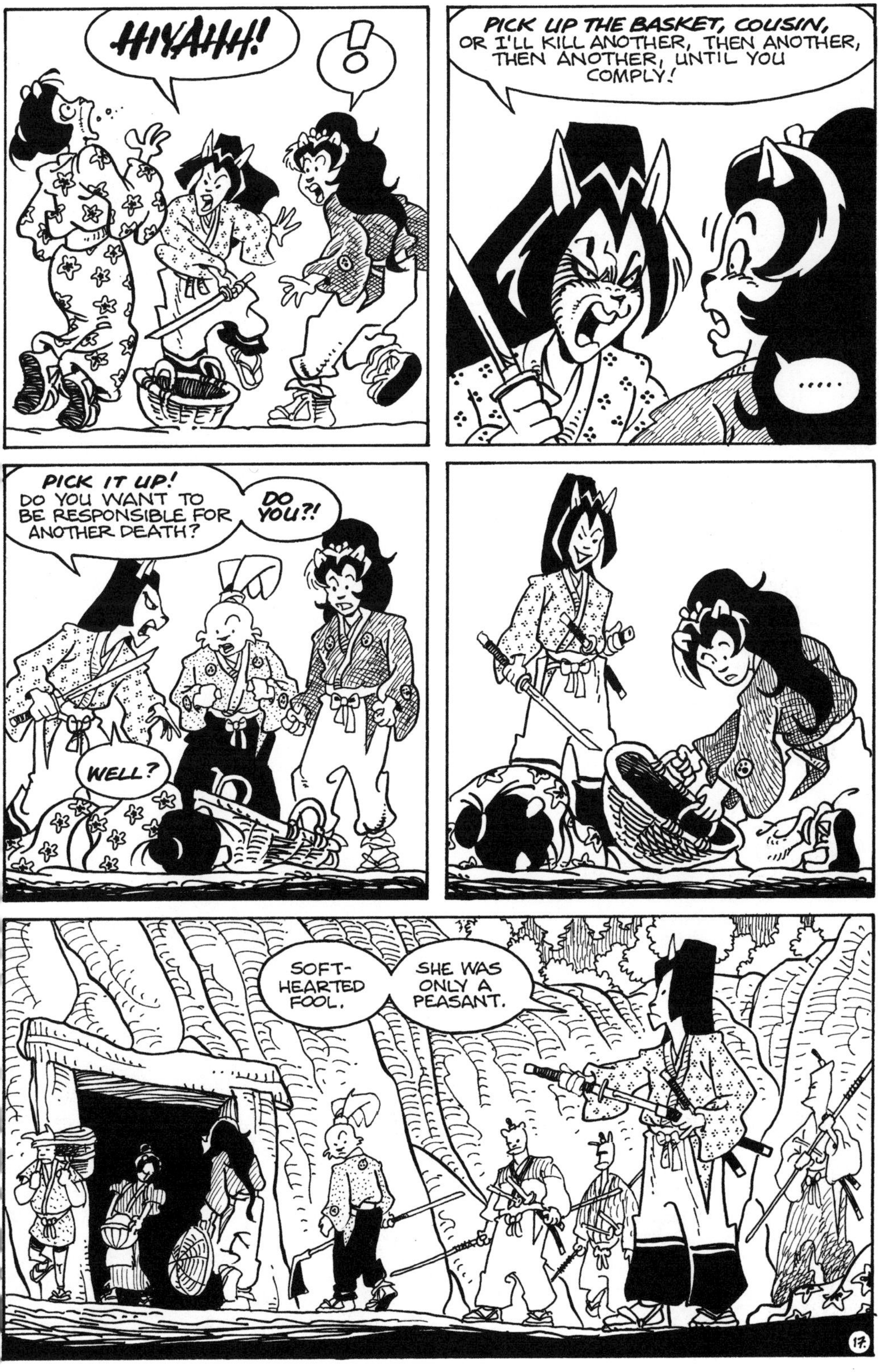
HIYAHH!
!
PICK UP THE BASKET, COUSIN, OR I'LL KILL ANOTHER, THEN ANOTHER, THEN ANOTHER, UNTIL YOU COMPLY!
.....
PICK IT UP! DO YOU WANT TO BE RESPONSIBLE FOR ANOTHER DEATH?
DO YOU?!
WELL?
SOFT-HEARTED FOOL.
SHE WAS ONLY A PEASANT.
17.

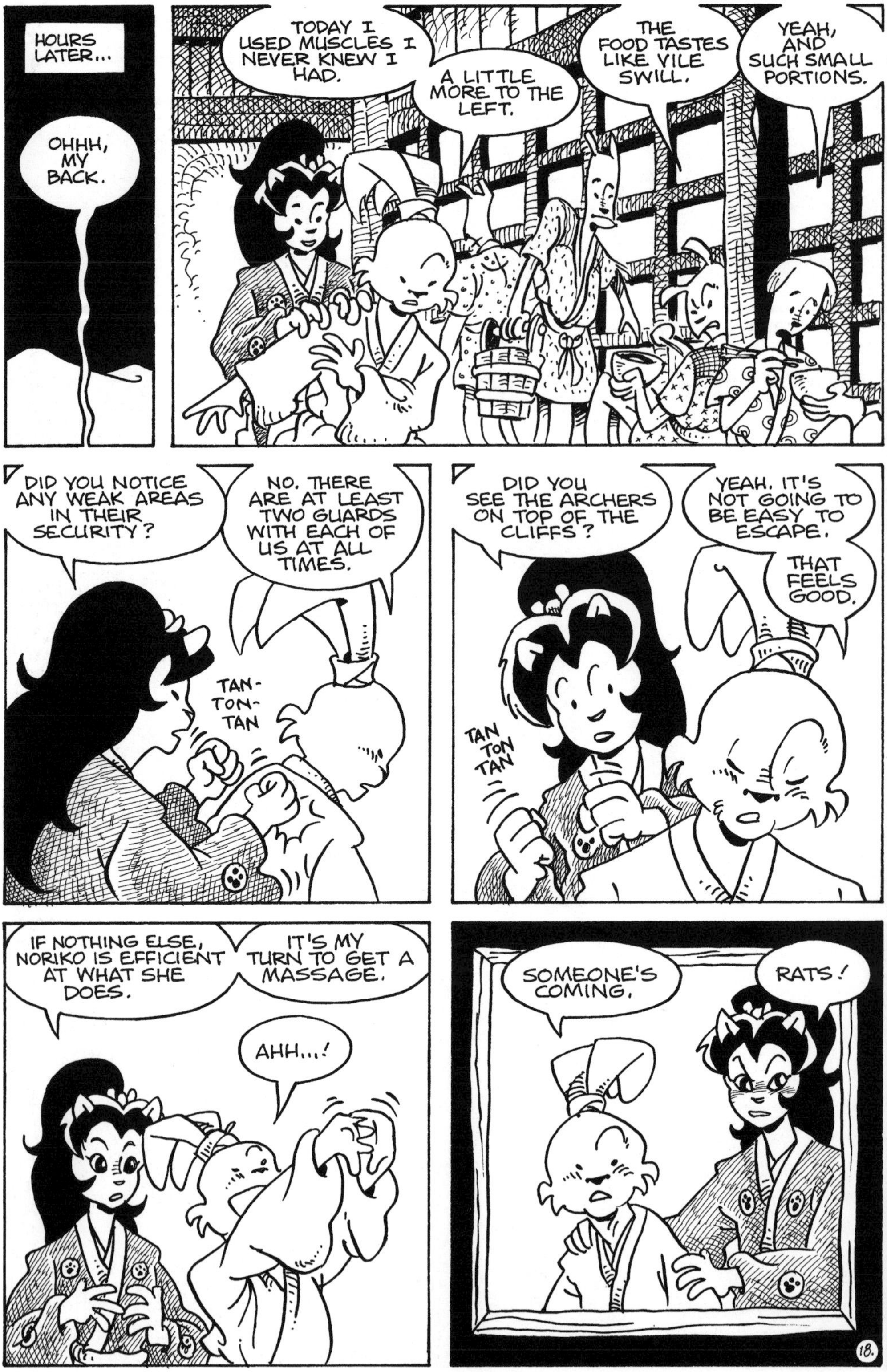
HOURS LATER...
OHHH, MY BACK.
TODAY I USED MUSCLES I NEVER KNEW I HAD.
A LITTLE MORE TO THE LEFT.
THE FOOD TASTES LIKE VILE SWILL.
YEAH, AND SUCH SMALL PORTIONS.
DID YOU NOTICE ANY WEAK AREAS IN THEIR SECURITY?
NO. THERE ARE AT LEAST TWO GUARDS WITH EACH OF US AT ALL TIMES.
TAN-TON-TAN
DID YOU SEE THE ARCHERS ON TOP OF THE CLIFFS?
YEAH. IT'S NOT GOING TO BE EASY TO ESCAPE.
THAT FEELS GOOD.
TAN TON TAN
IF NOTHING ELSE, NORIKO IS EFFICIENT AT WHAT SHE DOES.
IT'S MY TURN TO GET A MASSAGE.
AHH...!
SOMEONE'S COMING.
RATS!
18.

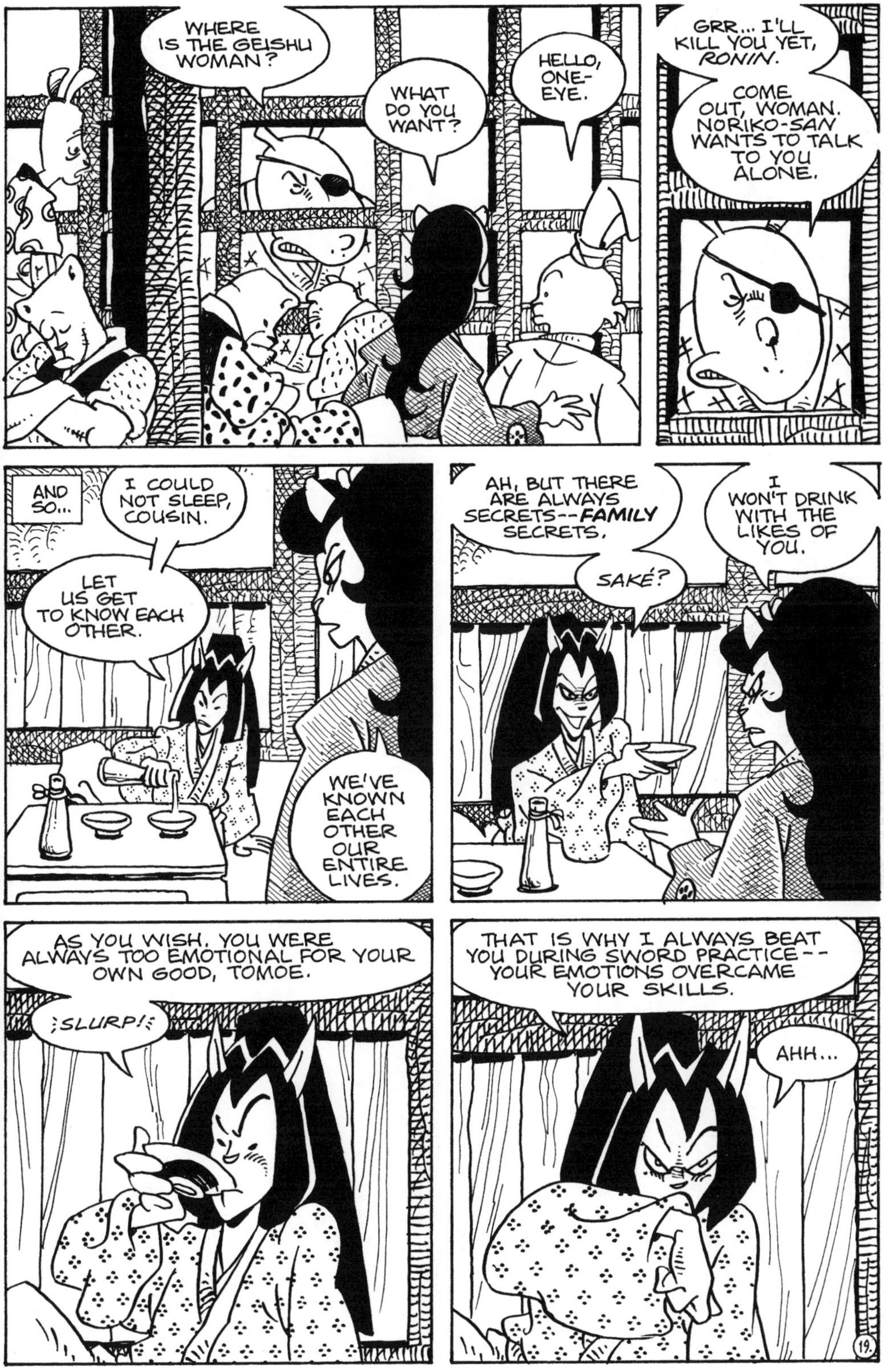
WHERE IS THE GEISHU WOMAN?
WHAT DO YOU WANT?
HELLO, ONE-EYE.
GRR... I'LL KILL YOU YET, *RONIN*.
COME OUT, WOMAN. NORIKO-*SAN* WANTS TO TALK TO YOU ALONE.
AND SO...
I COULD NOT SLEEP, COUSIN.
LET US GET TO KNOW EACH OTHER.
WE'VE KNOWN EACH OTHER OUR ENTIRE LIVES.
AH, BUT THERE ARE ALWAYS SECRETS--**FAMILY** SECRETS.
SAKÉ?
I WON'T DRINK WITH THE LIKES OF YOU.
AS YOU WISH. YOU WERE ALWAYS TOO EMOTIONAL FOR YOUR OWN GOOD, TOMOE.
SLURP!
THAT IS WHY I ALWAYS BEAT YOU DURING SWORD PRACTICE-- YOUR EMOTIONS OVERCAME YOUR SKILLS.
AHH...
19.

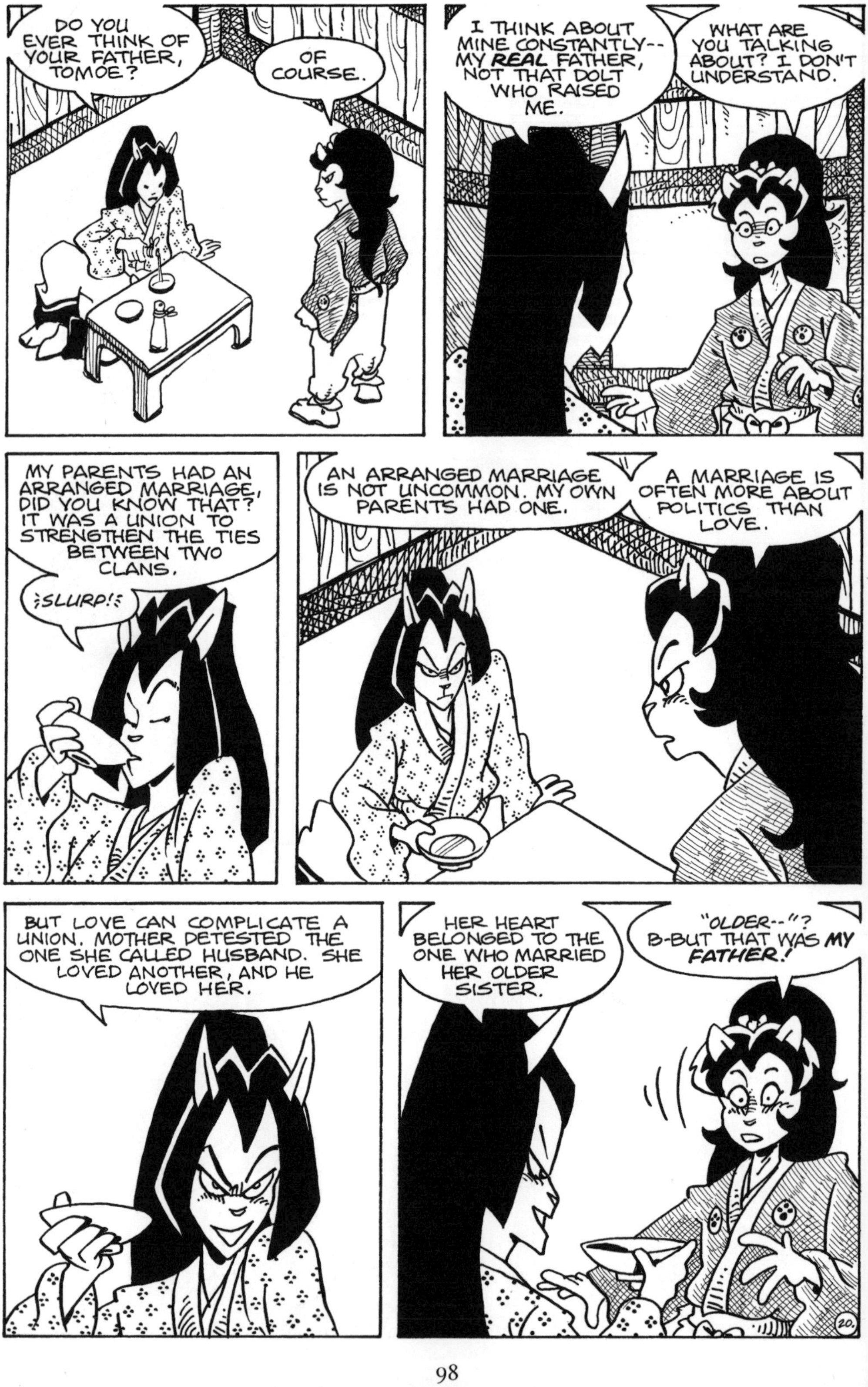
DO YOU EVER THINK OF YOUR FATHER, TOMOE?
OF COURSE.
I THINK ABOUT MINE CONSTANTLY-- MY REAL FATHER, NOT THAT DOLT WHO RAISED ME.
WHAT ARE YOU TALKING ABOUT? I DON'T UNDERSTAND.
MY PARENTS HAD AN ARRANGED MARRIAGE, DID YOU KNOW THAT? IT WAS A UNION TO STRENGTHEN THE TIES BETWEEN TWO CLANS.
SLURP!
AN ARRANGED MARRIAGE IS NOT UNCOMMON. MY OWN PARENTS HAD ONE.
A MARRIAGE IS OFTEN MORE ABOUT POLITICS THAN LOVE.
BUT LOVE CAN COMPLICATE A UNION. MOTHER DETESTED THE ONE SHE CALLED HUSBAND. SHE LOVED ANOTHER, AND HE LOVED HER.
HER HEART BELONGED TO THE ONE WHO MARRIED HER OLDER SISTER.
"OLDER--"? B-BUT THAT WAS MY FATHER!
20.

DID YOU EVER WONDER WHY, AFTER MOTHER DIED, I SPENT SO MUCH TIME WITH YOU AND YOUR FAMILY IN THE GEISHU PROVINCE?

MY FATHER COULD NOT BEAR THE SIGHT OF ME, SO HE SENT ME TO MY *REAL* FATHER.

"*REAL* F-FATHER"? BUT...BUT...THAT WOULD MEAN THAT YOU-- WE'RE....WE'RE...

SISTERS, TOMOE, WE ARE SISTERS, NOT COUSINS.

BUT YOUR FATHER NEVER ACKNOWLEDGED ME, AND YOUR MOTHER LOATHED ME.

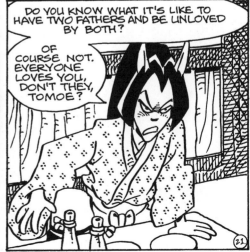

DO YOU KNOW WHAT IT'S LIKE TO HAVE TWO FATHERS AND BE UNLOVED BY BOTH?

OF COURSE NOT. EVERYONE LOVES YOU, DON'T THEY, TOMOE?

21.

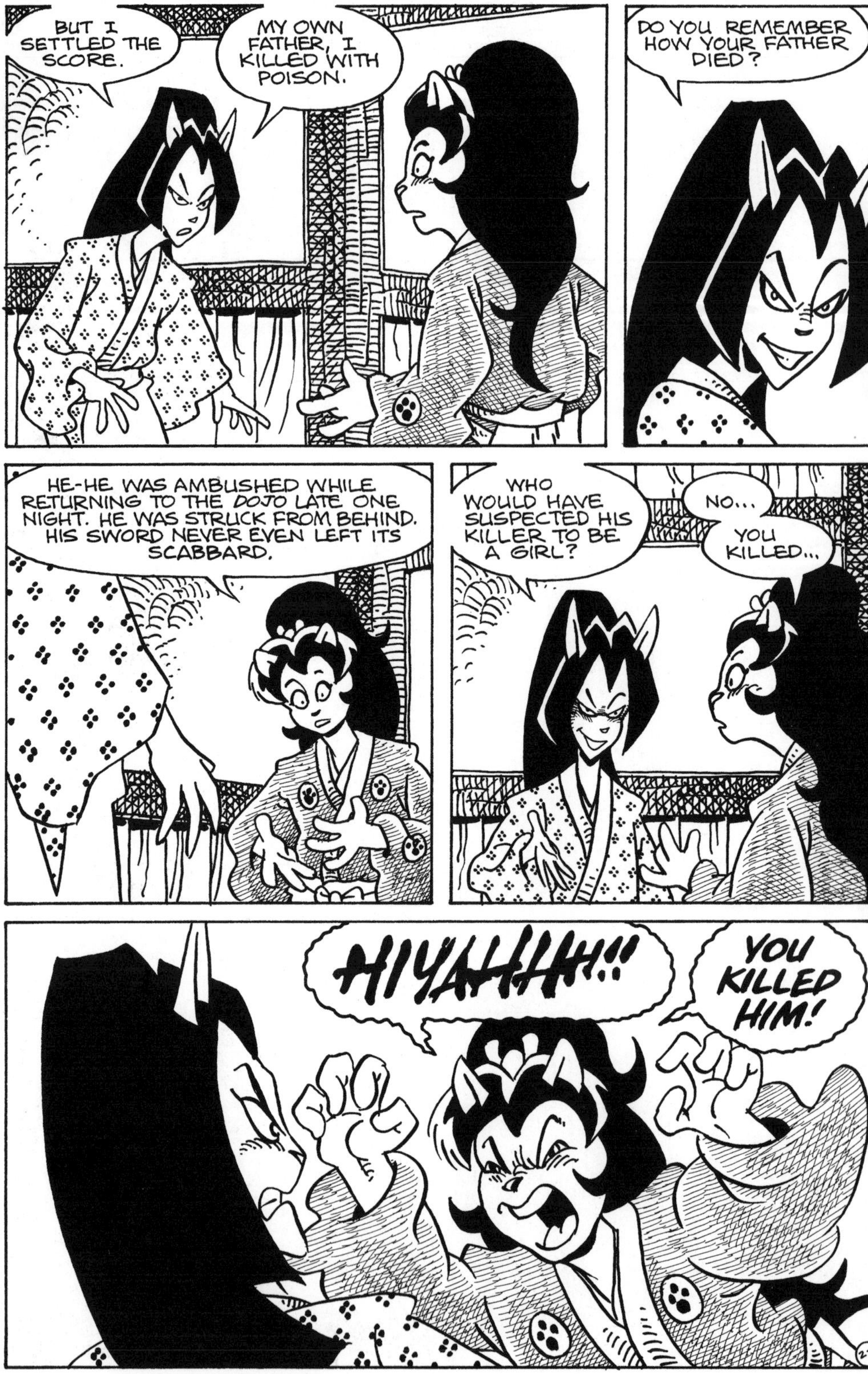
BUT I SETTLED THE SCORE.
MY OWN FATHER, I KILLED WITH POISON.
DO YOU REMEMBER HOW YOUR FATHER DIED?
HE-HE WAS AMBUSHED WHILE RETURNING TO THE DOJO LATE ONE NIGHT. HE WAS STRUCK FROM BEHIND. HIS SWORD NEVER EVEN LEFT ITS SCABBARD.
WHO WOULD HAVE SUSPECTED HIS KILLER TO BE A GIRL?
NO...
YOU KILLED...
HIYAHHH!!
YOU KILLED HIM!
22.

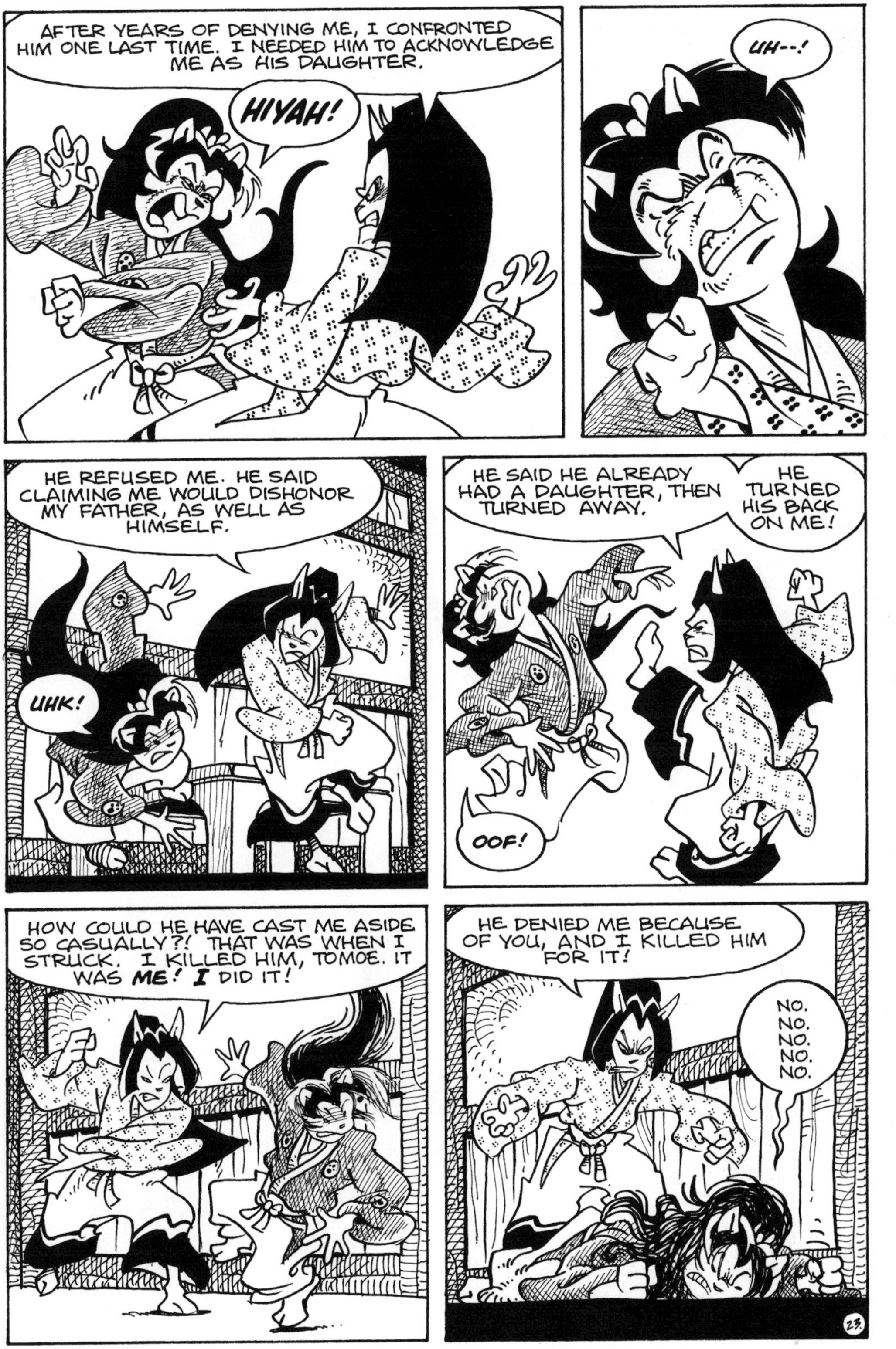
AFTER YEARS OF DENYING ME, I CONFRONTED HIM ONE LAST TIME. I NEEDED HIM TO ACKNOWLEDGE ME AS HIS DAUGHTER.
HIYAH!
UH--!
HE REFUSED ME. HE SAID CLAIMING ME WOULD DISHONOR MY FATHER, AS WELL AS HIMSELF.
UHK!
HE SAID HE ALREADY HAD A DAUGHTER, THEN TURNED AWAY.
HE TURNED HIS BACK ON ME!
OOF!
HOW COULD HE HAVE CAST ME ASIDE SO CASUALLY?! THAT WAS WHEN I STRUCK. I KILLED HIM, TOMOE. IT WAS ME! I DID IT!
HE DENIED ME BECAUSE OF YOU, AND I KILLED HIM FOR IT!
NO. NO. NO. NO. NO.
23.

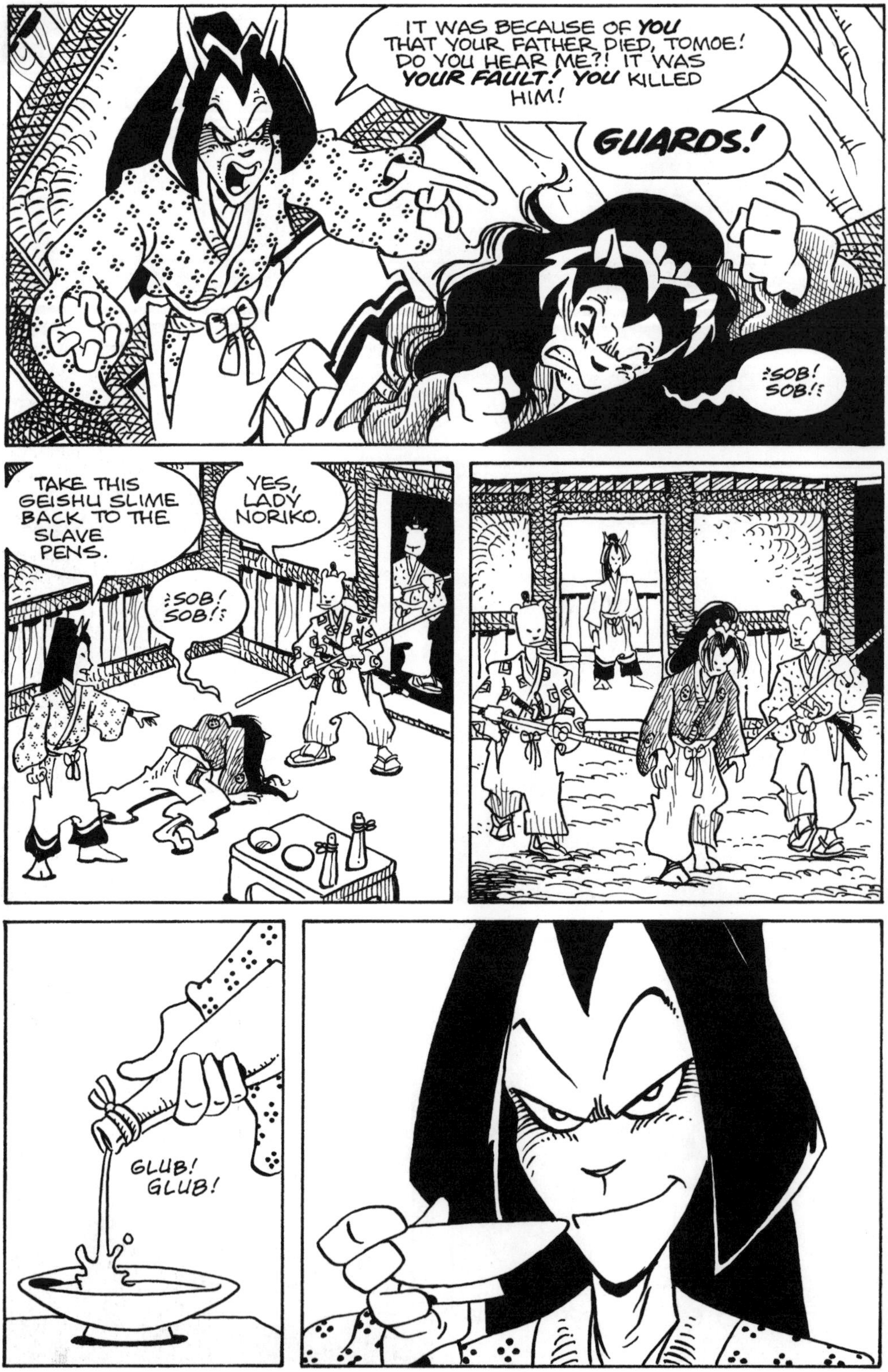
IT WAS BECAUSE OF YOU THAT YOUR FATHER DIED, TOMOE! DO YOU HEAR ME?! IT WAS YOUR FAULT! YOU KILLED HIM!
GUARDS!
SOB! SOB!
TAKE THIS GEISHU SLIME BACK TO THE SLAVE PENS.
YES, LADY NORIKO.
SOB! SOB!
GLUB! GLUB!

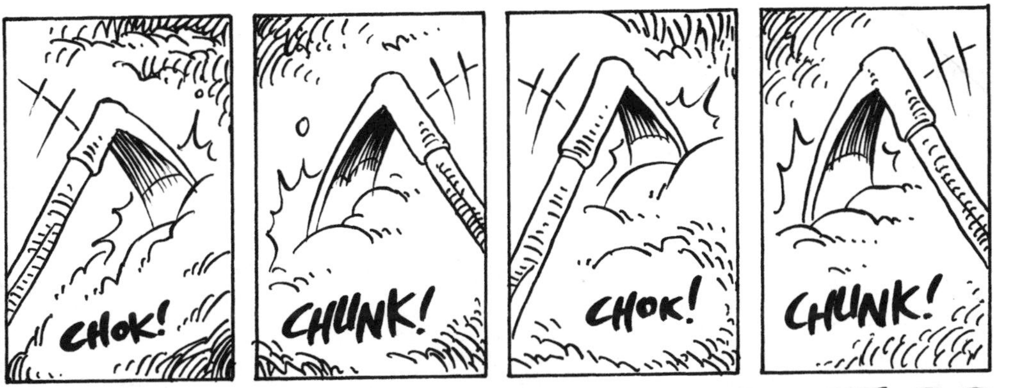
CHOK!
CHUNK!
CHOK!
CHUNK!

THE TREASURE of the MOTHER of MOUNTAINS

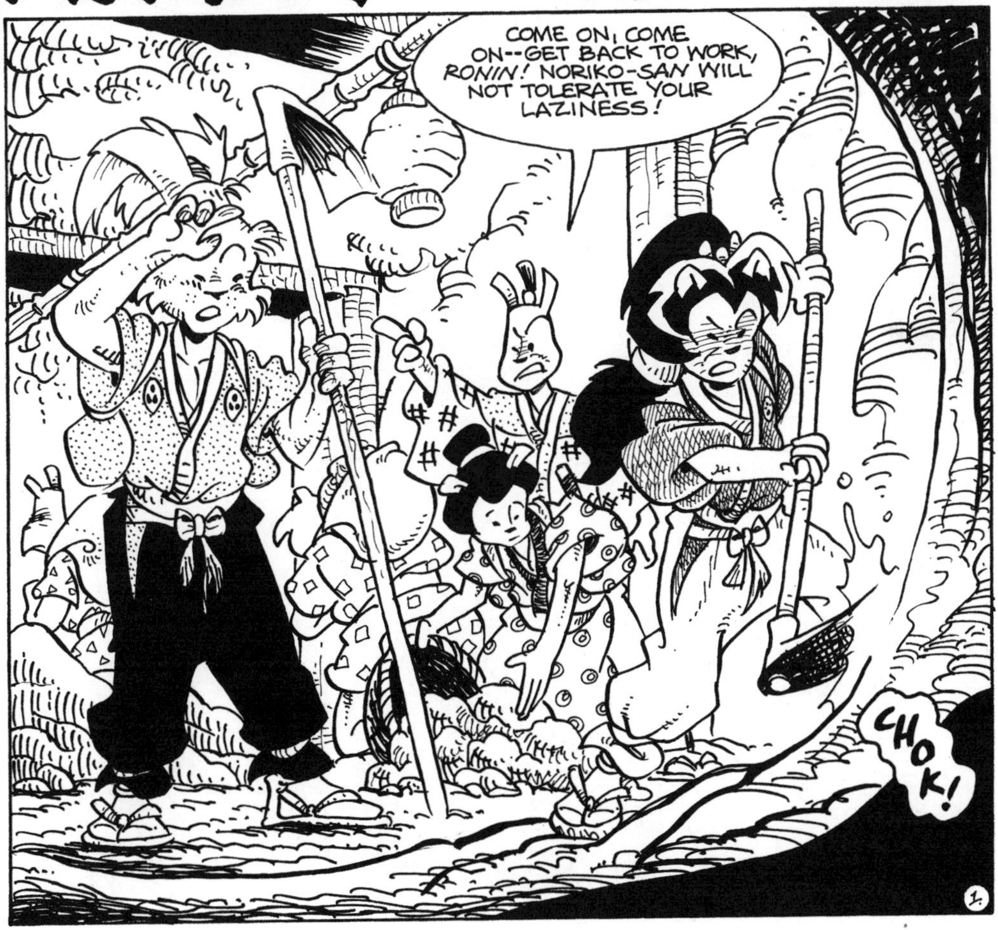
COME ON, COME ON--GET BACK TO WORK, *RONIN!* NORIKO-SAN WILL NOT TOLERATE YOUR LAZINESS!
CHOK!

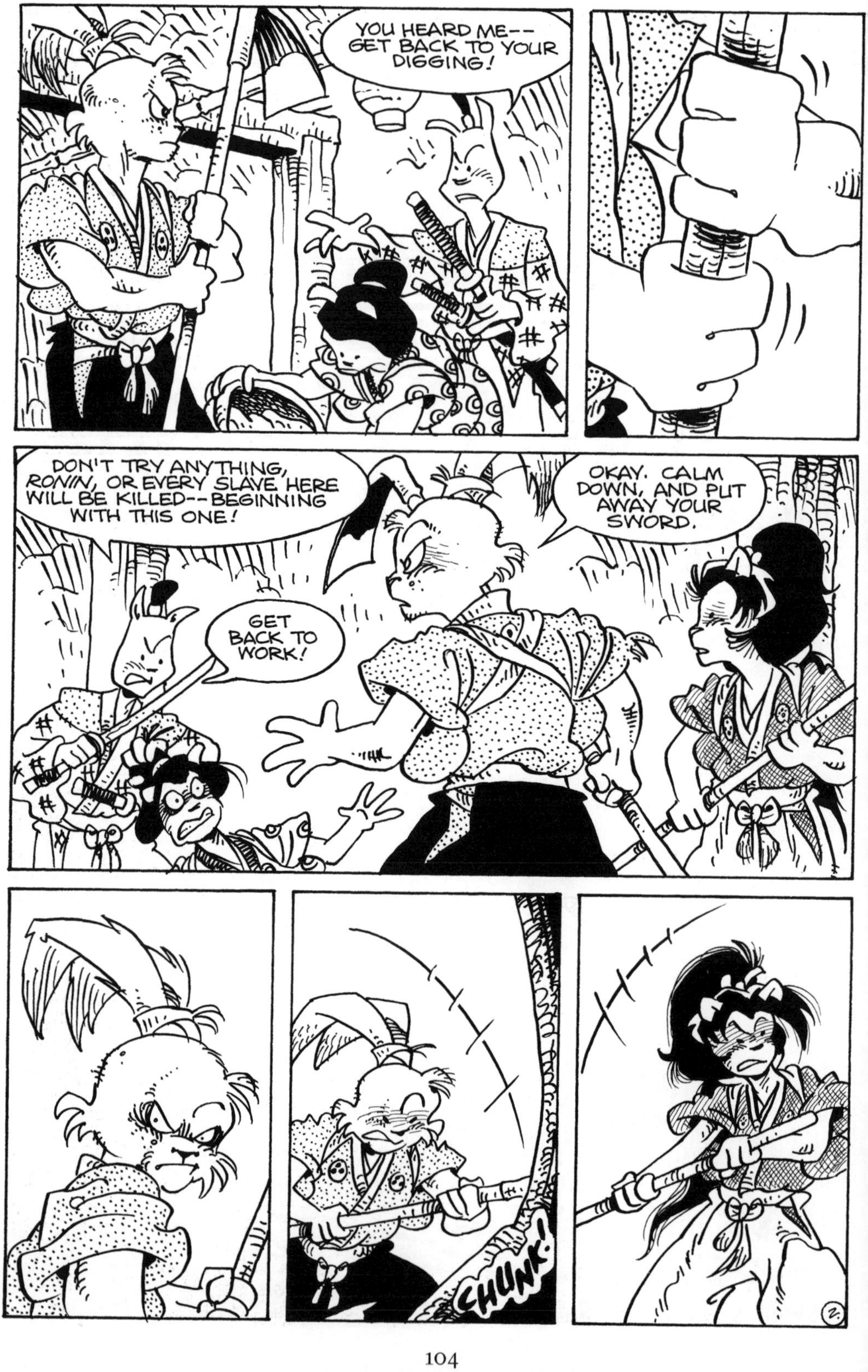
YOU HEARD ME-- GET BACK TO YOUR DIGGING!
DON'T TRY ANYTHING, *RONIN*, OR EVERY SLAVE HERE WILL BE KILLED--BEGINNING WITH THIS ONE!
OKAY. CALM DOWN, AND PUT AWAY YOUR SWORD.
GET BACK TO WORK!
CHUNK!

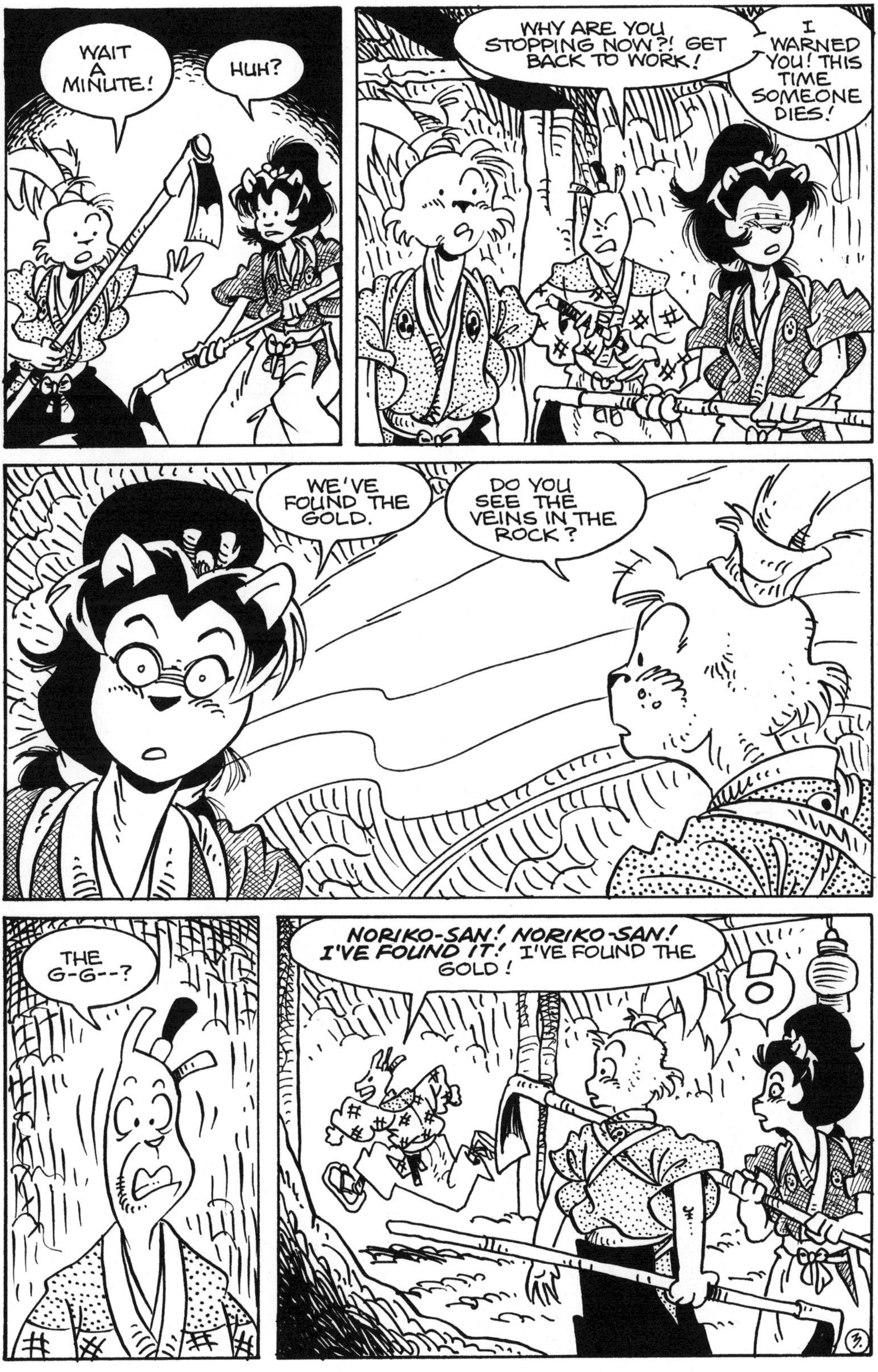

WAIT A MINUTE!
HUH?
WHY ARE YOU STOPPING NOW?! GET BACK TO WORK!
I WARNED YOU! THIS TIME SOMEONE DIES!
WE'VE FOUND THE GOLD.
DO YOU SEE THE VEINS IN THE ROCK?
THE G-G--?
NORIKO-SAN! NORIKO-SAN! I'VE FOUND IT! I'VE FOUND THE GOLD!
!
3.

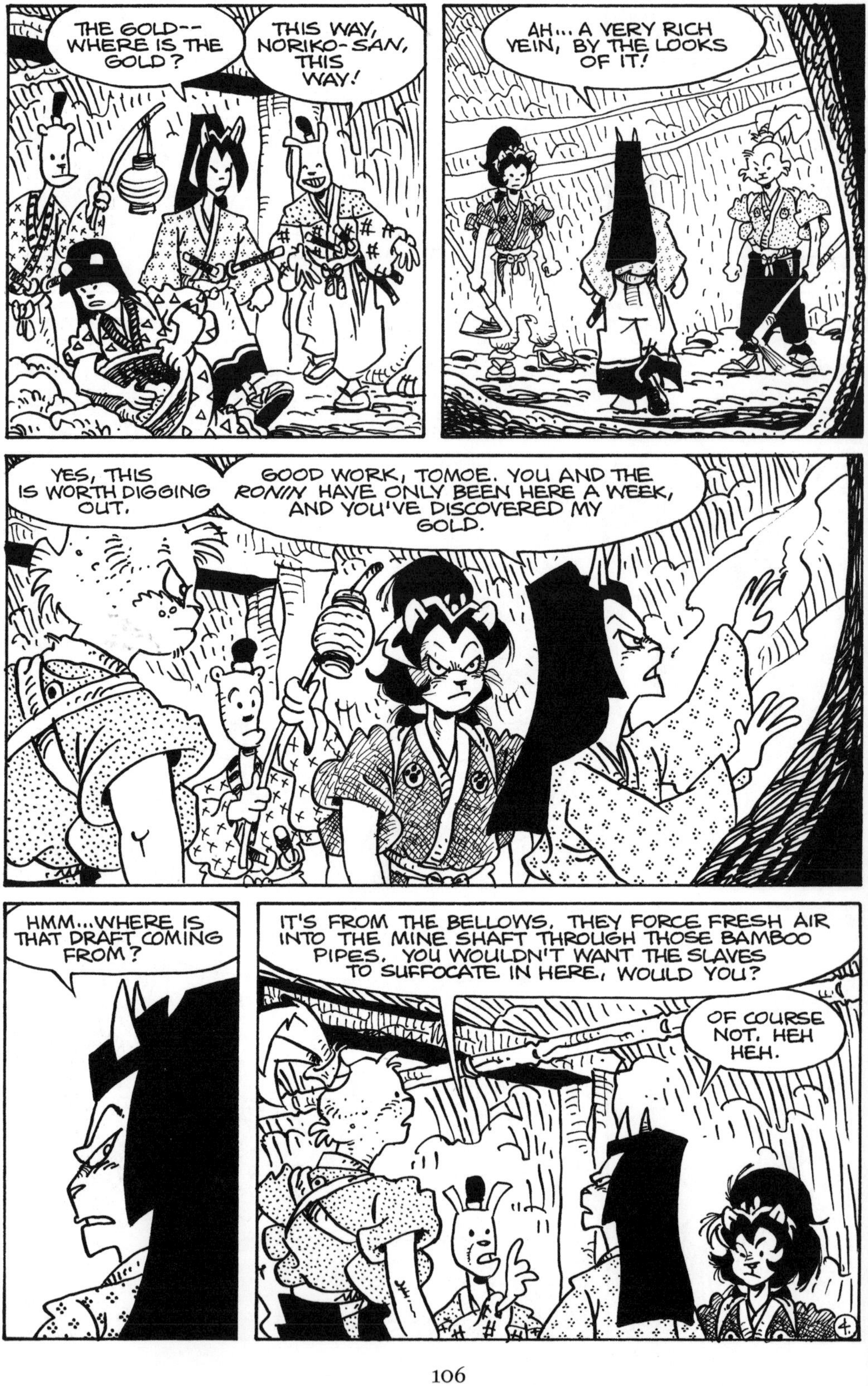
THE GOLD-- WHERE IS THE GOLD?
THIS WAY, NORIKO-SAN, THIS WAY!
AH... A VERY RICH VEIN, BY THE LOOKS OF IT!
YES, THIS IS WORTH DIGGING OUT.
GOOD WORK, TOMOE. YOU AND THE *RONIN* HAVE ONLY BEEN HERE A WEEK, AND YOU'VE DISCOVERED MY GOLD.
HMM...WHERE IS THAT DRAFT COMING FROM?
IT'S FROM THE BELLOWS. THEY FORCE FRESH AIR INTO THE MINE SHAFT THROUGH THOSE BAMBOO PIPES. YOU WOULDN'T WANT THE SLAVES TO SUFFOCATE IN HERE, WOULD YOU?
OF COURSE NOT. HEH HEH.
4.

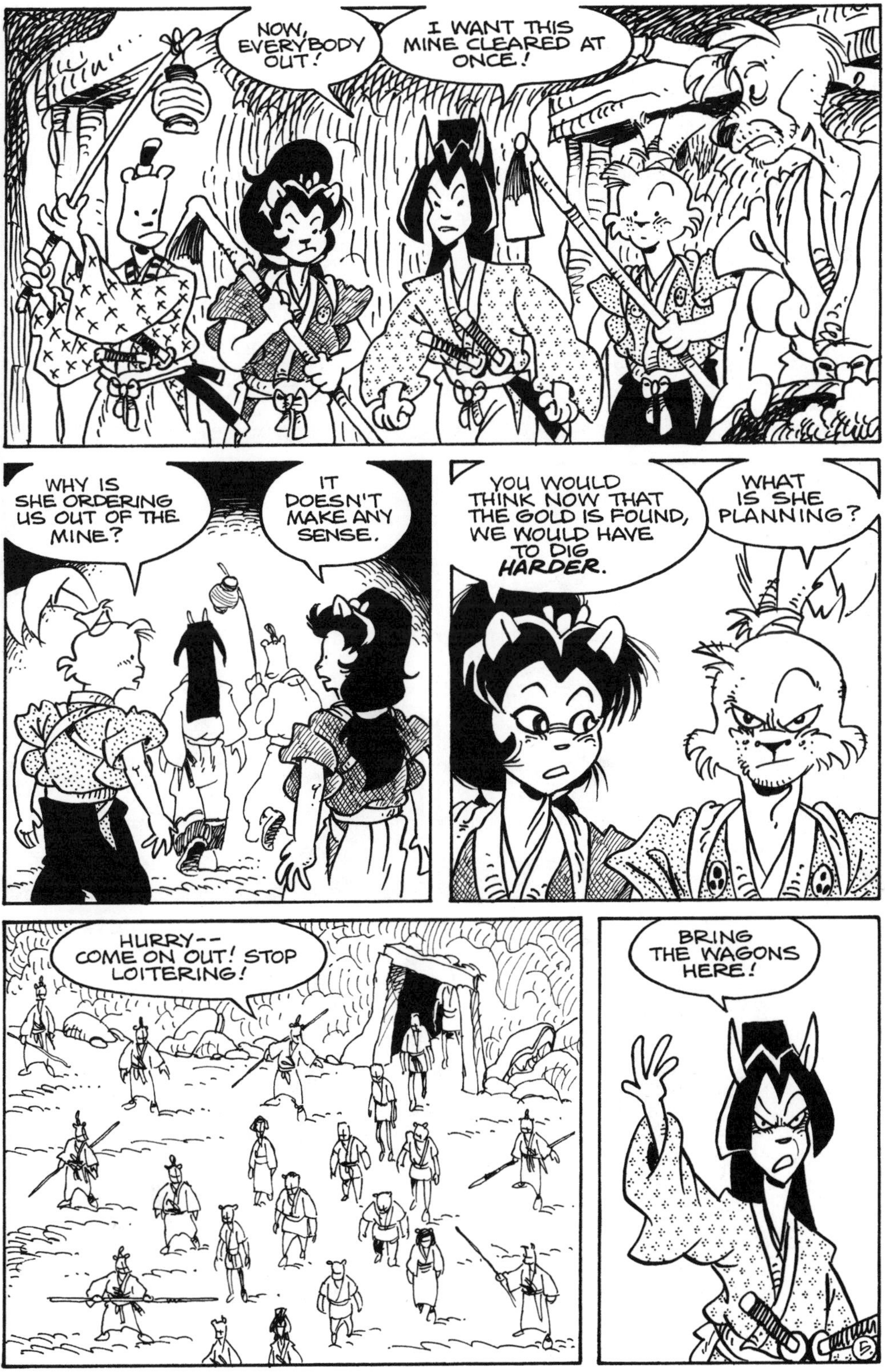
NOW, EVERYBODY OUT!
I WANT THIS MINE CLEARED AT ONCE!
WHY IS SHE ORDERING US OUT OF THE MINE?
IT DOESN'T MAKE ANY SENSE.
YOU WOULD THINK NOW THAT THE GOLD IS FOUND, WE WOULD HAVE TO DIG HARDER.
WHAT IS SHE PLANNING?
HURRY-- COME ON OUT! STOP LOITERING!
BRING THE WAGONS HERE!

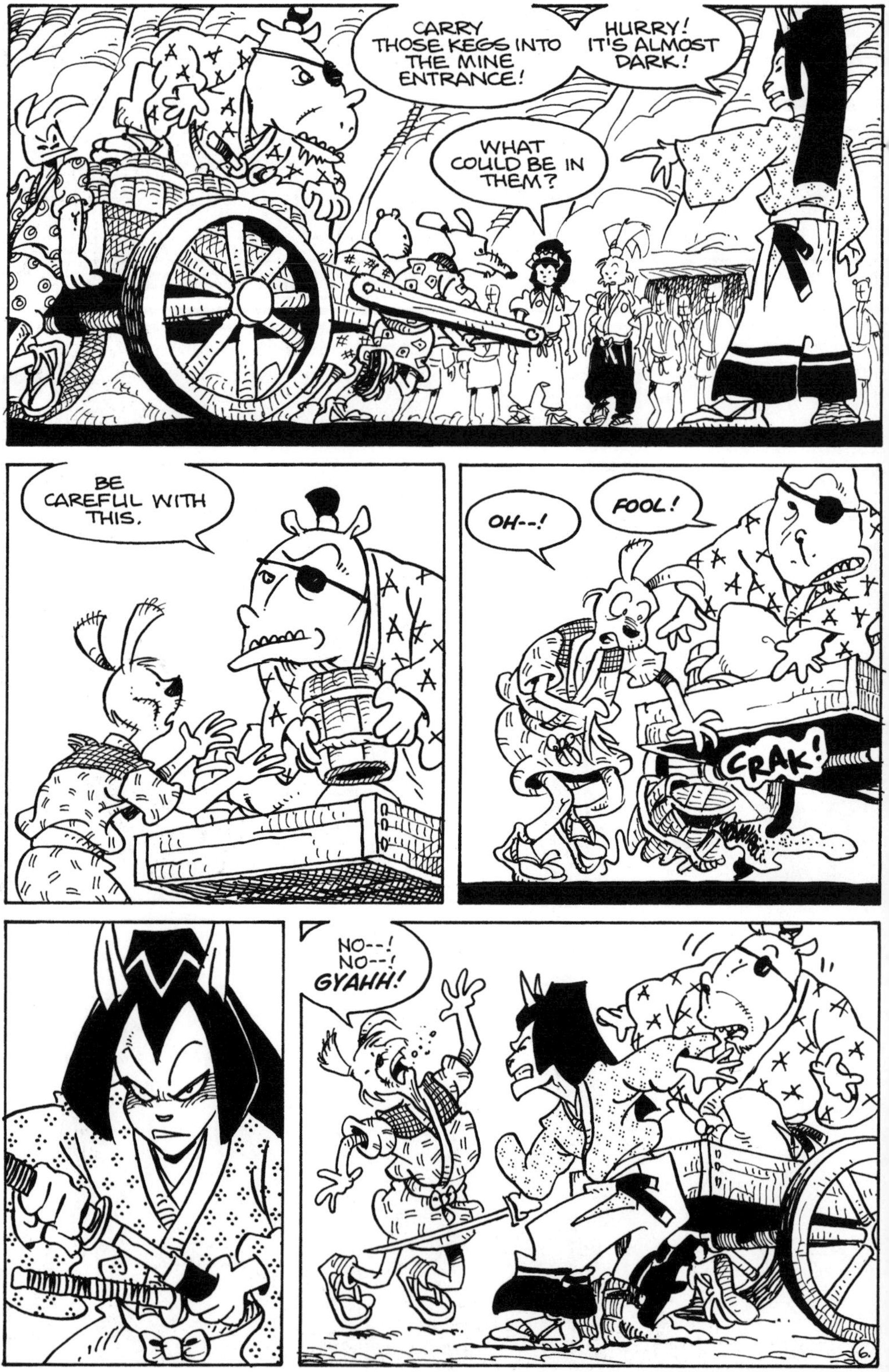
CARRY THOSE KEGS INTO THE MINE ENTRANCE!
HURRY! IT'S ALMOST DARK!
WHAT COULD BE IN THEM?
BE CAREFUL WITH THIS.
OH--!
FOOL!
CRAK!
NO--! NO--! GYAHH!
6.

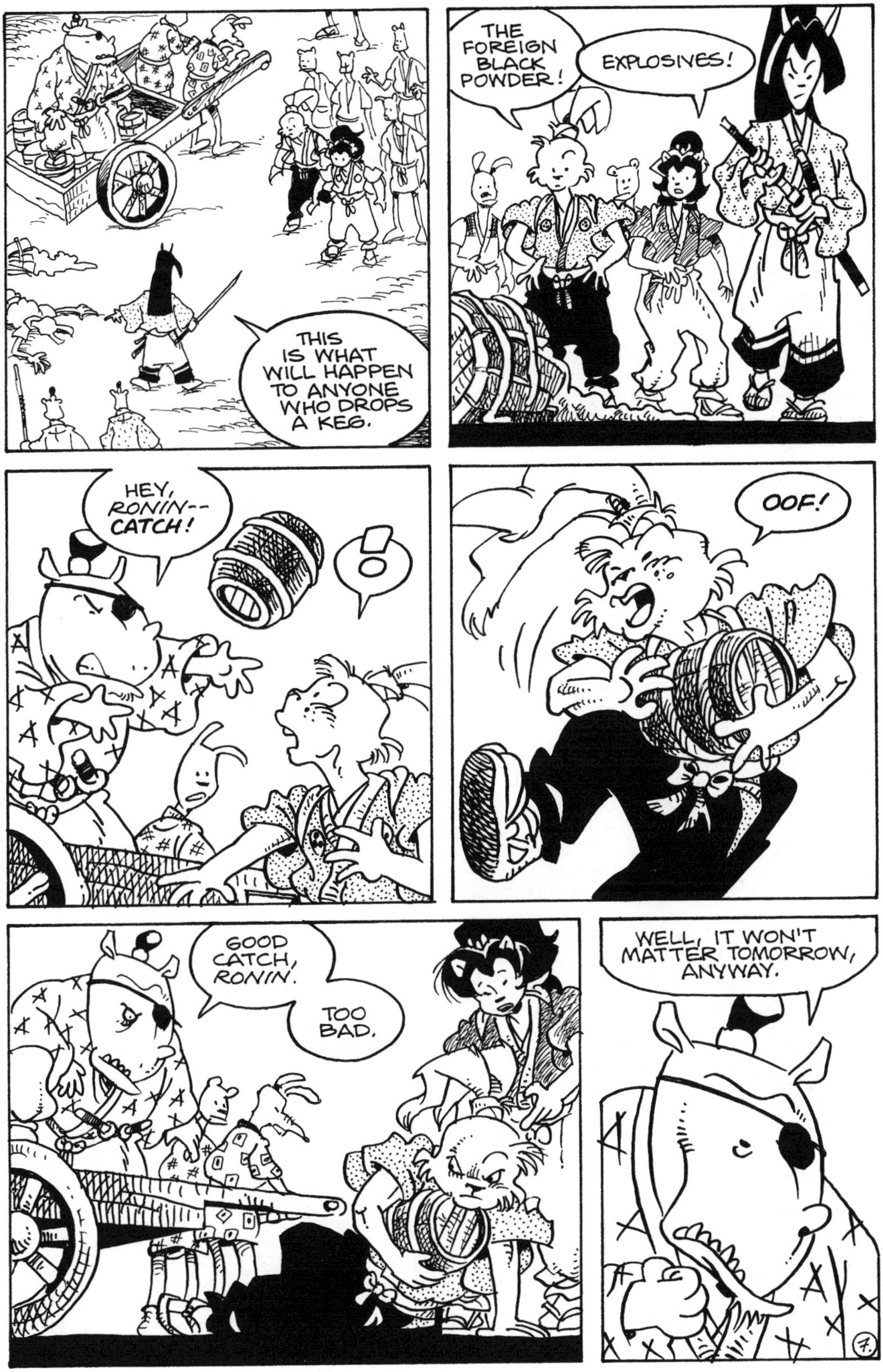

THIS IS WHAT WILL HAPPEN TO ANYONE WHO DROPS A KEG.
THE FOREIGN BLACK POWDER!
EXPLOSIVES!
HEY, RONIN-- CATCH!
!
OOF!
GOOD CATCH, RONIN.
TOO BAD.
WELL, IT WON'T MATTER TOMORROW, ANYWAY.
7.

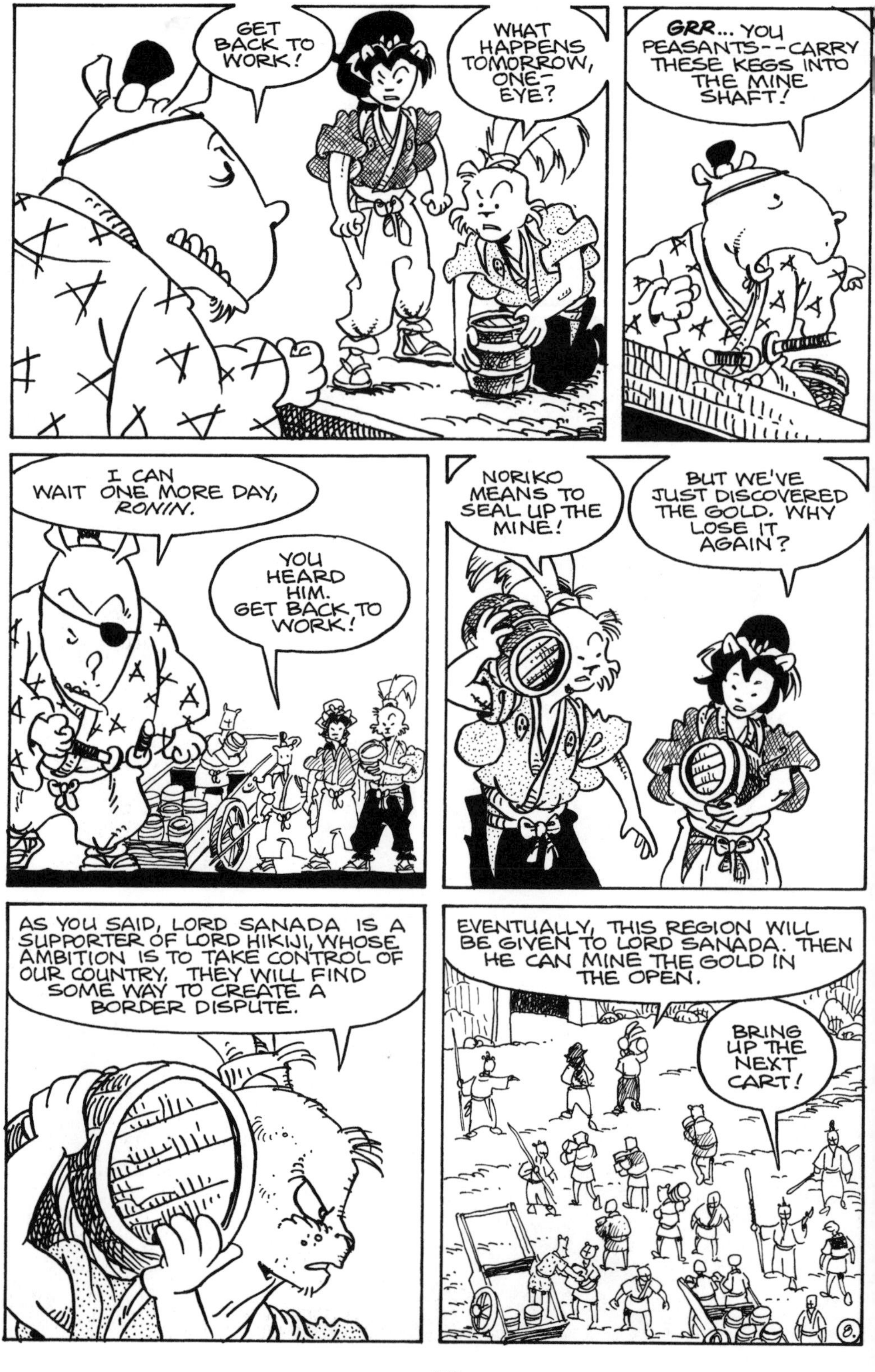

GET BACK TO WORK!
WHAT HAPPENS TOMORROW, ONE-EYE?
GRR... YOU PEASANTS--CARRY THESE KEGS INTO THE MINE SHAFT!
I CAN WAIT ONE MORE DAY, RONIN.
YOU HEARD HIM. GET BACK TO WORK!
NORIKO MEANS TO SEAL UP THE MINE!
BUT WE'VE JUST DISCOVERED THE GOLD. WHY LOSE IT AGAIN?
AS YOU SAID, LORD SANADA IS A SUPPORTER OF LORD HIKIJI, WHOSE AMBITION IS TO TAKE CONTROL OF OUR COUNTRY. THEY WILL FIND SOME WAY TO CREATE A BORDER DISPUTE.
EVENTUALLY, THIS REGION WILL BE GIVEN TO LORD SANADA. THEN HE CAN MINE THE GOLD IN THE OPEN.
BRING UP THE NEXT CART!
8.

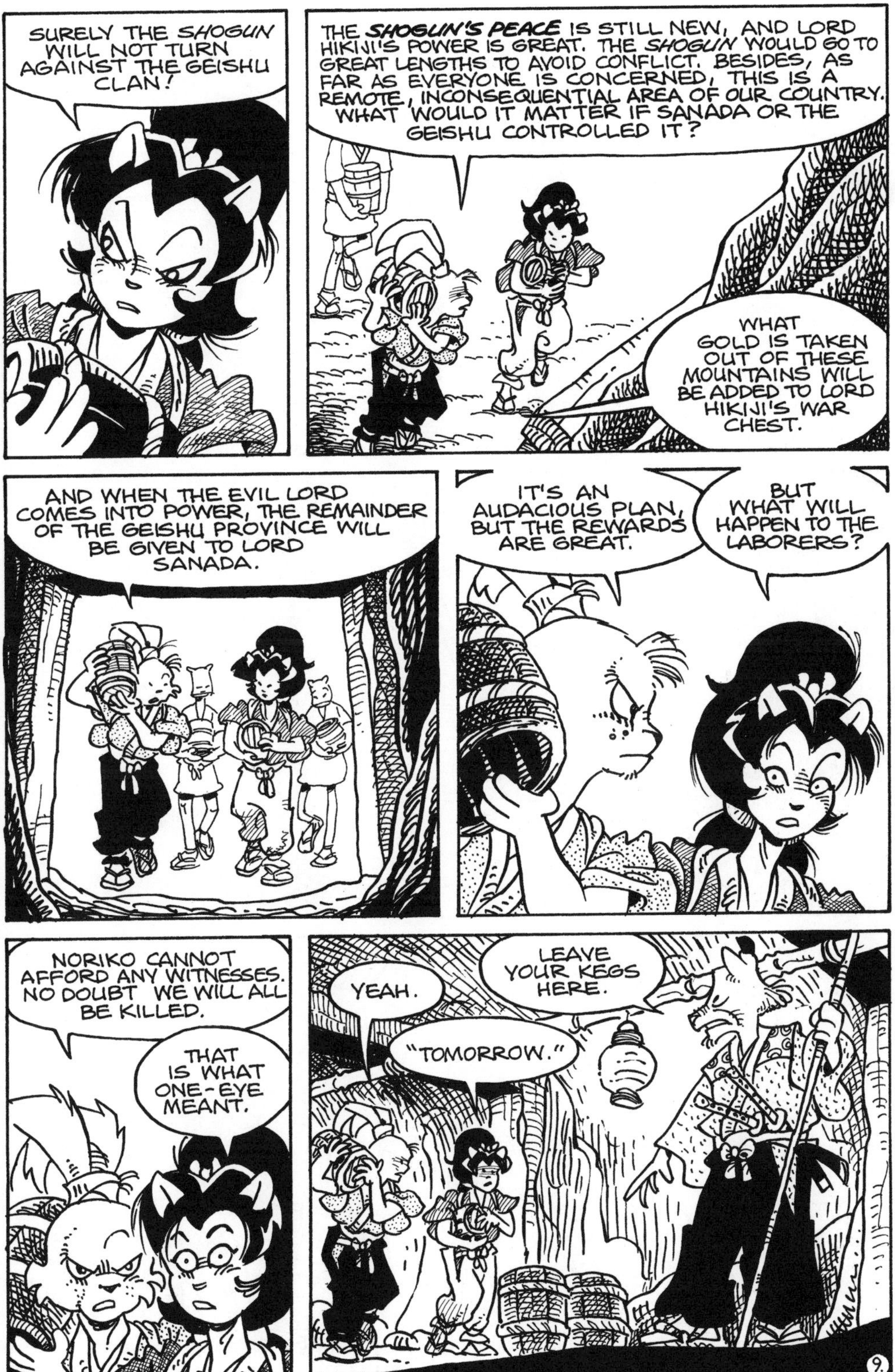
SURELY THE SHOGUN WILL NOT TURN AGAINST THE GEISHU CLAN!
THE SHOGUN'S PEACE IS STILL NEW, AND LORD HIKIJI'S POWER IS GREAT. THE SHOGUN WOULD GO TO GREAT LENGTHS TO AVOID CONFLICT. BESIDES, AS FAR AS EVERYONE IS CONCERNED, THIS IS A REMOTE, INCONSEQUENTIAL AREA OF OUR COUNTRY. WHAT WOULD IT MATTER IF SANADA OR THE GEISHU CONTROLLED IT?
WHAT GOLD IS TAKEN OUT OF THESE MOUNTAINS WILL BE ADDED TO LORD HIKIJI'S WAR CHEST.
AND WHEN THE EVIL LORD COMES INTO POWER, THE REMAINDER OF THE GEISHU PROVINCE WILL BE GIVEN TO LORD SANADA.
IT'S AN AUDACIOUS PLAN, BUT THE REWARDS ARE GREAT.
BUT WHAT WILL HAPPEN TO THE LABORERS?
NORIKO CANNOT AFFORD ANY WITNESSES. NO DOUBT WE WILL ALL BE KILLED.
THAT IS WHAT ONE-EYE MEANT.
LEAVE YOUR KEGS HERE.
YEAH.
"TOMORROW."
9.

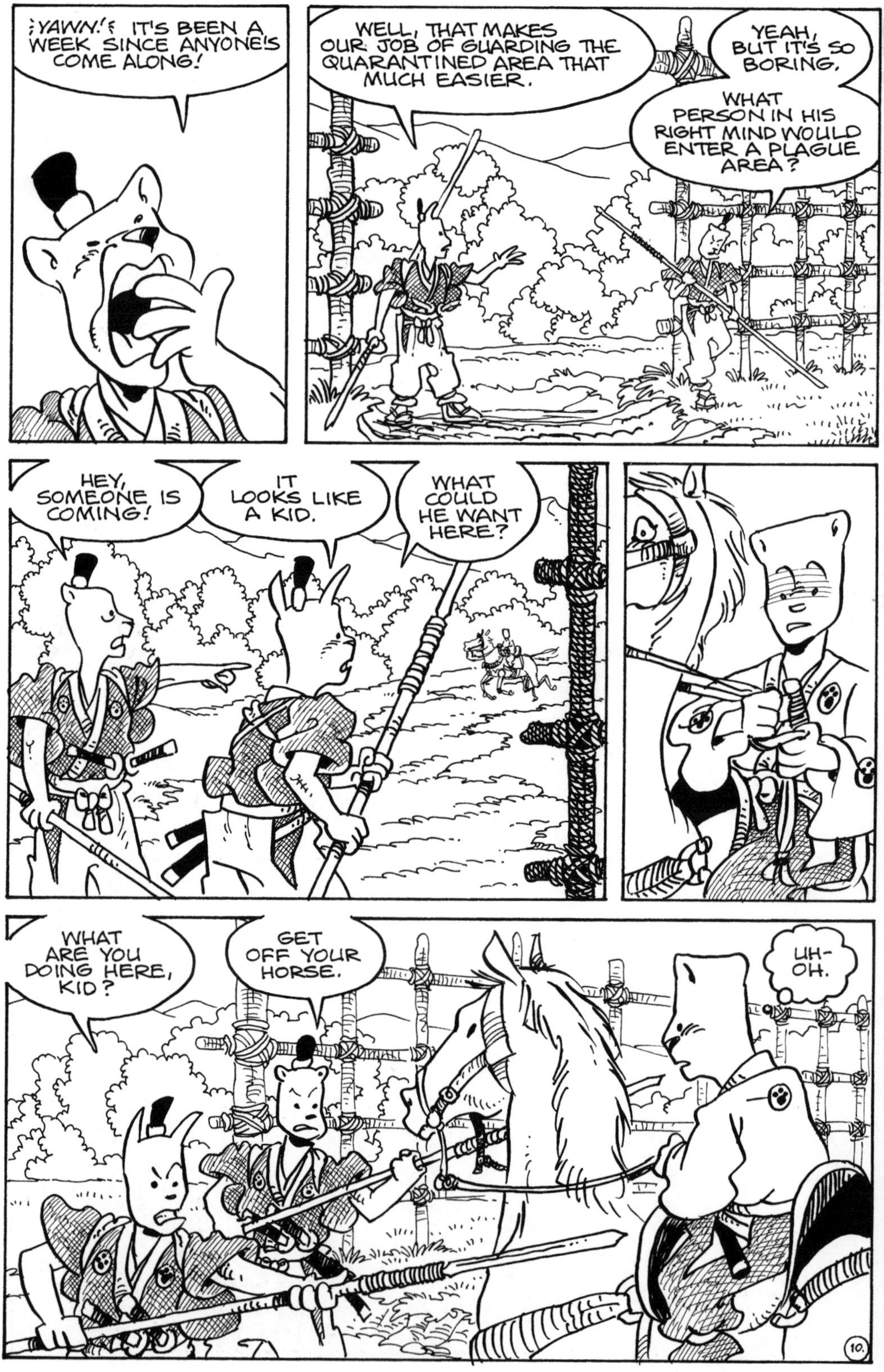
;YAWN!; IT'S BEEN A WEEK SINCE ANYONE'S COME ALONG!
WELL, THAT MAKES OUR JOB OF GUARDING THE QUARANTINED AREA THAT MUCH EASIER.
YEAH, BUT IT'S SO BORING.
WHAT PERSON IN HIS RIGHT MIND WOULD ENTER A PLAGUE AREA?
HEY, SOMEONE IS COMING!
IT LOOKS LIKE A KID.
WHAT COULD HE WANT HERE?
WHAT ARE YOU DOING HERE, KID?
GET OFF YOUR HORSE.
UH-OH.
10.

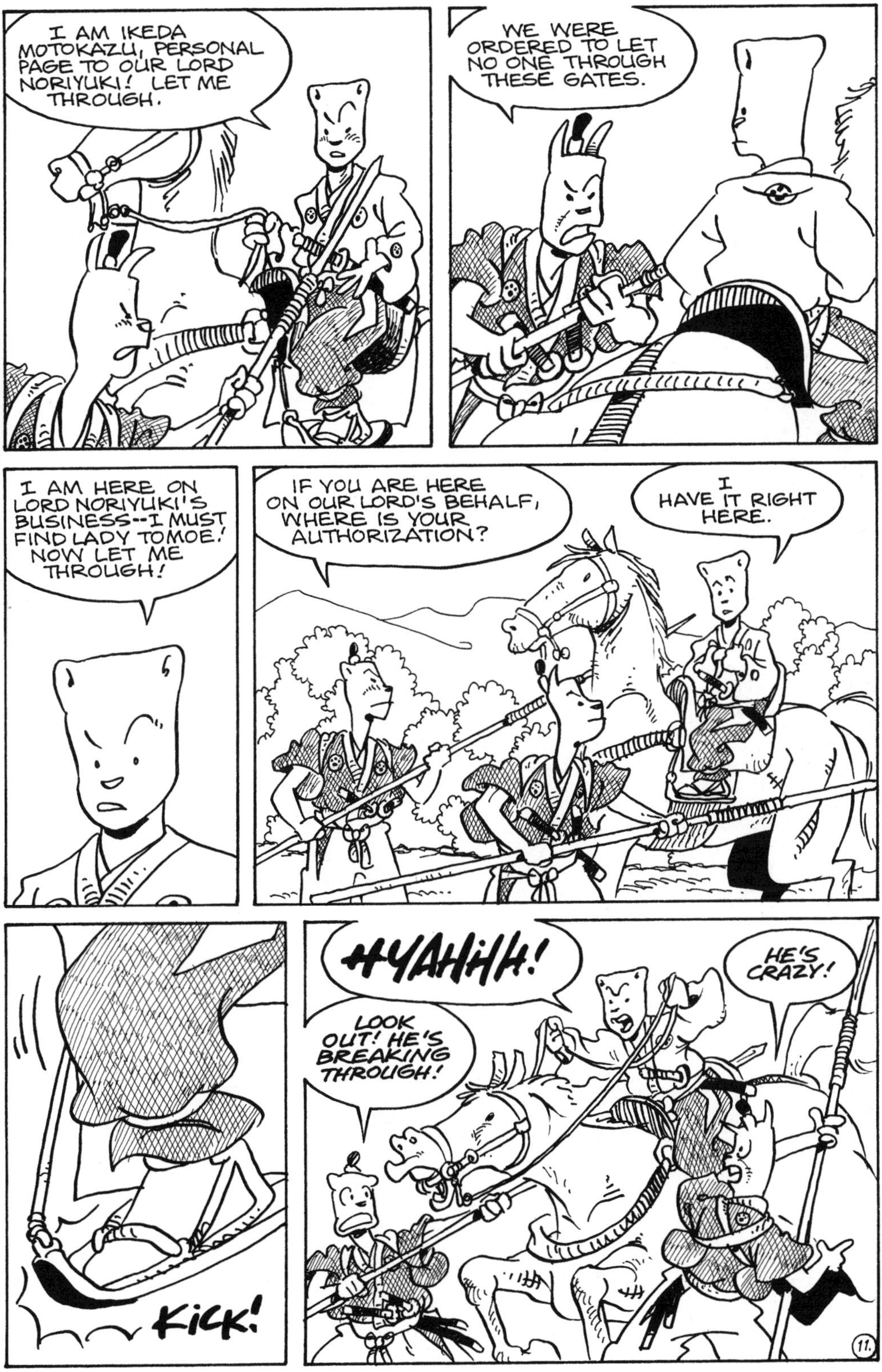

I AM IKEDA MOTOKAZU, PERSONAL PAGE TO OUR LORD NORIYUKI! LET ME THROUGH.
WE WERE ORDERED TO LET NO ONE THROUGH THESE GATES.
I AM HERE ON LORD NORIYUKI'S BUSINESS--I MUST FIND LADY TOMOE! NOW LET ME THROUGH!
IF YOU ARE HERE ON OUR LORD'S BEHALF, WHERE IS YOUR AUTHORIZATION?
I HAVE IT RIGHT HERE.
KICK!
HYAHHH!
LOOK OUT! HE'S BREAKING THROUGH!
HE'S CRAZY!
11.

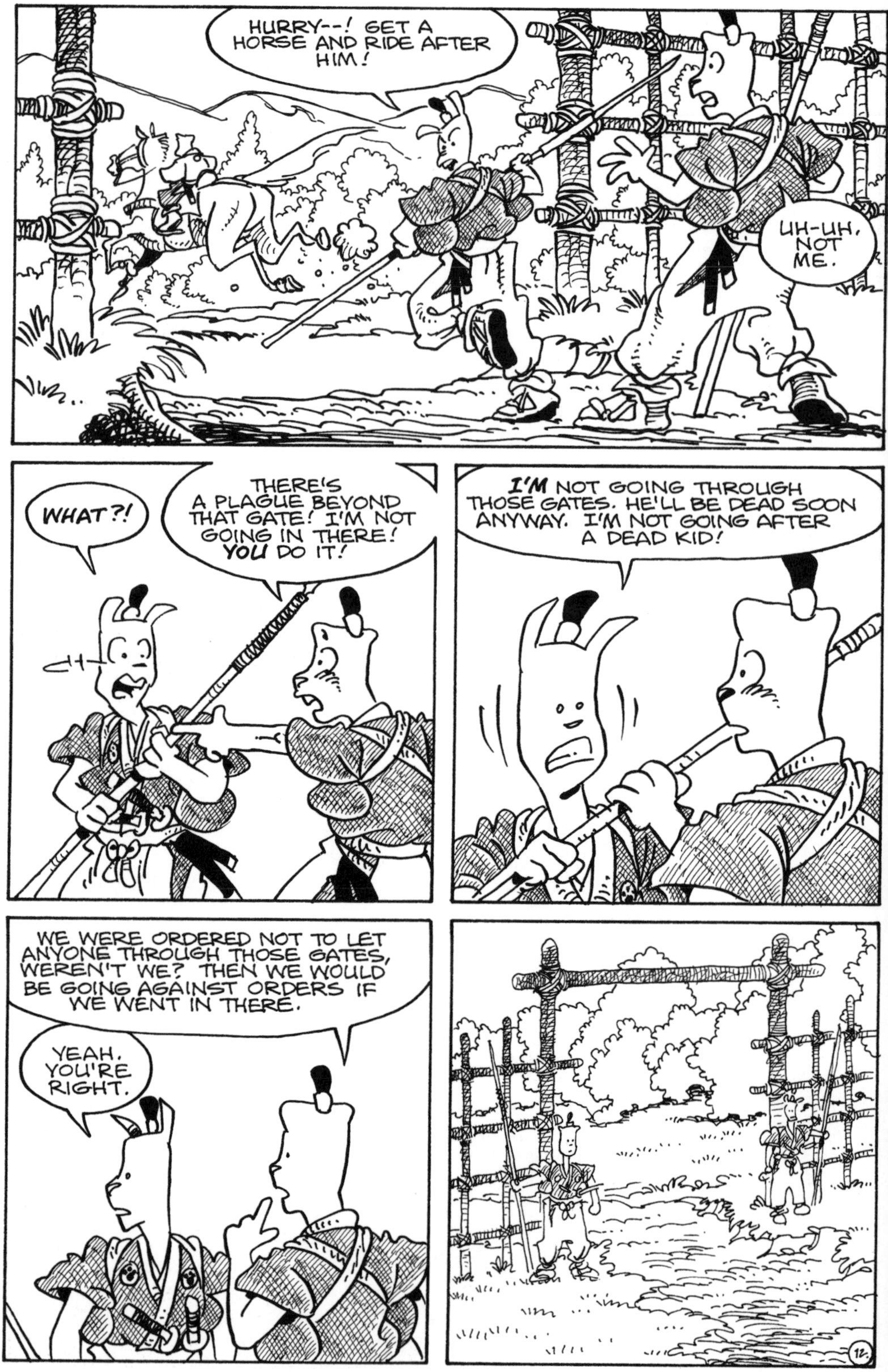
HURRY--! GET A HORSE AND RIDE AFTER HIM!
UH-UH, NOT ME.
WHAT?!
THERE'S A PLAGUE BEYOND THAT GATE! I'M NOT GOING IN THERE! YOU DO IT!
I'M NOT GOING THROUGH THOSE GATES. HE'LL BE DEAD SOON ANYWAY. I'M NOT GOING AFTER A DEAD KID!
WE WERE ORDERED NOT TO LET ANYONE THROUGH THOSE GATES, WEREN'T WE? THEN WE WOULD BE GOING AGAINST ORDERS IF WE WENT IN THERE.
YEAH. YOU'RE RIGHT.
12.

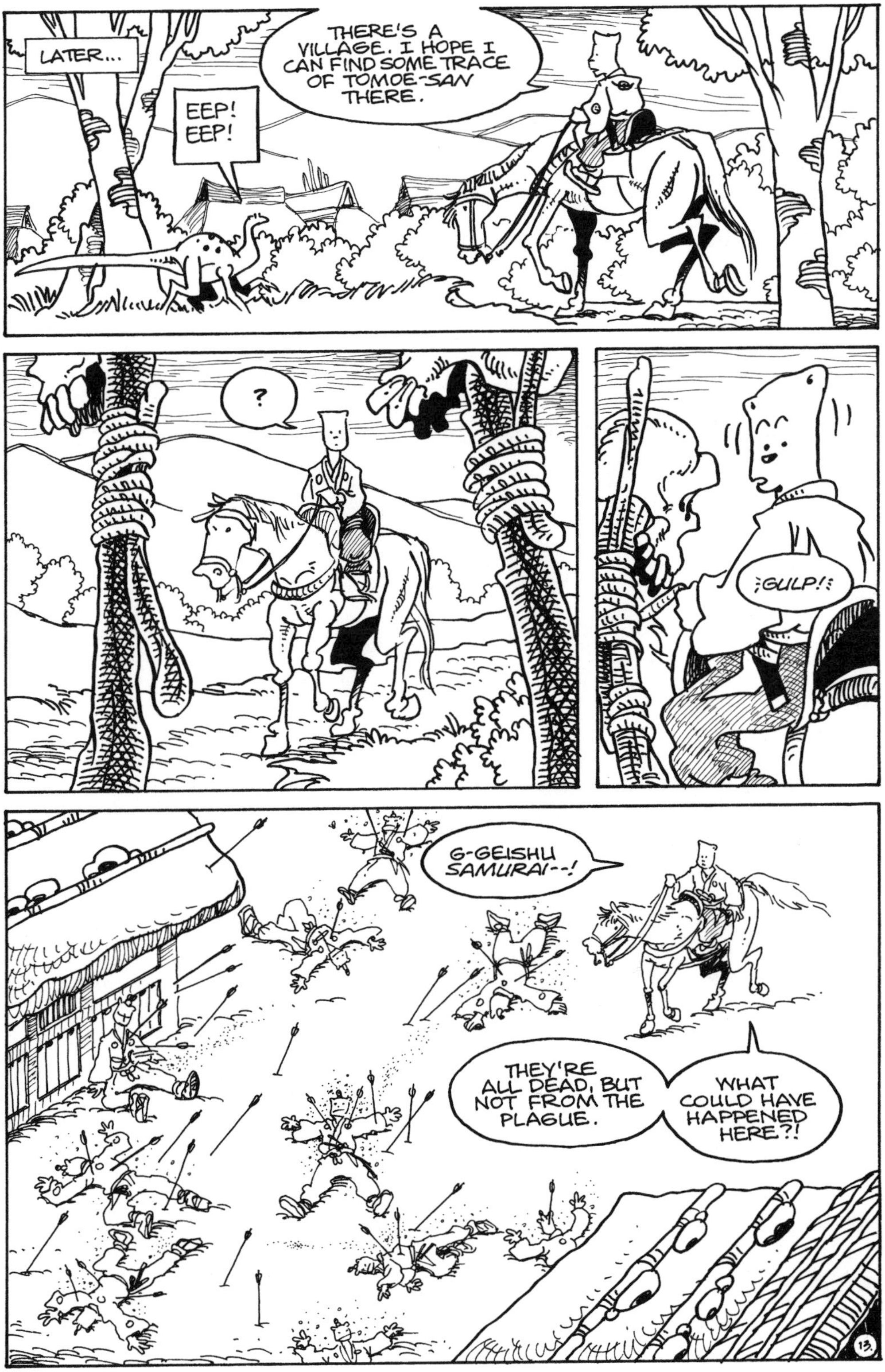
LATER...
EEP! EEP!
THERE'S A VILLAGE. I HOPE I CAN FIND SOME TRACE OF TOMOE-SAN THERE.
?
¡GULP!¡
G-GEISHU SAMURAI--!
THEY'RE ALL DEAD, BUT NOT FROM THE PLAGUE.
WHAT COULD HAVE HAPPENED HERE?!
13

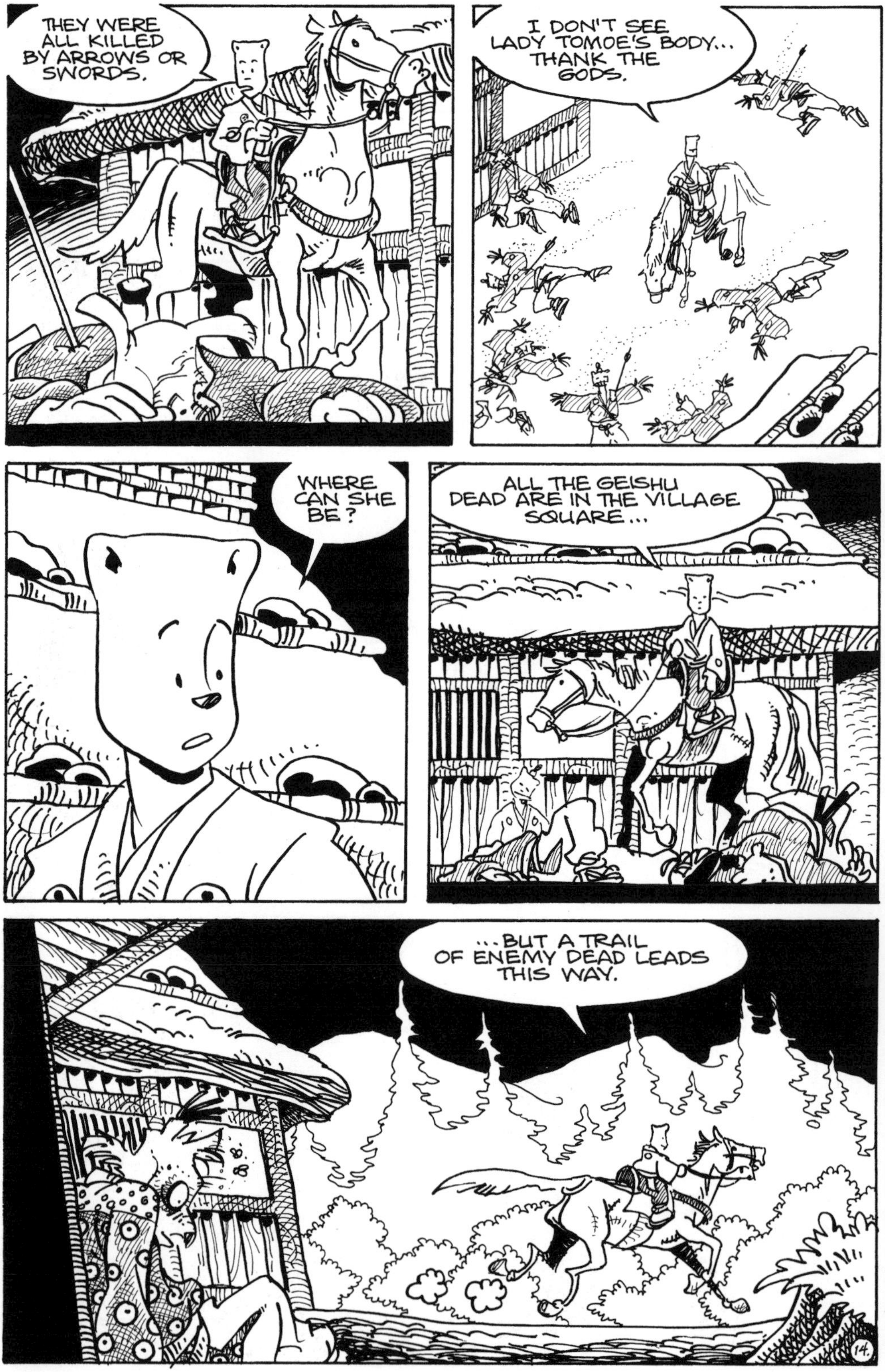
THEY WERE ALL KILLED BY ARROWS OR SWORDS.
I DON'T SEE LADY TOMOE'S BODY... THANK THE GODS.
WHERE CAN SHE BE?
ALL THE GEISHU DEAD ARE IN THE VILLAGE SQUARE...
...BUT A TRAIL OF ENEMY DEAD LEADS THIS WAY.
14.

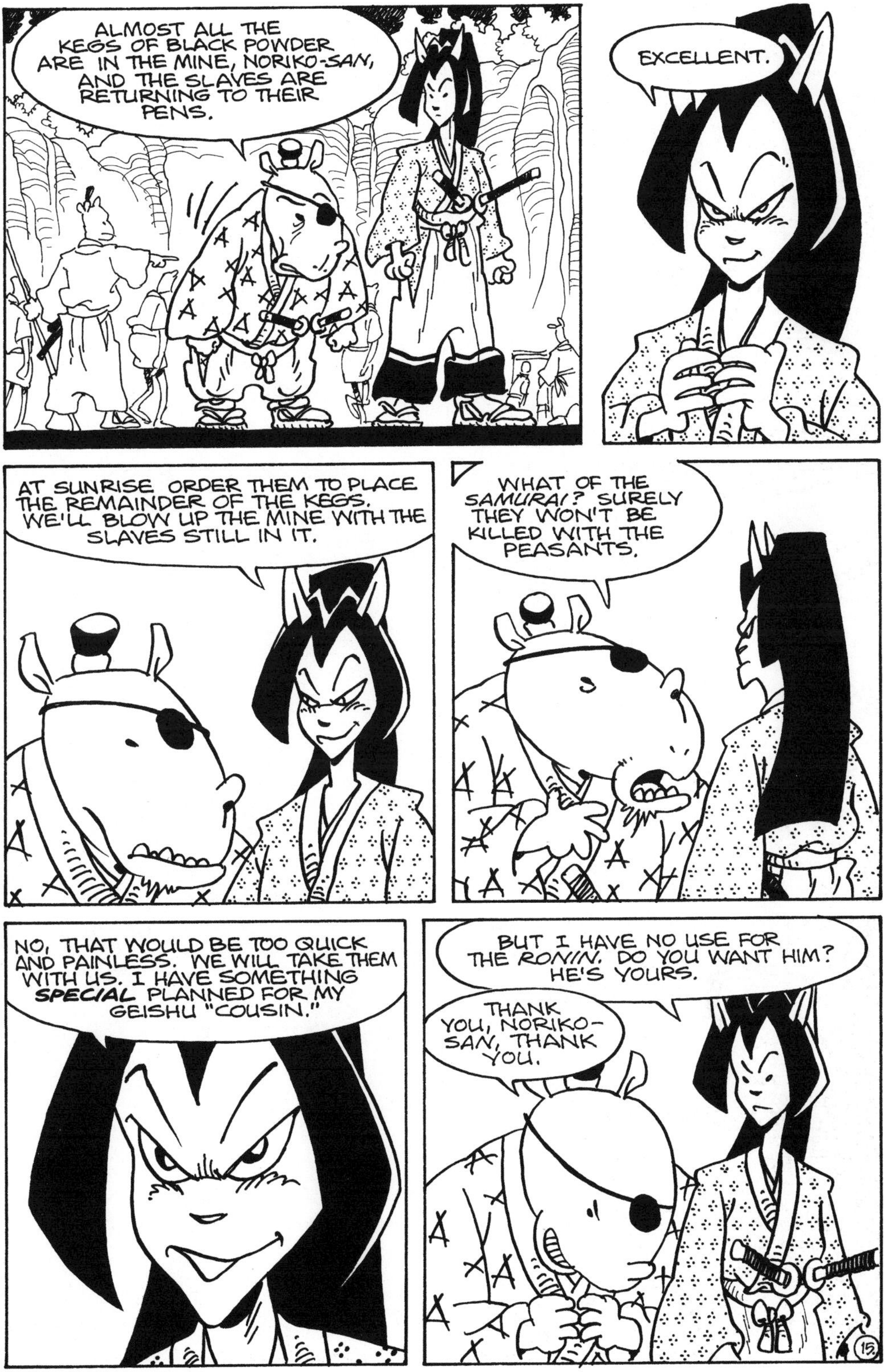
ALMOST ALL THE KEGS OF BLACK POWDER ARE IN THE MINE, NORIKO-SAN, AND THE SLAVES ARE RETURNING TO THEIR PENS.
EXCELLENT.
AT SUNRISE ORDER THEM TO PLACE THE REMAINDER OF THE KEGS. WE'LL BLOW UP THE MINE WITH THE SLAVES STILL IN IT.
WHAT OF THE SAMURAI? SURELY THEY WON'T BE KILLED WITH THE PEASANTS.
NO, THAT WOULD BE TOO QUICK AND PAINLESS. WE WILL TAKE THEM WITH US. I HAVE SOMETHING SPECIAL PLANNED FOR MY GEISHU "COUSIN."
BUT I HAVE NO USE FOR THE RONIN. DO YOU WANT HIM? HE'S YOURS.
THANK YOU, NORIKO-SAN, THANK YOU.
15

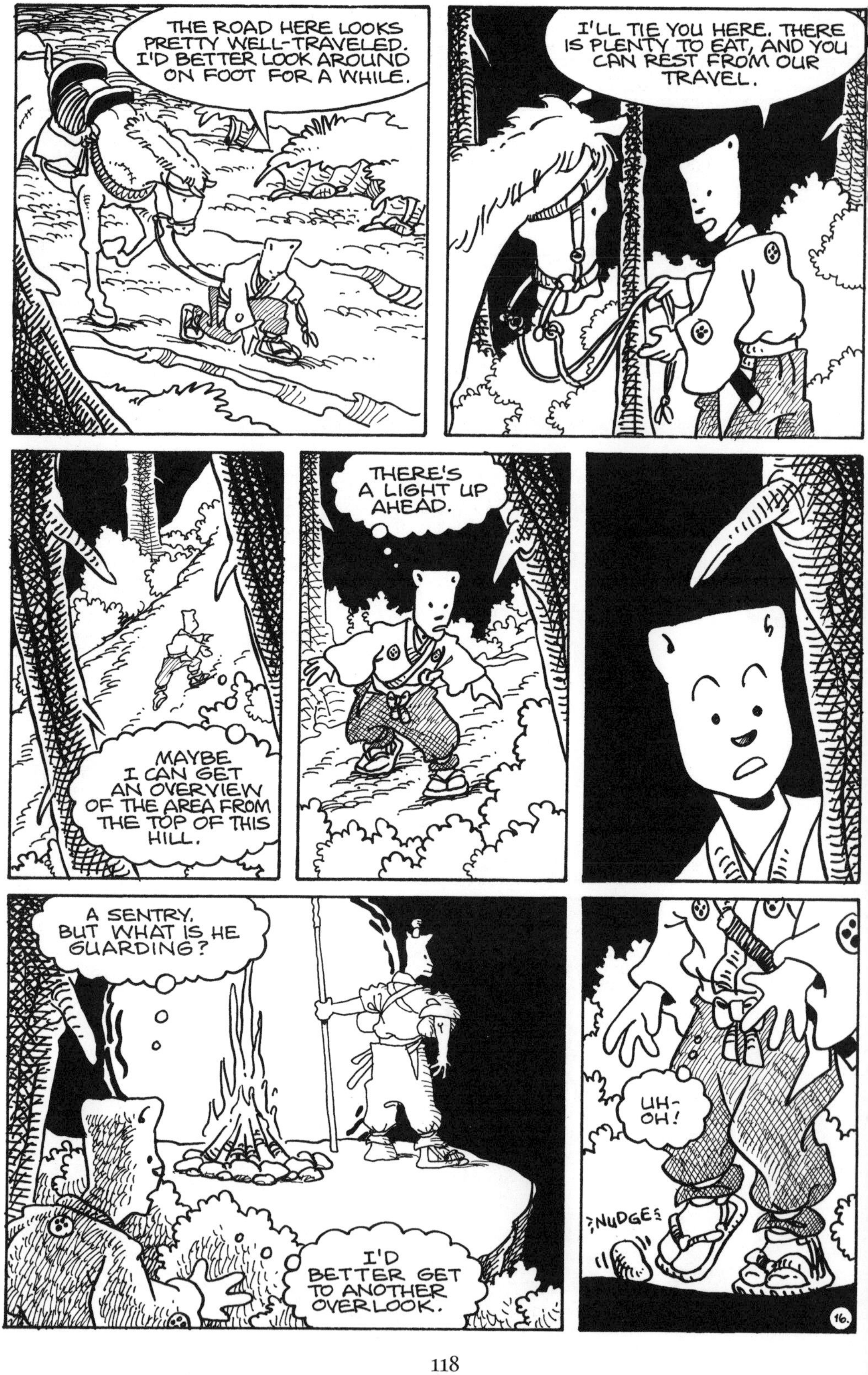
THE ROAD HERE LOOKS PRETTY WELL-TRAVELED. I'D BETTER LOOK AROUND ON FOOT FOR A WHILE.
I'LL TIE YOU HERE. THERE IS PLENTY TO EAT, AND YOU CAN REST FROM OUR TRAVEL.
MAYBE I CAN GET AN OVERVIEW OF THE AREA FROM THE TOP OF THIS HILL.
THERE'S A LIGHT UP AHEAD.
A SENTRY. BUT WHAT IS HE GUARDING?
I'D BETTER GET TO ANOTHER OVERLOOK.
UH-OH!
NUDGE
16.

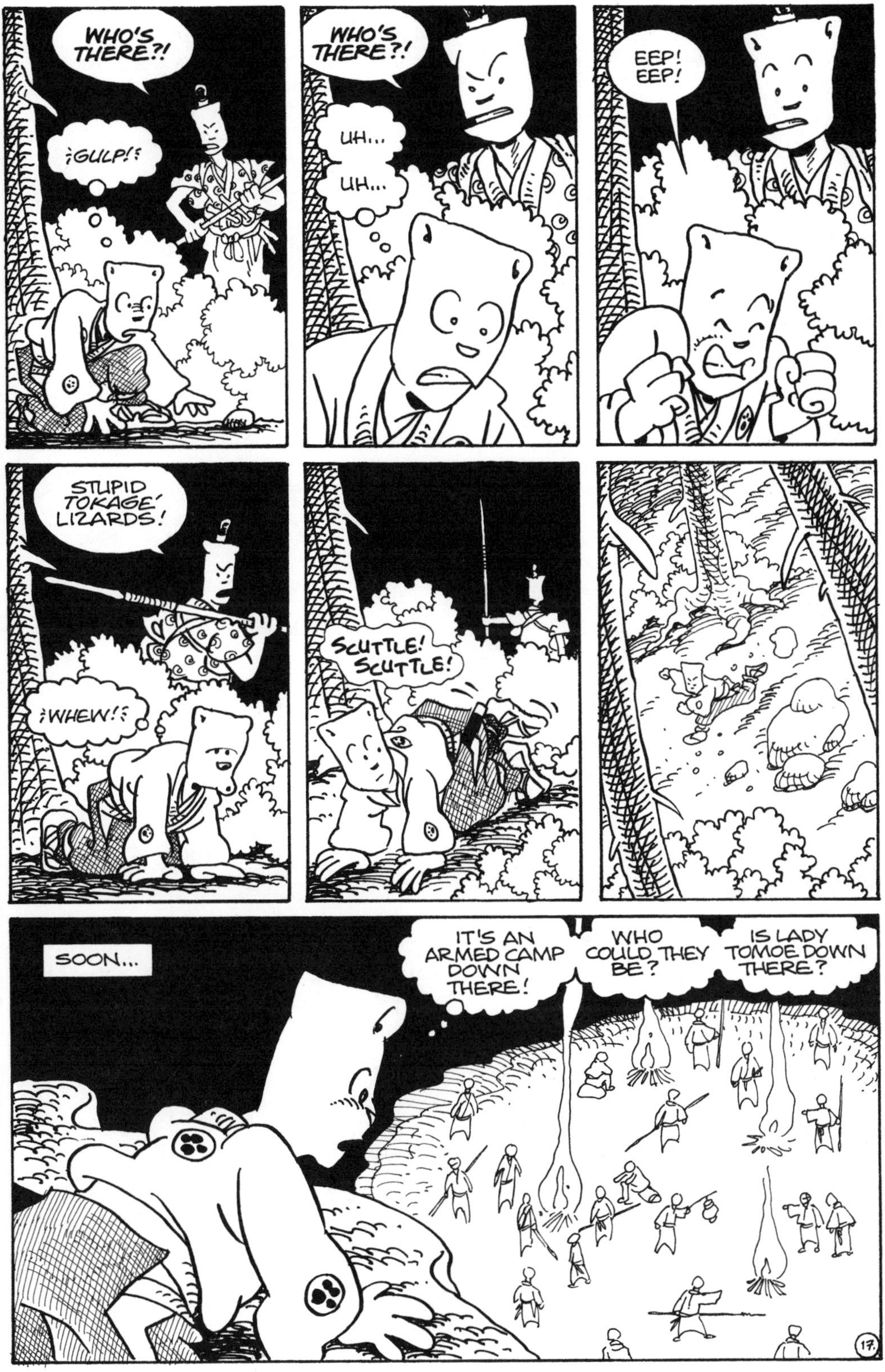
WHO'S THERE?!
¡GULP!¡
WHO'S THERE?!
UH...
UH...
EEP! EEP!
STUPID TOKAGE LIZARDS!
¡WHEW!¡
SCUTTLE! SCUTTLE!
SOON...
IT'S AN ARMED CAMP DOWN THERE!
WHO COULD THEY BE?
IS LADY TOMOE DOWN THERE?
17

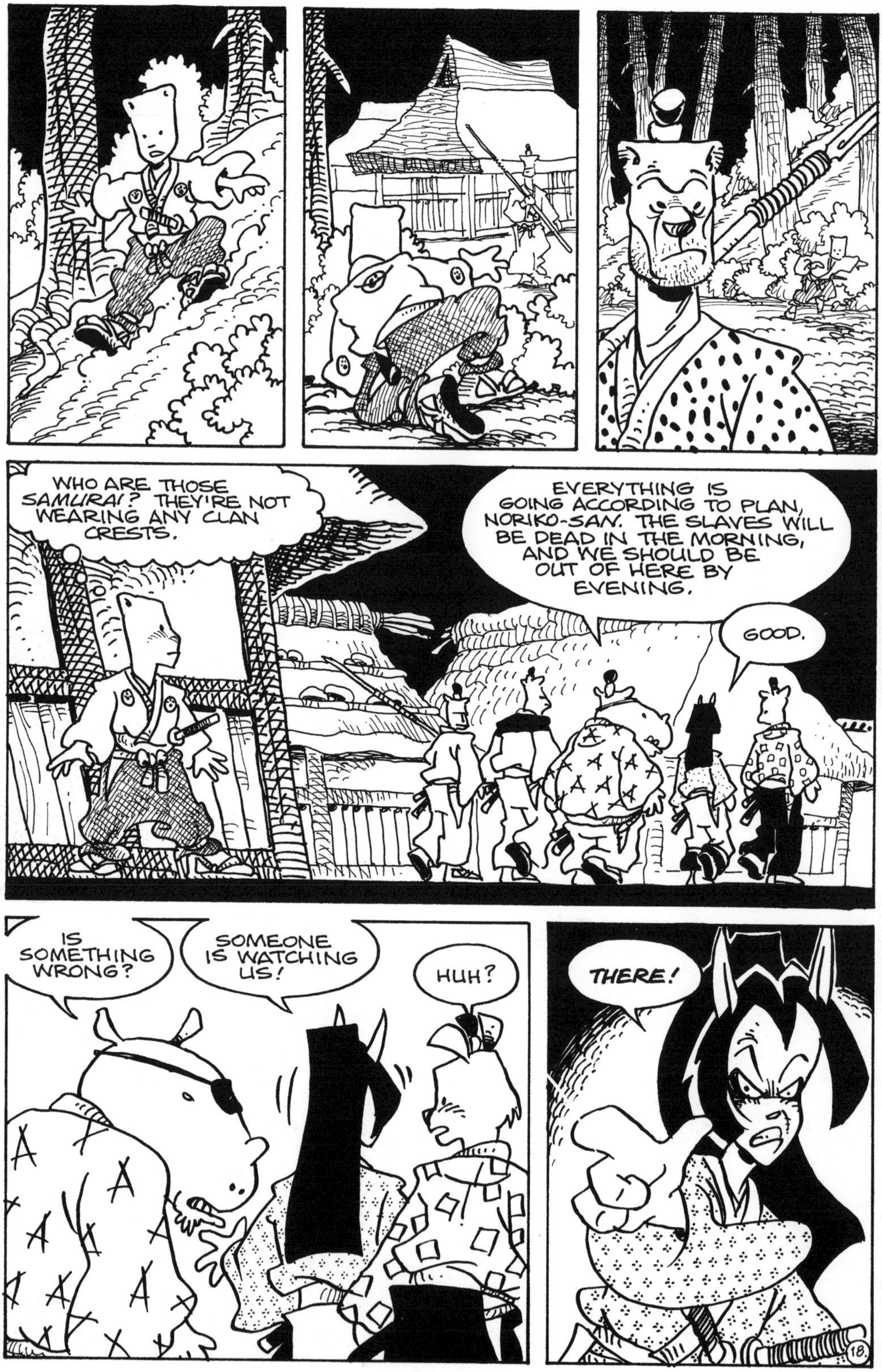
WHO ARE THOSE SAMURAI? THEY'RE NOT WEARING ANY CLAN CRESTS.
EVERYTHING IS GOING ACCORDING TO PLAN, NORIKO-SAN. THE SLAVES WILL BE DEAD IN THE MORNING, AND WE SHOULD BE OUT OF HERE BY EVENING.
GOOD.
IS SOMETHING WRONG?
SOMEONE IS WATCHING US!
HUH?
THERE!
18

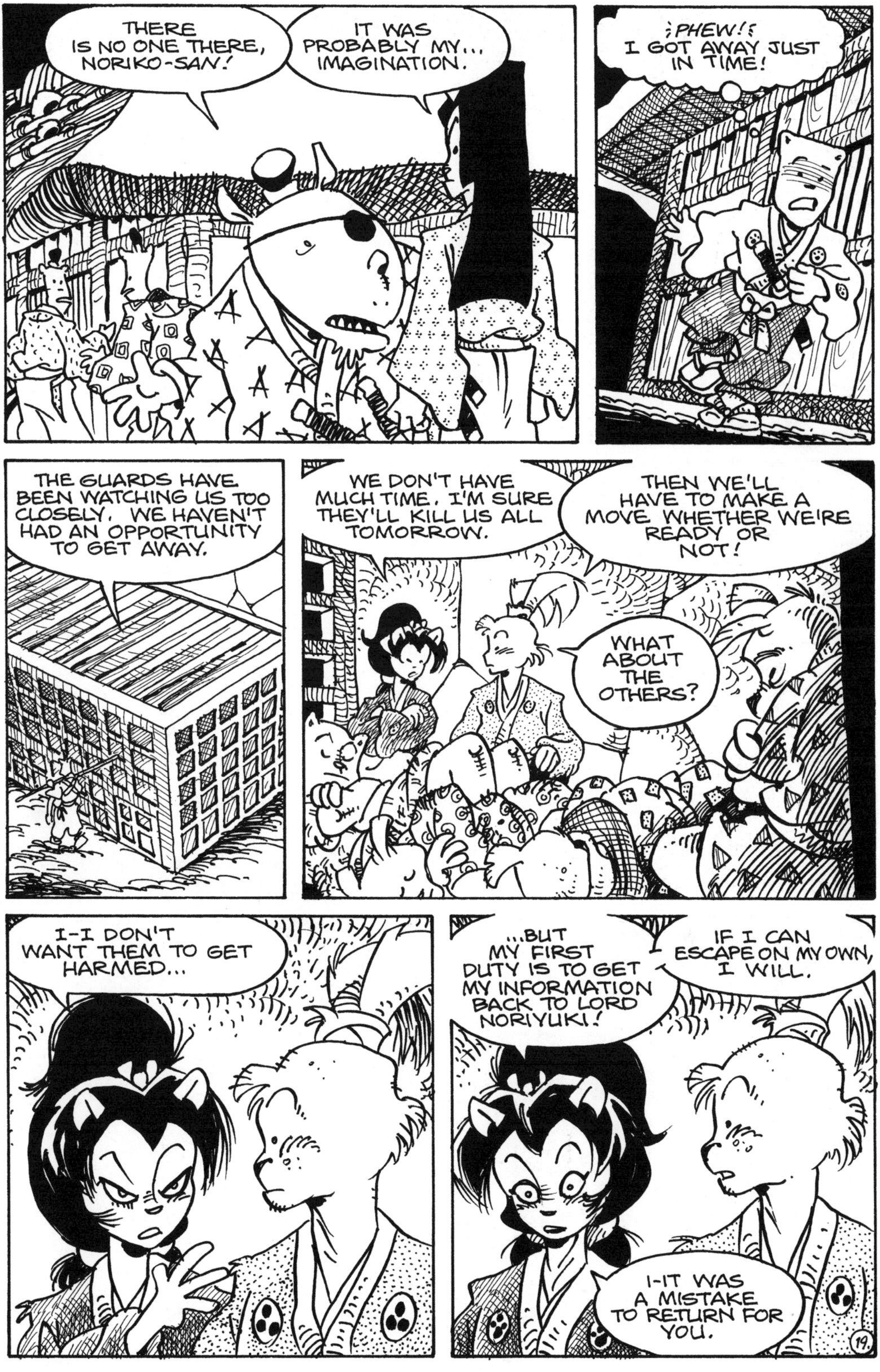
THERE IS NO ONE THERE, NORIKO-SAN!
IT WAS PROBABLY MY... IMAGINATION.
¡PHEW!¡ I GOT AWAY JUST IN TIME!
THE GUARDS HAVE BEEN WATCHING US TOO CLOSELY. WE HAVEN'T HAD AN OPPORTUNITY TO GET AWAY.
WE DON'T HAVE MUCH TIME. I'M SURE THEY'LL KILL US ALL TOMORROW.
THEN WE'LL HAVE TO MAKE A MOVE WHETHER WE'RE READY OR NOT!
WHAT ABOUT THE OTHERS?
I-I DON'T WANT THEM TO GET HARMED...
...BUT MY FIRST DUTY IS TO GET MY INFORMATION BACK TO LORD NORIYUKI!
IF I CAN ESCAPE ON MY OWN, I WILL.
I-IT WAS A MISTAKE TO RETURN FOR YOU.
19.

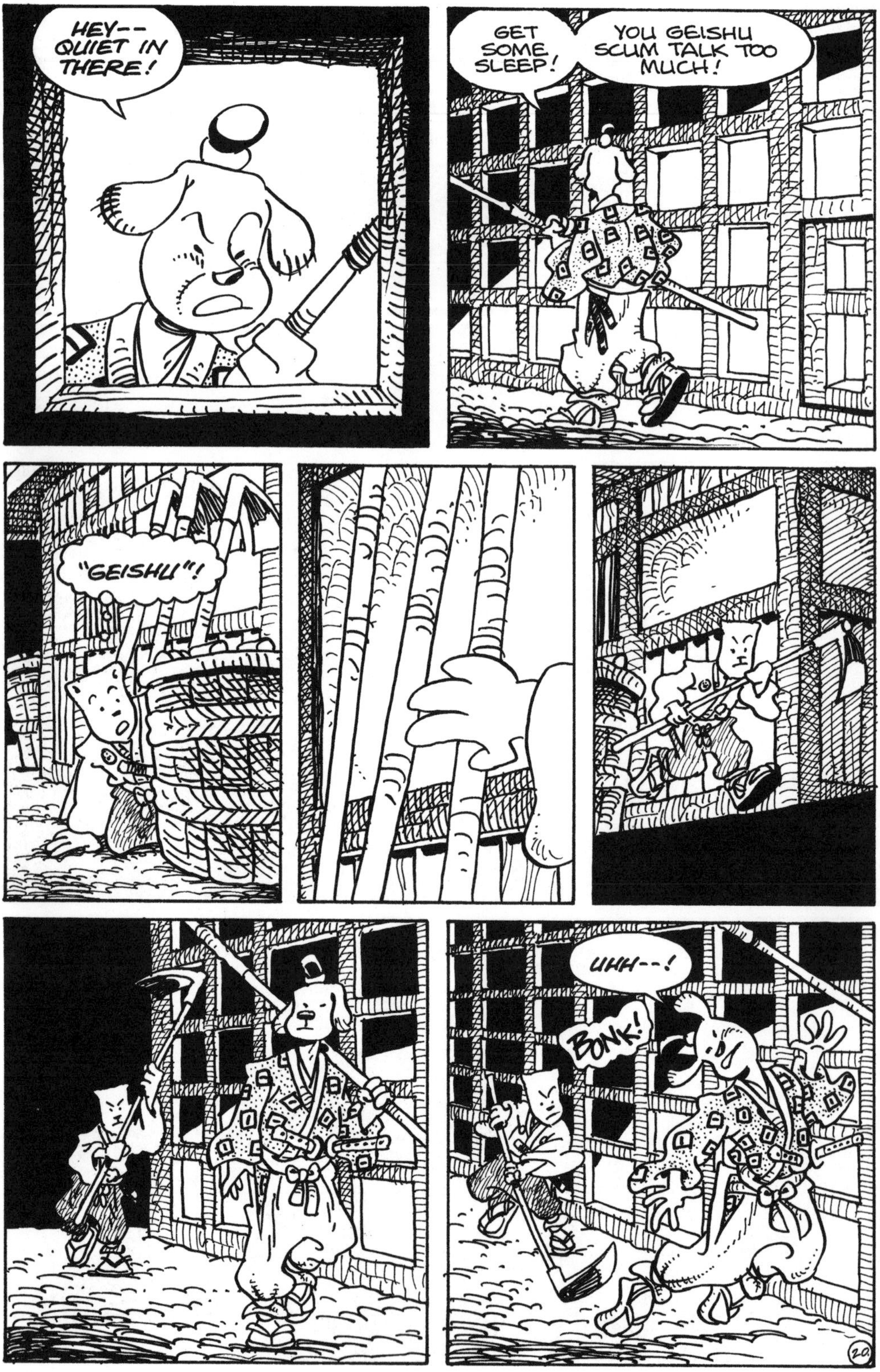
HEY-- QUIET IN THERE!
GET SOME SLEEP!
YOU GEISHU SCUM TALK TOO MUCH!
"GEISHU"!
UHH--!
BONK!
20

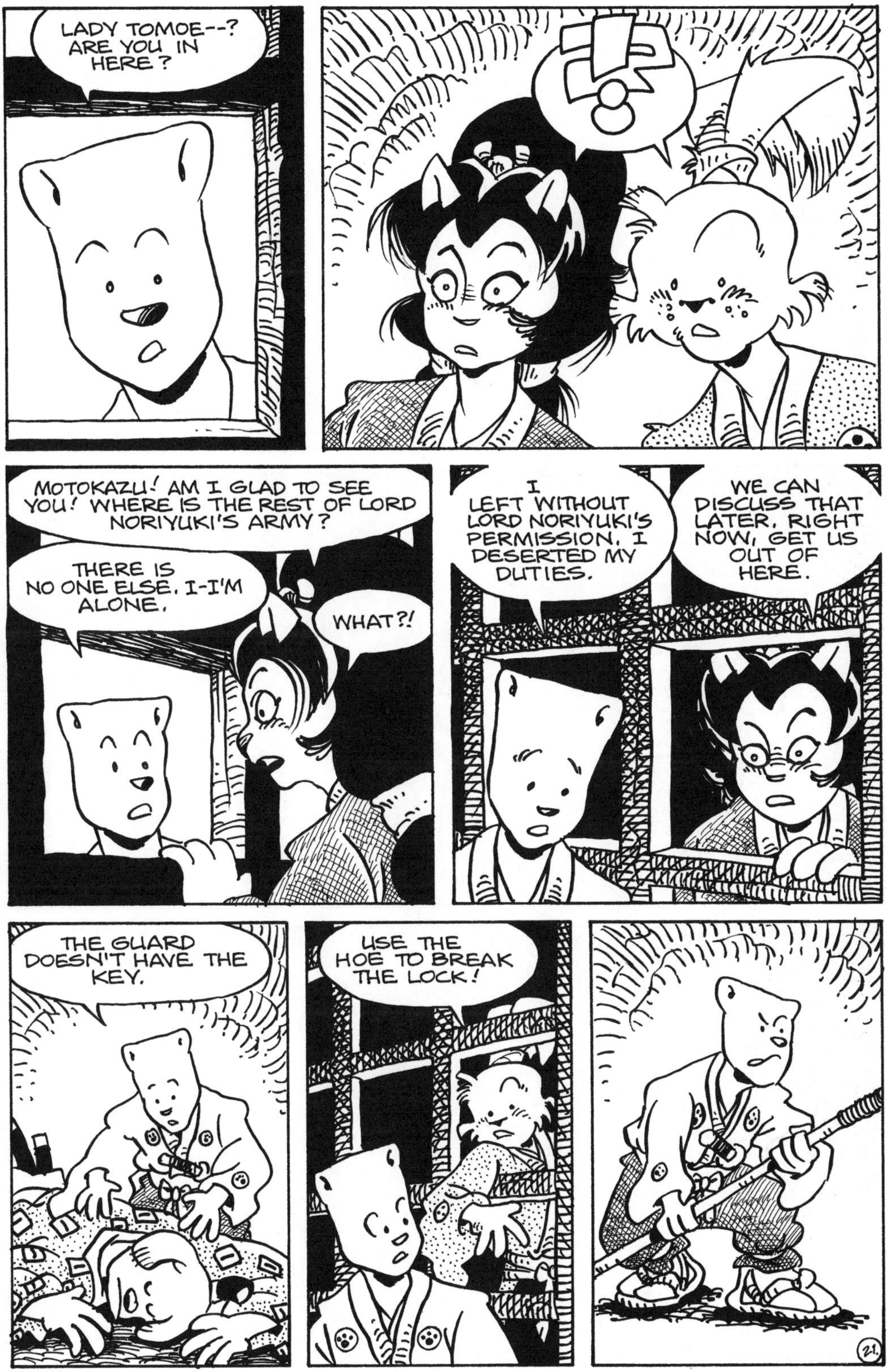

LADY TOMOE--? ARE YOU IN HERE?
MOTOKAZU! AM I GLAD TO SEE YOU! WHERE IS THE REST OF LORD NORIYUKI'S ARMY?
THERE IS NO ONE ELSE. I-I'M ALONE.
WHAT?!
I LEFT WITHOUT LORD NORIYUKI'S PERMISSION. I DESERTED MY DUTIES.
WE CAN DISCUSS THAT LATER. RIGHT NOW, GET US OUT OF HERE.
THE GUARD DOESN'T HAVE THE KEY.
USE THE HOE TO BREAK THE LOCK!
21.

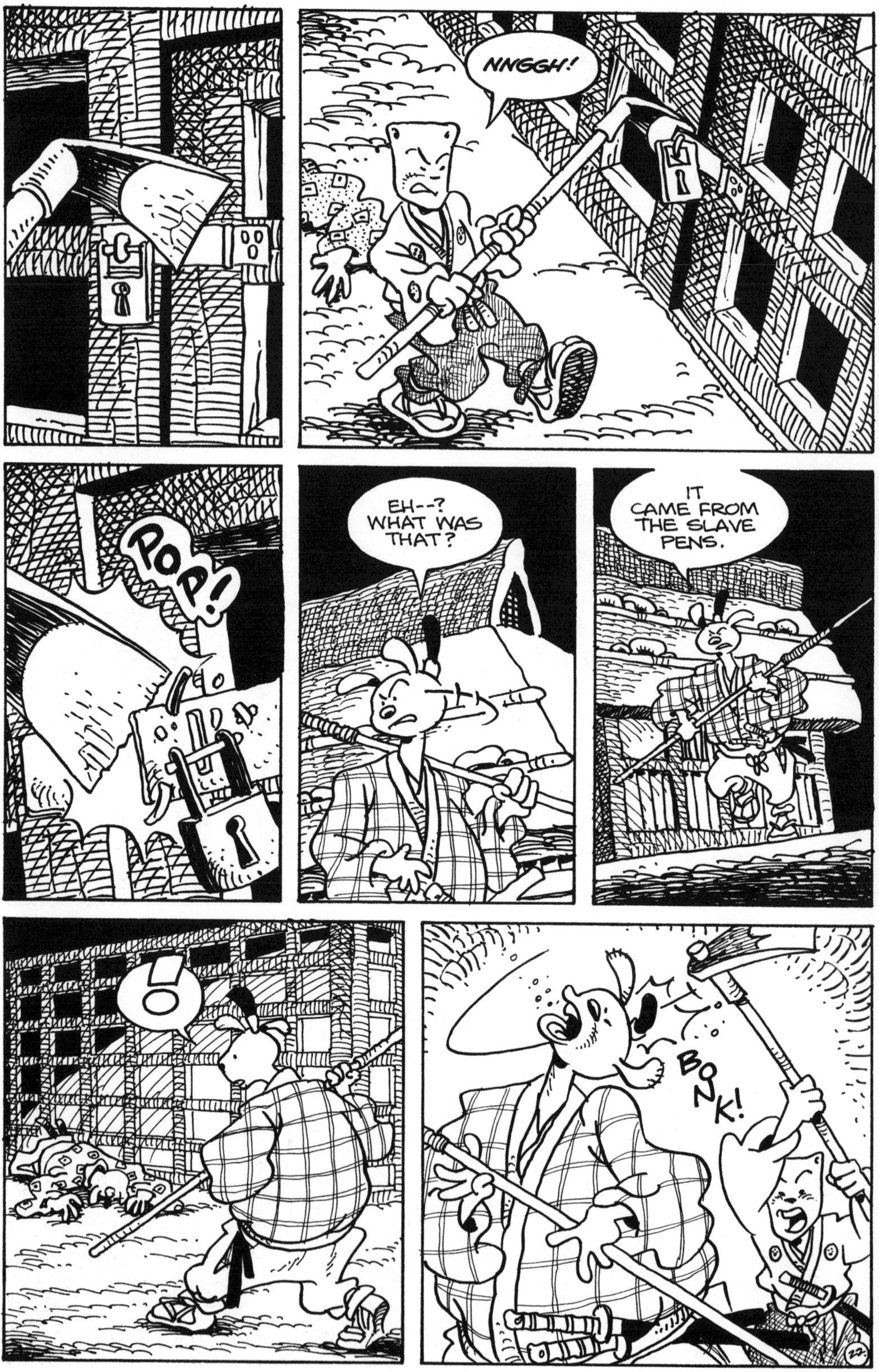
NNGGH!
POP!
EH--? WHAT WAS THAT?
IT CAME FROM THE SLAVE PENS.
!
BONK!

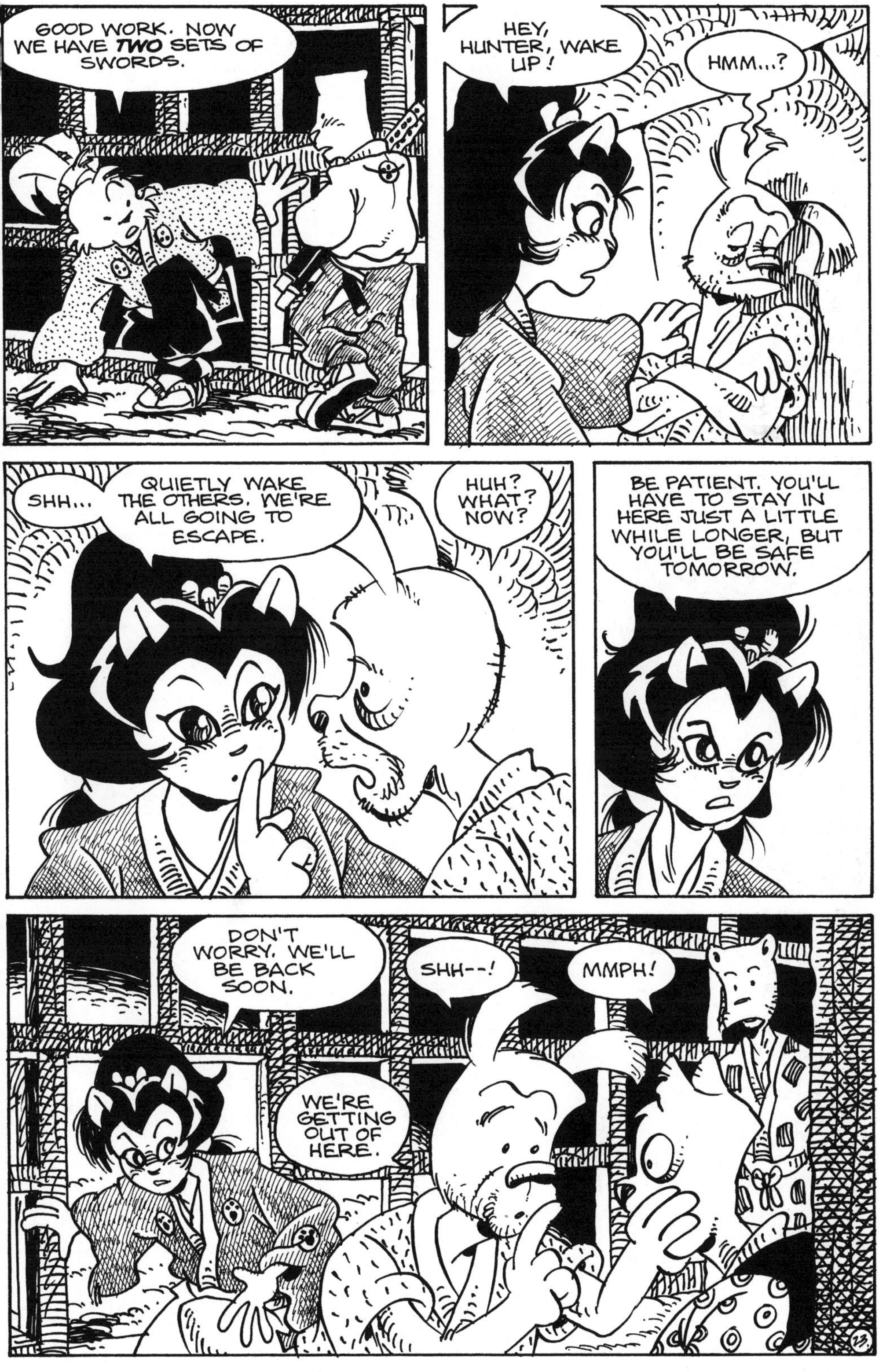
GOOD WORK. NOW WE HAVE **TWO** SETS OF SWORDS.
HEY, HUNTER, WAKE UP!
HMM...?
SHH...
QUIETLY WAKE THE OTHERS. WE'RE ALL GOING TO ESCAPE.
HUH? WHAT? NOW?
BE PATIENT. YOU'LL HAVE TO STAY IN HERE JUST A LITTLE WHILE LONGER, BUT YOU'LL BE SAFE TOMORROW.
DON'T WORRY. WE'LL BE BACK SOON.
WE'RE GETTING OUT OF HERE.
SHH--!
MMPH!

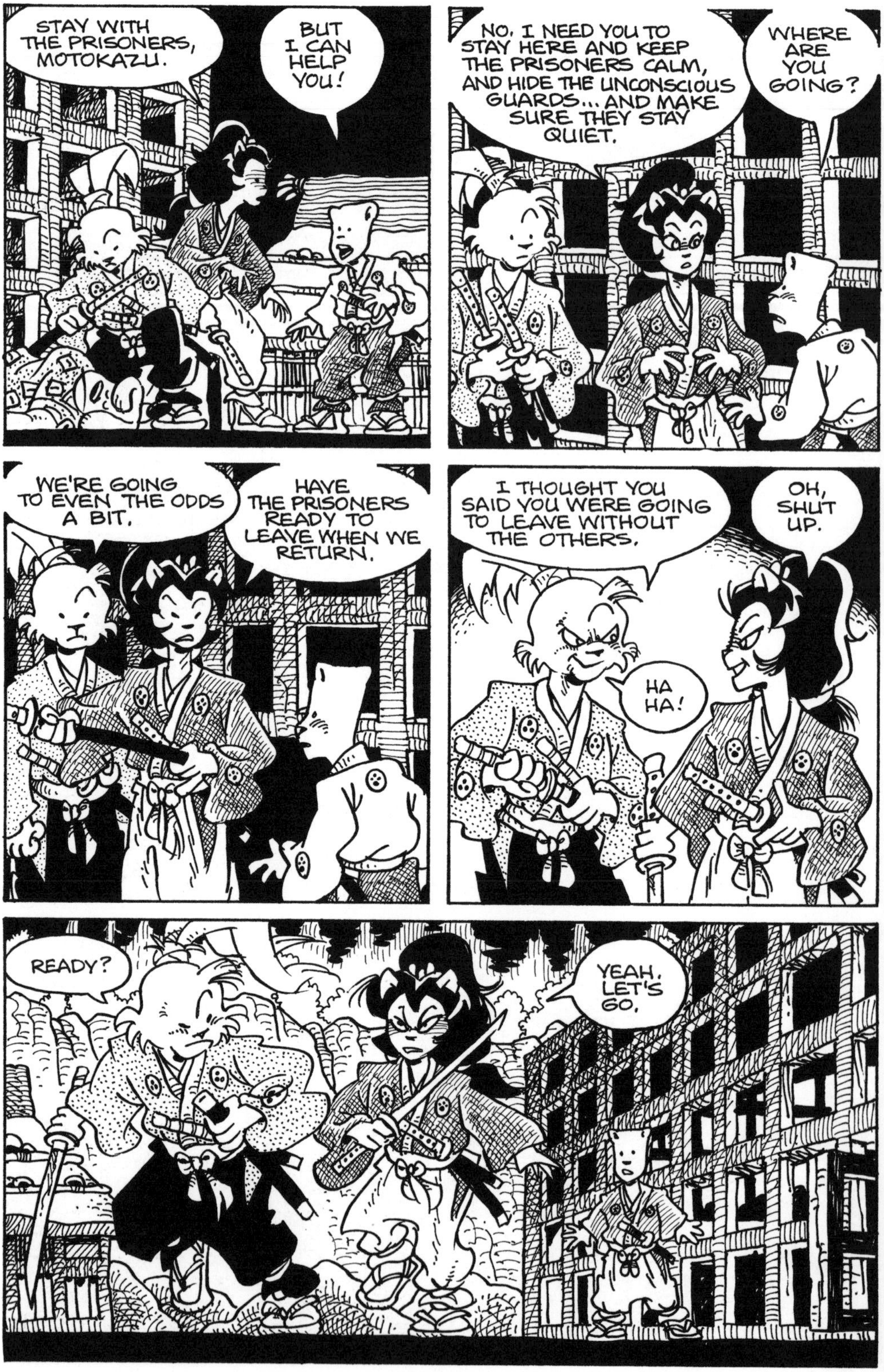
STAY WITH THE PRISONERS, MOTOKAZU.
BUT I CAN HELP YOU!
NO, I NEED YOU TO STAY HERE AND KEEP THE PRISONERS CALM, AND HIDE THE UNCONSCIOUS GUARDS... AND MAKE SURE THEY STAY QUIET.
WHERE ARE YOU GOING?
WE'RE GOING TO EVEN THE ODDS A BIT.
HAVE THE PRISONERS READY TO LEAVE WHEN WE RETURN.
I THOUGHT YOU SAID YOU WERE GOING TO LEAVE WITHOUT THE OTHERS.
OH, SHUT UP.
HA HA!
READY?
YEAH, LET'S GO.

THE TREASURE OF THE MOTHER OF MOUNTAINS

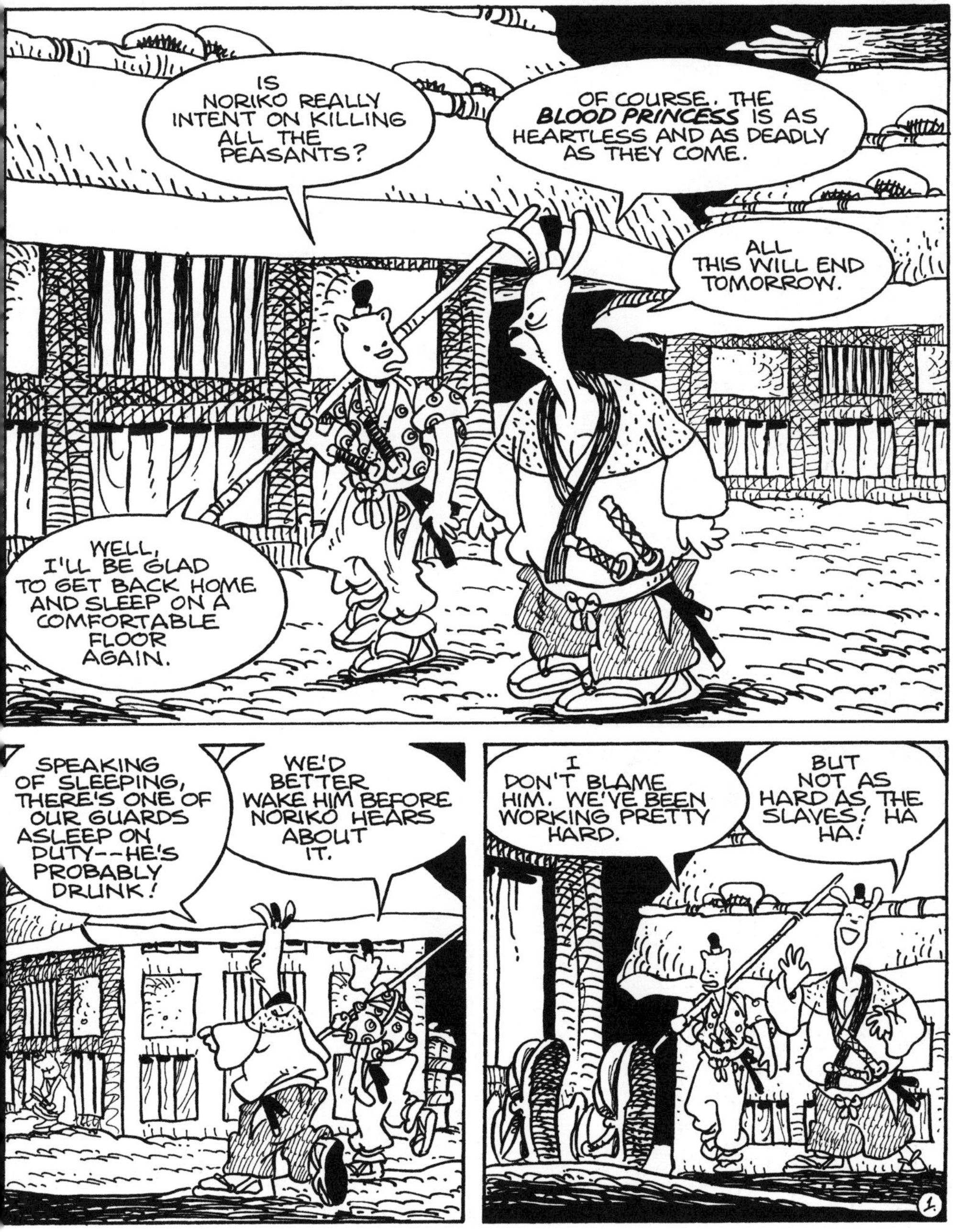
IS NORIKO REALLY INTENT ON KILLING ALL THE PEASANTS?
OF COURSE. THE BLOOD PRINCESS IS AS HEARTLESS AND AS DEADLY AS THEY COME.
ALL THIS WILL END TOMORROW.
WELL, I'LL BE GLAD TO GET BACK HOME AND SLEEP ON A COMFORTABLE FLOOR AGAIN.
SPEAKING OF SLEEPING, THERE'S ONE OF OUR GUARDS ASLEEP ON DUTY--HE'S PROBABLY DRUNK!
WE'D BETTER WAKE HIM BEFORE NORIKO HEARS ABOUT IT.
I DON'T BLAME HIM. WE'VE BEEN WORKING PRETTY HARD.
BUT NOT AS HARD AS THE SLAVES! HA HA!
1.

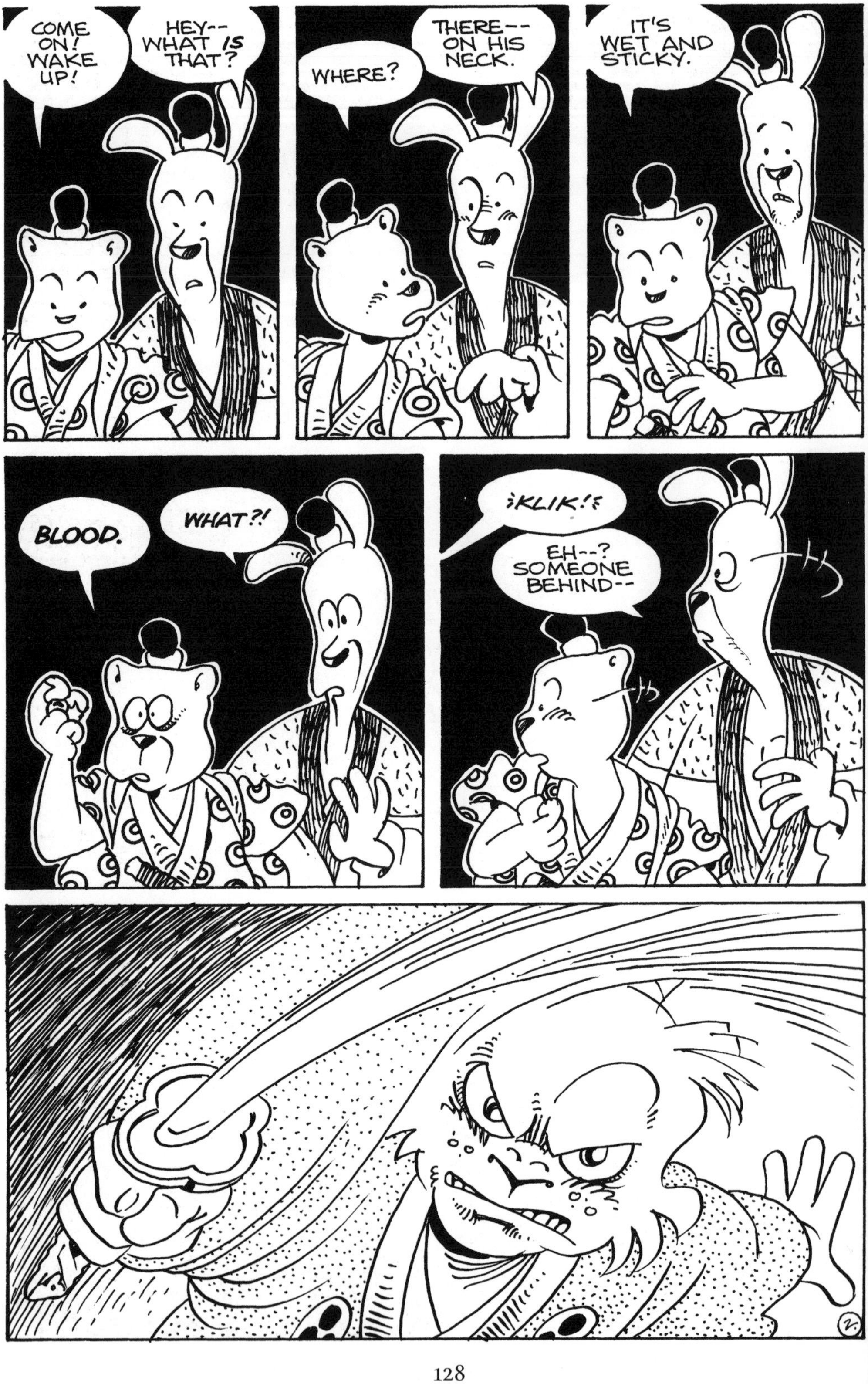
COME ON! WAKE UP!
HEY-- WHAT IS THAT?
WHERE?
THERE-- ON HIS NECK.
IT'S WET AND STICKY.
BLOOD.
WHAT?!
KLIK!
EH--? SOMEONE BEHIND--
2.

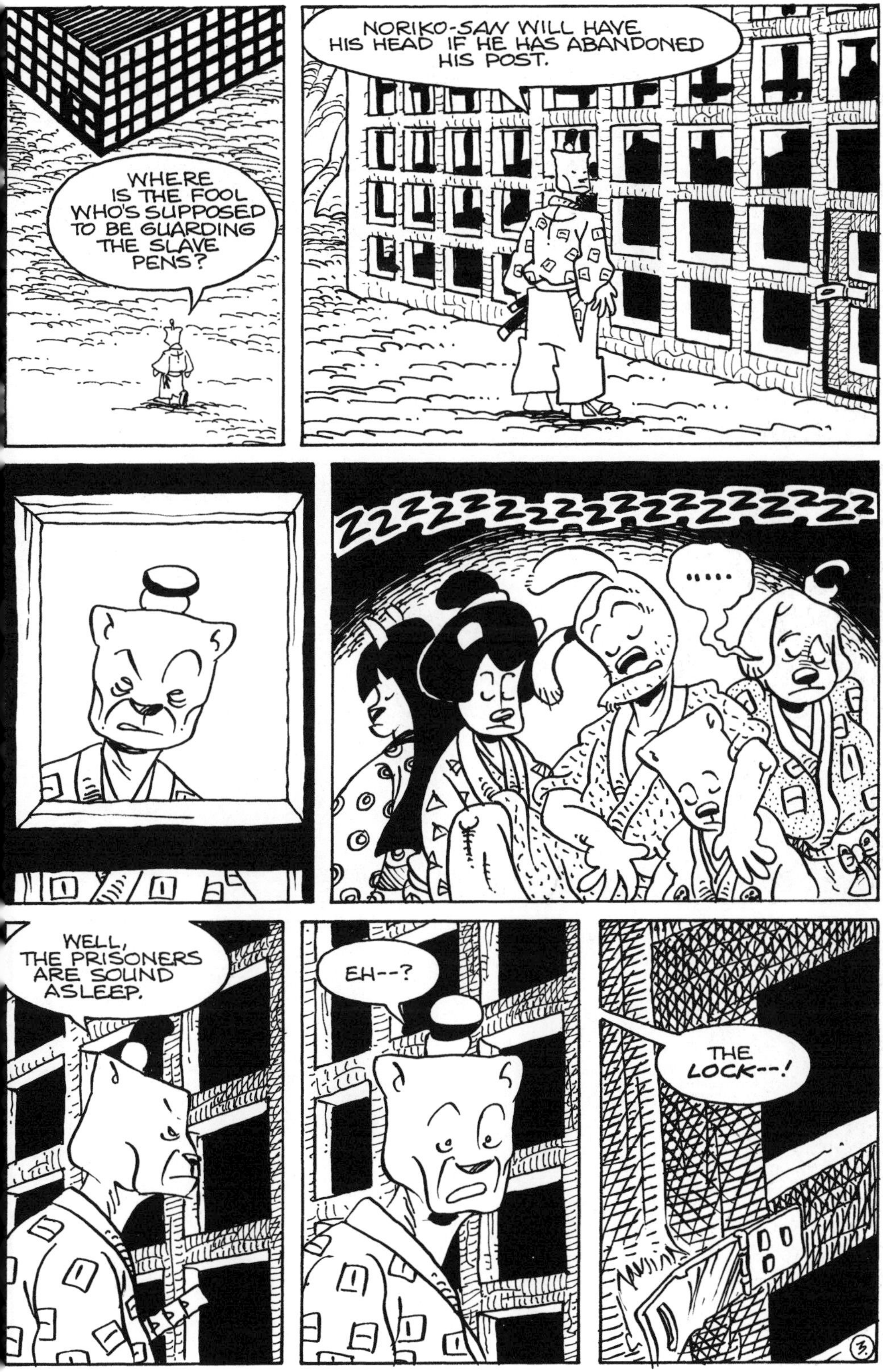
WHERE IS THE FOOL WHO'S SUPPOSED TO BE GUARDING THE SLAVE PENS?
NORIKO-SAN WILL HAVE HIS HEAD IF HE HAS ABANDONED HIS POST.
ZZZZZZZZZZZZZZZZZZZZ
.....
WELL, THE PRISONERS ARE SOUND ASLEEP.
EH--?
THE LOCK--!
3

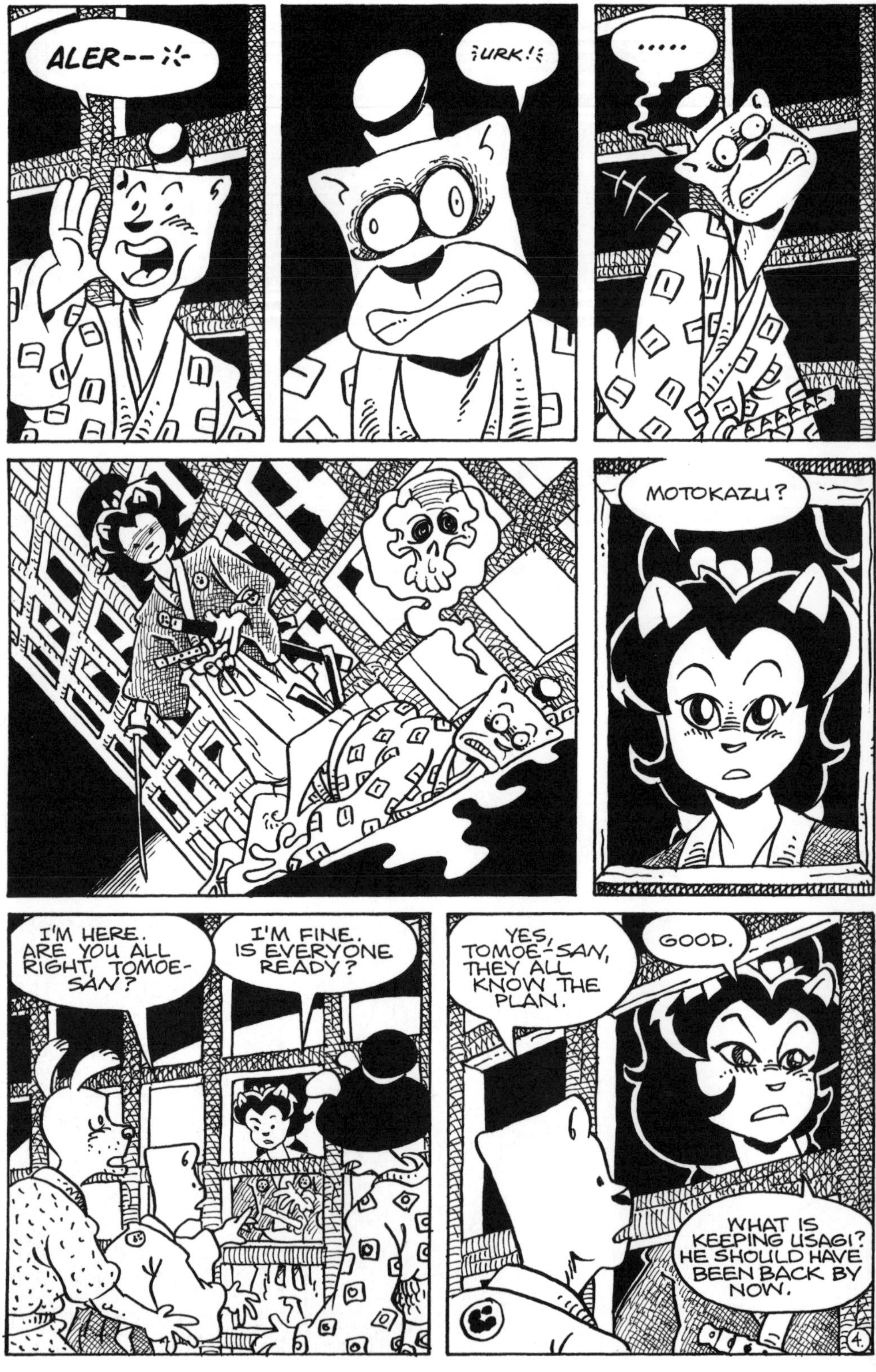
ALER--
URK!
.....
MOTOKAZU?
I'M HERE. ARE YOU ALL RIGHT, TOMOE-SAN?
I'M FINE. IS EVERYONE READY?
YES, TOMOE-SAN, THEY ALL KNOW THE PLAN.
GOOD.
WHAT IS KEEPING USAGI? HE SHOULD HAVE BEEN BACK BY NOW.
4.

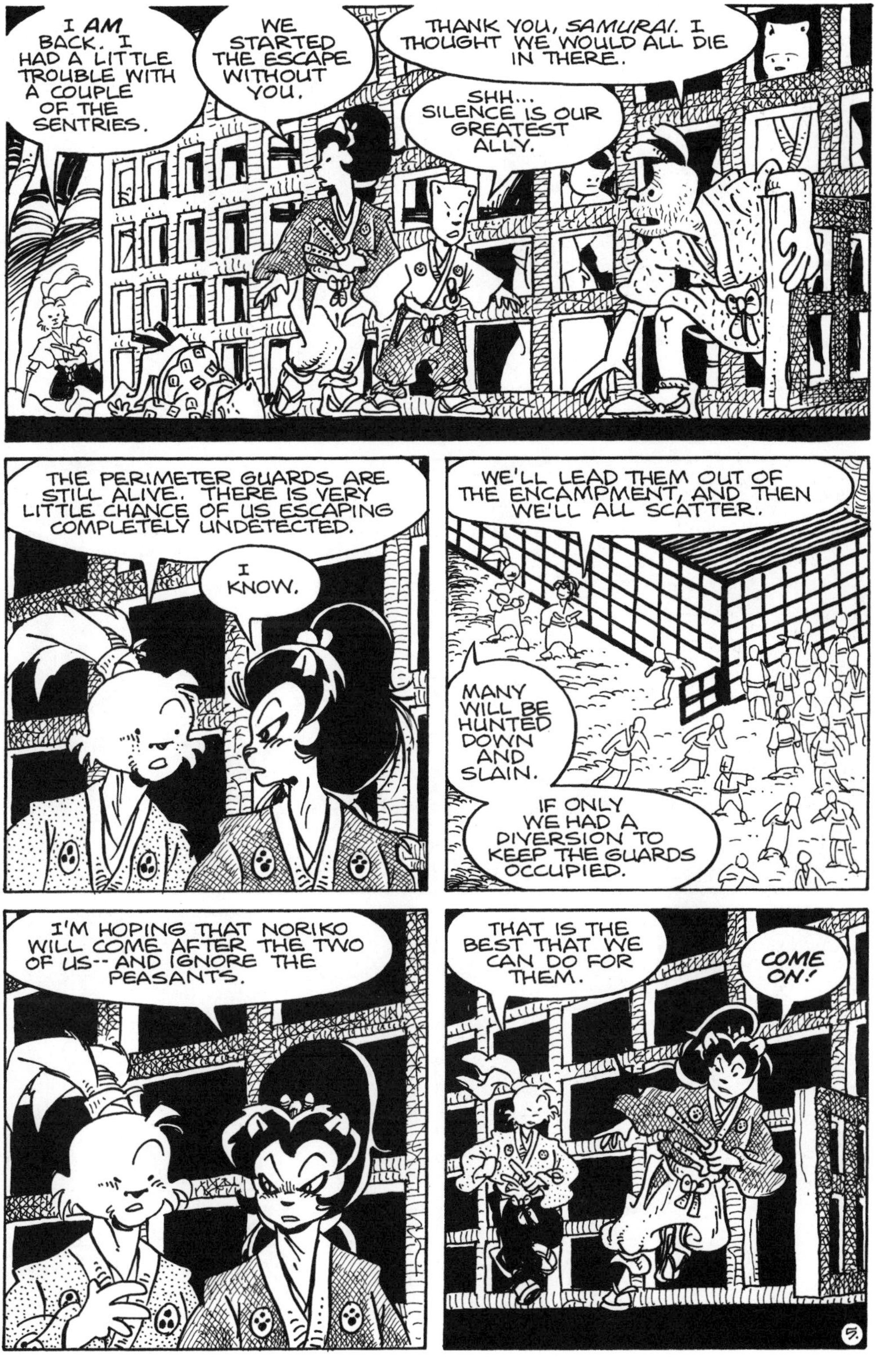
I AM BACK. I HAD A LITTLE TROUBLE WITH A COUPLE OF THE SENTRIES.
WE STARTED THE ESCAPE WITHOUT YOU.
THANK YOU, SAMURAI. I THOUGHT WE WOULD ALL DIE IN THERE.
SHH... SILENCE IS OUR GREATEST ALLY.
THE PERIMETER GUARDS ARE STILL ALIVE. THERE IS VERY LITTLE CHANCE OF US ESCAPING COMPLETELY UNDETECTED.
I KNOW.
WE'LL LEAD THEM OUT OF THE ENCAMPMENT, AND THEN WE'LL ALL SCATTER.
MANY WILL BE HUNTED DOWN AND SLAIN.
IF ONLY WE HAD A DIVERSION TO KEEP THE GUARDS OCCUPIED.
I'M HOPING THAT NORIKO WILL COME AFTER THE TWO OF US-- AND IGNORE THE PEASANTS.
THAT IS THE BEST THAT WE CAN DO FOR THEM.
COME ON!
5.

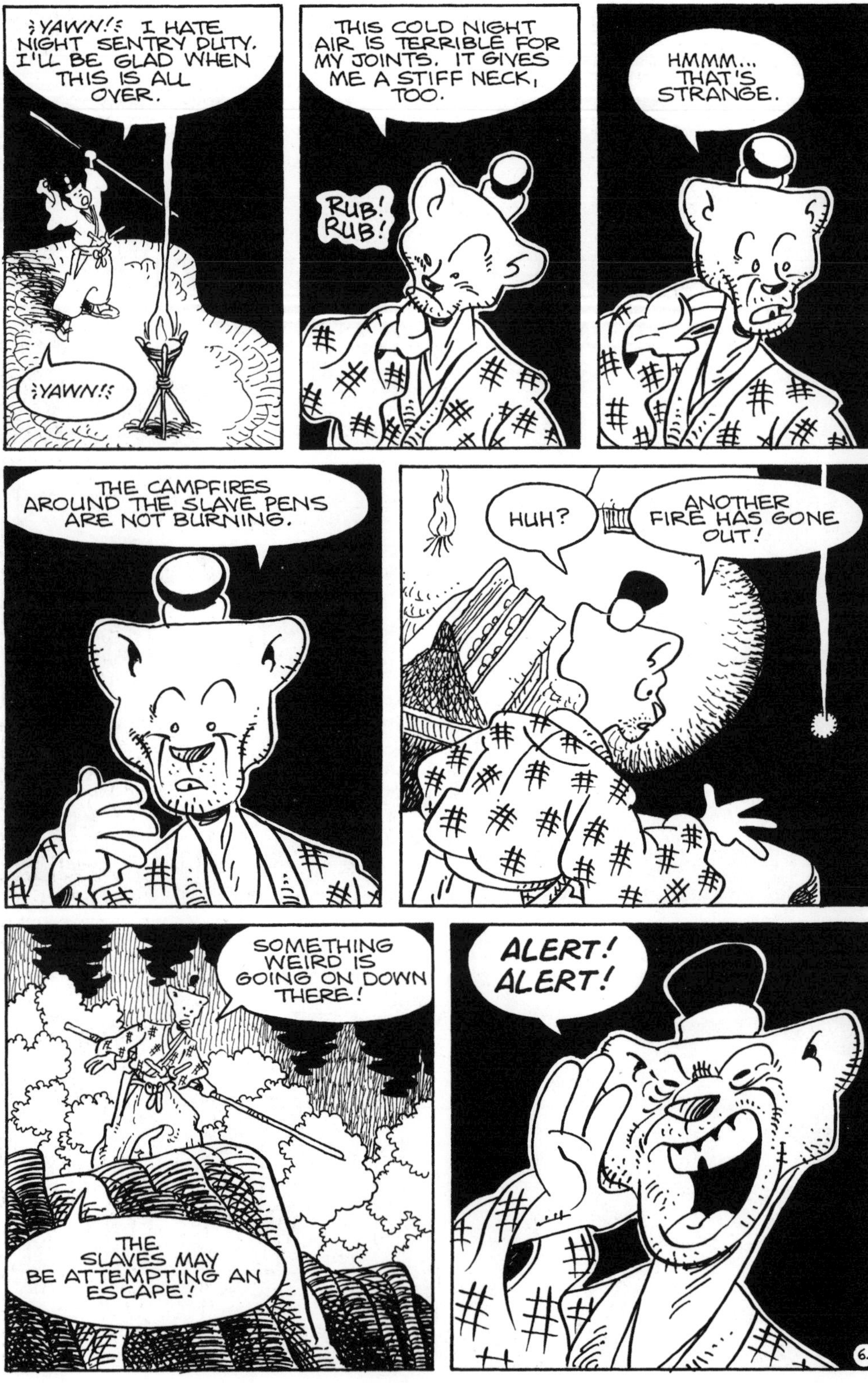

YAWN! I HATE NIGHT SENTRY DUTY. I'LL BE GLAD WHEN THIS IS ALL OVER.
YAWN!
THIS COLD NIGHT AIR IS TERRIBLE FOR MY JOINTS. IT GIVES ME A STIFF NECK, TOO.
RUB! RUB!
HMMM... THAT'S STRANGE.
THE CAMPFIRES AROUND THE SLAVE PENS ARE NOT BURNING.
HUH?
ANOTHER FIRE HAS GONE OUT!
SOMETHING WEIRD IS GOING ON DOWN THERE!
THE SLAVES MAY BE ATTEMPTING AN ESCAPE!
ALERT! ALERT!
6.

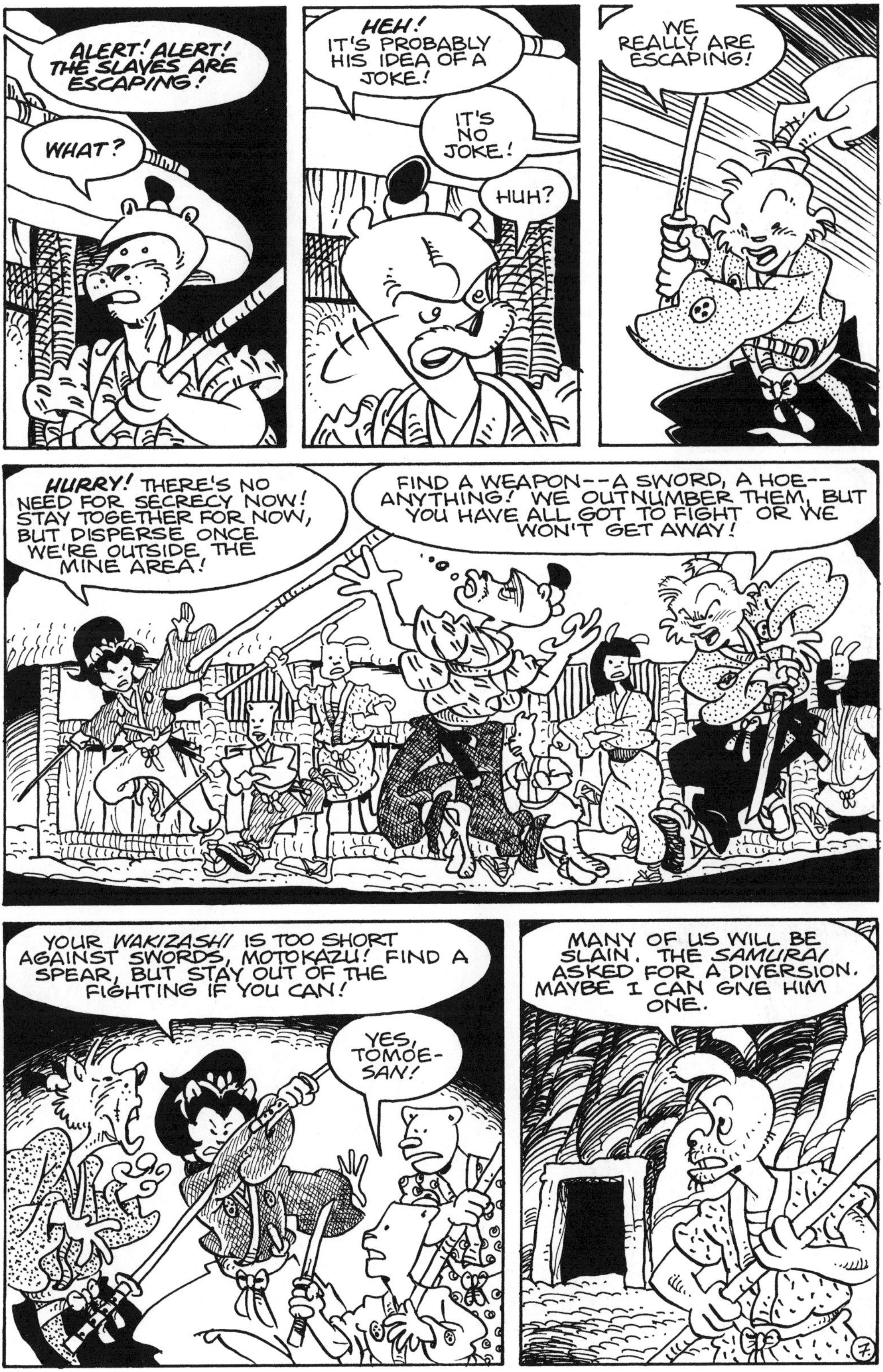
ALERT! ALERT! THE SLAVES ARE ESCAPING!
WHAT?
HEH! IT'S PROBABLY HIS IDEA OF A JOKE!
IT'S NO JOKE!
HUH?
WE REALLY ARE ESCAPING!
HURRY! THERE'S NO NEED FOR SECRECY NOW! STAY TOGETHER FOR NOW, BUT DISPERSE ONCE WE'RE OUTSIDE THE MINE AREA!
FIND A WEAPON--A SWORD, A HOE--ANYTHING! WE OUTNUMBER THEM, BUT YOU HAVE ALL GOT TO FIGHT OR WE WON'T GET AWAY!
YOUR WAKIZASHI IS TOO SHORT AGAINST SWORDS, MOTOKAZU! FIND A SPEAR, BUT STAY OUT OF THE FIGHTING IF YOU CAN!
YES, TOMOE-SAN!
MANY OF US WILL BE SLAIN. THE SAMURAI ASKED FOR A DIVERSION. MAYBE I CAN GIVE HIM ONE.
7.

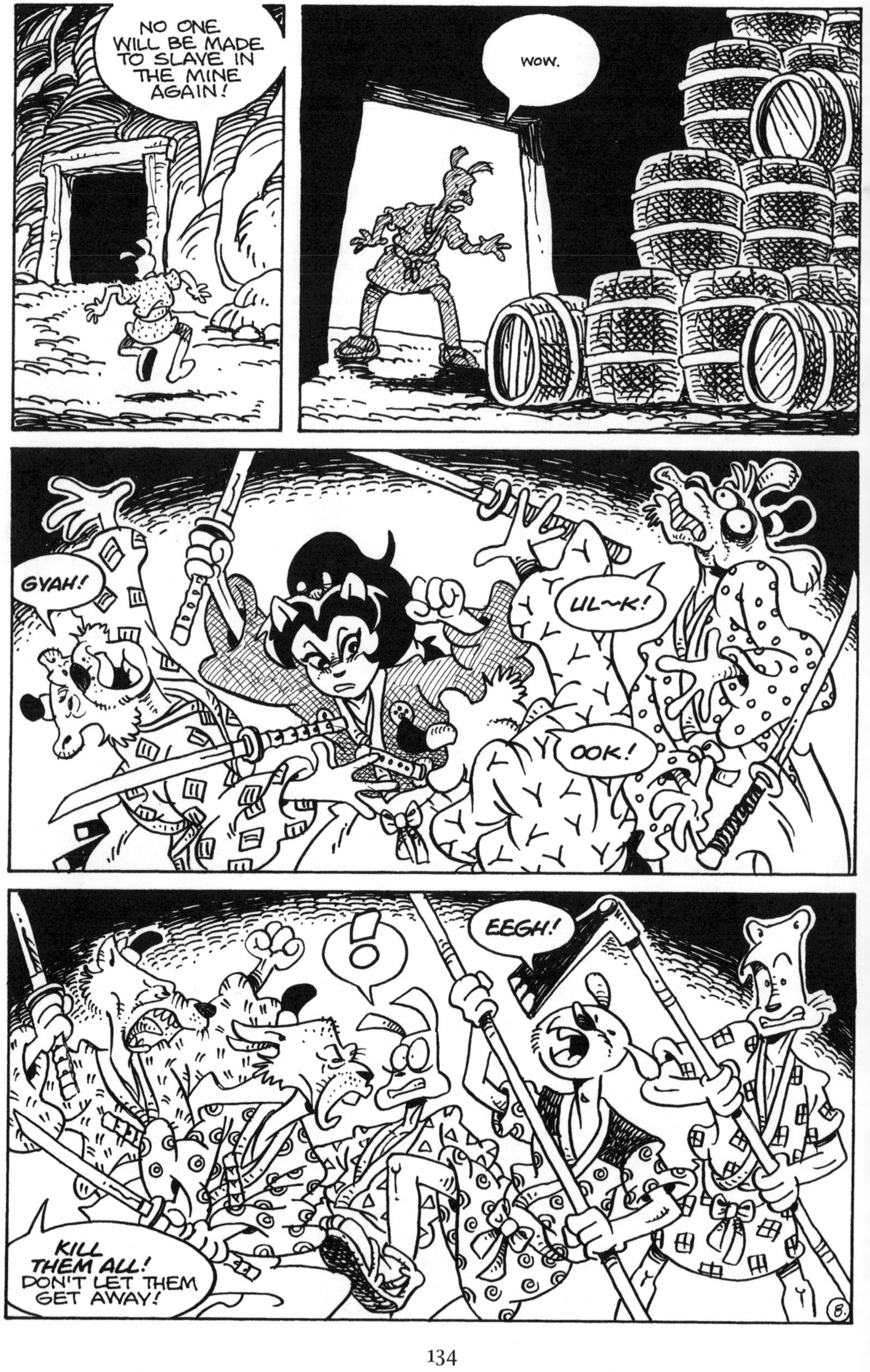
NO ONE WILL BE MADE TO SLAVE IN THE MINE AGAIN!
WOW.
GYAH!
UL~K!
OOK!
!
EEGH!
KILL THEM ALL! DON'T LET THEM GET AWAY!
8.

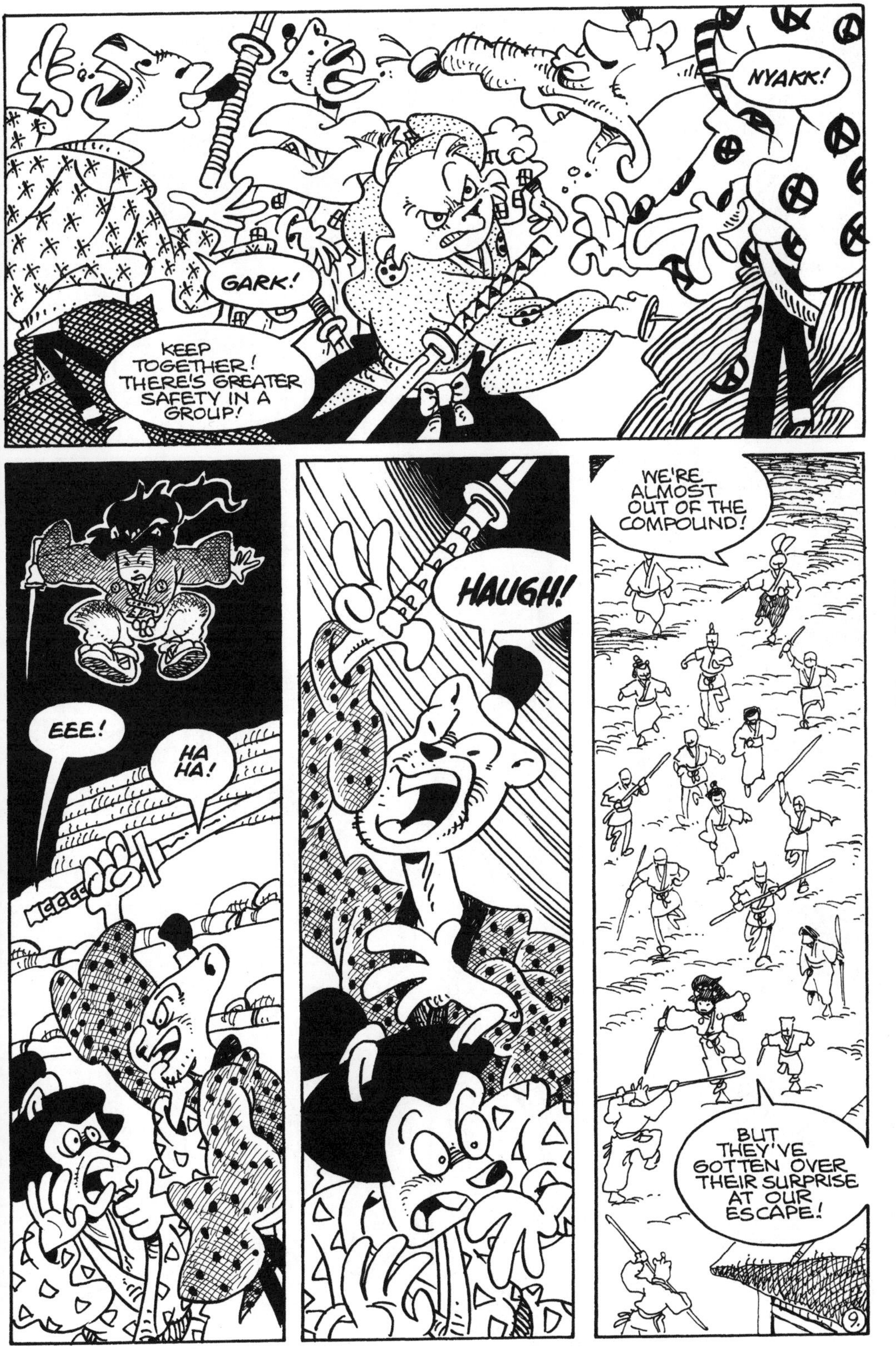
NYAKK!
GARK!
KEEP TOGETHER! THERE'S GREATER SAFETY IN A GROUP!
EEE!
HA HA!
HAUGH!
WE'RE ALMOST OUT OF THE COMPOUND!
BUT THEY'VE GOTTEN OVER THEIR SURPRISE AT OUR ESCAPE!
9.

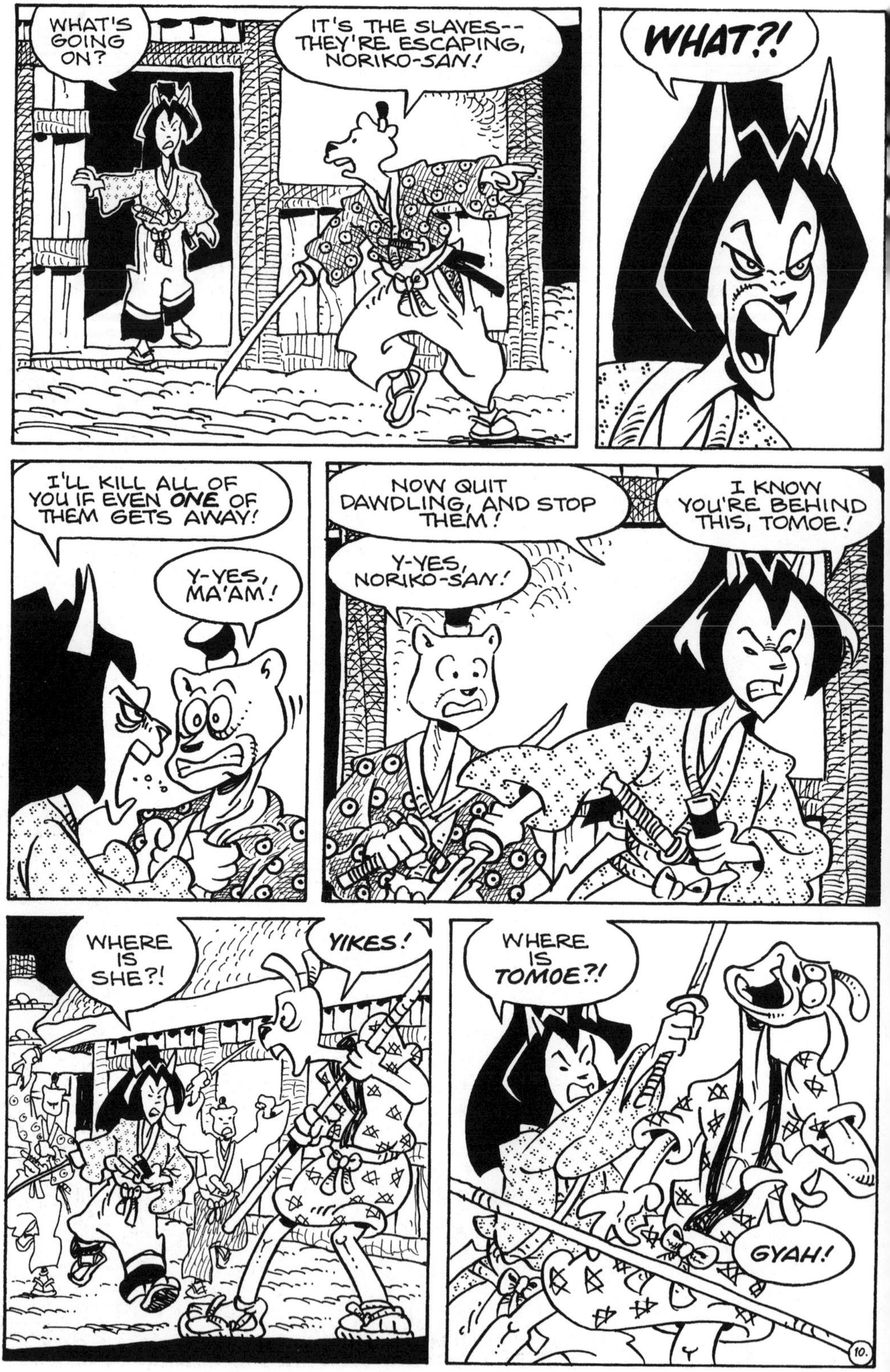

WHAT'S GOING ON?
IT'S THE SLAVES-- THEY'RE ESCAPING, NORIKO-SAN!
WHAT?!
I'LL KILL ALL OF YOU IF EVEN ONE OF THEM GETS AWAY!
Y-YES, MA'AM!
NOW QUIT DAWDLING, AND STOP THEM!
Y-YES, NORIKO-SAN!
I KNOW YOU'RE BEHIND THIS, TOMOE!
WHERE IS SHE?!
YIKES!
WHERE IS TOMOE?!
GYAH!
10.

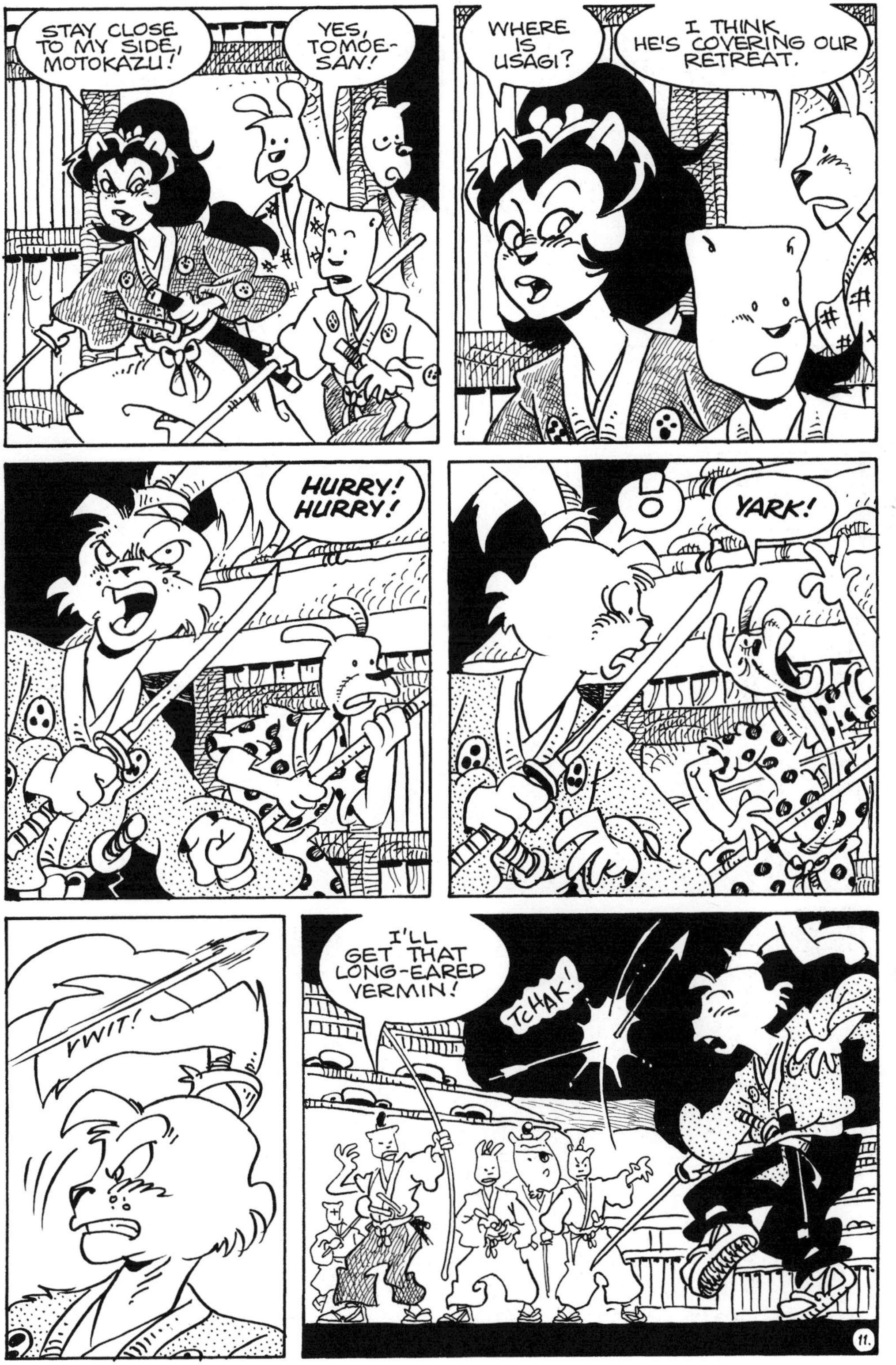

STAY CLOSE TO MY SIDE, MOTOKAZU!
YES, TOMOE-SAN!
WHERE IS USAGI?
I THINK HE'S COVERING OUR RETREAT.
HURRY! HURRY!
!
YARK!
YWIT!
I'LL GET THAT LONG-EARED VERMIN!
TCHAK!
11.

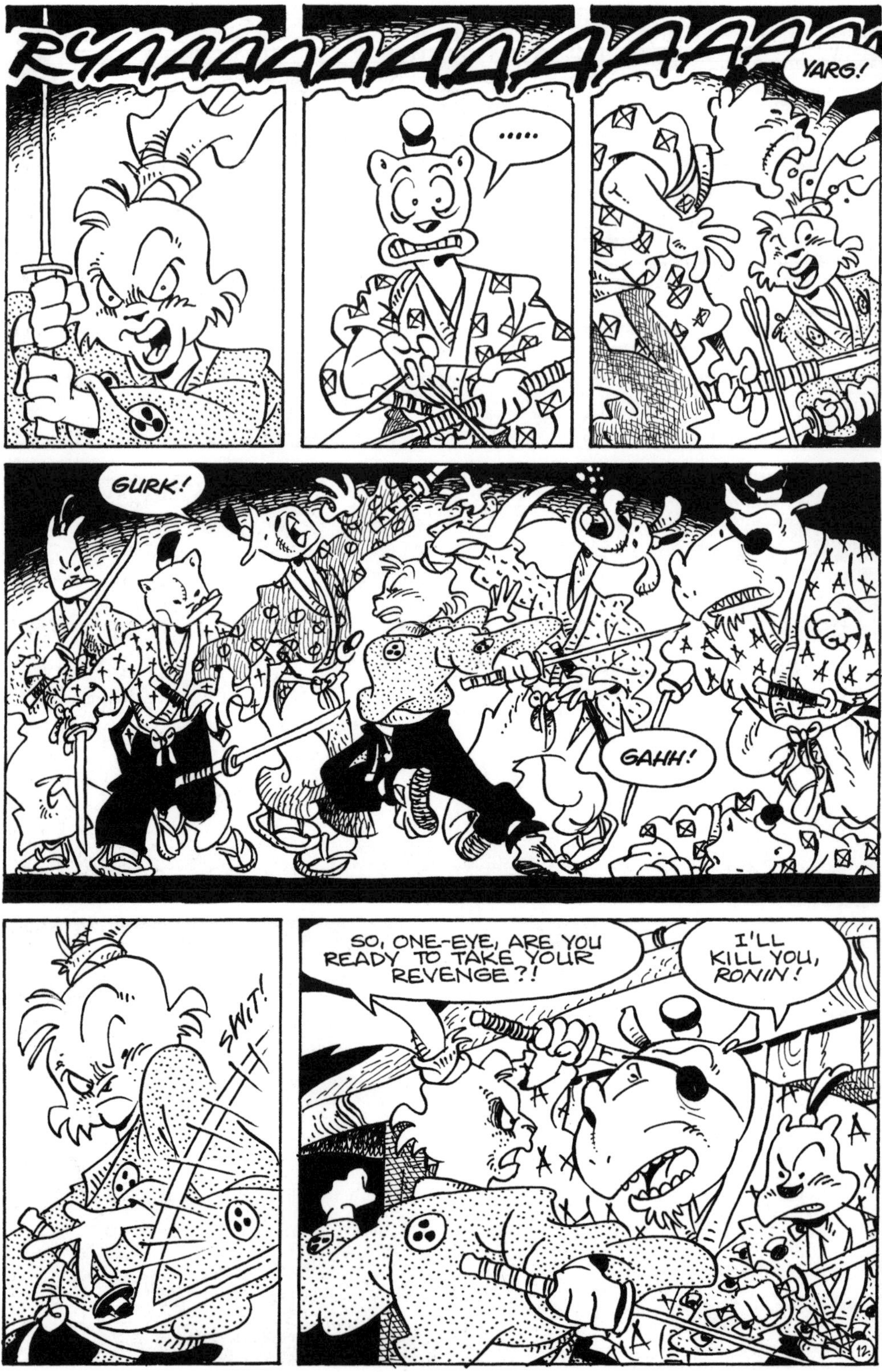
RYAAAAAAAAAAAAAA
......
YARG!
GURK!
GAHH!
SWIT!
SO, ONE-EYE, ARE YOU READY TO TAKE YOUR REVENGE?!
I'LL KILL YOU, *RONIN*!
12.

WE'LL NOT DIE IN THE MINE.

SOON, THERE WON'T EVEN BE A MINE.

AND ITS DESTRUCTION WILL DISTRACT THE GUARDS SO WE CAN GET AWAY.

I NEED A TORCH.

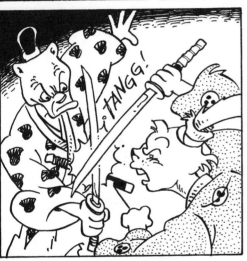

iTANGG!

OOK!

HOLD STILL, YOU!

HEY--! WATCH OUT! ARE YOU TRYING TO KILL ME?!

STOP HIDING BEHIND THE OTHERS, ONE-EYE!

ULK!

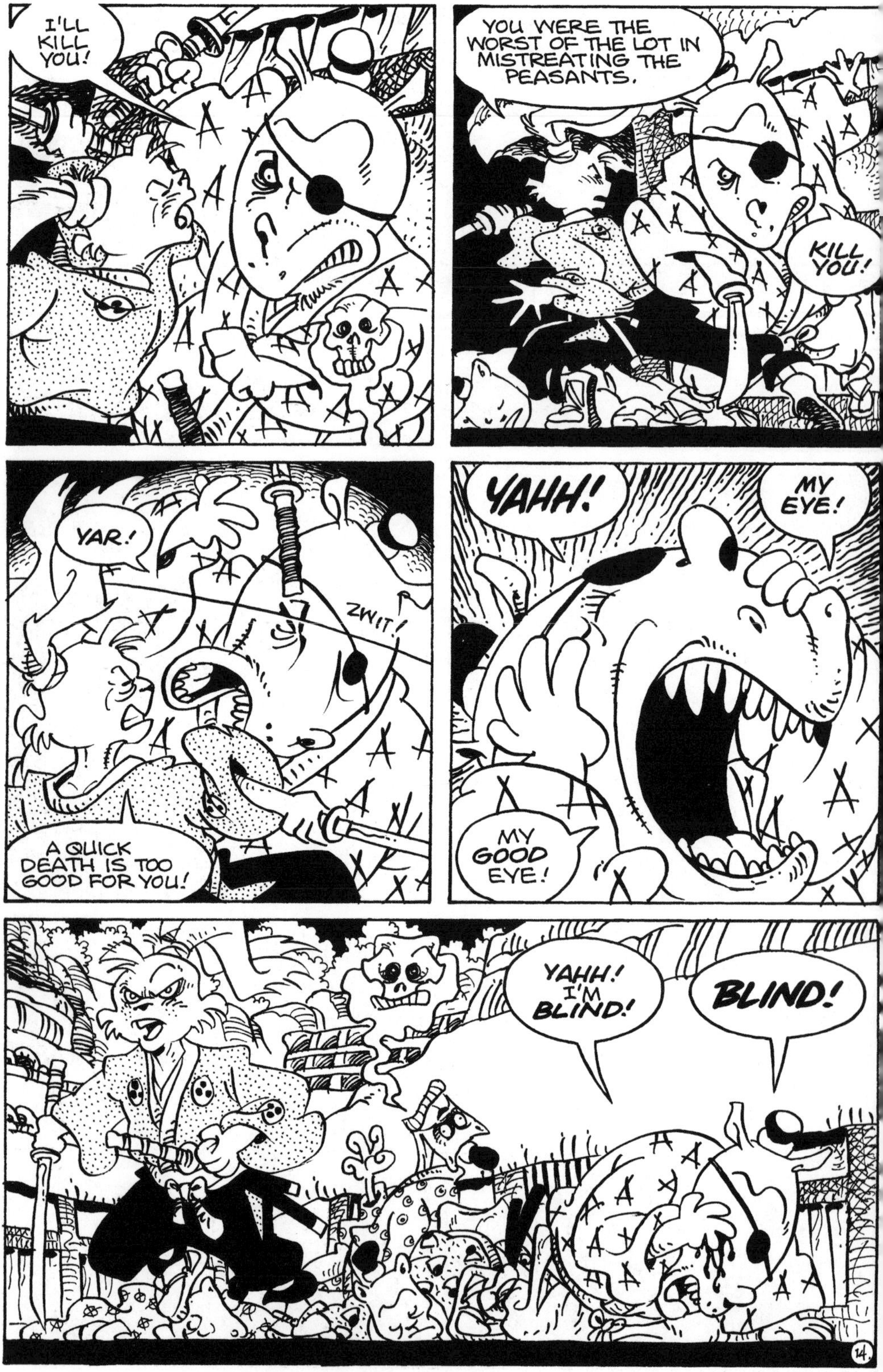
I'LL KILL YOU!
YOU WERE THE WORST OF THE LOT IN MISTREATING THE PEASANTS.
KILL YOU!
YAR!
ZWIT!
A QUICK DEATH IS TOO GOOD FOR YOU!
YAHH!
MY EYE!
MY GOOD EYE!
YAHH! I'M BLIND!
BLIND!
14.

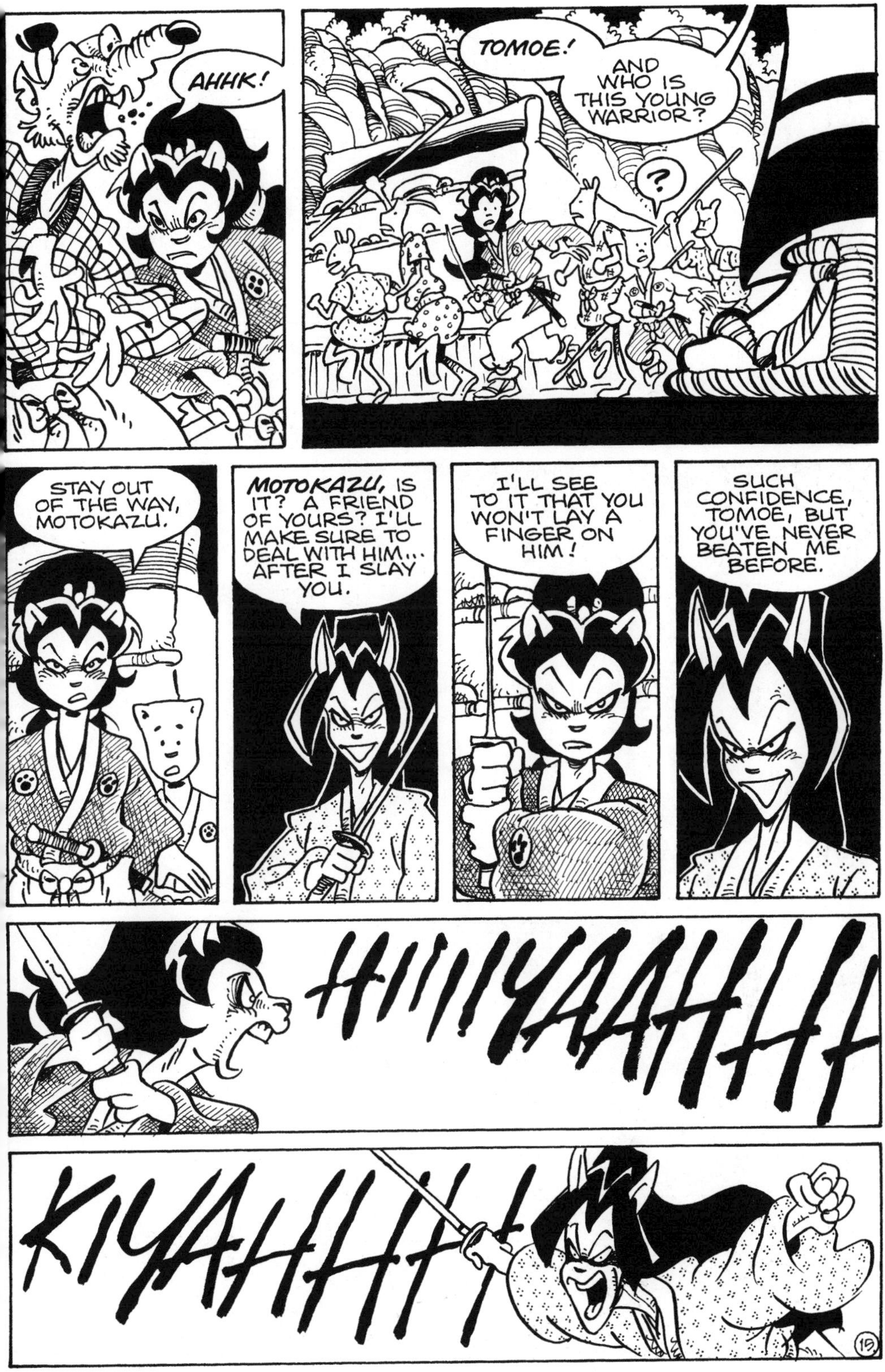
AHHK!
TOMOE!
AND WHO IS THIS YOUNG WARRIOR?
?
STAY OUT OF THE WAY, MOTOKAZU.
MOTOKAZU, IS IT? A FRIEND OF YOURS? I'LL MAKE SURE TO DEAL WITH HIM... AFTER I SLAY YOU.
I'LL SEE TO IT THAT YOU WON'T LAY A FINGER ON HIM!
SUCH CONFIDENCE, TOMOE, BUT YOU'VE NEVER BEATEN ME BEFORE.
HIIIIYAAHHH
KIYAHHHH
15

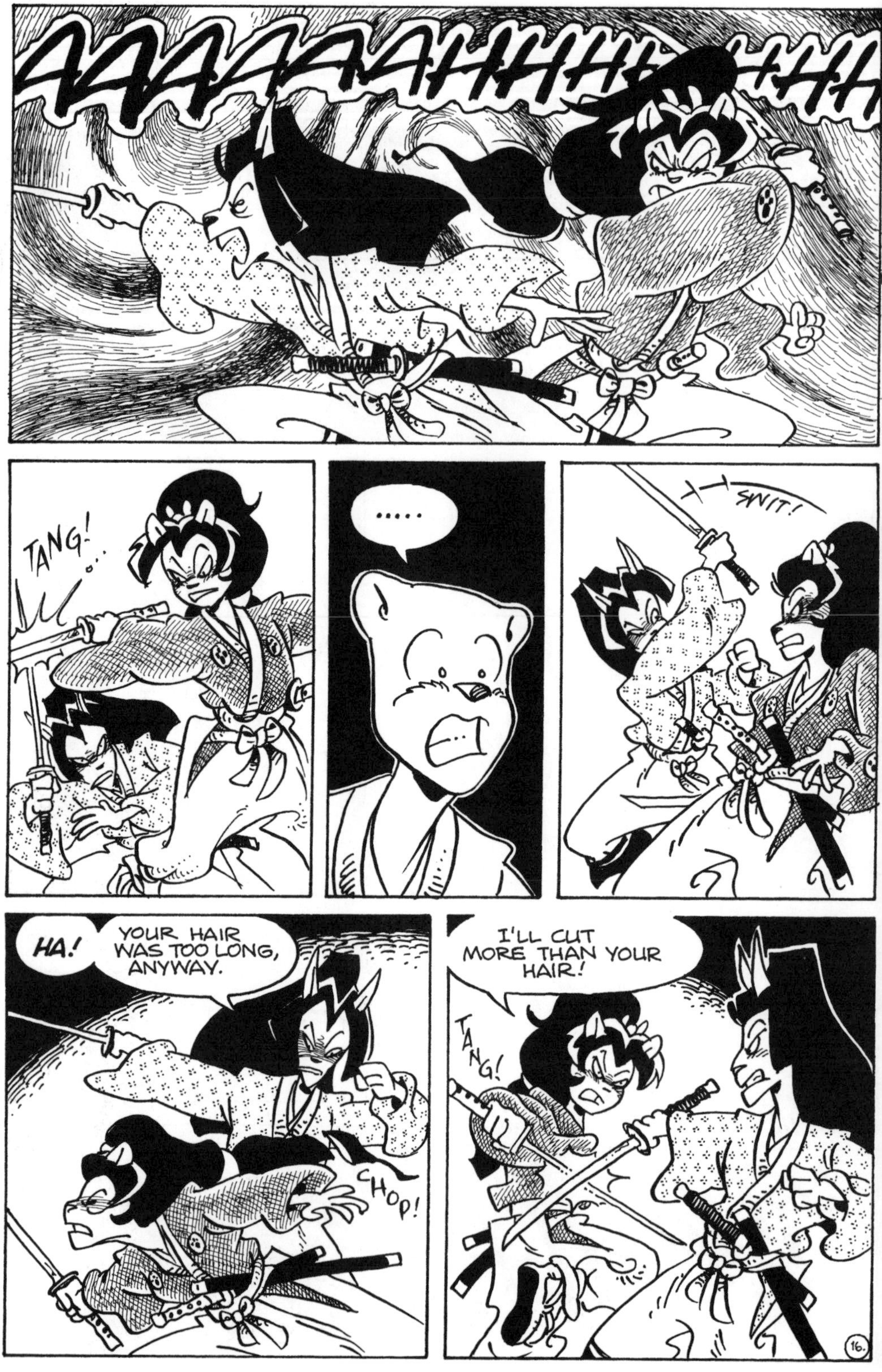
AAAAAAAHHHHHHHHHHH
TANG!
.....
SNIT!
HA!
YOUR HAIR WAS TOO LONG, ANYWAY.
CHOP!
I'LL CUT MORE THAN YOUR HAIR!
TANG!
16.

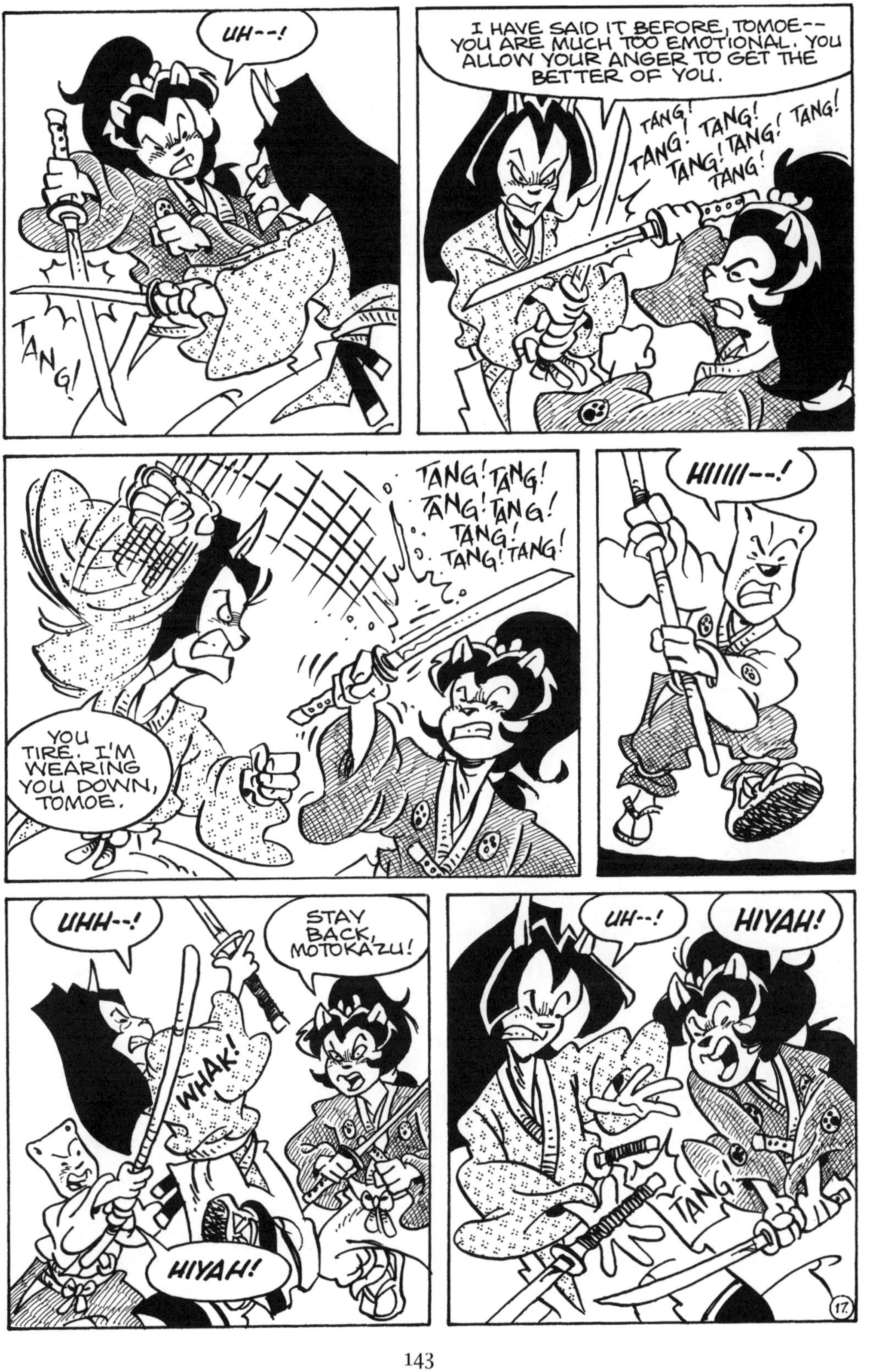
UH--!
TANG!
I HAVE SAID IT BEFORE, TOMOE-- YOU ARE MUCH TOO EMOTIONAL. YOU ALLOW YOUR ANGER TO GET THE BETTER OF YOU.
TANG! TANG! TANG! TANG! TANG! TANG! TANG! TANG!
TANG! TANG! TANG! TANG! TANG! TANG! TANG!
YOU TIRE. I'M WEARING YOU DOWN, TOMOE.
HIIIII--!
UHH--!
STAY BACK, MOTOKAZU!
WHAK!
HIYAH!
UH--!
HIYAH!
TANG!
17

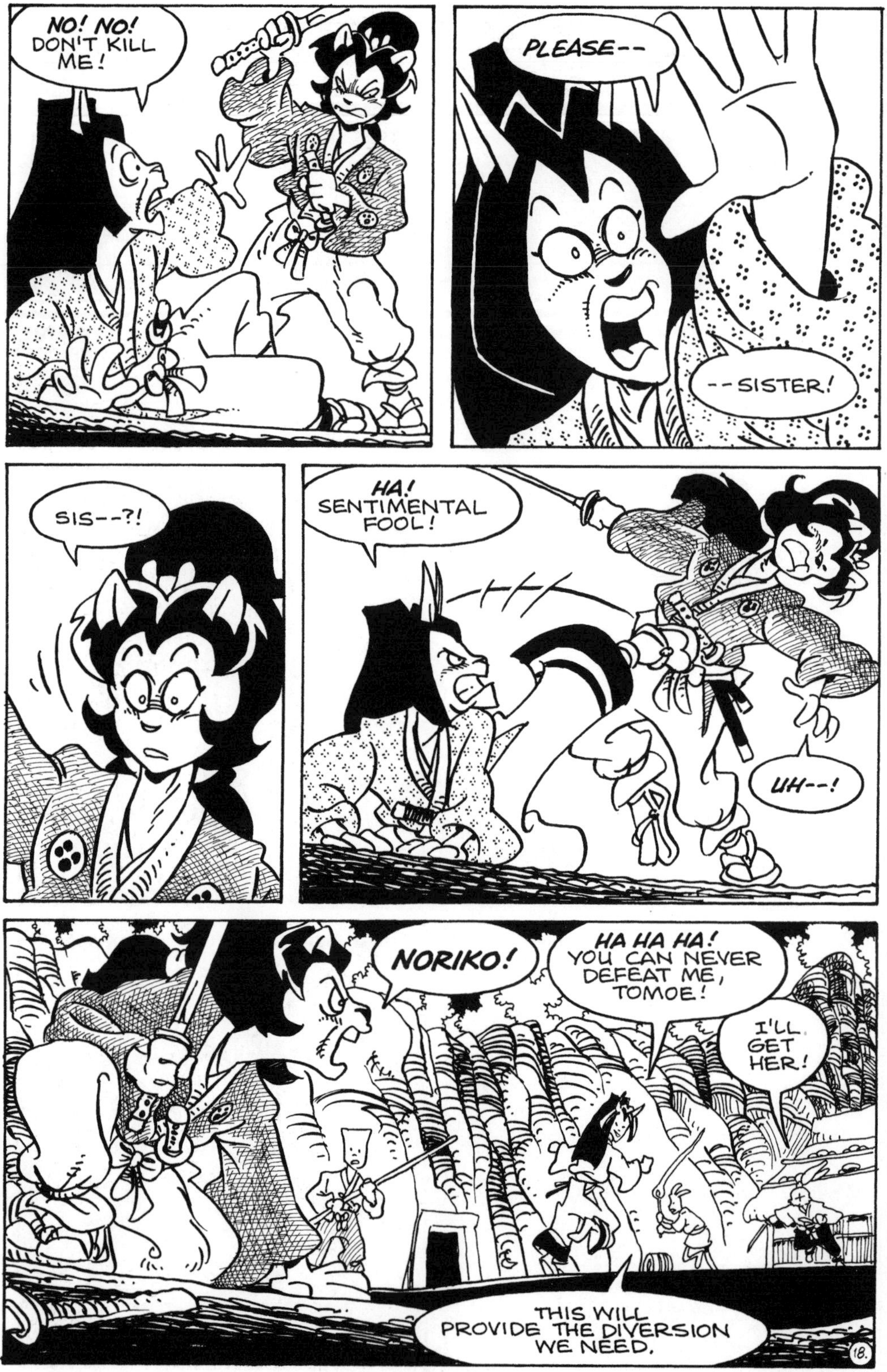

NO! NO! DON'T KILL ME!
PLEASE--
--SISTER!
SIS--?!
HA! SENTIMENTAL FOOL!
UH--!
NORIKO!
HA HA HA! YOU CAN NEVER DEFEAT ME, TOMOE!
I'LL GET HER!
THIS WILL PROVIDE THE DIVERSION WE NEED.
18.

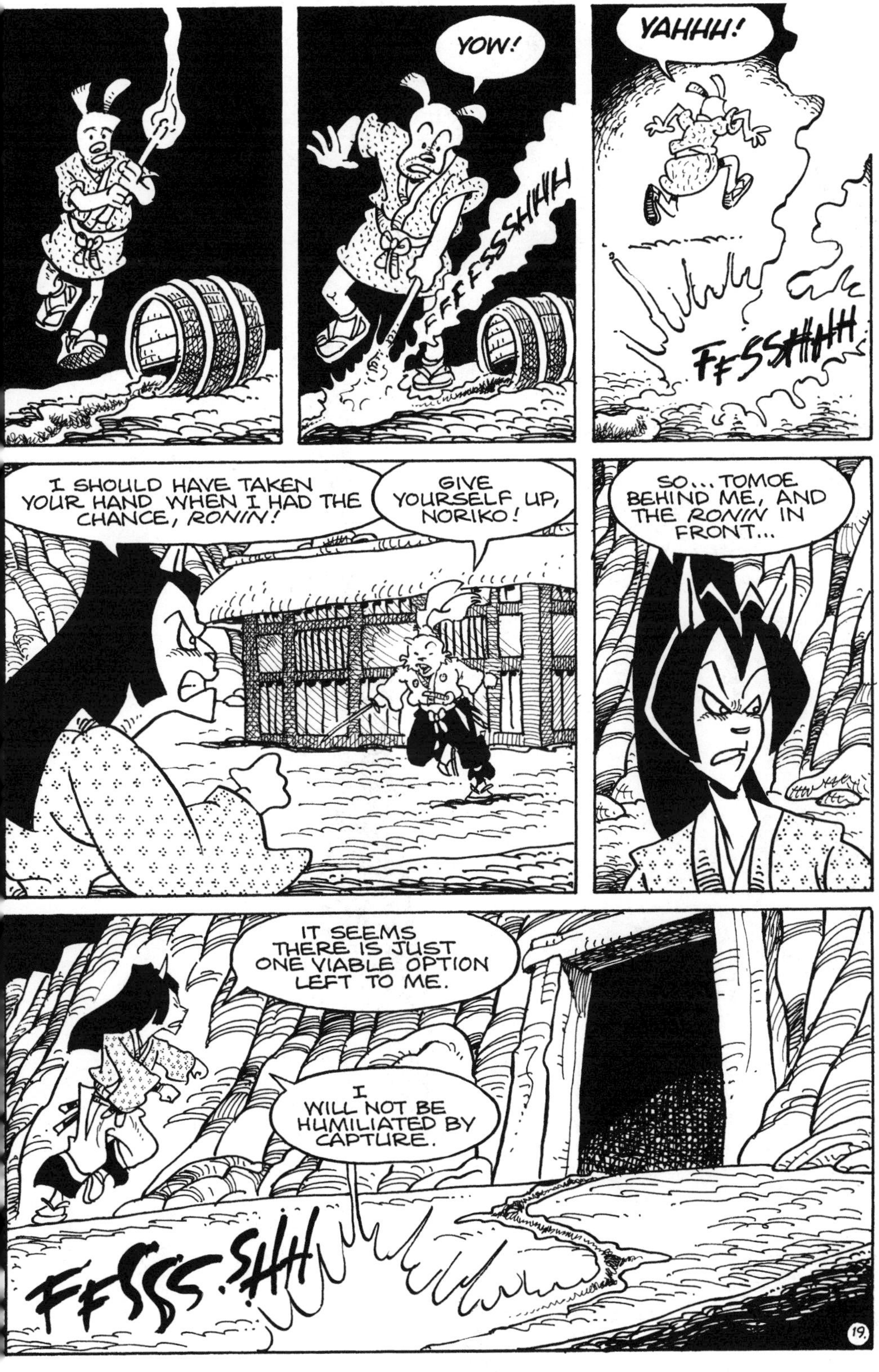
YOW!
FFFFSSSHHH
YAHHH!
FFSSHHHH
I SHOULD HAVE TAKEN YOUR HAND WHEN I HAD THE CHANCE, *RONIN*!
GIVE YOURSELF UP, NORIKO!
SO...TOMOE BEHIND ME, AND THE *RONIN* IN FRONT...
IT SEEMS THERE IS JUST ONE VIABLE OPTION LEFT TO ME.
I WILL NOT BE HUMILIATED BY CAPTURE.
FFSSS.SHH
19.

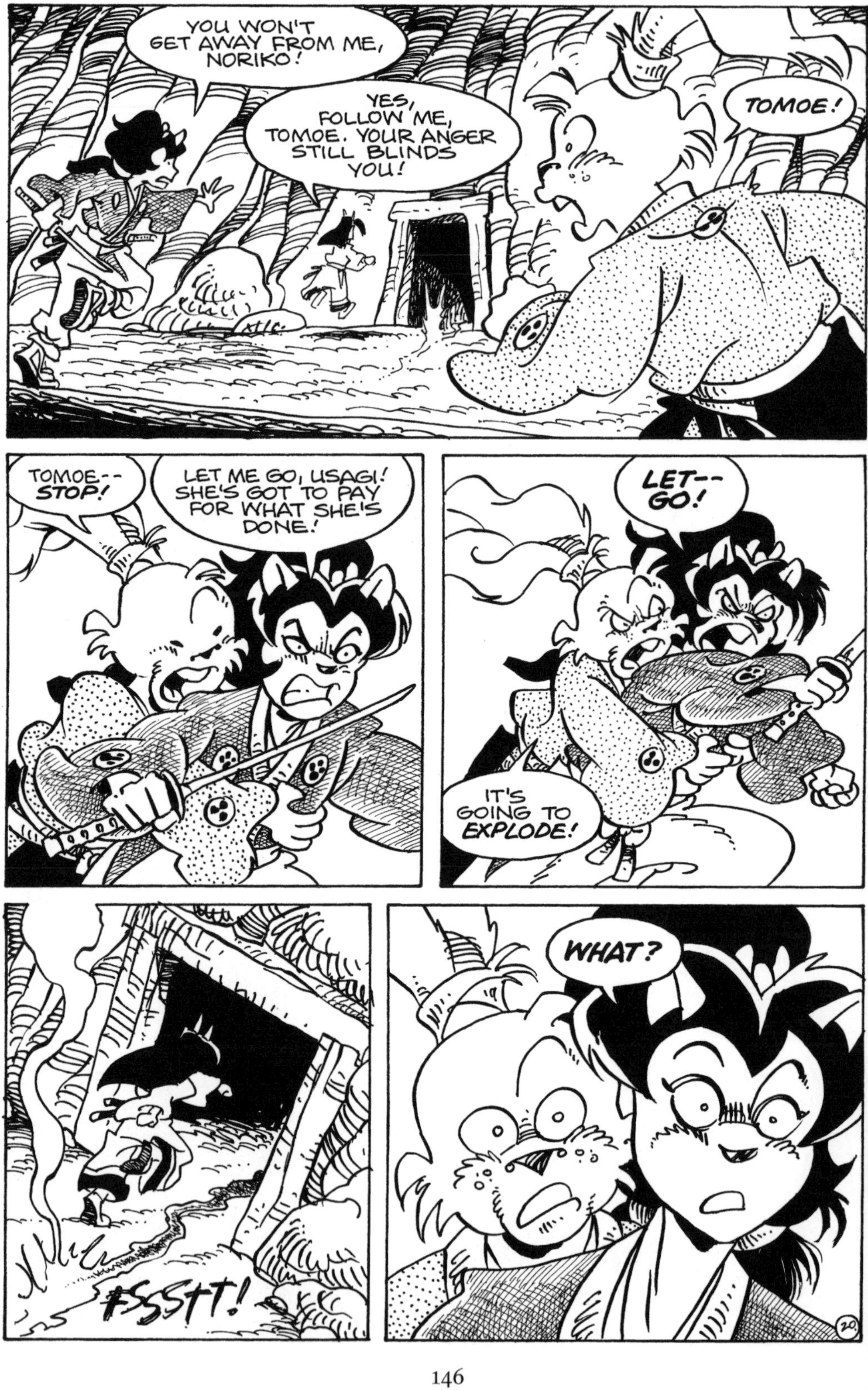
YOU WON'T GET AWAY FROM ME, NORIKO!
YES, FOLLOW ME, TOMOE. YOUR ANGER STILL BLINDS YOU!
TOMOE!
TOMOE-- STOP!
LET ME GO, USAGI! SHE'S GOT TO PAY FOR WHAT SHE'S DONE!
LET-- GO!
IT'S GOING TO EXPLODE!
FSSTT!
WHAT?
20

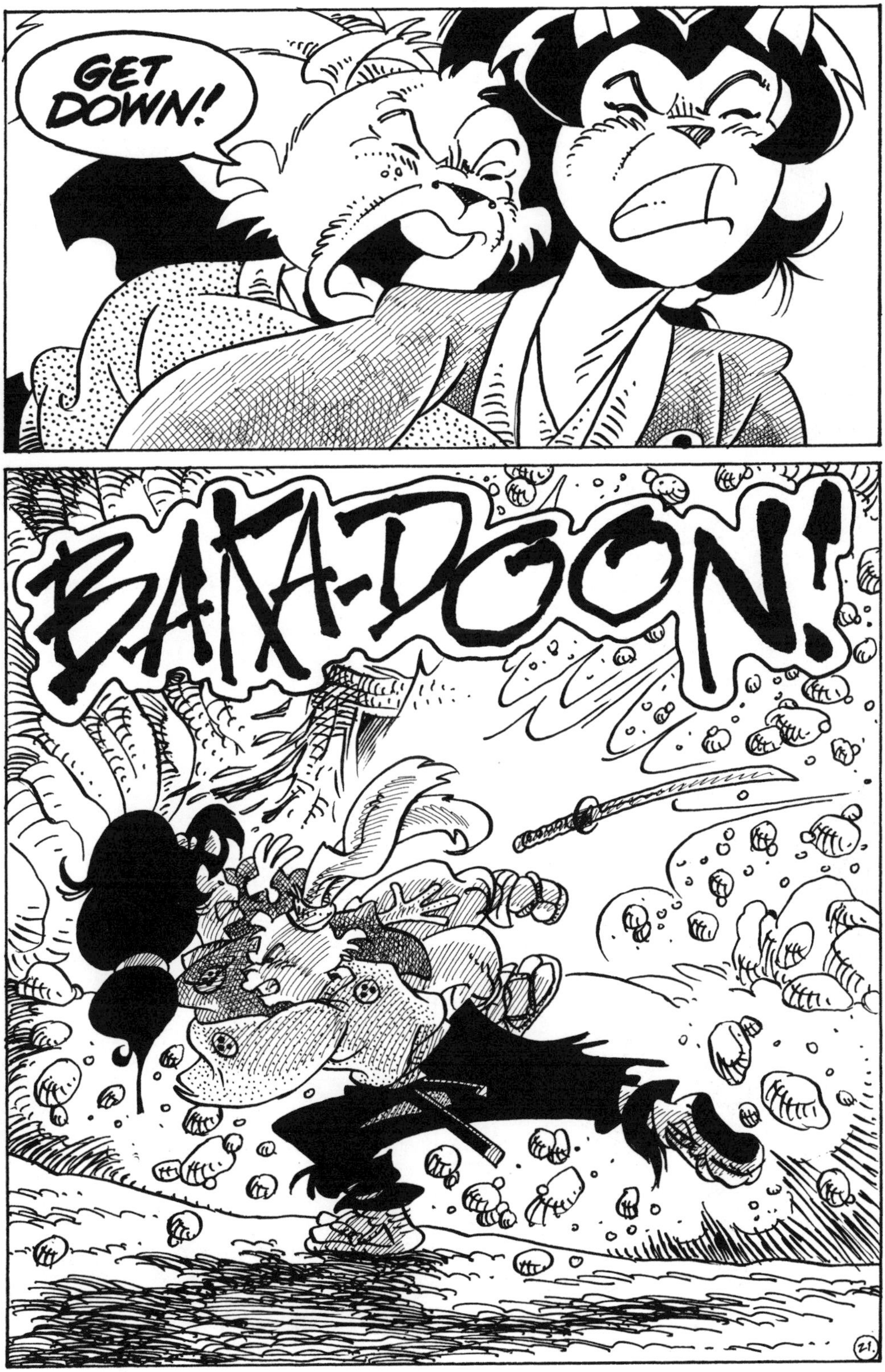
GET DOWN!
BAKA-DOON!
21.

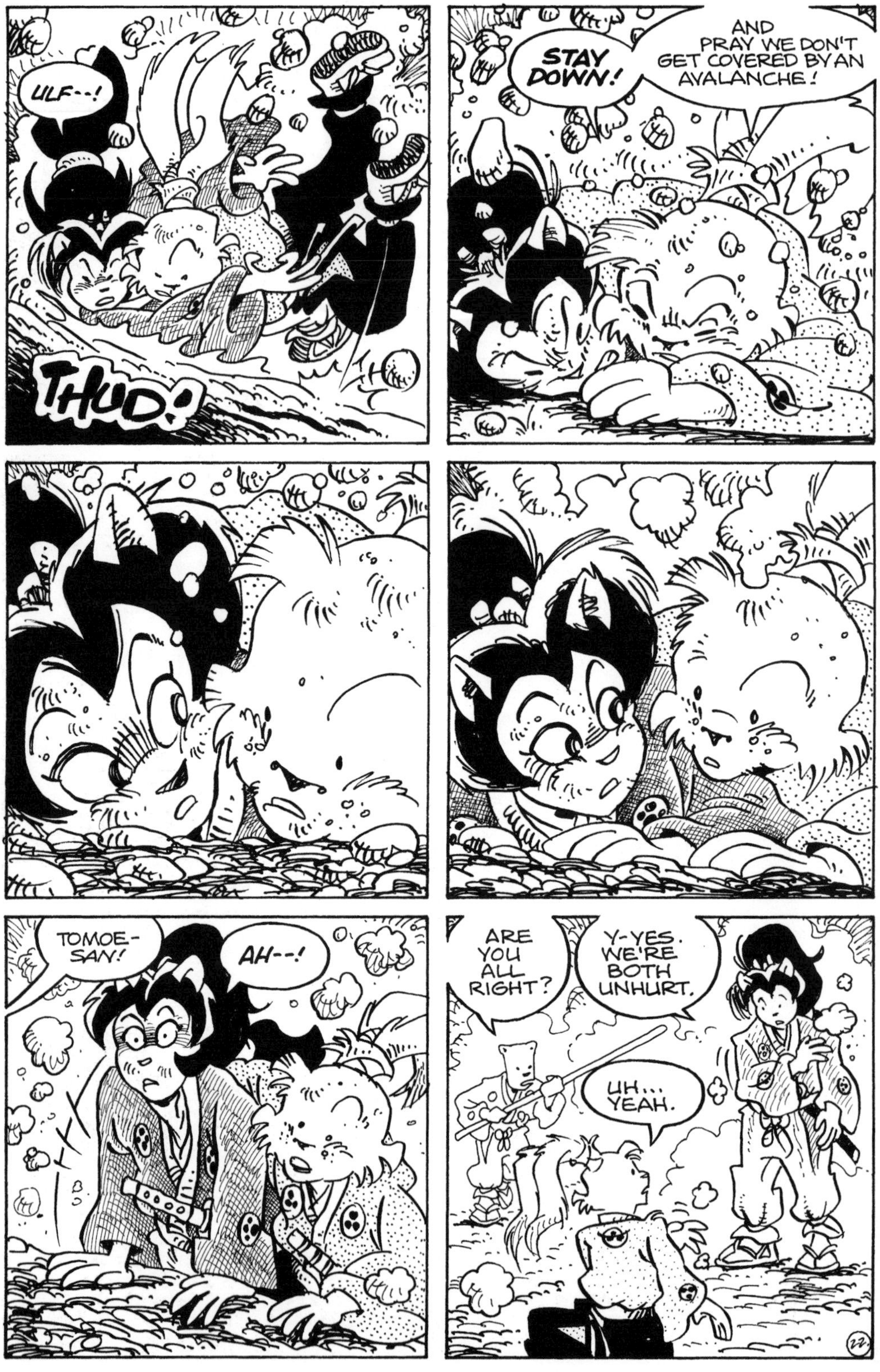
ULF--!
THUD!
STAY DOWN!
AND PRAY WE DON'T GET COVERED BY AN AVALANCHE!
TOMOE-SAN!
AH--!
ARE YOU ALL RIGHT?
Y-YES. WE'RE BOTH UNHURT.
UH... YEAH.
22

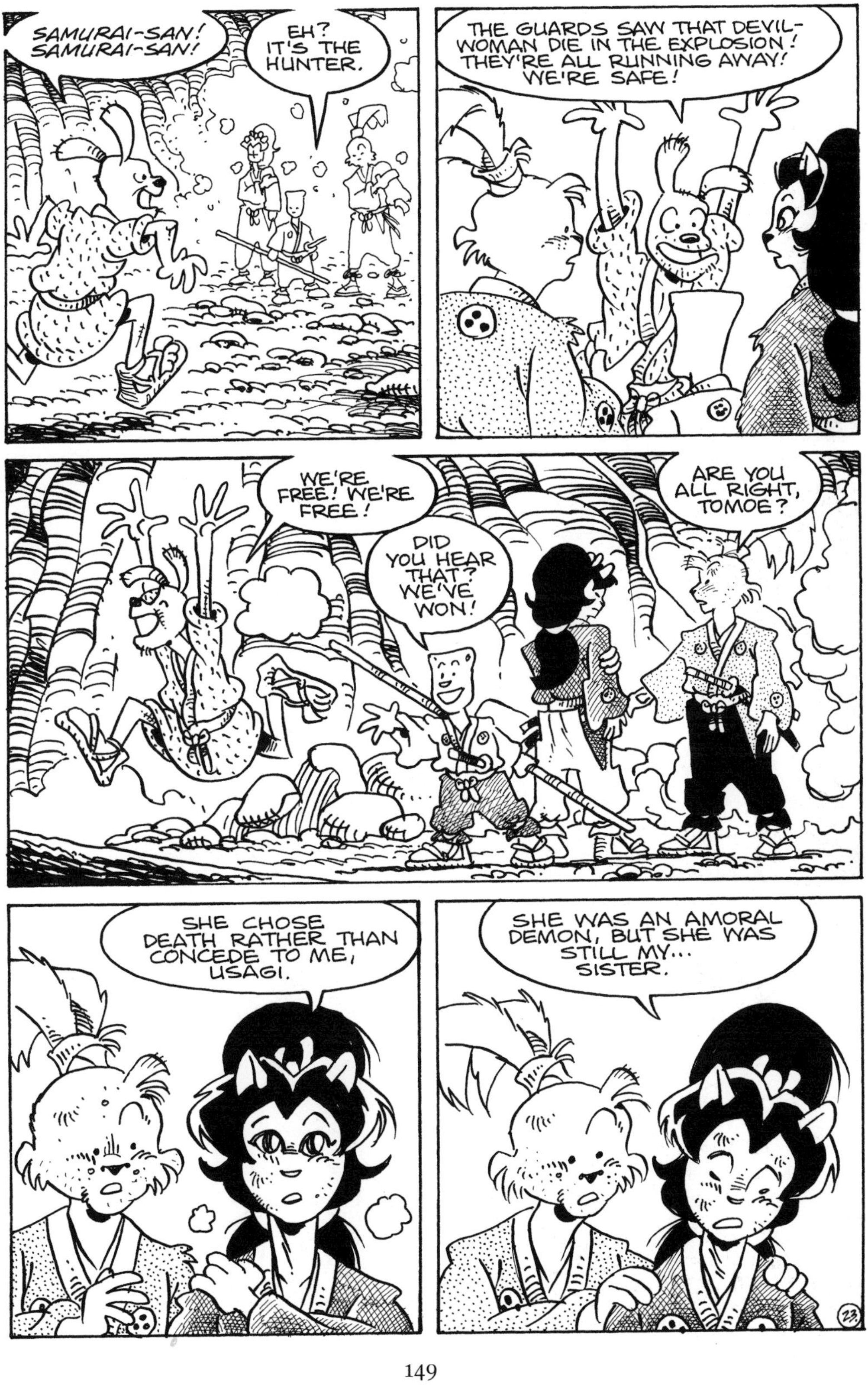

SAMURAI-SAN! SAMURAI-SAN!
EH? IT'S THE HUNTER.
THE GUARDS SAW THAT DEVIL-WOMAN DIE IN THE EXPLOSION! THEY'RE ALL RUNNING AWAY! WE'RE SAFE!
WE'RE FREE! WE'RE FREE!
DID YOU HEAR THAT? WE'VE WON!
ARE YOU ALL RIGHT, TOMOE?
SHE CHOSE DEATH RATHER THAN CONCEDE TO ME, USAGI.
SHE WAS AN AMORAL DEMON, BUT SHE WAS STILL MY... SISTER.
23

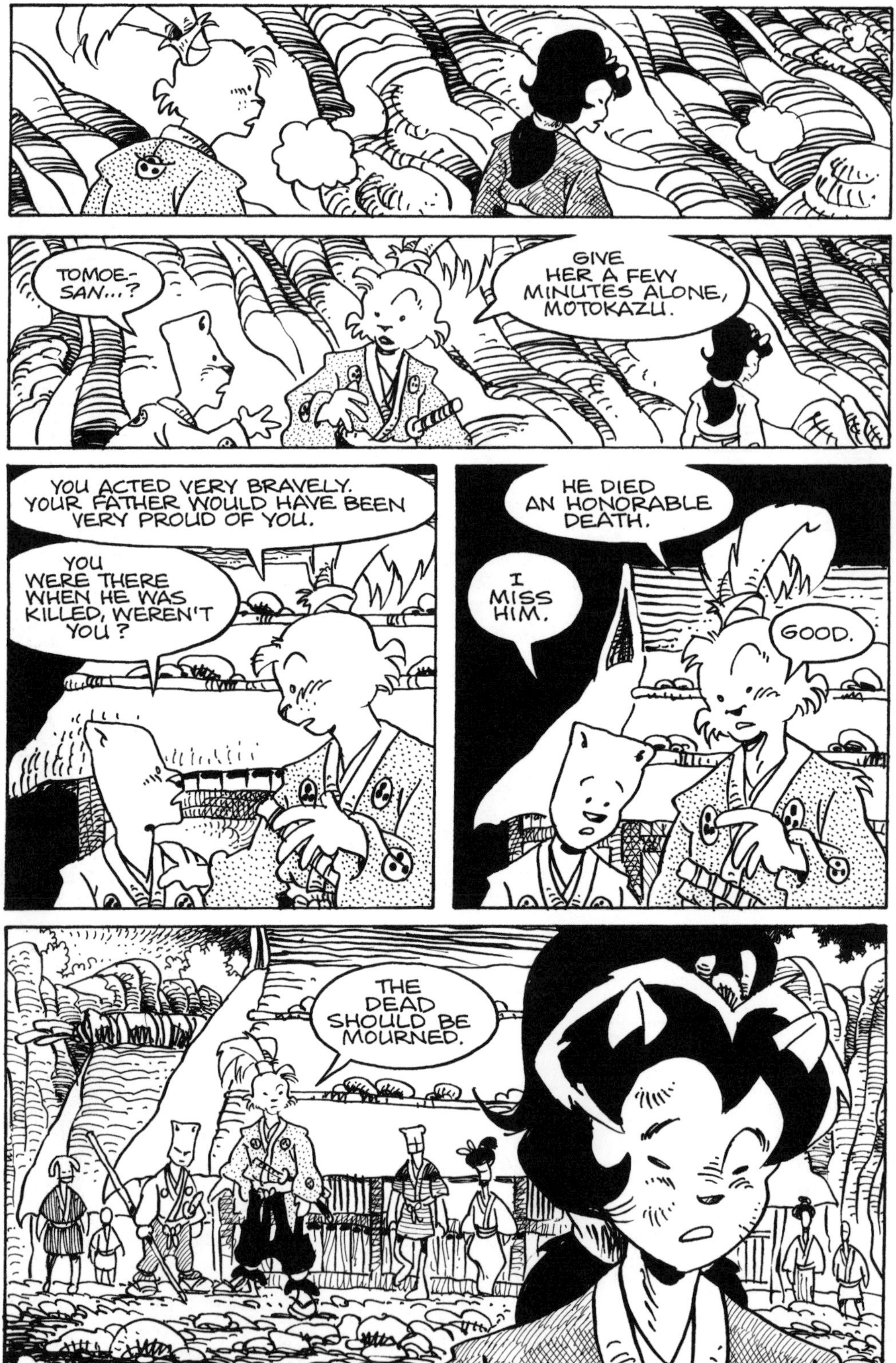
TOMOE-SAN...?
GIVE HER A FEW MINUTES ALONE, MOTOKAZU.
YOU ACTED VERY BRAVELY. YOUR FATHER WOULD HAVE BEEN VERY PROUD OF YOU.
YOU WERE THERE WHEN HE WAS KILLED, WEREN'T YOU?
HE DIED AN HONORABLE DEATH.
I MISS HIM.
GOOD.
THE DEAD SHOULD BE MOURNED.

THE TREASURE of the MOTHER of MOUNTAINS

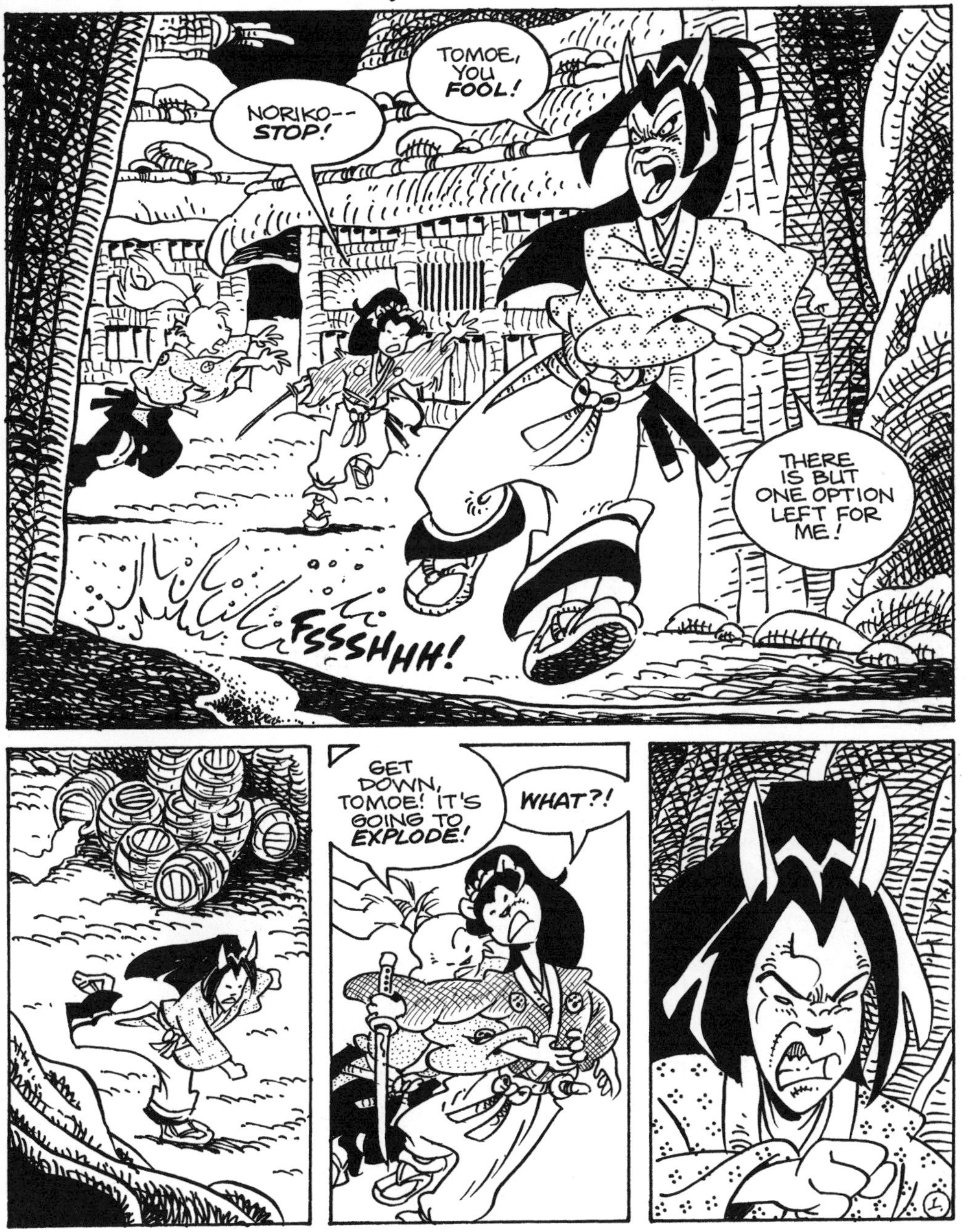
NORIKO--
STOP!
TOMOE, YOU FOOL!
THERE IS BUT ONE OPTION LEFT FOR ME!
FSSSHHH!
GET DOWN, TOMOE! IT'S GOING TO EXPLODE!
WHAT?!
1

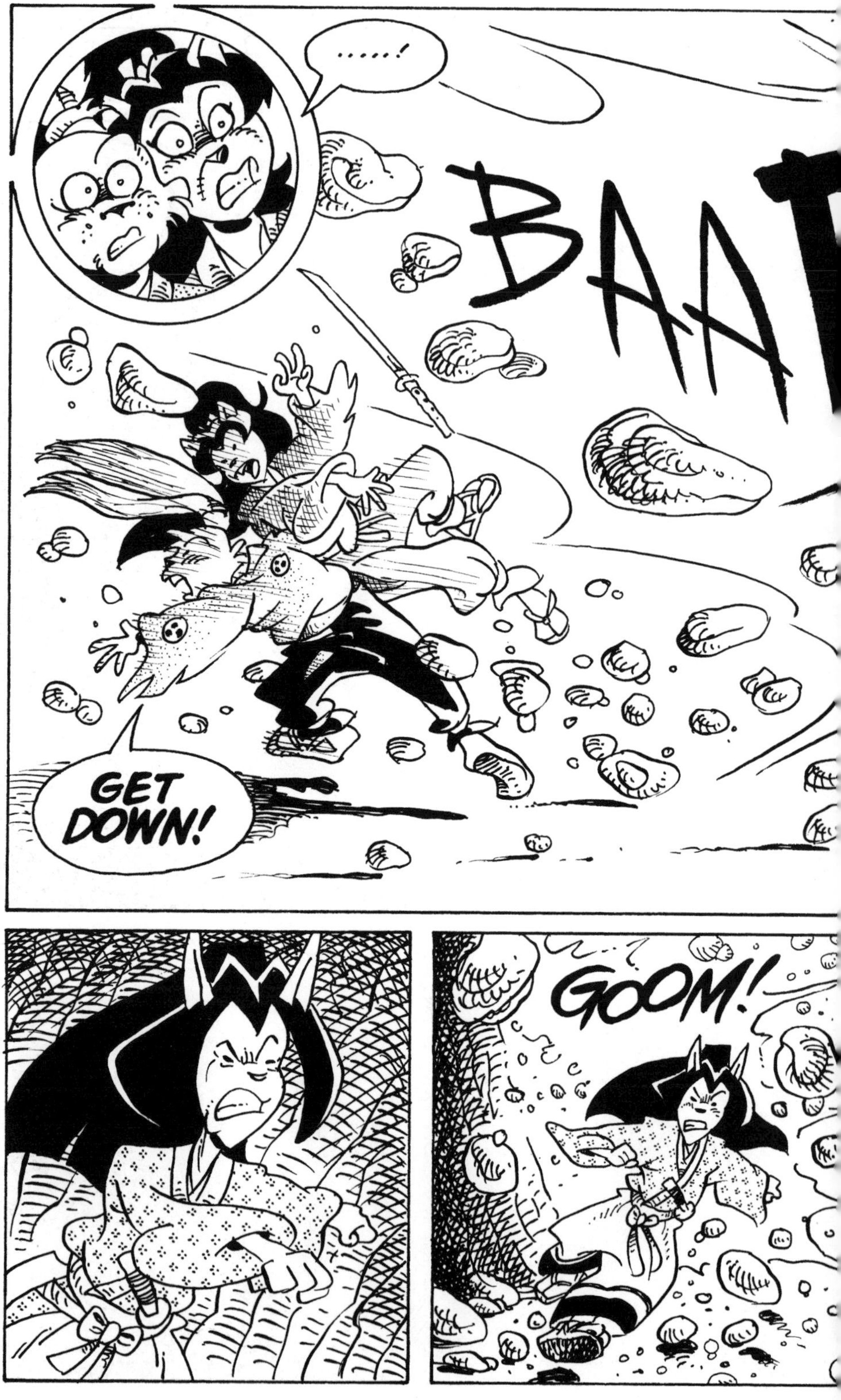

......!
BAA
GET DOWN!
GOOM!

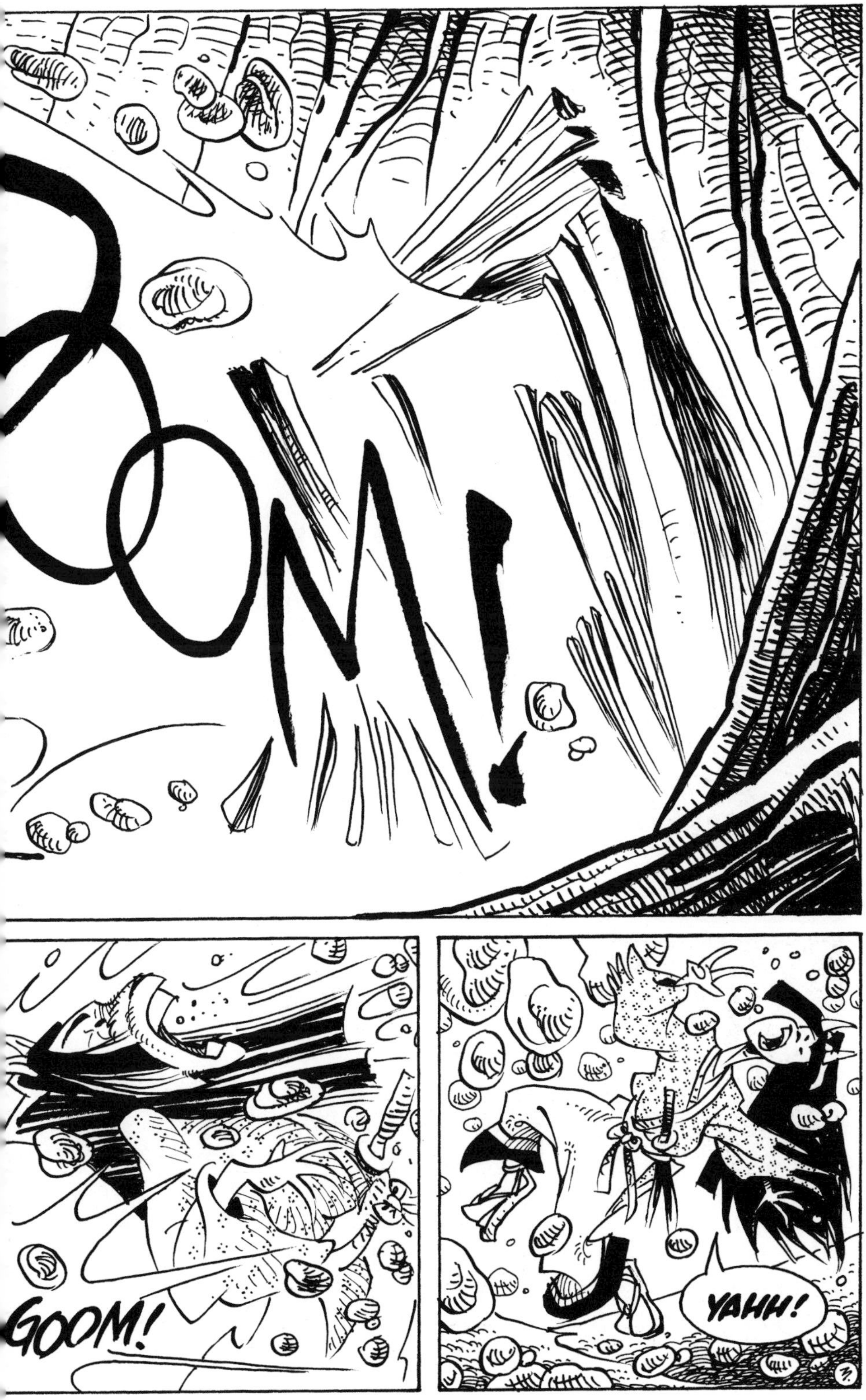
GOOM!
YAHH!

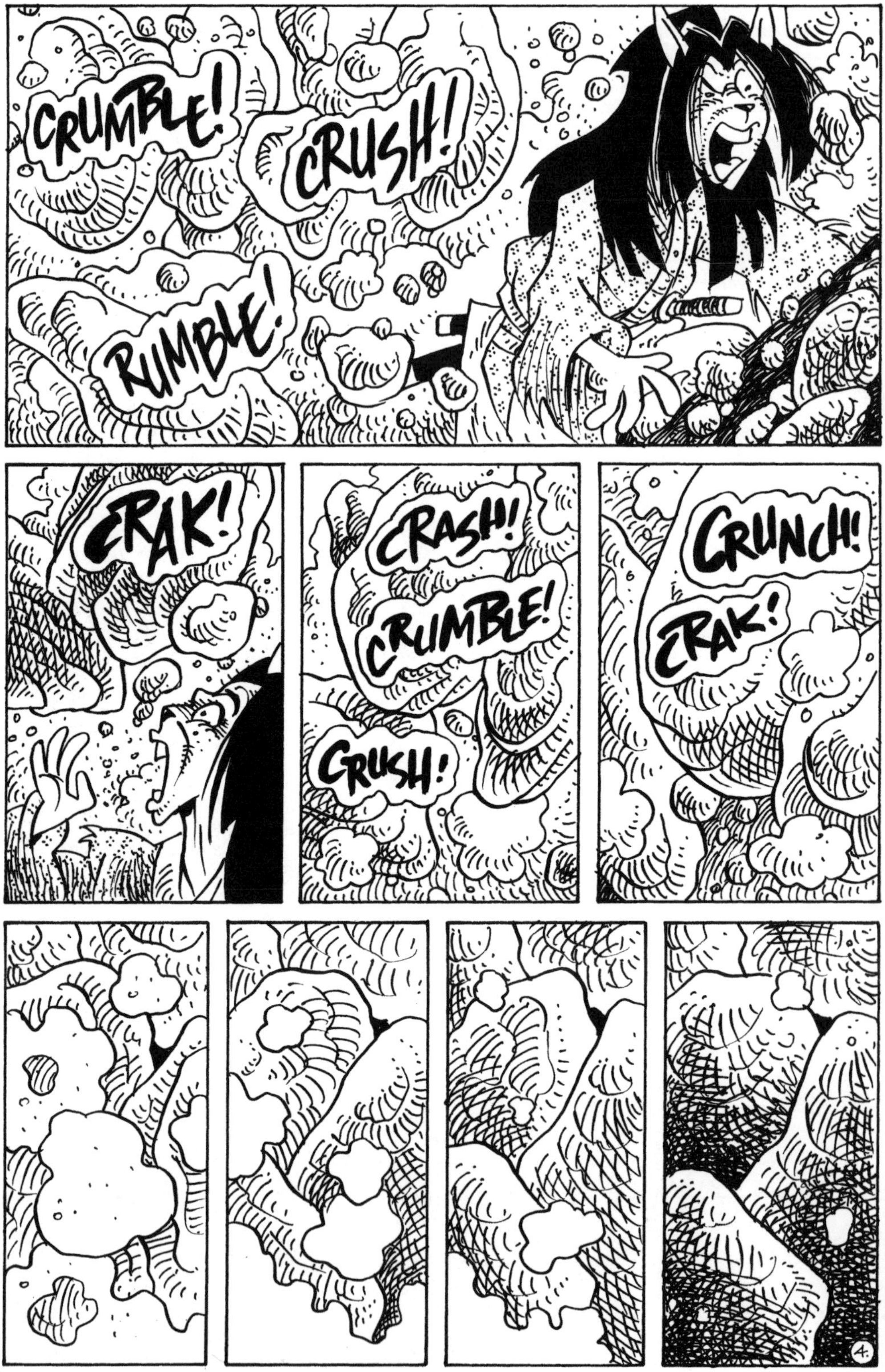
CRUMBLE!
CRUSH!
RUMBLE!
CRAK!
CRASH!
CRUMBLE!
CRUSH!
CRUNCH!
CRAK!
4.

.....

UHH...

I'M ALIVE... HOW LONG HAVE I BEEN BURIED HERE?

IT WILL TAKE MORE THAN AN EXPLOSION TO KILL ME, DEAR TOMOE.

MY FOOT IS TRAPPED... PROBABLY BROKEN.

¡UGH!

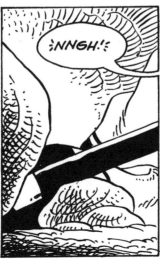

¡NNGH!

CRAK! THUD!

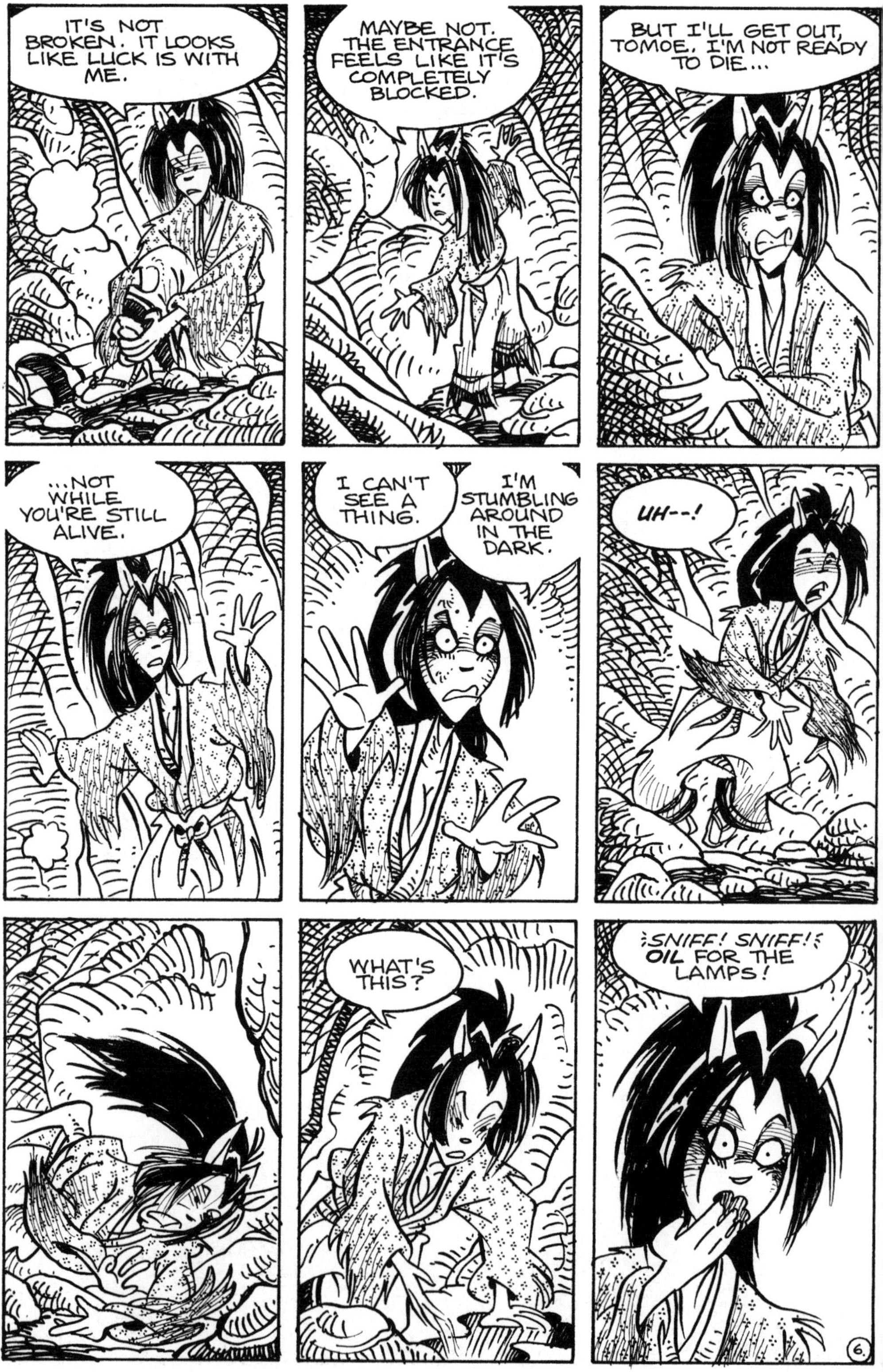
IT'S NOT BROKEN. IT LOOKS LIKE LUCK IS WITH ME.
MAYBE NOT. THE ENTRANCE FEELS LIKE IT'S COMPLETELY BLOCKED.
BUT I'LL GET OUT, TOMOE. I'M NOT READY TO DIE...
...NOT WHILE YOU'RE STILL ALIVE.
I CAN'T SEE A THING.
I'M STUMBLING AROUND IN THE DARK.
UH--!
WHAT'S THIS?
SNIFF! SNIFF! OIL FOR THE LAMPS!
6.

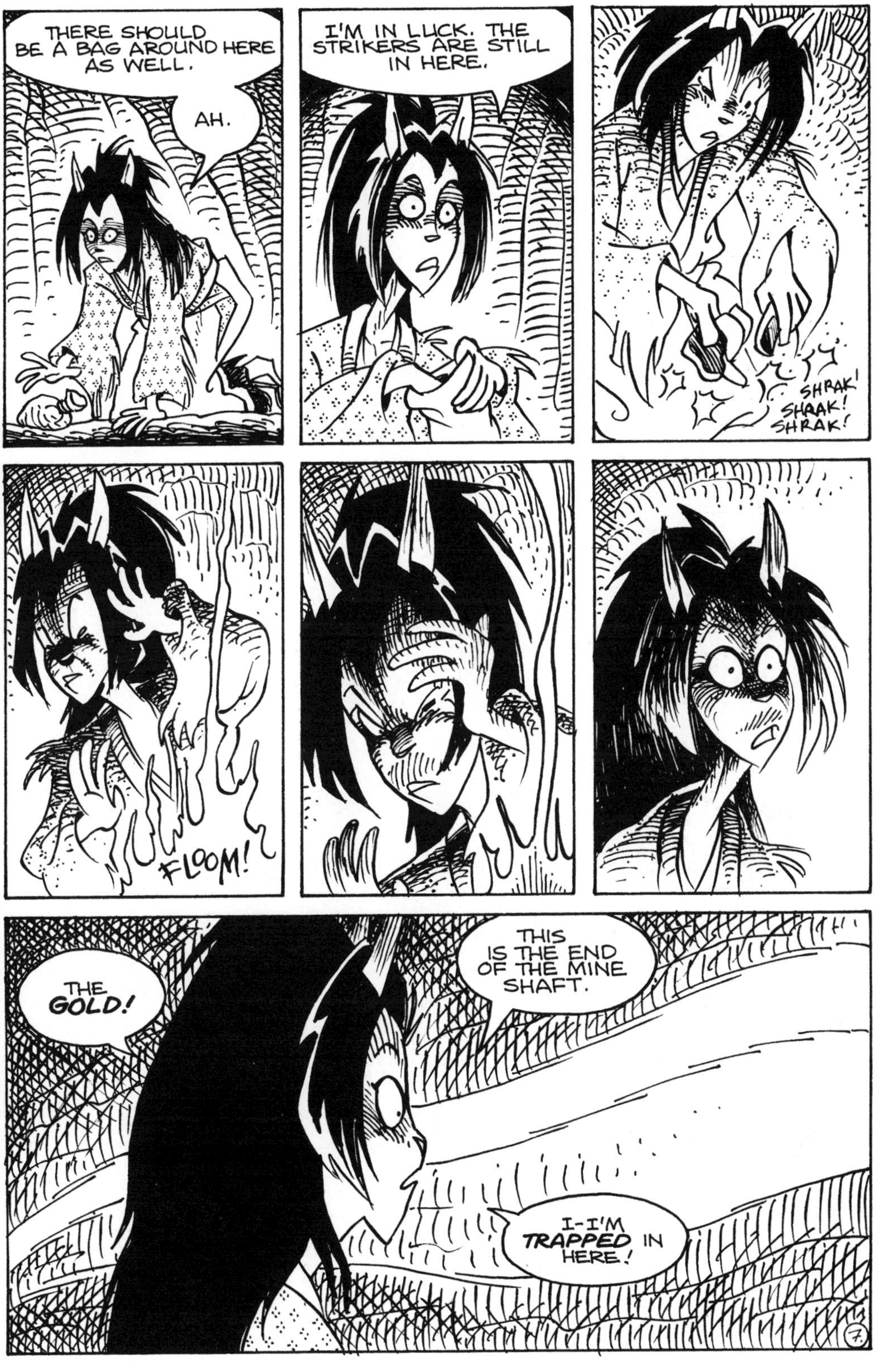

THERE SHOULD BE A BAG AROUND HERE AS WELL.
AH.
I'M IN LUCK. THE STRIKERS ARE STILL IN HERE.
SHRAK! SHRAK! SHRAK!
FLOOM!
THE GOLD!
THIS IS THE END OF THE MINE SHAFT.
I-I'M TRAPPED IN HERE!
7

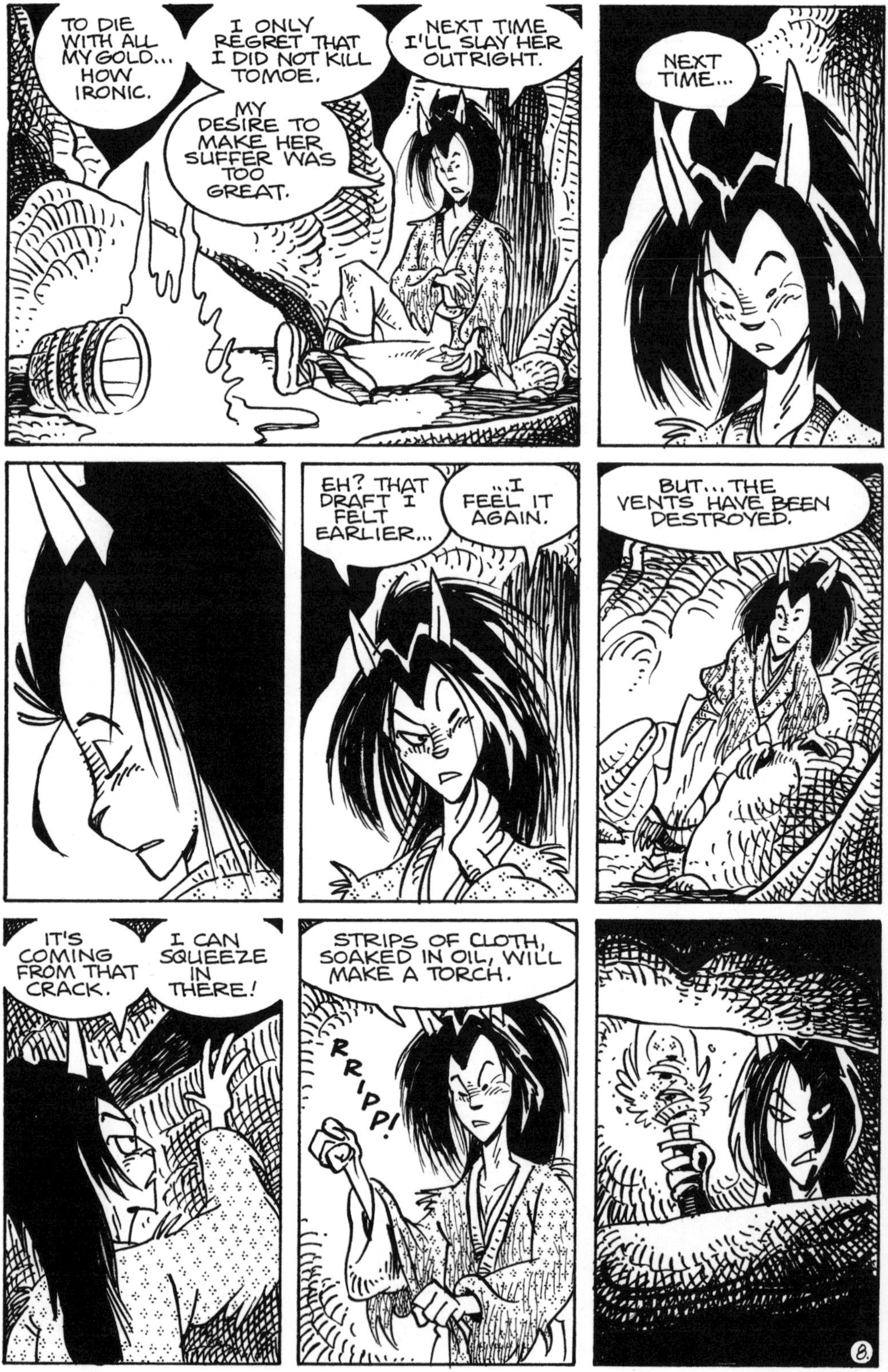
TO DIE WITH ALL MY GOLD... HOW IRONIC.
I ONLY REGRET THAT I DID NOT KILL TOMOE.
MY DESIRE TO MAKE HER SUFFER WAS TOO GREAT.
NEXT TIME I'LL SLAY HER OUTRIGHT.
NEXT TIME...
EH? THAT DRAFT I FELT EARLIER...
...I FEEL IT AGAIN.
BUT...THE VENTS HAVE BEEN DESTROYED.
IT'S COMING FROM THAT CRACK.
I CAN SQUEEZE IN THERE!
STRIPS OF CLOTH, SOAKED IN OIL, WILL MAKE A TORCH.
RRIPP!
8.

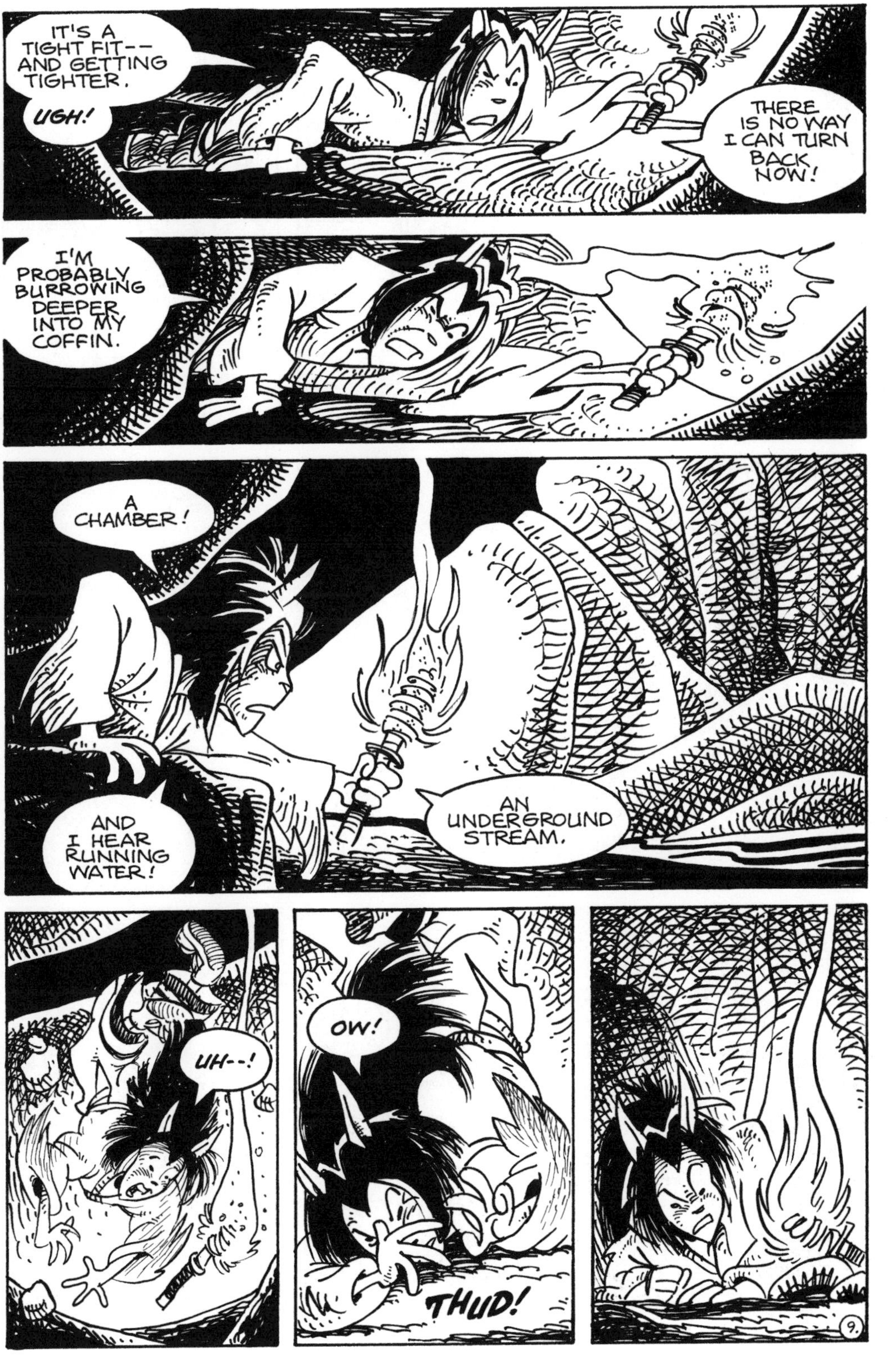
IT'S A TIGHT FIT-- AND GETTING TIGHTER.
UGH!
THERE IS NO WAY I CAN TURN BACK NOW!
I'M PROBABLY BURROWING DEEPER INTO MY COFFIN.
A CHAMBER!
AND I HEAR RUNNING WATER!
AN UNDERGROUND STREAM.
UH--!
OW!
THUD!
9.

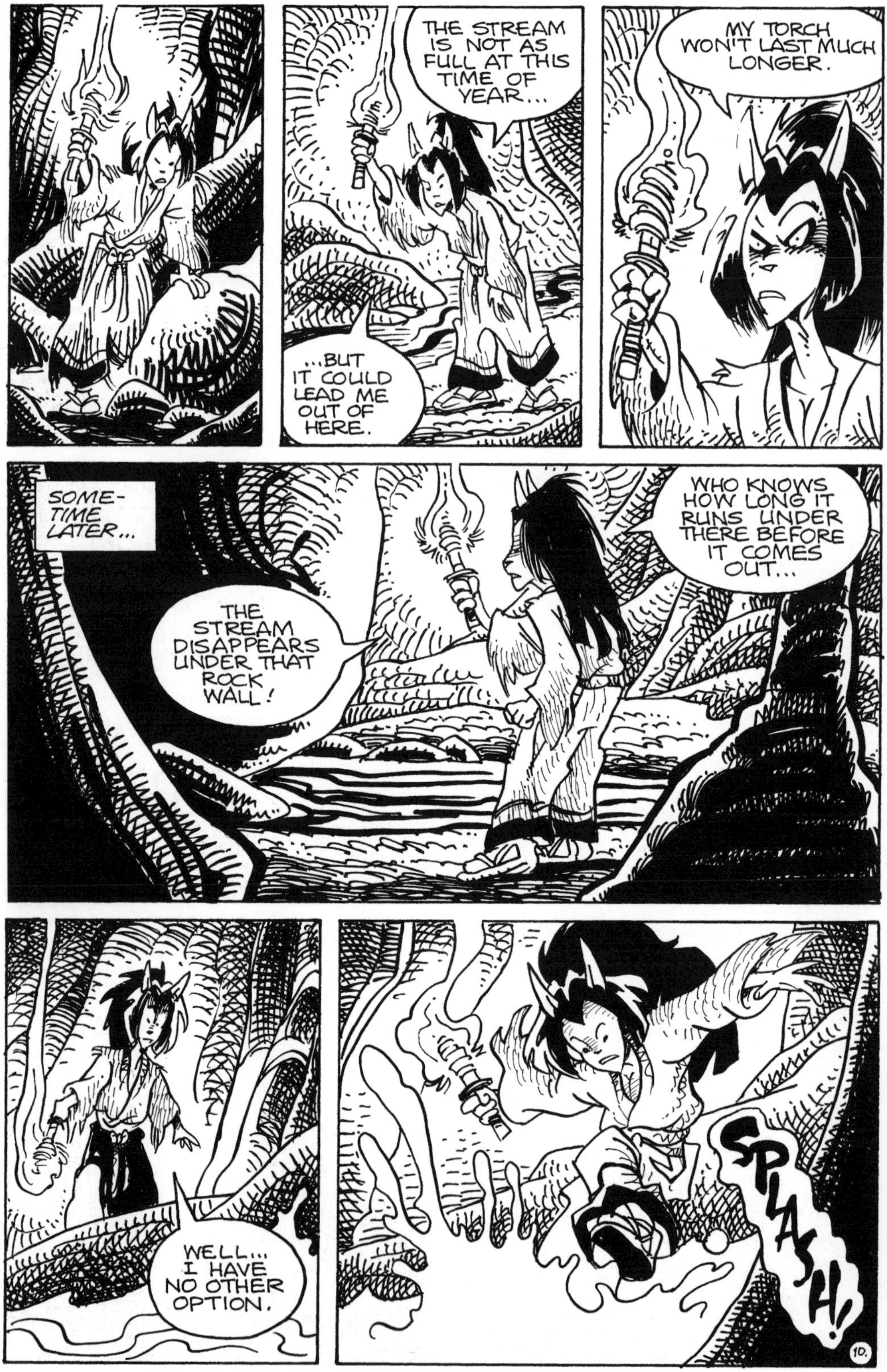
THE STREAM IS NOT AS FULL AT THIS TIME OF YEAR...
...BUT IT COULD LEAD ME OUT OF HERE.
MY TORCH WON'T LAST MUCH LONGER.
SOME-TIME LATER...
THE STREAM DISAPPEARS UNDER THAT ROCK WALL!
WHO KNOWS HOW LONG IT RUNS UNDER THERE BEFORE IT COMES OUT...
WELL... I HAVE NO OTHER OPTION.
SPLASH!
10.

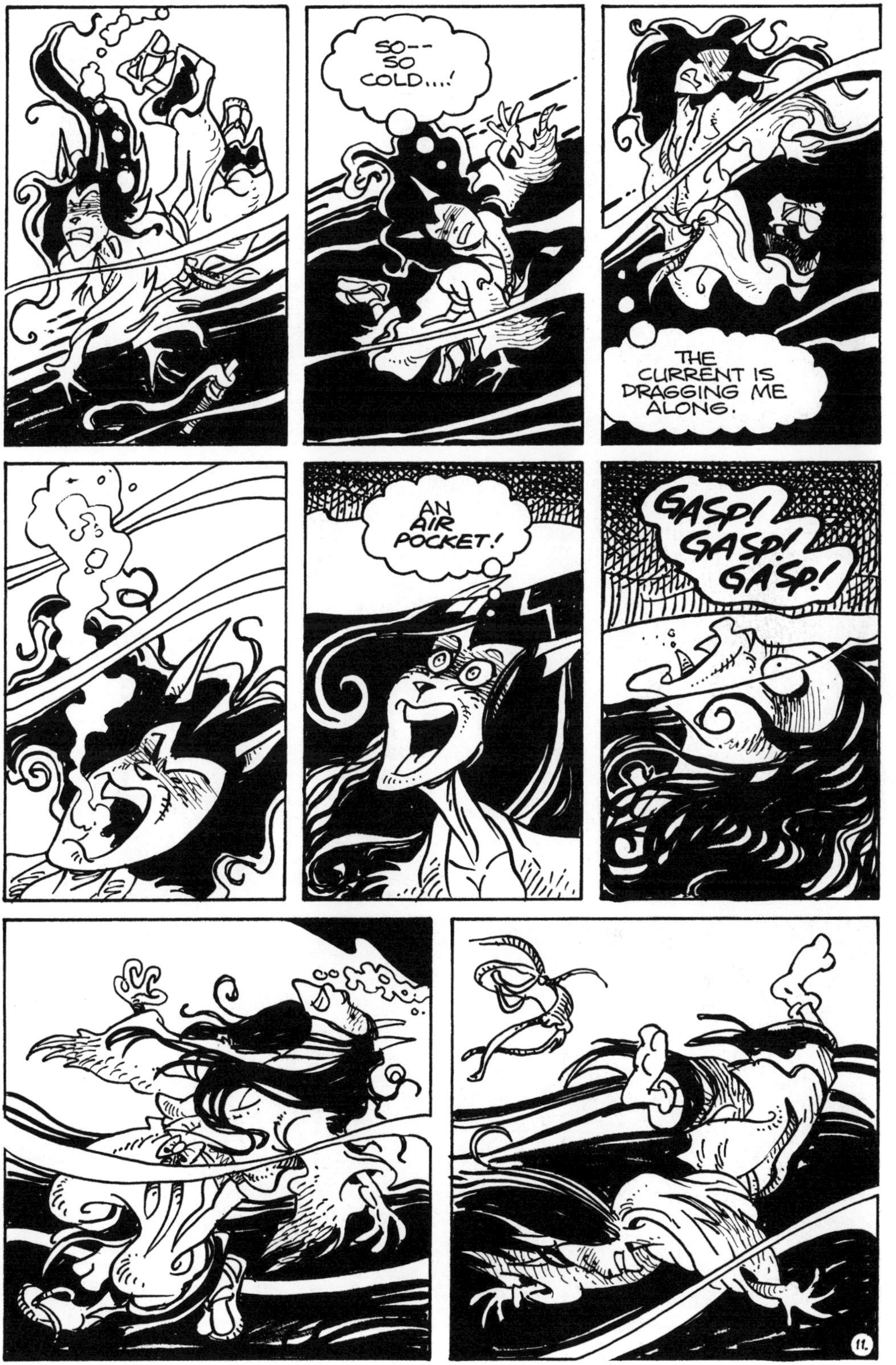
SO-- SO COLD....!
THE CURRENT IS DRAGGING ME ALONG.
AN AIR POCKET!
GASP! GASP! GASP!
11.

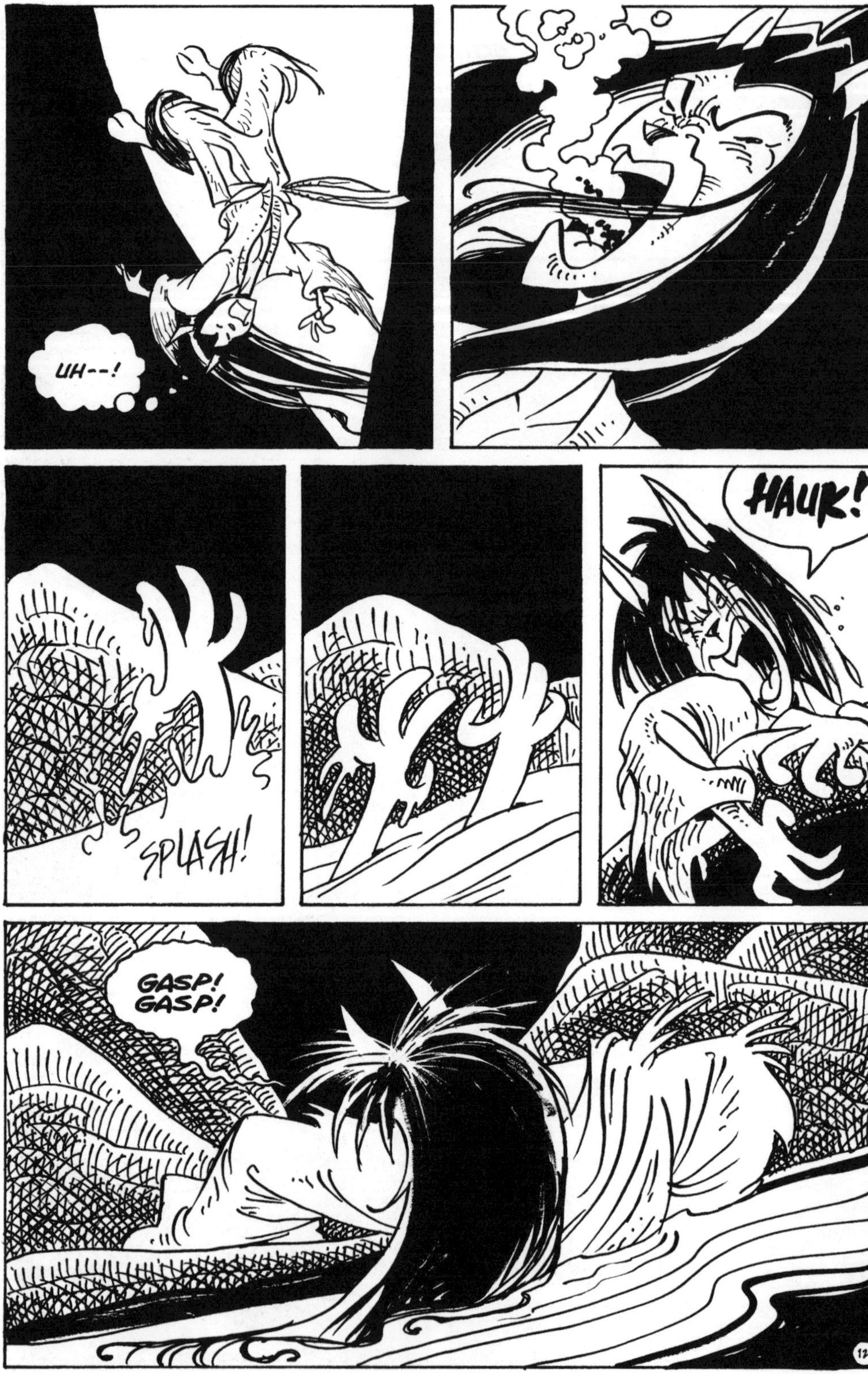
UH--!
SPLASH!
HAUK!
GASP! GASP!
12.

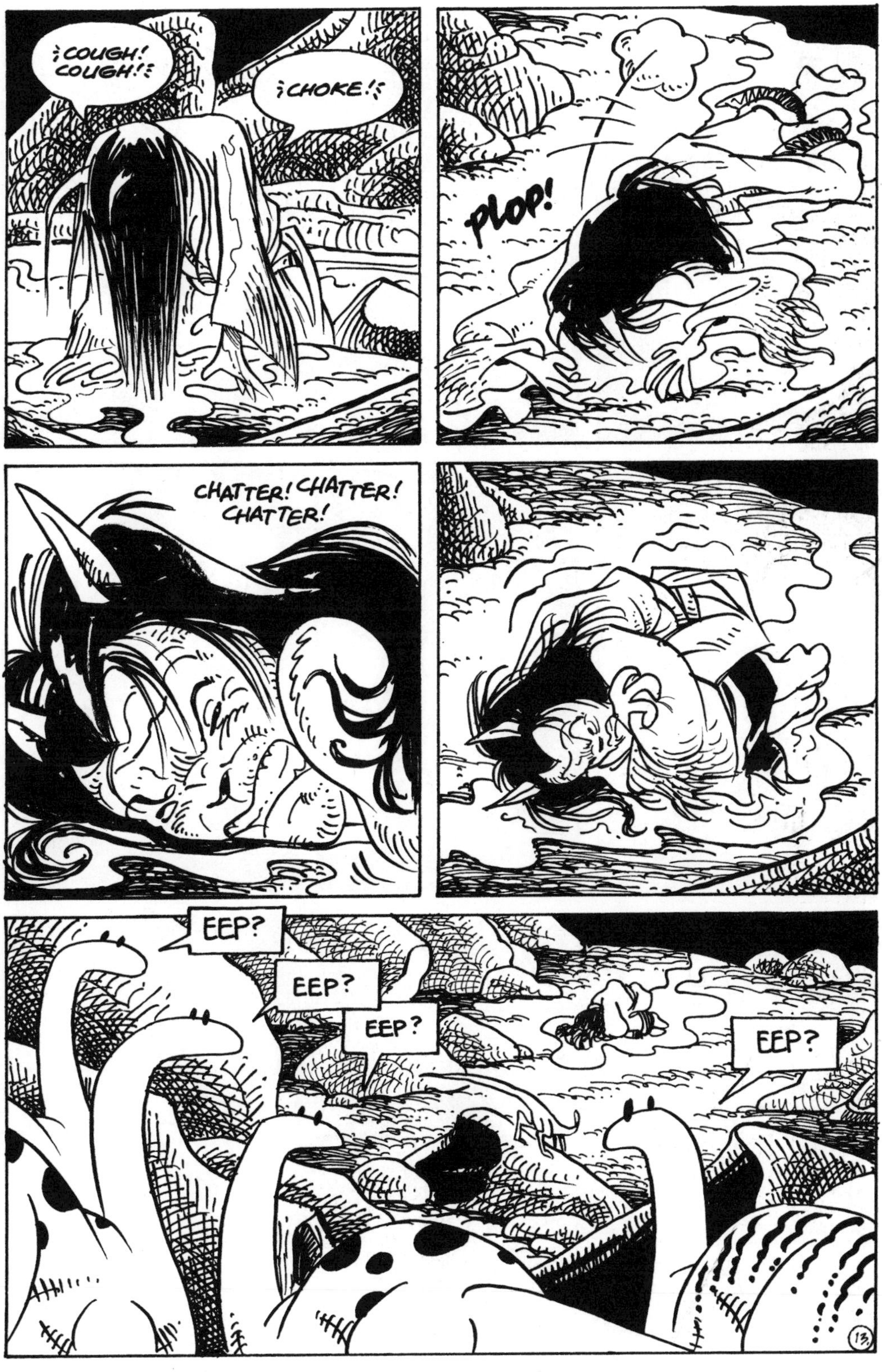
¡COUGH! COUGH!¡
¡CHOKE!¡
PLOP!
CHATTER! CHATTER! CHATTER!
EEP?
EEP?
EEP?
EEP?
13

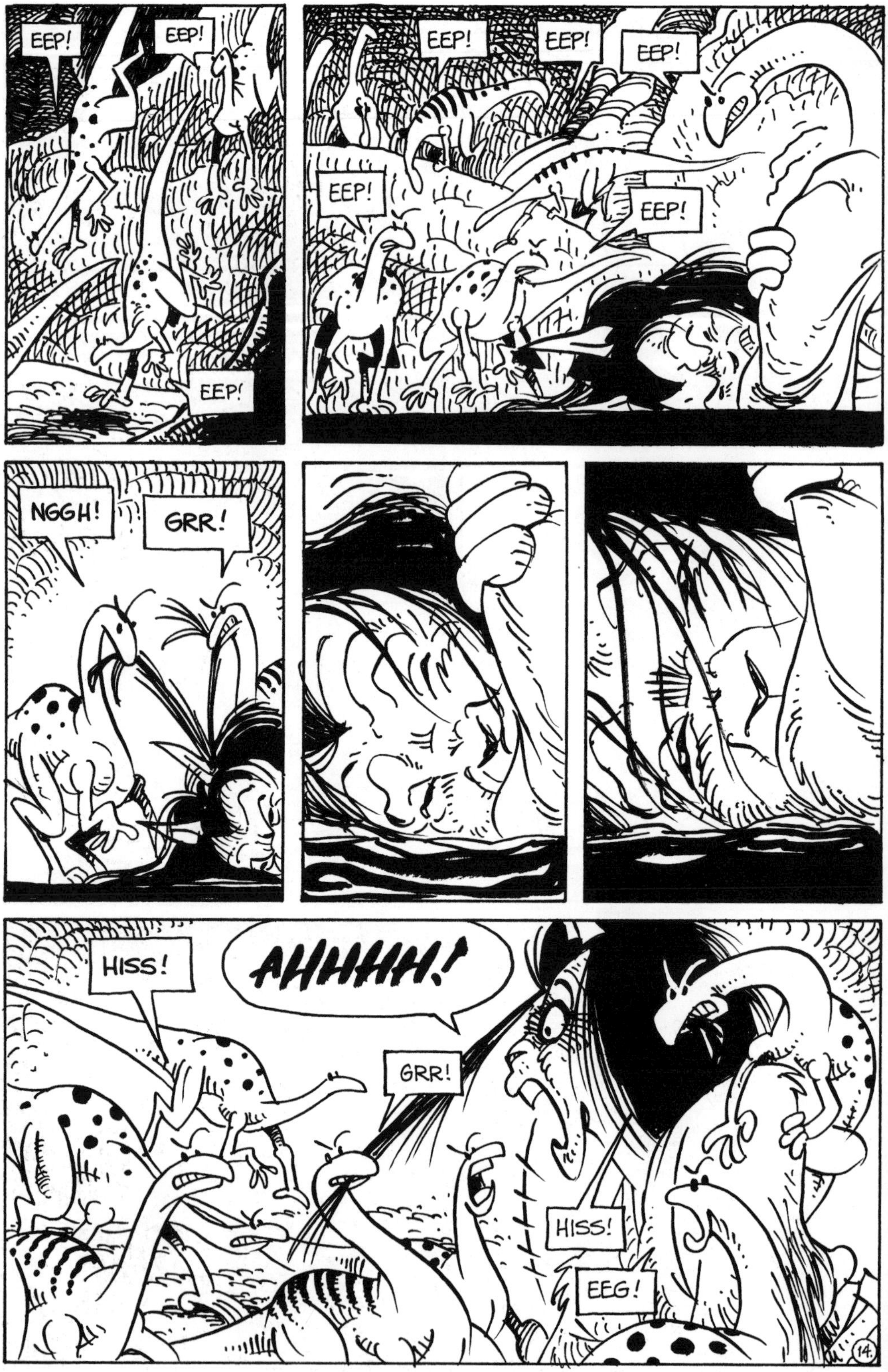
EEP!
EEP!
EEP!
EEP!
EEP!
EEP!
EEP!
EEP!
NGGH!
GRR!
HISS!
AHHHH!
GRR!
HISS!
EEG!
14.

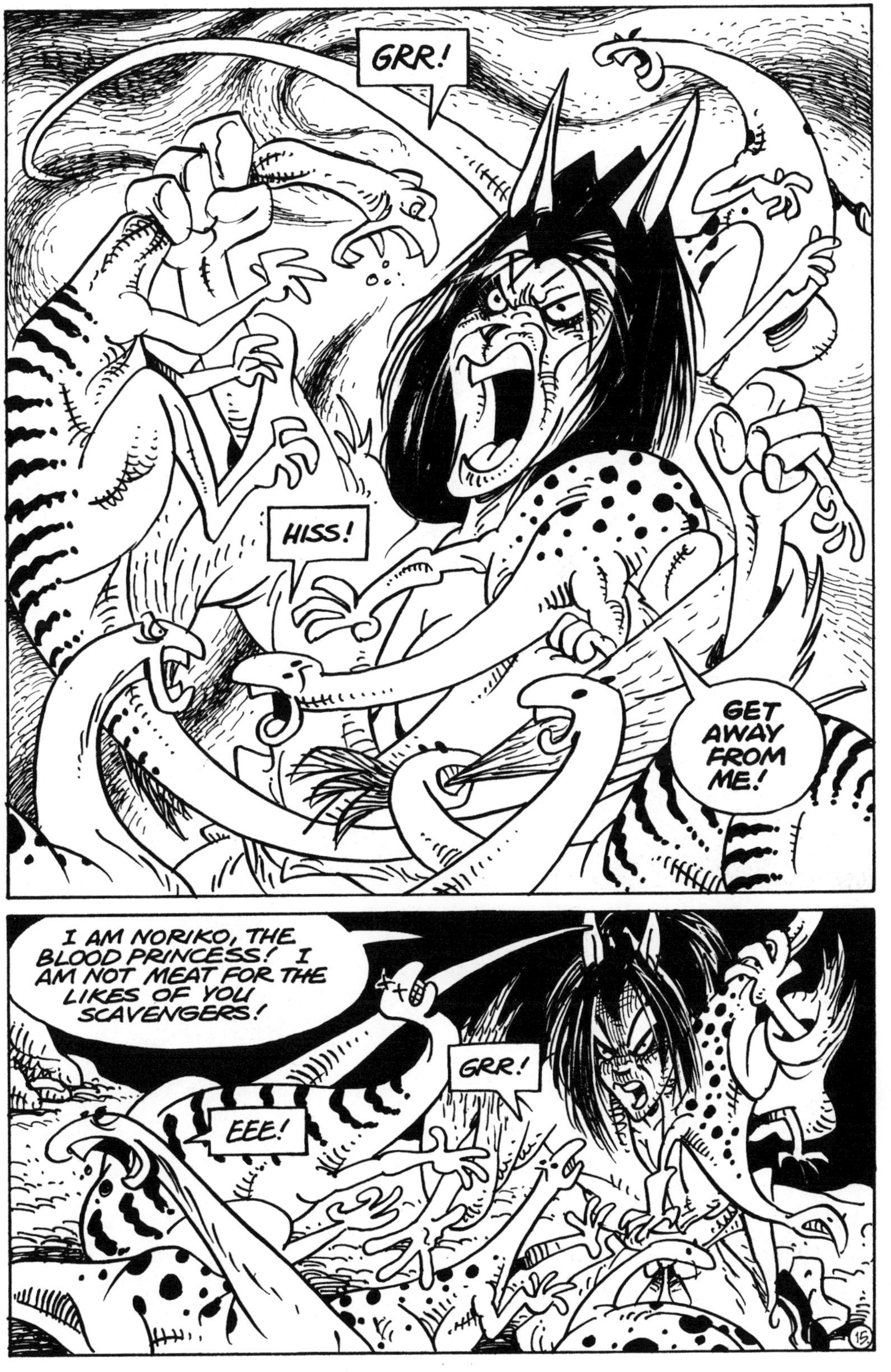
GRR!
HISS!
GET AWAY FROM ME!
I AM NORIKO, THE BLOOD PRINCESS! I AM NOT MEAT FOR THE LIKES OF YOU SCAVENGERS!
GRR!
EEE!
15

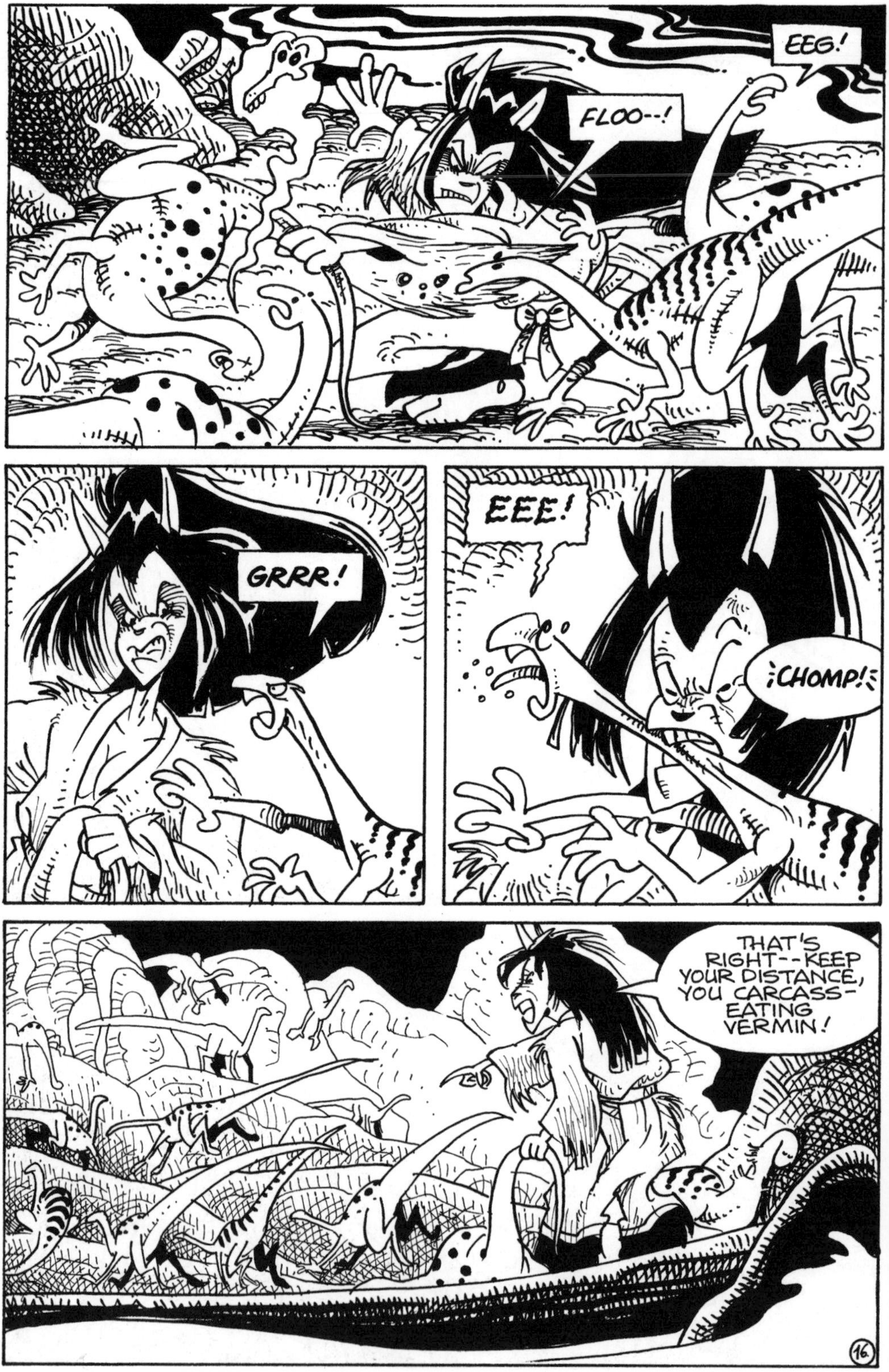
FLOO--!
EEG!
GRRR!
EEE!
¡CHOMP!
THAT'S RIGHT--KEEP YOUR DISTANCE, YOU CARCASS-EATING VERMIN!
16.

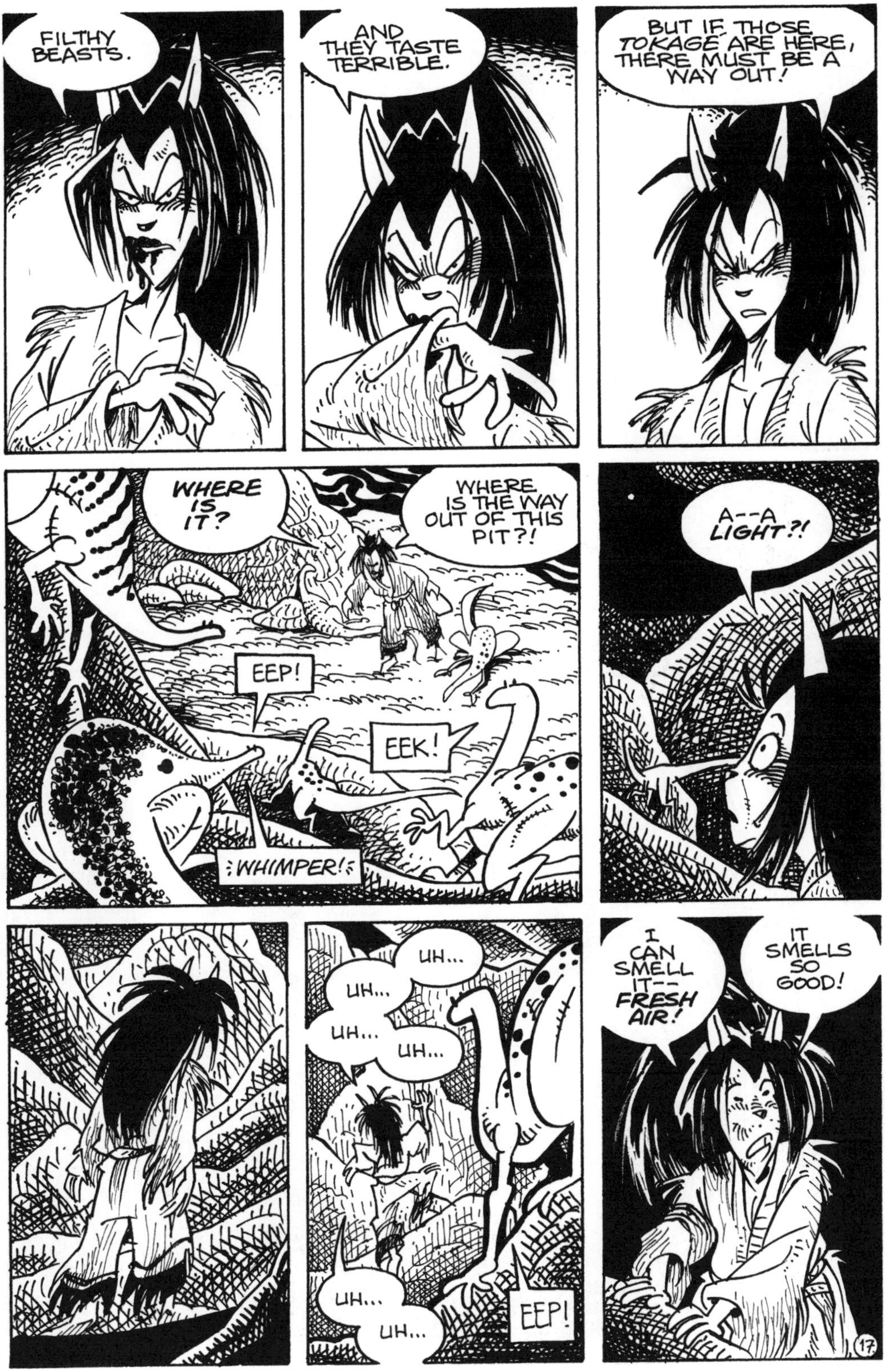

FILTHY BEASTS.
AND THEY TASTE TERRIBLE.
BUT IF THOSE *TOKAGE* ARE HERE, THERE MUST BE A WAY OUT!
WHERE IS IT?
WHERE IS THE WAY OUT OF THIS PIT?!
EEP!
EEK!
WHIMPER!
A--A LIGHT?!
UH...
UH...
UH...
UH...
UH...
UH...
EEP!
I CAN SMELL IT-- FRESH AIR!
IT SMELLS SO GOOD!
17

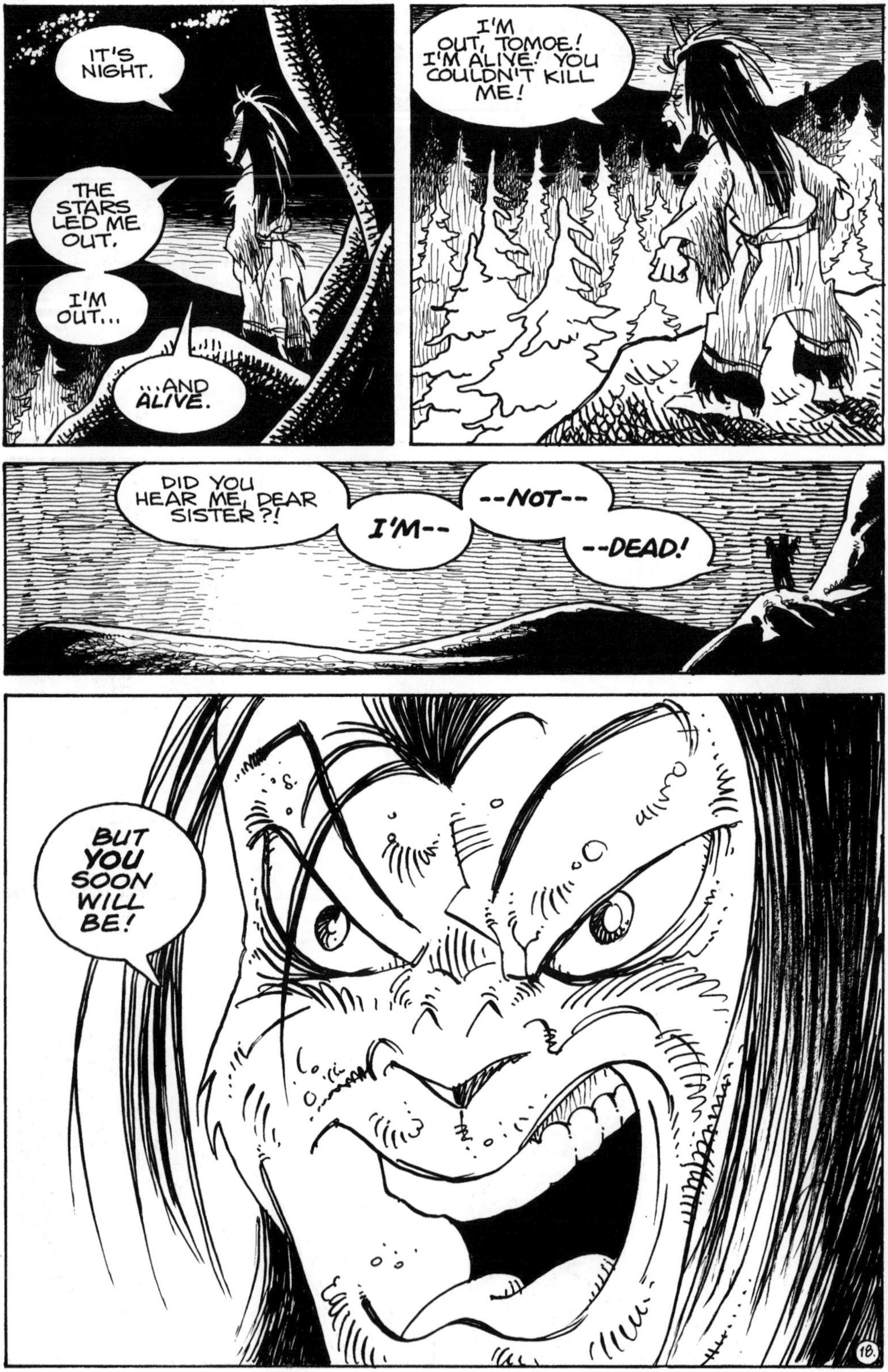
IT'S NIGHT.
THE STARS LED ME OUT.
I'M OUT...
...AND ALIVE.
I'M OUT, TOMOE! I'M ALIVE! YOU COULDN'T KILL ME!
DID YOU HEAR ME, DEAR SISTER?!
I'M--
--NOT--
--DEAD!
BUT YOU SOON WILL BE!
18.

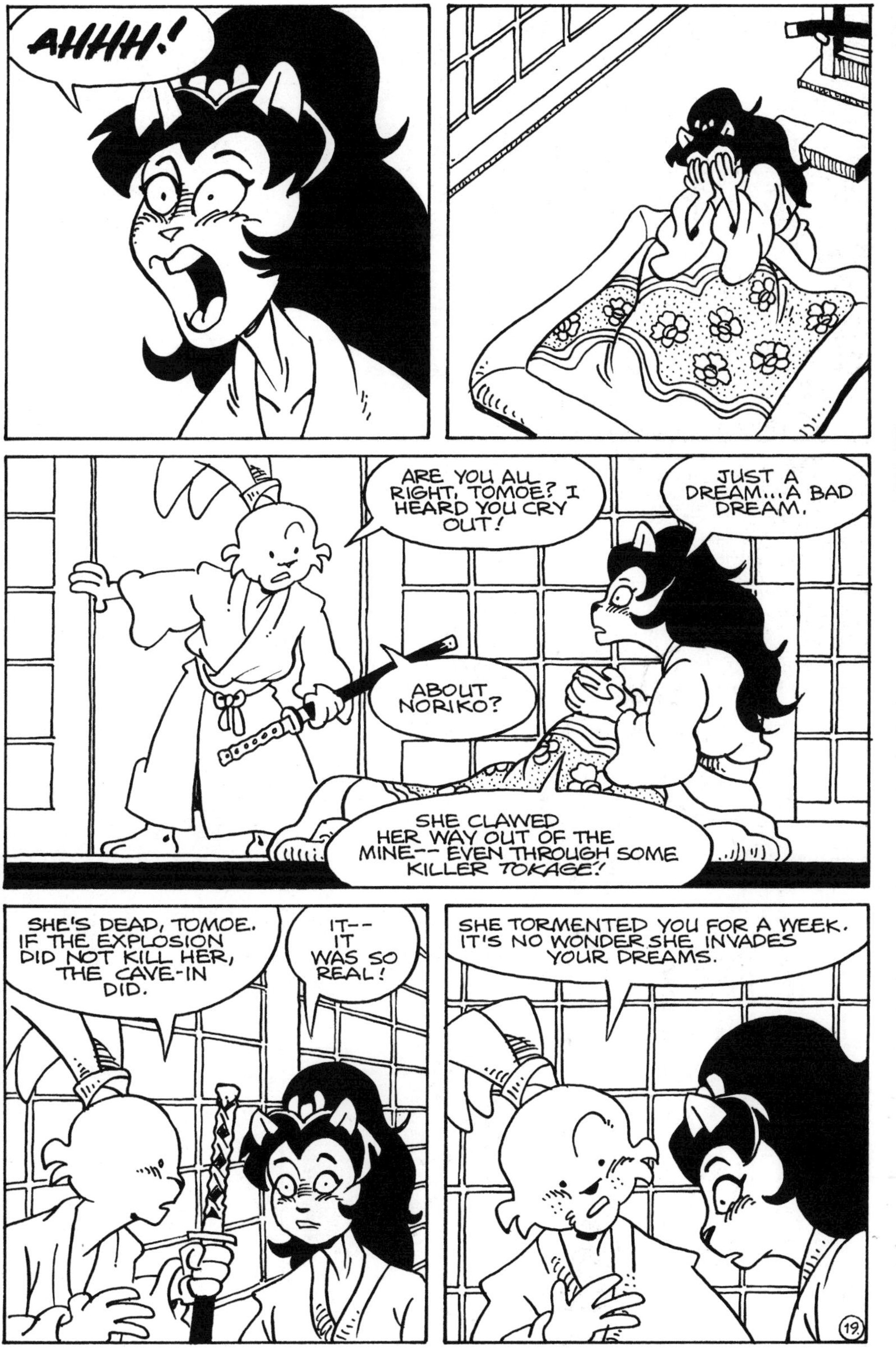
AHHH!
ARE YOU ALL RIGHT, TOMOE? I HEARD YOU CRY OUT!
JUST A DREAM...A BAD DREAM.
ABOUT NORIKO?
SHE CLAWED HER WAY OUT OF THE MINE-- EVEN THROUGH SOME KILLER TOKAGE!
SHE'S DEAD, TOMOE. IF THE EXPLOSION DID NOT KILL HER, THE CAVE-IN DID.
IT-- IT WAS SO REAL!
SHE TORMENTED YOU FOR A WEEK. IT'S NO WONDER SHE INVADES YOUR DREAMS.
19

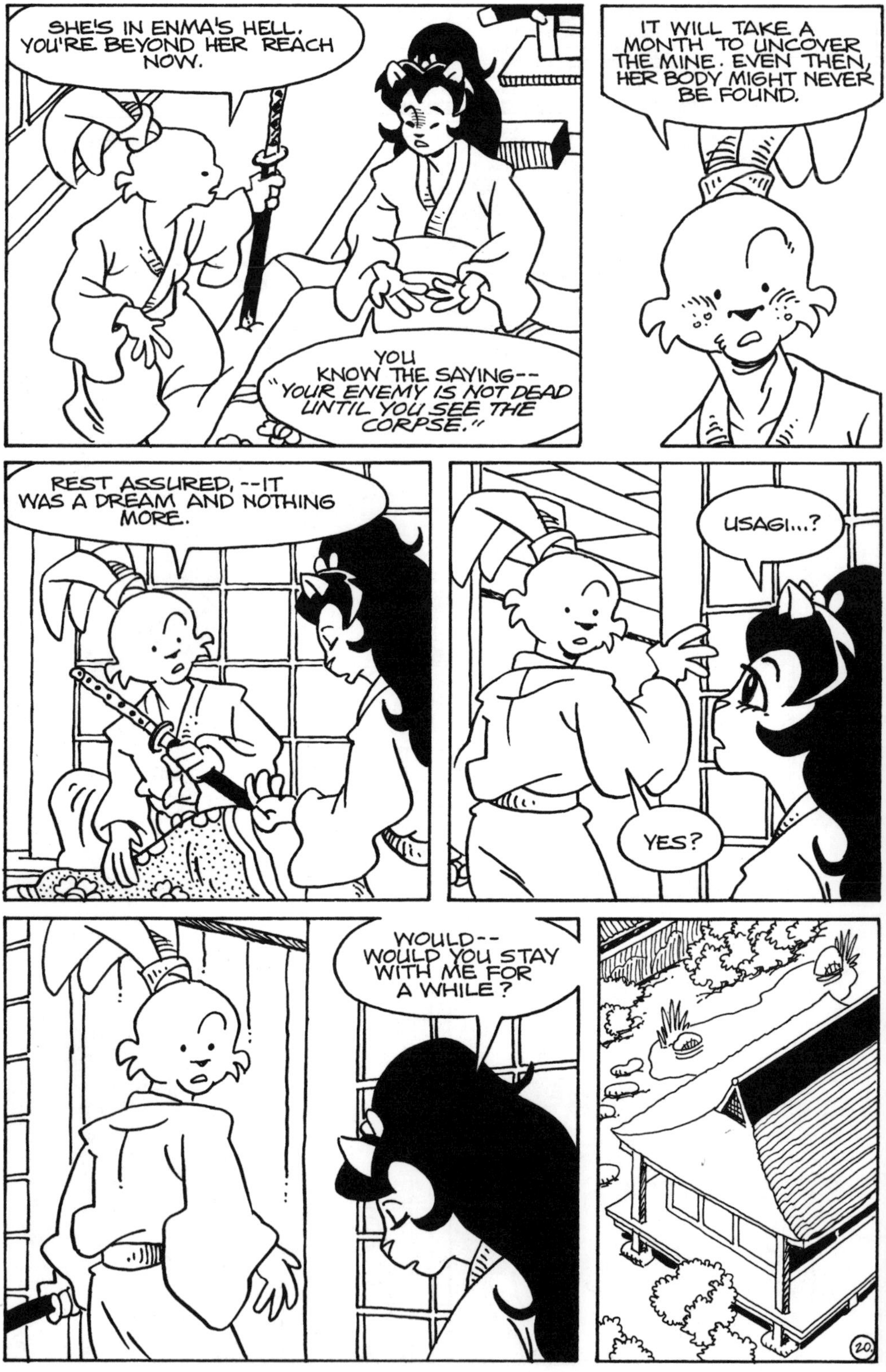
SHE'S IN ENMA'S HELL. YOU'RE BEYOND HER REACH NOW.
YOU KNOW THE SAYING-- "YOUR ENEMY IS NOT DEAD UNTIL YOU SEE THE CORPSE."
IT WILL TAKE A MONTH TO UNCOVER THE MINE. EVEN THEN, HER BODY MIGHT NEVER BE FOUND.
REST ASSURED, --IT WAS A DREAM AND NOTHING MORE.
USAGI...?
YES?
WOULD-- WOULD YOU STAY WITH ME FOR A WHILE?
20

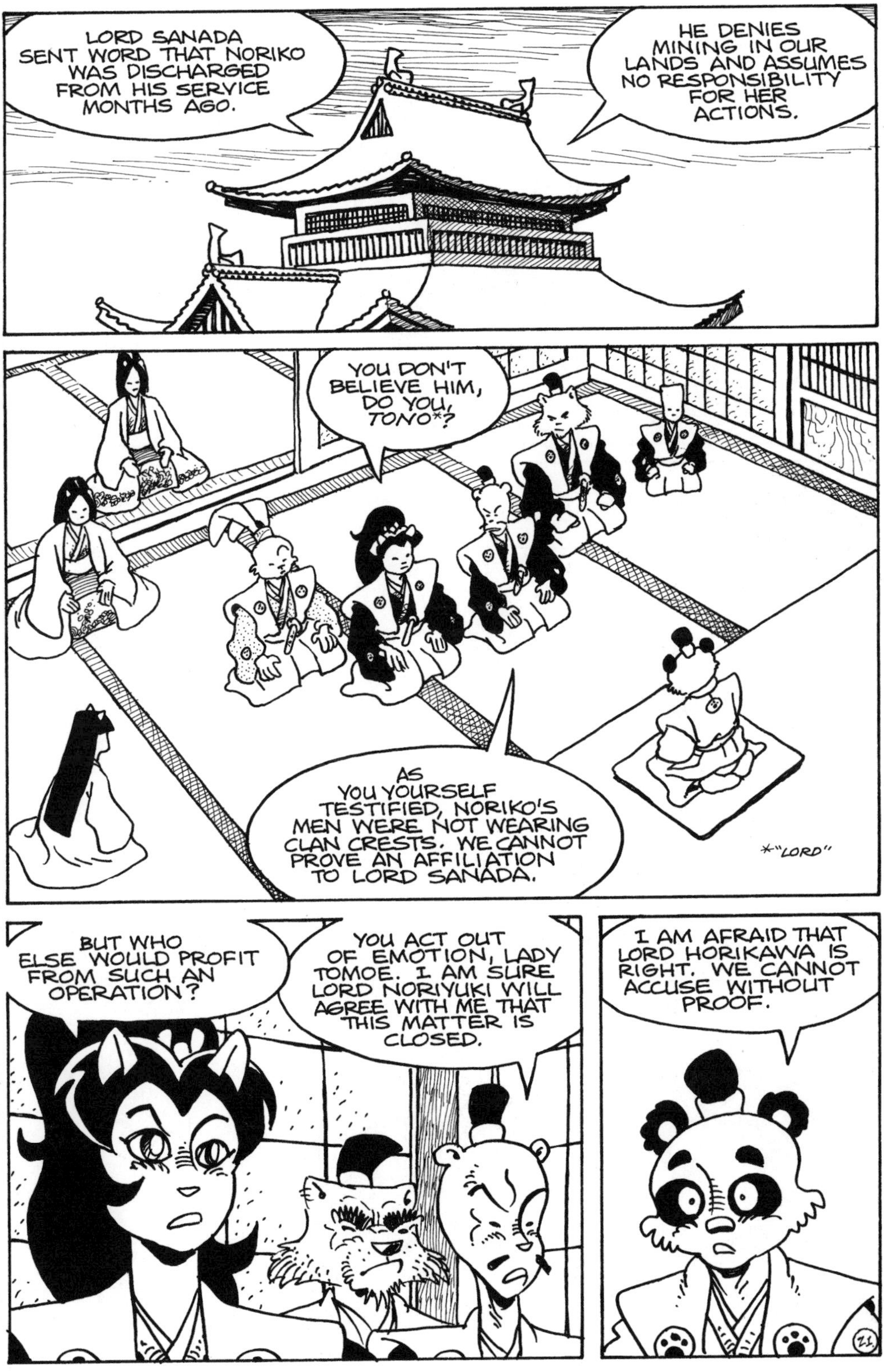
LORD SANADA SENT WORD THAT NORIKO WAS DISCHARGED FROM HIS SERVICE MONTHS AGO.
HE DENIES MINING IN OUR LANDS AND ASSUMES NO RESPONSIBILITY FOR HER ACTIONS.
YOU DON'T BELIEVE HIM, DO YOU, *TONO**?
AS YOU YOURSELF TESTIFIED, NORIKO'S MEN WERE NOT WEARING CLAN CRESTS. WE CANNOT PROVE AN AFFILIATION TO LORD SANADA.
*"LORD"
BUT WHO ELSE WOULD PROFIT FROM SUCH AN OPERATION?
YOU ACT OUT OF EMOTION, LADY TOMOE. I AM SURE LORD NORIYUKI WILL AGREE WITH ME THAT THIS MATTER IS CLOSED.
I AM AFRAID THAT LORD HORIKAWA IS RIGHT. WE CANNOT ACCUSE WITHOUT PROOF.
21

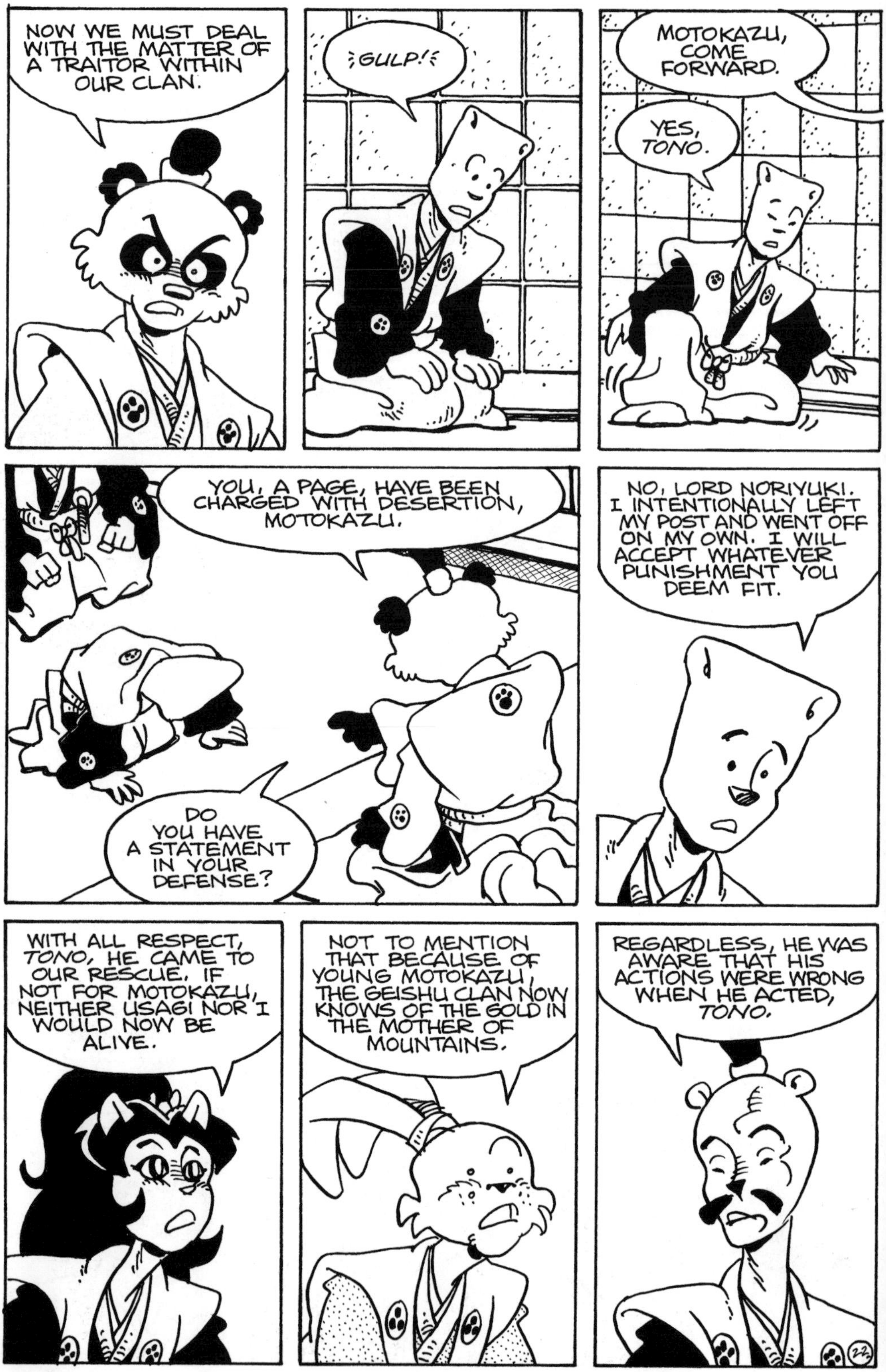
NOW WE MUST DEAL WITH THE MATTER OF A TRAITOR WITHIN OUR CLAN.
GULP!
MOTOKAZU, COME FORWARD.
YES, TONO.
YOU, A PAGE, HAVE BEEN CHARGED WITH DESERTION, MOTOKAZU.
DO YOU HAVE A STATEMENT IN YOUR DEFENSE?
NO, LORD NORIYUKI. I INTENTIONALLY LEFT MY POST AND WENT OFF ON MY OWN. I WILL ACCEPT WHATEVER PUNISHMENT YOU DEEM FIT.
WITH ALL RESPECT, TONO, HE CAME TO OUR RESCUE. IF NOT FOR MOTOKAZU, NEITHER USAGI NOR I WOULD NOW BE ALIVE.
NOT TO MENTION THAT BECAUSE OF YOUNG MOTOKAZU, THE GEISHU CLAN NOW KNOWS OF THE GOLD IN THE MOTHER OF MOUNTAINS.
REGARDLESS, HE WAS AWARE THAT HIS ACTIONS WERE WRONG WHEN HE ACTED, TONO.
22

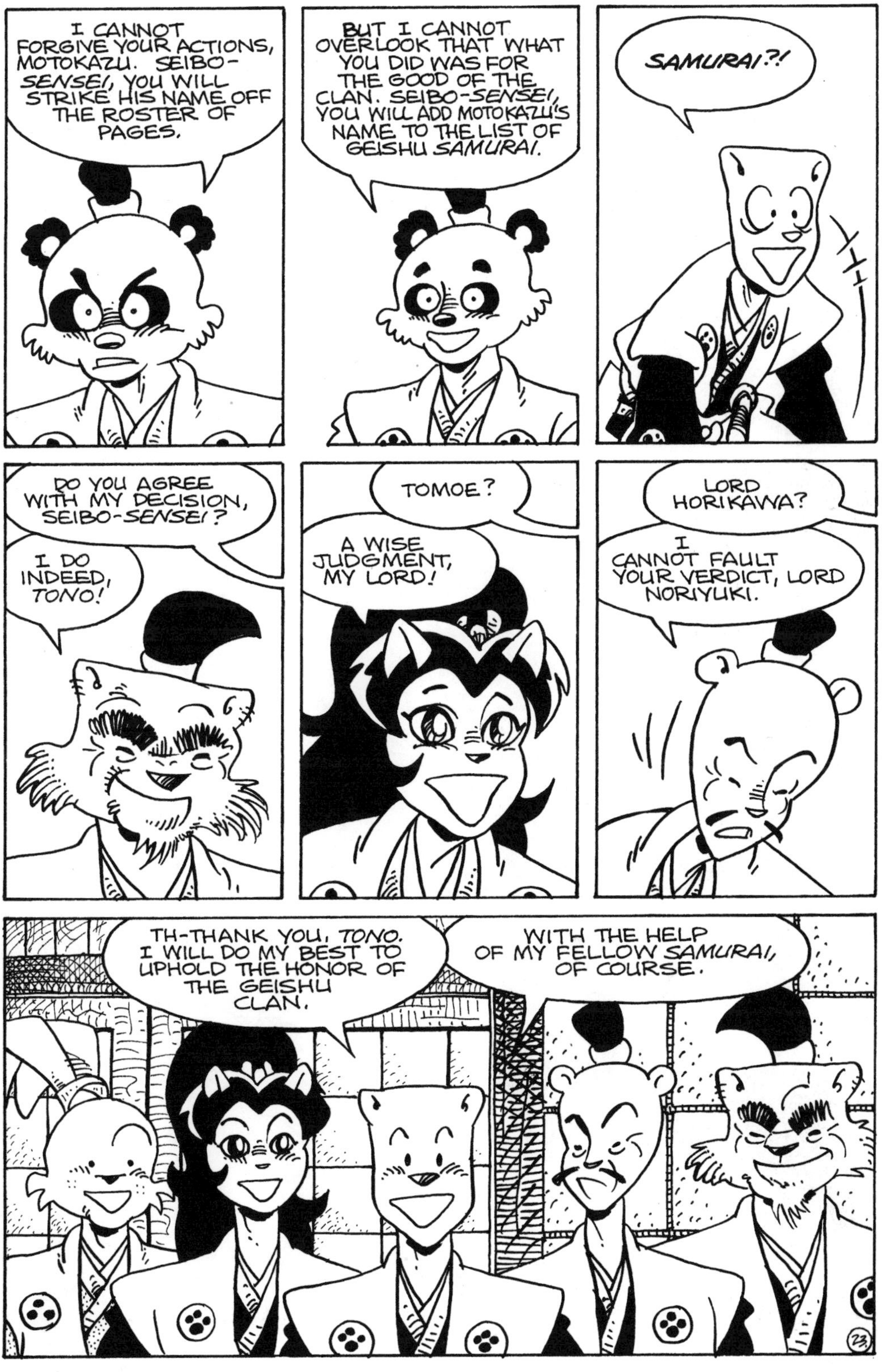
I CANNOT FORGIVE YOUR ACTIONS, MOTOKAZU. SEIBO-SENSEI, YOU WILL STRIKE HIS NAME OFF THE ROSTER OF PAGES.
BUT I CANNOT OVERLOOK THAT WHAT YOU DID WAS FOR THE GOOD OF THE CLAN. SEIBO-SENSEI, YOU WILL ADD MOTOKAZU'S NAME TO THE LIST OF GEISHU SAMURAI.
SAMURAI?!
DO YOU AGREE WITH MY DECISION, SEIBO-SENSEI?
I DO INDEED, TONO!
TOMOE?
A WISE JUDGMENT, MY LORD!
LORD HORIKAWA?
I CANNOT FAULT YOUR VERDICT, LORD NORIYUKI.
TH-THANK YOU, TONO. I WILL DO MY BEST TO UPHOLD THE HONOR OF THE GEISHU CLAN.
WITH THE HELP OF MY FELLOW SAMURAI, OF COURSE.
23

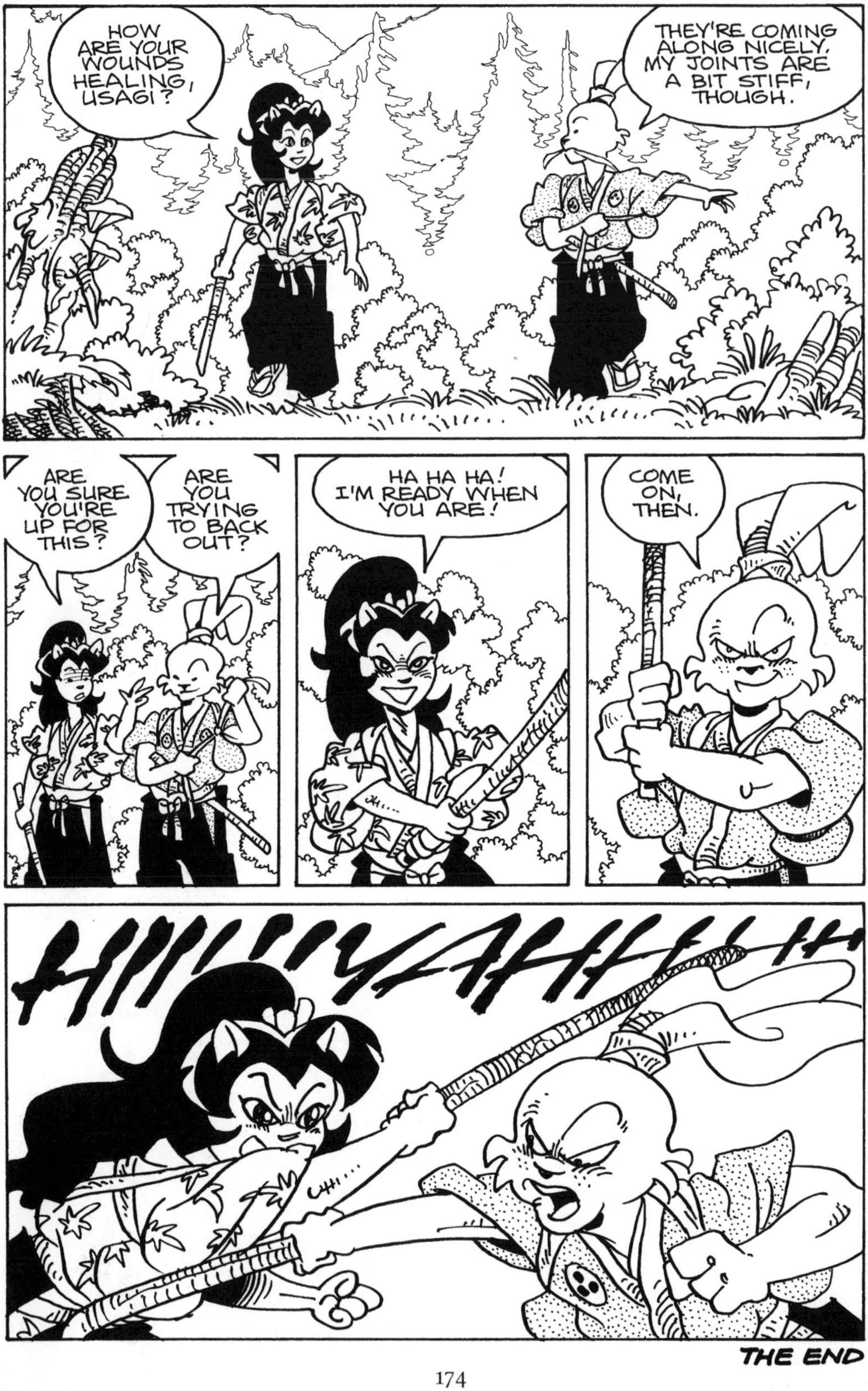
HOW ARE YOUR WOUNDS HEALING, USAGI?
THEY'RE COMING ALONG NICELY. MY JOINTS ARE A BIT STIFF, THOUGH.
ARE YOU SURE YOU'RE UP FOR THIS?
ARE YOU TRYING TO BACK OUT?
HA HA HA! I'M READY WHEN YOU ARE!
COME ON, THEN.
HIIIIYAHHH
THE END

Usagi Yojimbo

Story Notes

WHAT'S THIS?!
I-I CAN'T BELIEVE IT! A GROMWELL BUSH!
HOORAY! THIS IS THE BEST DAY OF MY LIFE!

I first heard of the Japanese gromwell in a television documentary about the mountains of Japan. The shrub grows in the presence of gold, and there is a speck of gold in its berries as well as fine gold powder in its leaves. There are two other native Japanese plants that share the same properties—the spicebrush and the Japanese beech. The roots of these plants absorb gold from underground water and then distribute the metal throughout their systems to their leaves.

A January 25, 1993, article in the *American Metal Market* reported that the Metal Mining Industry Association of Japan, an affiliate of the trade ministry, had been studying the gold content in plants that grew above twelve mines. This project began in 1987. Studying these plants would be much more cost-effective than random drilling.

The Mother of Mountains was first conceived as a minor story arc, but as I worked with Noriko, she gradually came to life with a definite personality and tragic backstory. The story changed from an events-driven story to one that is character-driven. Subplots were thrown in with Motokazu, Lord Horikawa, and the suggestion of Tomoe's marriage.

The role of the woman in the samurai class was just as strict and regulated as that of the man. In earliest times, there are records of women leading men into battle: Empress Jingu led the invasion of Korea while pregnant. However, by Usagi's time, women of the military class did not go into battle but were submissive to their husbands or fathers and usually oversaw the samurai household. They were still expected to be proficient with weapons such as the *yari* (straight spear) and *naginata* (curved spear). One of these hung over the door in every samurai home. They carried a *kaiken* (short dagger), which would be used for defense or to commit *seppuku* (ritualized suicide).

Tomoe Ame was inspired by Tomoe Gozen, consort of Kiso Yoshinaka during the Gempei War. She helped lead the Minamoto forces, even killing several of the enemy in single combat. At the Battle of Azazu-no-Hara, she was almost captured by Uchida Iyeyoshi. He had seized and ripped a part of her sleeve. Angered, she attacked him, cut off his head, and later presented it to her husband.

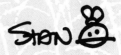

Gallery

The following pages feature Stan Sakai's cover art from issues eighty-three through eighty-nine of Dark Horse's Usagi Yojimbo Volume Three *series.*

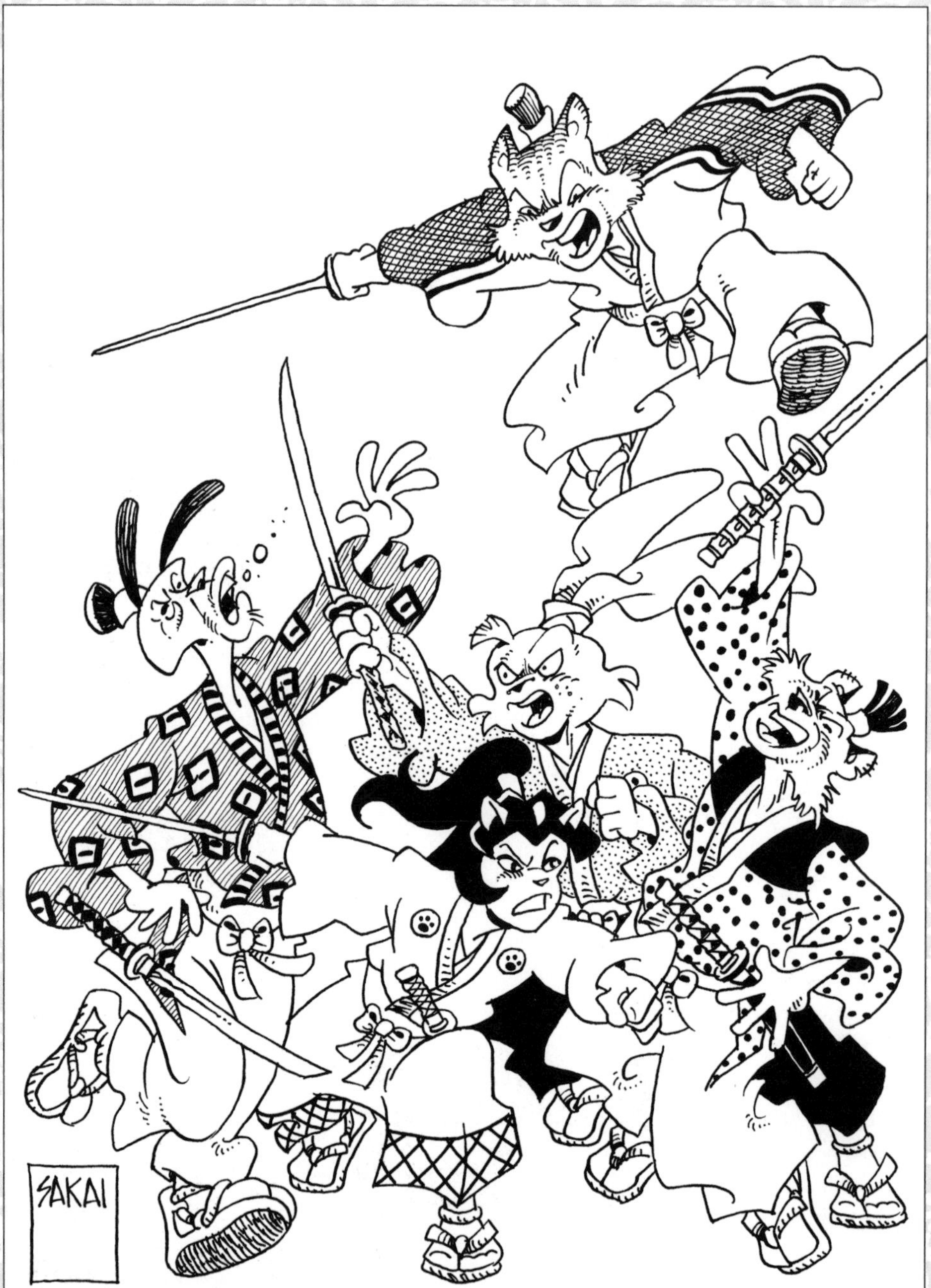

SAKAI

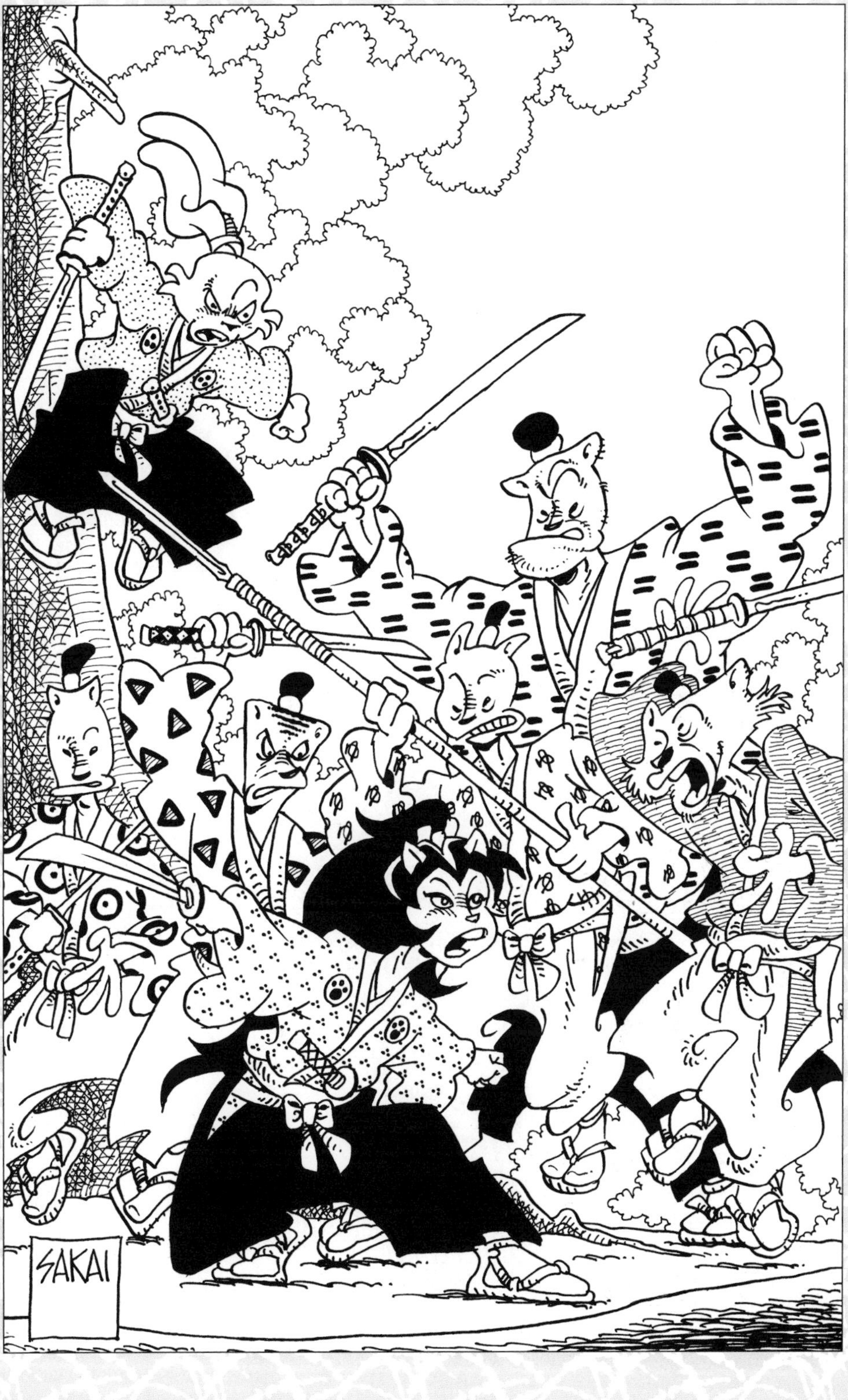
SAKAI

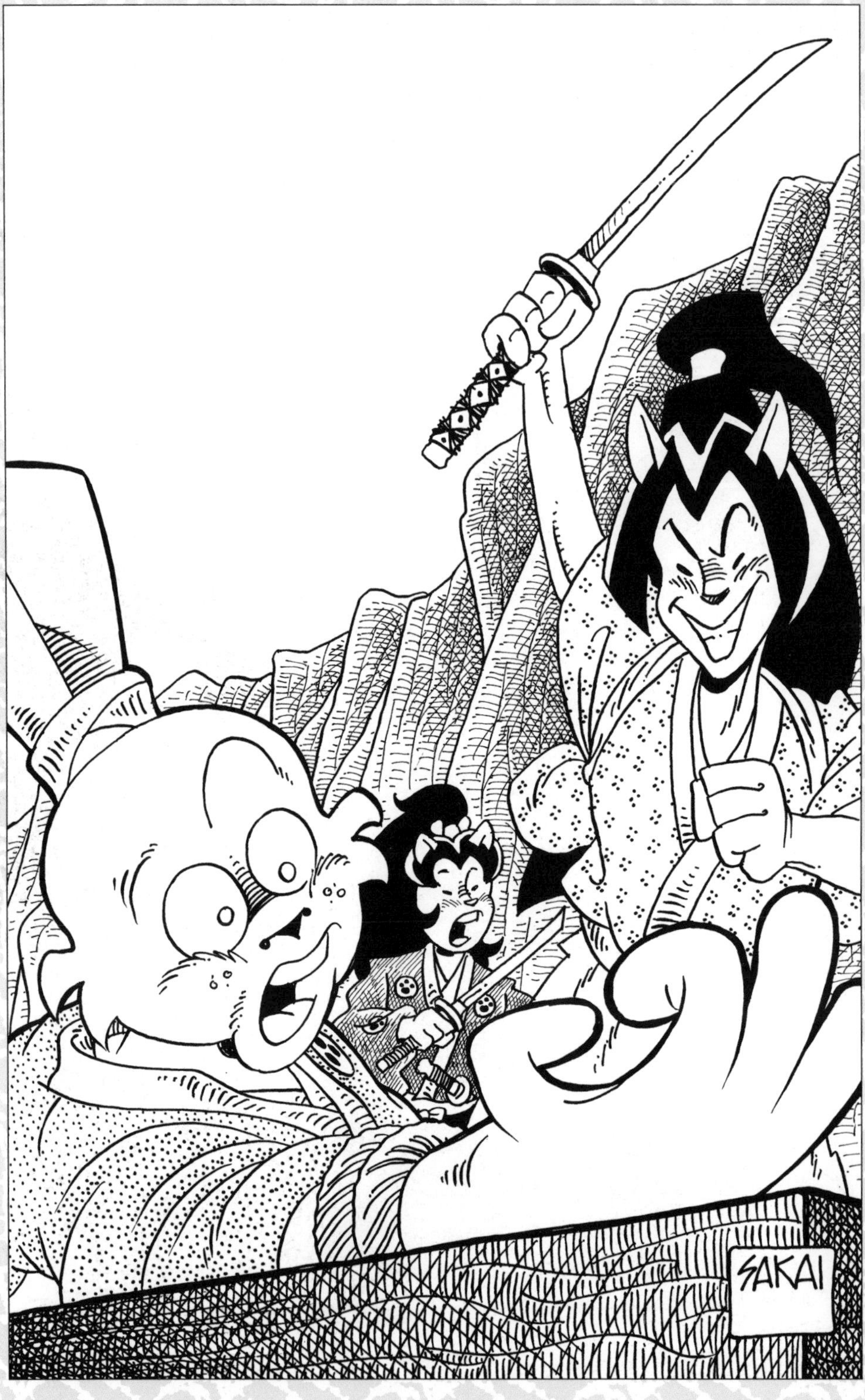
SAKAI

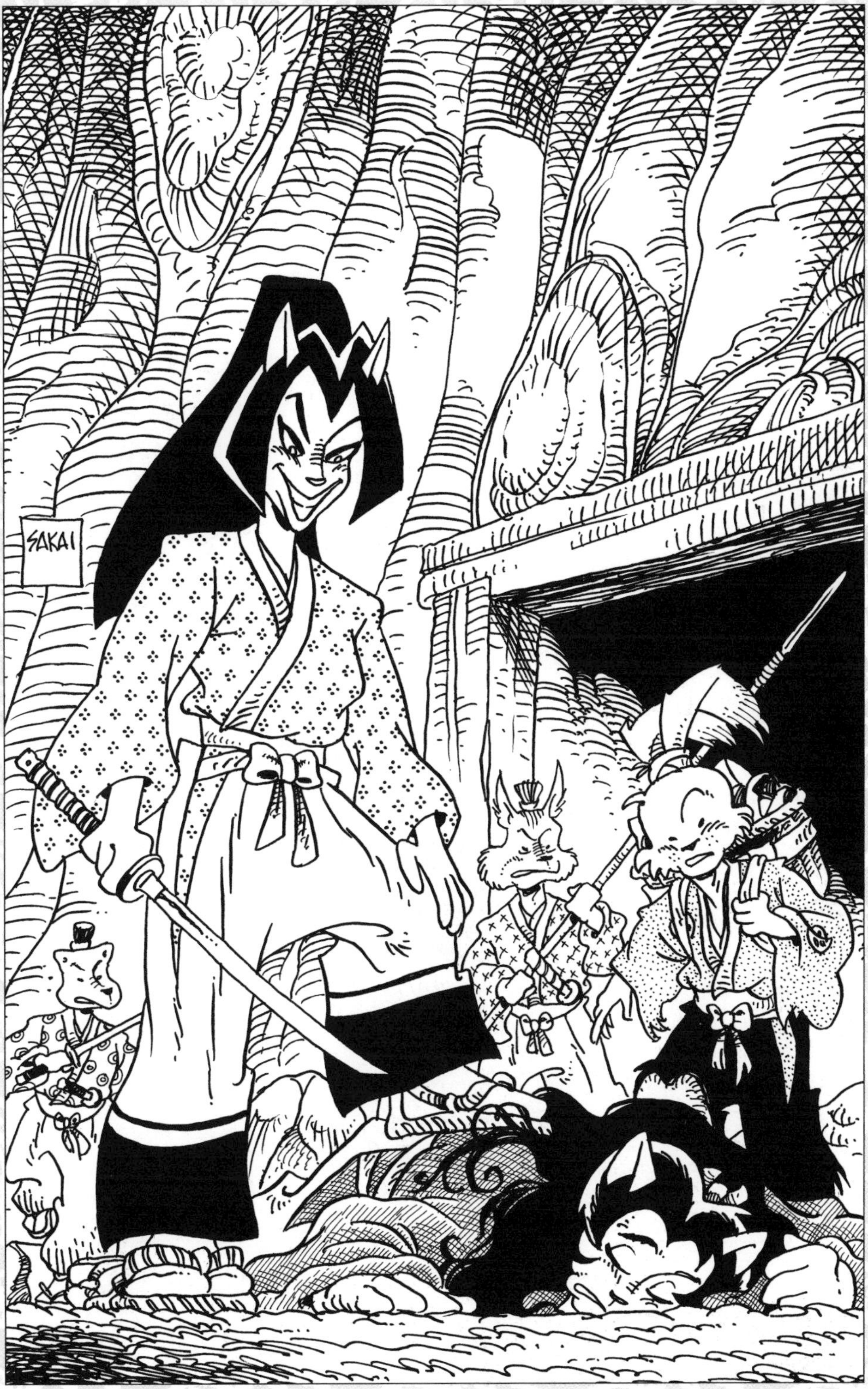
SAKAI

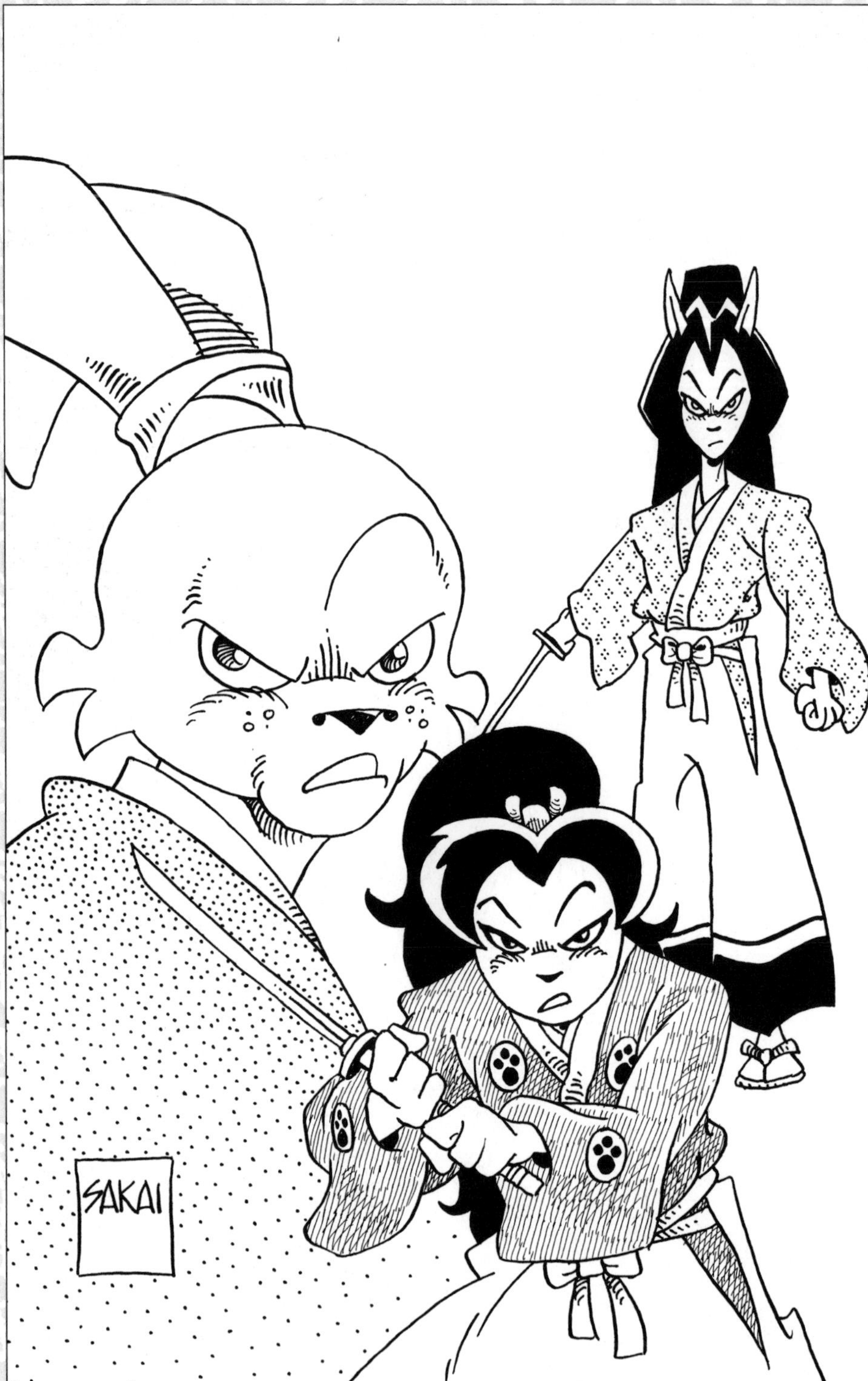
SAKAI

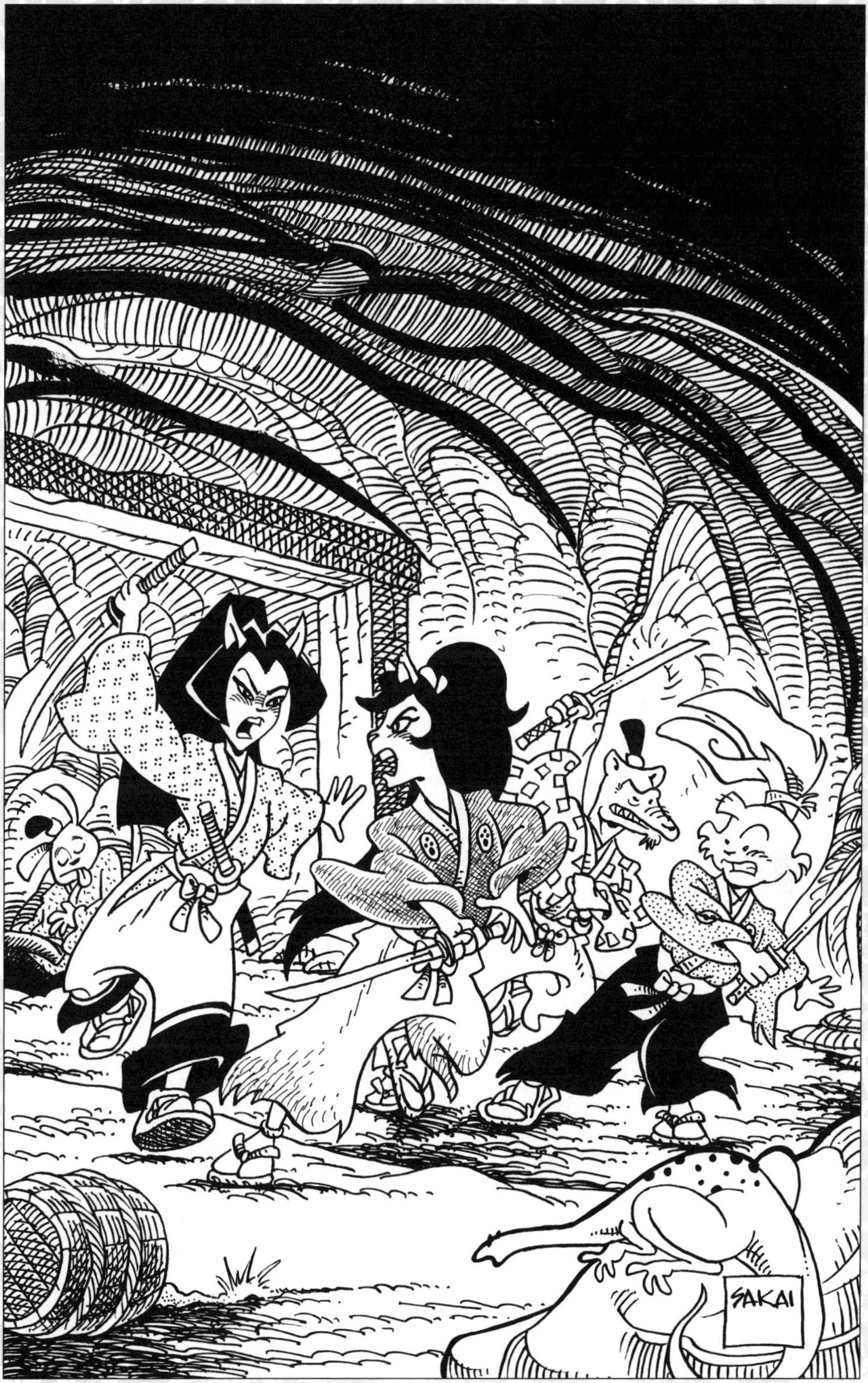
SAKAI

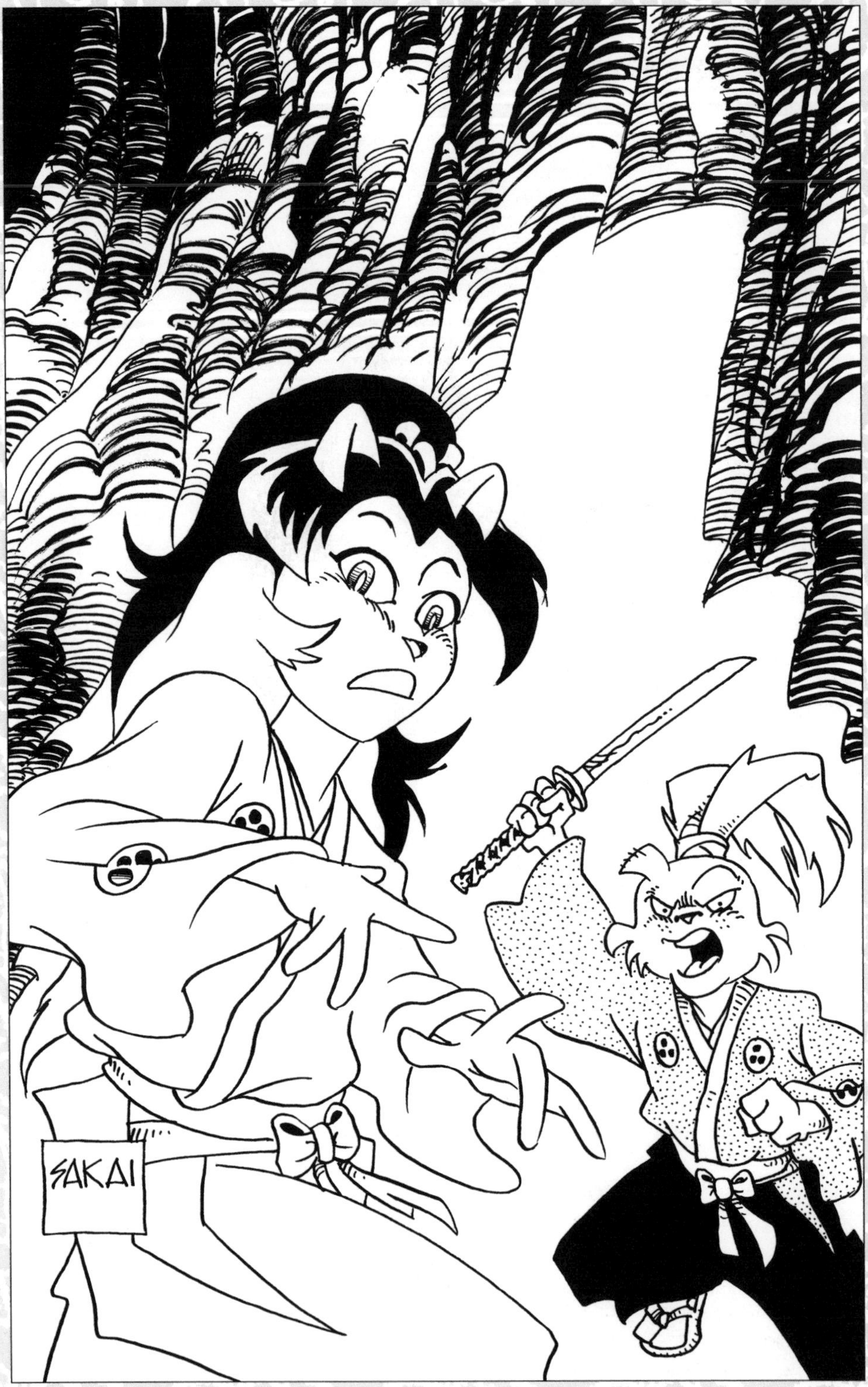
SAKAI

Biography

Stan Sakai

Stan Sakai at Mont Saint-Michel in France, 2006. *Photo by Stéphane "Fanfan" Heude.*

Stan Sakai was born in Kyoto, Japan, grew up in Hawaii, and now lives in California with his wife, Sharon, and two children, Hannah and Matthew. He received a Fine Arts degree from the University of Hawaii and furthered his studies at Art Center College of Design in Pasadena, California.

His creation, Usagi Yojimbo, first appeared in comics in 1984. Since then, Usagi has been on television as a guest of the Teenage Mutant Ninja Turtles and has been made into toys, seen on clothing, and featured in a series of graphic novel collections.

In 1991, Stan created *Space Usagi*, a series dealing with samurai in a futuristic setting, featuring the adventures of a descendant of the original Usagi.

Stan is also an award-winning letterer for his work on Sergio Aragonés's *Groo*, the "Spider-Man" Sunday newspaper strips, and *Usagi Yojimbo*.

Stan is the recipient of a Parents' Choice Award, an Inkpot Award, an American Library Association Award, a Harvey Award, four Spanish Haxtur Awards, and several Eisner Awards. In 2003 he received the prestigious National Cartoonists Society Award in the Comic Book Division.

Usagi Yojimbo

Books by Stan Sakai

From Dark Horse Comics
DarkHorse.com

Book 8: Shades of Death
Book 9: Daisho
Book 10: The Brink of Life and Death
Book 11: Seasons
Book 12: Grasscutter
Book 13: Grey Shadows
Book 14: Demon Mask
Book 15: Grasscutter II — Journey to Atsuta Shrine
Book 16: The Shrouded Moon
Book 17: Duel at Kitanoji
Book 18: Travels with Jotaro
Book 19: Fathers and Sons
Book 20: Glimpses of Death
Book 21: The Mother of Mountains
Book 22: Tomoe's Story
Book 23: Bridge of Tears
Book 24: Return of the Black Soul
Book 25: Fox Hunt
Space Usagi
Usagi Yojimbo: Yokai

From Fantagraphics Books
fantagraphics.com

Book 1: The Ronin
Book 2: Samurai
Book 3: The Wanderer's Road
Book 4: The Dragon Bellow Conspiracy
Book 5: Lone Goat and Kid
Book 6: Circles
Book 7: Gen's Story